OXFORD ENGLISH DRAMA

General Editor: MICHAEL CORDNER

Associate General Editors: PETER HOLLAND · MARTIN WIGGINS

THE RELAPSE
AND OTHER PLAYS

JOHN VANBRUGH (1664–1726) is remembered today more for his work as an architect than for his achievement as one of the best playwrights of his generation. By 1699 he had commenced designs for Lord Carlisle's Castle Howard in Yorkshire, working in collaboration with Nicholas Hawksmoor. His fame as the architect of Blenheim was to lead to commissions at Claremont for the Duke of Newcastle, Kimbolton for the Manchester family, and Stowe for Viscount Cobham. He was knighted in September 1714.

The Relapse, the first of his comedies of marital disharmony, had its première at Drury Lane in 1696, enjoying a successful opening run of six nights, and was followed rapidly by *Aesop* and *The Provoked Wife*. In 1698 Drury Lane mounted his two-act version of Dancourt's *La Maison de campagne* (1688) as *The Country House*. With the exception of *The Confederacy* in 1705, his subsequent plays were not to repeat the successes of his early years. His collected plays of 1719 did not include *A Journey to London*, an uncompleted play found amongst his papers after his death and published in the present volume.

BREAN HAMMOND is Professor of English at the University of Nottingham. He is the author of many books and articles on seventeenth- and eighteenth-century writing.

MICHAEL CORDNER is Reader in the Department of English and Related Literature at the University of York. He has edited George Farquhar's *The Beaux' Stratagem*, the *Complete Plays* of Sir George Etherege, and, for Oxford English Drama, *Four Restoration Marriage Plays* and Sheridan's *The School for Scandal and Other Plays*. He is writing books on *The Comedy of Marriage* and *Shakespeare and the Actor*.

PETER HOLLAND is Professor of Shakespeare Studies and Director of the Shakespeare Institute, University of Birmingham.

MARTIN WIGGINS is a fellow of the Shakespeare Institute and Lecturer in English at the University of Birmingham.

D0721760

OXFORD ENGLISH DRAMA

OXFORD WORLD'S CLASSICS

JOHN VANBRUGH

The Relapse
The Provoked Wife
The Confederacy
A Journey to London
The Country House

Edited with an Introduction and Notes by
BREAN HAMMOND

OXFORD
UNIVERSITY PRESS

OXFORD
UNIVERSITY PRESS

Great Clarendon Street, Oxford OX2 6DP

Oxford University Press is a department of the University of Oxford.
It furthers the University's objective of excellence in research, scholarship,
and education by publishing worldwide in

Oxford New York

Auckland Bangkok Buenos Aires Cape Town Chennai
Dar es Salaam Delhi Hong Kong Istanbul Karachi Kolkata
Kuala Lumpur Madrid Melbourne Mexico City Mumbai Nairobi
São Paulo Shanghai Taipei Toyko Toronto

Oxford is a registered trade mark of Oxford University Press
in the UK and in certain other countries

Published in the United States
by Oxford University Press Inc., New York

First published as an Oxford World's Classics paperback 2004
Reissued 2009

British Library Cataloguing in Publication Data

Data available

Library of Congress Cataloging in Publication Data

Data available

ISBN 978–0–19–955569–7

1

Typeset by RefineCatch Limited, Bungay, Suffolk
Printed in Great Britain by Clays Ltd, St Ives plc

CONTENTS

INTRODUCTION

Vanbrugh in context

Vanbrugh's main preoccupation, in his major plays, is with the nature of the marriage bond; reconciling it with affection and sexual appetite, and establishing gender advantage within it. If today our problem lies in coming to terms with the realization that the nuclear family model is outdated and no longer describes the social reality in which very many people live, Vanbrugh's society was grappling with the nuclear model as emergent, not as residual. By the close of the seventeenth century, marriage amongst people of wealth and position was no longer primarily dynastic, contracted for the sake of augmenting landed estates and the getting of heirs to inherit them. Questions of affection were higher on the agenda in what social historian Lawrence Stone has called 'companionate marriages'.[1] Love as a motive for marriage, monogamy as a necessary condition of the married state, and social compatibility after the marriage was solemnized, were higher-profile considerations than they had been earlier in the century. It was not taken for granted, however, that all unions be spiritually fulfilling in those ways; and society agonized about how far it was in male and female nature for such conditions to prevail. Marriages that had been properly solemnized in church, and even 'clandestine' marriages (such as Young Fashion's to Hoyden in *The Relapse*) that took place in the presence of a clergyman but not with full publicity and parental consent in the wife's parish of birth, were very difficult to dissolve if they were not working out. And of course the odds in marriage law were very heavily stacked in favour of the male gender. Lawrence Stone formulates it thus:

It is easy to forget that under the patriarchal system of values, as expressed in the enacted law as it endured until the nineteenth century, a married woman was the nearest approximation in a free society to a slave. Her person, her property both real and personal, her earnings, and her children all passed on marriage into the absolute control of her husband. The latter could use her sexually as and when he wished, and beat her (within reason) or confine her for disobedience to any orders. The children were entirely at the disposal of

[1] Lawrence Stone, *The Family, Sex and Marriage* (London: Weidenfeld & Nicolson, 1977).

the father, who was legally empowered to remove them, put them to work, or marry them, just as he thought fit, without consulting the wishes of his wife. He could even debar his wife from ever setting eyes on them or writing to them.[2]

So it behoved women to be very careful.

The personal was political in this arena of social life. Just as today debates about equal rights for homosexual and heterosexual partnerships are not questions solely confined to what goes on behind closed bedroom doors, but have profound consequences for the law and the nature of the state, questions raised about marriage in plays of the seventeenth century's final decade were not merely questions about private life. There was perhaps a more direct connection between imaginative representations in theatrical art and social behaviour during Vanbrugh's period than there is now because courtiers were 'role models' in more than a metaphorical sense. Lord Rochester was presumed to be the inspiration for several theatrical roles in plays by Etherege, Crowne, and Lee. There is a suggestion that Lord Foppington's affected drawl might have been based on the voice of Robert Spencer, second Earl Sunderland.[3] When Wycherley presents the role of Horner in the 1675 play *The Country Wife*, a libertine who disguises his seductive obsession behind a rumour of impotence and, thus cloaked, exploits the willing innocence of a naive country girl (Margery Pinchwife, a character somewhere in Vanbrugh's mind when he created Hoyden), analogies could be drawn with aspects of the king's own conduct. By the 1690s, however, in the immediate aftermath of the so-called 'Revolution', the court was assuming a very different complexion. William III and his consort Mary used a 'clean up society' campaign for moral reform as one means of legitimizing a reign that did not seem legitimate to many English people. It was an attempt to capture the hearts and minds of solid middle-station burghers, a public relations initiative pursued through royal proclamation and the sermons and writings of the higher clergy. Tony Claydon's study of this subject outlines the principal ways in which William's propagandists 'attempted to legitimate the regime by proving that it was reforming many different areas of national life'. His publicists showed that the new monarch had cleared the court of sin and made the royal household an appropriately virtuous engine of reform. The king himself promoted a series of fasts and thanksgivings, assuming an

---

[2] Lawrence Stone, *Road to Divorce: England 1530–1837* (Oxford: OUP, 1990), 13.

[3] Kerry Downes, *Sir John Vanbrugh* (London: Sidgwick & Jackson, 1987), 131.

Old Testament patriarch role, turning his people towards God; and royal patronage was given to initiatives aimed at reforming the nation's manners through statute law.[4]

The effect of William's campaign in the 1690s was precisely to politicize the personal. Towards the end of the decade, the Commons was thanking the king for his declaration of an intention to discourage profanity and immorality 'which chiefly by the neglect and ill example of too many magistrates are like a general contagion diffused and spread throughout the kingdom'.[5] Leave was given on 26 February 1699 to introduce a bill 'for the more effectual suppressing profaneness, immorality and debauchery' that would make adultery a misdemeanour punishable by common law—which was rejected, according to Stone, on the grounds that it might be used to disgrace politicians by members of the opposing party![6] The temper of the times is epitomized in this zealous attempt to render the ethical conduct of individuals within marriage the legitimate province of the law.

Against this general milieu, the 'marital disharmony' comedies of Sir John Vanbrugh must be understood. More than by any previously performed play or plays, Vanbrugh was tempted into writing for the theatre by a perceived need to take a stand against a constraining and unconvincing view of marital relations that threatened to make it impossible for comedy to perform its age-old mission: of making us laugh at things as they are. Commencing around 1691, and for reasons that make sense against the background sketched above, a series of plays were written in which marital disharmony was explored more seriously than it ever had been before. The postures of older sex comedy, such as held the stage for a while in the 1670s and 1680s but influenced the popular imagination for much longer, were far too brittle for a society beginning to accept that married couples really had to find a way to live fulfilled lives together. Thomas Southerne's *The Wives Excuse* was the first and best of them, and it echoed in Vanbrugh's imagination. Structurally, it is a fascinating play in being largely unplotted. It revolves round a series of open-plan, free-form scenes mostly centring on social gatherings. It creates an atmosphere hardly replicated before *fin de siècle* Russia, in the plays of Gorky and Chekhov. Act 1, for example, is set around a newly fashionable 'music

---

[4] Tony Claydon, *William III and the Godly Revolution*, Cambridge Studies in Early Modern British History, ed. Anthony Fletcher, John Guy, and John Morrill (Cambridge: CUP, 1996), 90 ff.

[5] *Collection of the Parliamentary Debates in England, from 1668–1740*, Dec. 1698.

[6] Stone, *Road to Divorce*, 246.

meeting', and begins with a below-stairs view of the occasion from footmen and pages. The view is established in Act 1 that the Friendalls' marriage is a sham. Although Mrs Friendall is faithful, everyone agrees that her husband deserves to be a cuckold. Through a ruse contrived by Lovemore, who has Ruffle insult Friendall by boxing his ears, he is exposed as a coward, occasioning this speech from Mrs Friendall:

How despicable a condition must that matrimony be, when the husband, whom we look upon as a sanctuary for a woman's honour, must be obliged to the discretion and management of a wife for the security of his own! Have a care of thinking that way; for, in a married state, as in the public, we tie ourselves up, indeed, but to be protected in our persons, fortunes and honours by those very laws that restrain us in other things; for few will obey, but for the benefit they receive from the government.[7]

In character, sentiment, and situation, the play resonates with devices that haunted Vanbrugh's imagination and were replicated in *The Relapse* and *The Provoked Wife*. Amanda in *The Relapse* owes something to Mrs Friendall when she also refuses to be seduced by the arguments of a rake. Mrs Friendall is a woman married to a cowardly husband crying out to be cuckolded; this is Lady Brute's situation in *The Provoked Wife*. *The Wives Excuse* incorporates a moment of self-reflexivity worthy of Pirandello, when Friendall pesters the playwright Welvile to find out what he is writing, and Welvile describes precisely the play in which they are both characters. Similar moments are achieved in *The Relapse* when Loveless reports his meeting with Berinthia at a play whose plot mirrors the one he is actually in; and in *The Provoked Wife* when Lady Brute and Bellinda discuss immorality on the contemporary stage and the question of how women should allow their reactions to it to be manifest. Southerne's character Courtall, a gallant who makes a point of being impervious to love, may have influenced that of Heartfree in *The Provoked Wife*. Vanbrugh's own provocation, however, was found in a much inferior play staged in 1696, Colley Cibber's *Love's Last Shift*.

Love's Last Shift dramatizes the fifth-act repentance of a bankrupt gamester, the whoring, drunken rake Loveless, who has abandoned his wife Amanda but on returning home has been tricked into bedding her under the pretence that she is a top-class whore. When they have

---

[7] Richard Southerne, *The Wives Excuse; or Cuckolds Make Themselves* (1692), from *Four Restoration Marriage Plays*, ed. Michael Cordner with Ronald Clayton (Oxford World's Classics, Oxford: OUP, 1995), 2.2.79–86.

scaled the heights of pleasure, she reveals her true identity as the faithful wife who has dressed in mourning for him ever since he absconded a decade previously. Act 5 Scene 2 begins with Amanda in soliloquy, having charmed her husband to a madness of impure desire. Using a quasi-religious language of virtue and holy martyrdom, she prepares herself to slip the disguise. A famous repentance/conversion scenario follows. Theatre historians sometimes present this play as if, single-handedly, it ushered in a new dramatic era of the 'sentimental', introducing a new strain of generically modified comedy that kicked the more cynical, smuttier 'Restoration' comedy into touch. Untenably simplistic though this is, one can certainly argue that Cibber's play is influenced by the Williamite moral crusade discussed above and is a somewhat unsubtle attempt to accommodate a new middle-class ethic to the stage. Aspects of Cibber's work that are sometimes described as 'sentimental' will include the assumption that good always triumphs over evil and that vicious men are capable of being permanently converted to goodness. Such attitudes are frequently expressed by Cibber in a language of religious ecstasy and conversion.[8] Vanbrugh's hasty composition of a sequel to this play, entitled *The Relapse*, in which Loveless relapses into his former habits and is shown carrying off a (very quietly) protesting Berinthia into the bedroom, suggests both a negative and a positive response to Cibber. Guided by an insistent moral direction but implying a grossly implausible psychology, Cibber's plays are suspected by Vanbrugh to be actually as cynical as any dramatic form they have been argued to displace. In Act 1 of *Love's Last Shift*, Loveless's reason for leaving his wife is introduced thus:

the World to me is a Garden stockt with all sorts of Fruit, where the greatest Pleasure we can take, is in the Variety of Taste: but a Wife is an Eternal Apple-tree; after a pull or two, you are sure to set your Teeth on Edge. (1.1.42–5)

Despite its final-act moralizing, the libertine whose views these are has only been brought round by a sparkling performance from his wife in bed! How can this conceivably be the bedrock upon which a permanent religious conversion to chastity and monogamy is founded? People are just not like that, says the negative hypothesis of *The Relapse*. Positively, Vanbrugh responded to one magnificent dramatic creation in Cibber's play—the role Cibber wrote for himself and acted himself:

---

[8] See Colley Cibber, *Three Sentimental Comedies*, ed. and introd. Maureen Sullivan (New Haven: Yale UP, 1973), p. xxvi.

Sir Novelty Fashion. One of the period's best definitions of the fop or beau is afforded by Berinthia in *The Relapse* when she distinguishes the beau from the man of sense for Amanda's benefit thus:

> These have brains; the beau has none.
> These are in love with their mistress; the beau with himself.
> They take care of her reputation; he's industrious to destroy it.
> They are decent; he's a fop.
> They are sound; he's rotten.
> They are men; he's an ass.

(2.1.489–94)

Sir Novelty Fashion is the ultimate narcissist: heterosexual, but so artificial and self-regarding as to lose sight of other-directed sexuality altogether; male, but so dandified, so much the creature of his dancing, singing, and fencing-masters, his tailor, milliner, perfumier, wig-maker, and valet, that he has lost touch not only with gender but with humanity and, as Sir William Witwoud says in *Love's Last Shift*, 'Heaven made you a man, and they [his entourage] have made a monster of you' (3.1.175). This liminal creature Vanbrugh endows with a knighthood, and as Lord Foppington he is required to outdo Cibber's own most excessive imaginings. Although the occupation 'playwright' was never one that Vanbrugh would have owned— rather he defined himself as a gentleman-amateur whose theatrical writing was thrown off in order to show the professionals that he could in a few spare hours beat them at their own game—he was precipitated into writing for the stage by seeing the medium's potential to explore the truth of the marriage predicament; and by its capacity to endow character with enduring, independent life beyond the stage.

Vanbrugh succeeded only too well. In 1698, Jeremy Collier published his *A Short View of the Immorality, and Profaneness of the English Stage* in which Vanbrugh's plays were excoriated above all others for their venality and blasphemy. Collier made the interesting point that the subplot of *The Relapse* in which Foppington figures is really the main plot in terms of its sheer stage presence (one might compare Shakespeare's *Othello* where Iago always threatens to act Othello off the stage); and some later adaptations have certainly suggested that this might be true. But just as Cibber's *Love's Last Shift* is credited with too much cultural power, so the effect of Collier's attack is often grossly exaggerated. Although Cibber's play is also a target for Collier, they are often yoked together as part of a two-pronged attack on robust comedy that ushered in sentimentalism.[9] His attack did draw from Vanbrugh, however, a very interesting defence. *A Short Vindication of* The Relapse *and* The Provoked Wife *from Immorality and Profaneness* was published in June 1698. One set of arguments is a traditional defence of the satirist's art, entirely familiar and predictable:

The Stage is a Glass for the World to view itself in; People ought therefore to see themselves as they are; if it makes their Faces too Fair, they won't know they are Dirty, and by consequence will neglect to wash 'em.[10]

A second set of arguments is more interesting and has set the agenda for subsequent commentary on the play. What is at issue, Vanbrugh argues, is the real nature of religion and therefore the real nature of religious theatre. Throughout his attack, Vanbrugh contends, Collier mistakes the trappings and outward show of religion for its inner ethical and devotional inspiration; indeed, Vanbrugh goes so far as to say that *The Relapse* is a religious play whose true theme is based on the Lord's Prayer: 'Lead us not into Temptation'. Recent discussions of Collier's battle with the playwrights Vanbrugh and Congreve tend to give the preacher the victory. The density of his textual citation was a new and important contribution to literary-critical method (even if that was hardly his intention), and it duped the playwrights into accepting his premiss that the basis of theatre must be ethical instruction. Instead of showing that Collier took his place in a long line of quasi-puritan enemies to the theatre, the tendency of whose remarks would destroy comedy itself and close playhouses, they undertook a point-by-point refutation of Collier's charges, a refutation largely in bad faith and a strain on credulity.[11] It was a hot controversy. In a pamphlet entitled 'Will Pierre's Answer [to Julian]', dated 'Behind the Scenes, Lincoln's-Inn Fields, Nov. 5, 1701', Tom Brown wrote:

There has a terrible Enemy arose to the Stage, an abdicated Divine . . . There is yet a greater Mischief befal'n the Stage; here are Societies set up for *Reformation of Manners*; Troops of *Informers*, who are maintain'd by Perjury, serve

---

[9] Robert D. Hume has recently argued that this entirely distorts and overplays Collier's influence, in Robert D. Hume, 'Jeremy Collier and the Future of the London Theatre in 1698', *Studies in Philology*, 96.4 (1999), 480–511.

[10] Sir John Vanbrugh, *A Short Vindication of* The Relapse *and* The Provoked Wife *from Immorality and Profaneness* (1698) in *The Complete Works of Sir John Vanbrugh*, ed. Bonamy Dobrée and Geoffrey Webb, 4 vols. (London: Nonesuch Press, 1927), i. 206.

[11] See for instance Michael Cordner's excellent discussion in 'Playwright versus Priest: Profanity and the Wit of Restoration Comedy', from Deborah Payne Fisk (ed.), *Cambridge Companion to English Restoration Theatre* (Cambridge: CUP, 2000), 209–25.

God for Gain, and ferret out Whores for Subsistence . . . These worthy
Gentlemen, for promoting the Interest of the Crown-Office, and some such
honest Place; pick harmless words out of Plays, to indict the Players and
squeeze twenty Pound a Week out of them, if they can, for their exposing
Pride, Vanity, Hypocrisie, Usury, Oppression, cheating, and other darling
Vices of the Master Reformers . . .[12]

Very soon, *The Provoked Wife* was in trouble. Luttrell reports that:

an Information is brought in the kings bench against 12 of the players, viz.
Mrs Bracegirdle, Mrs Barry, Mr Batterton, Mr Vanbruggen, &c. for using
indecent expressions in some late plays, particularly The Provok'd Wife, and
are to be tried the latter end of the term.[13]

An anonymous broadside called *The Proceedings and Tryals of the
Players in Lincoln's-Inn-Fields Held at the King's-Bench Bar at Westminster on Munday the 16th of February 1701/2* (London, 1702)
describes the actors being fined £5 each after testimony from audience
members was taken. The Attorney-General specifically declared that
the prosecution 'was not to suppress ye Acting of Plays . . . but for ye
Reformation of ye Stage'.[14] Vanbrugh, at least, was more interested in
reforming the stage.

The Relapse

In *The Relapse* (performed November 1696), Vanbrugh projects Cibber's central couple, Amanda and Loveless, into a future life beyond
the latter's repentance and conversion. He shows that it only takes a
move from the country to the town, and one attractive, willing woman
called Berinthia to puncture the spiritual rhetoric of the prequel.
Throughout the opening scene, Loveless's supposedly philosophical
arguments for the view that happiness is to be found in retirement and
peace of mind are all ambiguous and can all as easily be applied in
support of the opposite hypothesis. His self-image as locked in a
heroic struggle against vice and his own fallen nature, borders on
the ridiculous. Meanwhile, Amanda's virtue comes under siege
from Worthy, in collaboration with Berinthia whose function is to

---

[12] *The Works of Mr Tho. Brown*, 4th edn. (London, 1715), ii. 55–7.

[13] Narcissus Luttrell, *A Brief Historical Relation of State Affairs from September, 1678
to April 1714*, 6 vols. (Oxford, 1857), v. 111.

[14] *The London Stage Part II (1700–29)*, 2.1.51–2. (Draft copy annotated by Judith
Milhous and Robert Hume, Covent Garden Theatre Museum. I am grateful to Professor Hume for permission to use and quote from this edition.)

undermine her resistance from within. The scenes between the women are curiously double-edged. Female intimacy creates a confessional atmosphere, enabling Vanbrugh to put frank words into their mouths about the predicament of being female in a censorious, hypocritical, and repressive society; yet confidentiality is a tool for betraying confidence—Berinthia is soon acting as Worthy's pimp. Amanda triumphantly survives her temptation, however (and imagistically, Worthy is represented as a satanic tempter); more than that, her virtue reaches out to embrace her would-be seducer who, although he admits it might only be temporary, confesses that his coarse desires have been refined into spirituality by his contact with her. Critical discussion of this storyline focuses on the relationship between a bankrupt conventional morality and the language in which such an outmoded system of belief has been traditionally expressed.[15] The language works by a quasi-metaphorical transferring of pious religious formulas to a context of vicious practice. In 5.2, for example, when Berinthia tells Worthy that Amanda is now receptive to his advances, there is almost a mock-Annunciation:

WORTHY (*kneeling*) Thou angel of light, let me fall down and adore thee!
BERINTHIA Thou minister of darkness, get up again, for I hate to see the
 devil at his devotions. (ll. 59–62)

How far, in the end, does this process undercut traditional ways of thinking about religion and gender? Does the play simply reinforce the endemic double standard by showing that, however tempted, Amanda does not fall? 'Woman', if not every particular woman, has a higher nature, and this is enough to ground the entire apparatus of patriarchy? That is probably the critical consensus. For Derek Hughes, the play is a socially conservative one that, however it deploys a language of fixed and eternal absolutes into ambiguity, flux and self-subversion, permits traditional moral values to survive.[16] Hughes himself emphasizes, however, the strength of Amanda's fascination with 'morally alien lifestyles', and almost the last word in the play is given to a cynical travesty of Cibber's final masque. Vanbrugh's 'Dialogue between Cupid and Hymen' has the imp of sensuous love, Cupid, berating the god of marriage, Hymen, for spoiling everyone's fun.

---

[15] For a brilliant exposition of this, see Alan Roper, 'Language and Action in *The Way of the World*, *Love's Last Shift* and *The Relapse*', *English Literary History*, 40 (1973), 44–69 (54).
[16] Derek Hughes, *English Drama, 1660–1700* (Oxford: Clarendon Press, 1996), ch. 11.

Hymen replies that this would only be true if he demanded *monogamous* marriage; since he doesn't, Cupid and he are on the same side. Marriage is the perfect cover for adultery.

Such a venal account is supported by the other plot, in which Lord Foppington's younger brother (Young Fashion) abetted by the sodomitical pimp Coupler and his Cervantic servant Lory, impersonates Foppington at Clumsy Hall in order to gain the hand of Sir Tunbelly Clumsy's heiress daughter Hoyden. To an extent, the play's representation of Clumsy Hall and its booby occupants is the standard late-century account of the country as seen through metropolitan eyes: Kent is next-door to hell. Guests are welcomed into a fortified redoubt by armed servants and baying hounds, where they are as likely to be cast into a dungeon as invited to dine. Not everyone agrees, however, that Clumsy Hall is a bad place to be. For some, Clumsy Hall might represent an escape from the womb-like sterility of Loveless and Amanda's country retirement, and from the virility-obsessed masculine world of London society. It has even seemed to be a realm dominated by mother figures such as Hoyden's Nurse and mythic versions of femininity, Hoyden playing Persephone to Nurse's Demeter, displaying 'an overpowering vitality at all points in the life-cycle, from hungry baby to (future) prolific and nurturing mother'.[17]

Yet it goes well beyond this. The saturnalian sense of a world turned upside-down, an arbitrary realm of pain and violence at the centre of which is a cold moral nullity, overcomes Drougge's matriarchal cycle of fertility. Although Hoyden has a stage energy and presence that rivals Foppington's, her relationship with her Nurse is a parody of Juliet's in Shakespeare's tragedy. Shortly after Hoyden has run off to 'put on [her] laced smock', though she is 'whipped till the blood run down [her] heels for't', she responds to her Nurse's caution that she should not fall in love with her gallant: 'Love him? Why, do you think I love him, Nurse? I'cod I would not care if he were hanged, so I were but once married to him' (4.1.6–8). As for Young Fashion, he is perfectly happy for Hoyden to chase whatever town gallants she fancies once he is in possession of her fortune. The Nurse's description, to Young Fashion whom they believe to be Lord Foppington, of the baby Hoyden's feeding habits, is the grossest possible parody of the maternal—the baby as parasite:

[17] Helga Drougge, ' "The Deep Reserves of Man": Anxiety in Vanbrugh's *The Relapse*', *Studies in English Literature*, 34 (1994), 507–22 (515).

Eh, God's blessing on the sweet face on't; how it used to hang at this poor teat, and suck and squeeze, and kick and sprawl it would, till the belly on't was so full, it would drop off like a leech. (4.1.87–9)

She is as much a mother as Parson Bull is a clergyman. Both have to be bribed into witnessing Young Fashion's corrupt, clandestine marriage to Hoyden by a gap-toothed, homosexual pander Coupler, who, to erode certainties further, was played by a woman in the original production. In this extraordinary cartoon world, even Foppington, whose narcissism creates its own universe wherever he goes, can make very little impression—cannot even succeed in passing himself off as what he actually is.

The Provoked Wife

Amanda's intact virtue is an inadequate vaccination in a plague-ridden world. In *The Provoked Wife*, first performed probably in late April 1697, the strain of idealism represented by Amanda's survival as a chaste wife is even further weakened. Sir John Brute's marriage to Lady Brute is just as bad as his name and their reasons for marrying would lead us to expect: he married her because she wouldn't sleep with him otherwise, and she him for his money. Sir John's hatred for the married state has grown into a predominant humour, the motivating force of his drunken, dissolute conduct. His desire to beat women is a minor leitmotif in the play, and there are two scenes in which he is represented with his cronies attacking and robbing innocent bystanders, impersonating the clergy and behaving with appalling insubordination towards the bench: all this he does in the name of 'liberty and property'—a Whig slogan quite meaningless coming from his lips because his tendencies are entirely anarchic, or absolutist, except when it comes to protecting his own property in his wife.[18] From the opening scene, Lady Brute is constructing arguments to persuade herself that in such circumstances as Brute provides, the marriage vows cannot mean anything. Her lover Constant does not encounter the resistance, therefore, that Worthy in *The Relapse* experiences. When in 3.1 Constant argues that virtue cannot be equated with sexual continence, but is a far more charitable, extroverted, active quality, this is not obviously to be dismissed as a specious rake's charter:

[18] The inconsistency in Brute's attitude towards property and the law is very well elucidated by Michael Cordner in his introduction to *Sir John Vanbrugh: Four Comedies* (Harmondsworth: Penguin, 1989), 19–21.

Virtue consists in goodness, honour, gratitude, sincerity and pity, and not in peevish, snarling, strait-laced chastity. True virtue, wheresoe'er it moves, still carries an intrinsic worth about it, and is in every place, and in each sex, of equal value. So is not continence, you see, that phantom of honour, which men in every age have so contemned, they have thrown it amongst the women to scrabble for. (ll. 345–51)

True, he overreaches himself a little in that final sentence and has some difficulty later in his argument, but the point is that this does persuade Lady Brute and in 4.4 it is made absolutely clear that she would have yielded to Constant in the arbour in Spring Garden if they had not been interrupted by the spying Lady Fancyfull. Strictly speaking, Sir John is not cuckolded; but his other predominant character trait is cowardice, and Constant makes it icily clear that should he ever choose to question his wife's constancy, he is likely to end up on the point of a sword. The implication here is that Constant will take this action whether Lady Brute stays chaste or not. He leaves Sir John in 5.2 to consider the injustice of thus being made a compliant cuckold, with which the audience might have some sympathy if earlier in the scene Sir John had not committed a virtual rape upon his wife and if he had not fallen asleep before he finishes his meditation. In 5.5, in another Falstaffian speech, he accepts the terms of the unstated treaty the men make. Discretion is the better part of valour. He will ask no awkward questions in the interests of staying alive—now, or (it is implied) in future.

Bleak; yet *The Provoked Wife* embodies a weak, almost undiscernible strain of idealistic hope. Like Benedick in Shakespeare's *Much Ado About Nothing*, Constant's crony Heartfree is a sworn bachelor, enemy to love, whose function is to provide an ironic commentary upon lovers less impervious than himself. He has developed a metaphorical x-ray vision that he uses to strip arrogant women, strutting in their finery, down to their underwear: and he tries to see them from the inside out, imagining what is going on in their devious inner thoughts rather than taking them at face value. An actual example of this is staged, when Heartfree offers to meet the grotesquely affected Lady Fancyfull in St James's Park—not for the assignation that she imagines, but to advise her to behave more like a human being because her natural endowments are considerable. Heartfree's hard-boiled cynicism is clearly soft-centred: why would he go out of his way to reform Lady Fancyfull if it were not that he is frustrated by her refusal, and the world's, to realize its potential? And so the play is structured round a moment of reversal in 4.2 similar to *Much Ado*, when Heartfree, like Benedick, has sheepishly to admit that he is in love with Bellinda. So Heartfree cannot quite subscribe to the refrain from the masque in *The Relapse* to the effect that 'Constancy's an empty sound'. He has to believe in the theory that marriage is an ideal state where the partners are perfectly matched, and that such marriages are possible. In 5.4, the two gallants squeeze out of the play's impasse by convincing themselves that 'A man of real worth scarce ever is a cuckold but by his own fault. Women are not naturally lewd; there must be something to urge 'em to it.' Superficially darker than *The Relapse*, there is a little more chewing-gum and sticking-plaster here for the broken social relationships in the play's universe.

In the role of the Frenchified coquette Lady Fancyfull, Vanbrugh attempts to provide a virtuoso part for an actress on a par with that of Lord Foppington. For all her strutting and posturing, Lady Fancyfull has at heart a chilling sterility. In 2.2, a song of her own composition is sung, imagining her beauty destroying the world, leaving only gods to celebrate her achievements. She explains that the lyrics came to her in a dream: 'I dreamt that by an unanimous vote I was chosen queen of that pale world [the moon]; and that the first time I appeared upon my throne—all my subjects fell in love with me' (2.1). She is the sexual tease who must have the adulation of the crowd, but being scorned by the man she loves, turns into her own obverse—the prude whose main aim in life is to prevent the sexual union of others. Frequently treated cruelly in the play, the important comment that Amanda makes on Foppington applies to her also: 'it moves my pity more than my mirth, to see a man whom nature has made no fool be so very industrious to pass for an ass' (2.1). Often in Vanbrugh's plays, characters are invited to tell the audience how they pass their day: Foppington's day is a set-piece aria in *The Relapse*, and in the revised version of 4.3 that in all probability Vanbrugh himself wrote for *The Provoked Wife*, Sir John Brute describes how he puts in his day when, disguised as his own wife, he is cross-examined by the bench. *A Journey to London* has a sequence in which a 'coquette' and a 'prude' give contrasting descriptions of how they intend to pass their time amidst the diversions of the town. In *The Confederacy*, the two female protagonists Araminta and Clarissa freely confess that plaguing their husbands is a way of passing time that would otherwise hang very heavy on their hands. This repeated preoccupation suggests that Vanbrugh perceived boredom as life's greatest enemy. Measuring of time into segments that mark its passing, and the need to inject interest into one's day, indicates the spiritual barrenness inherent in social forms: and this malaise at the heart of society is one of Vanbrugh's most serious theatrical ideas. As has been noticed, there is a resonant phrase that occurs in Vanbrugh's letters when he speaks of being ''twixt jest and earnest', and if that cast of mind moves his writing towards the darker end of the comic spectrum, issuing in black comedy, this realization is what sets him apart.[19]

A Journey to London

These are the only completed original plays that Vanbrugh wrote. Although A Journey to London is not next in chronological order, being his last, unfinished play first published posthumously in 1728, we will discuss it now because it is not an adaptation from any other source. Theatrically, this play shapes up to be less directly controversial than The Provoked Wife, though like the earlier play there is an interest in the psychology of the female who is at once coquette and prude—who is at once provocative and discouraging to men; and in the town/country collision already dramatized in The Relapse. The Headpieces are a gentrified country family who believe that their finances can be repaired by moving to London where Sir Francis has gained a parliamentary seat. Squire Humphry, the son, is a gormandizing lubber, and Miss Betty, the daughter, is a pert baggage: he is his father's favourite, she her mother's. Their country boobyism is revealed in their choice of Mrs Motherly's house for lodgings—she is obviously a bawd; and it results in several comic incidents that show them being systematically tricked and beaten in their collision with metropolitan manners and practices. Such incidents as the theft of the family's supper, a delicious 'goose pie', Squire Humphry's complete indifference to the fate of the servants as against that of the pie, and the wonderfully circumstantial account given by the servant James of the Headpieces' caravanserai entering London, ensure the play's vitality; but there is nevertheless a very stifling ideology and static dramatic structure. Their Uncle Richard is an authorial 'raissonneur' figure, whose opening speech places his family's folly so firmly that much of the dramatic interest is removed. Colonel Courtly, seducer of Mrs Motherly's niece Martilla, is introduced, and his next target is seen to be Lady Headpiece. In the second plot, the Loverules are an incompatible aristocratic couple, he trying to run a rational household and she addicted to the gambling

---

[19] See Lincoln B. Faller, 'Between Jest and Earnest: The Comedy of Sir John Vanbrugh', Modern Philology (Aug. 1974), 17–29.

game of hazard. Lady Arabella Loverule's character as a coquette is strongly contrasted to that of Clarinda as a 'prude', who wishes to live a sober life. She has a natural partner in Sir Charles, friend of Lord Loverule, whose advice to the peer is to seek a divorce from his wife and who though no longer in the grip of his youthful idealism about women, would still marry if he could find 'a cheerful companion, an agreeable intimate, a useful assistant, a faithful friend, and (in time perhaps) a tender mother' (2.1). The extant script ends with a detailed dramatization of the game of hazard that brings both plots together since both women are players: Sir Francis interrupts to accuse one of the players, Captain Toupee, of cheating.

Heavy-handedly patriarchal, this play might be a product of an uncertain political and social environment. If, as Frank McCormick has argued, this play was written around 1715–17, the period of the Old Pretender's Jacobite invasion and the political fallout of its aftermath, there is some explanation for the complete reversal of sympathy for oppressed women painted into matrimonial corners by boorish husbands that we see in the earlier plays.[20] All of the women in this play are nasty pieces of work, save the 'sober' Clarinda (the word having overtones of Quakerism); several of the men are sensible and the play urges them to get a grip on their womenfolk in whatever way they can. In previous plays by Vanbrugh, there has been a party political undercurrent. Lord Foppington in *The Relapse* is a Whig grandee who has exploited his connections to buy his title, whereas his brother, Young Fashion, is a Jacobite—the party with the more romantic, swashbuckling reputation. In 1696, a year in which there was a Jacobite-inspired plot to assassinate King William that had as its informal headquarters the Blue Posts Tavern where Sir John Brute's night on the town starts, Vanbrugh's plays were highly topical. By the time he started work on *A Journey to London*, however, he appears unwilling to flirt with the social danger involved in any toleration of Jacobitism. This is a heavily-policed text with a 'lock up your daughters' mentality. Sir Francis's most egregious folly is his being unwittingly led into a Jacobite lobby during a vote in the Commons, and his constant harping upon the refrain 'the good of the country' simply shows how politically naive he is. Vanbrugh's old associate Colley Cibber informs us that the play was due to end with Lord

---

[20] Frank McCormick, 'Vanbrugh and the Duke of Newcastle: The Genesis of the Loverule Plot in *A Journey to London*', *Bulletin of Research in the Humanities*, 86 (1983), 216–22.

Loverule actually expelling his errant wife from the household: and it is certainly difficult to see this play coming to anything other than a conventionally male-dominated conclusion.

The Confederacy

The Confederacy is an adaptation from a French original, Florent Dancourt's *Les Bourgeoises à la mode* first performed in Paris in 1692, but it is a tribute to Vanbrugh's skill as a translator that he has contrived to 'English' the play so thoroughly. Given the excellent comic opportunities it offers for actresses, this play is long overdue for a professional production, though John Bull's recent claim that it is an 'undeservedly ignored masterpiece, not just a postscript to [Vanbrugh's] career, but its culmination' is an overstatement resting, in my view, on the misconceived premiss that 'it seeks to open up the class parameters of a London world in a way that reflected the changes in the structure of contemporary theatre audiences'.[21] Its ambience is not at all contemporary. Rather, it is as if Vanbrugh has cast it back to Jacobean London, to the early years of King James I's reign when the comic stage was dominated by 'city comedy' of the kind written by Thomas Middleton and even Ben Jonson. To a far more explicit extent than any other play by Vanbrugh this one is obsessed by social status. Intelligence appears to be inversely proportional to social rank, however, in the play's dramatic universe. Pert, aspiring servants Brass and Flippanta are the shakers and movers of the plot, and the implausibly symmetrical 'coney-catching' devices that they use to ensnare their masters to their mistresses give this play the feeling of a 'period piece' even in 1705 when it was first performed. A previous editor of the play, Thomas E. Lowderbaugh, has made a close study of the relationship between *The Confederacy* and its source in Dancourt, concluding that the principal difference lies in the level of sheer aggression and violence in Vanbrugh, communicated through the dominant imagery of death and militarism that controls the play.[22] This is, as he says, 'guided by a particular vision of human nature, of the way humans relate—or do not relate—to each other' (p. 17); but that is a vision considerably at odds with the polite urbanity of developing early-century mores. The stripped-down, schematic—almost cartoonish—

---

[21] John Bull, *Vanbrugh and Farquhar* (Basingstoke: Macmillan, 1998), 76.

[22] Thomas E. Lowderbaugh, 'A Critical Edition of Sir John Vanbrugh's *The Confederacy*'. Unpublished University of Maryland Ph.D. thesis, 1976.

nature of the characters and the plot devices here suggests an older, less sophisticated society. John Downes the Drury Lane prompter's comment that 'the Nice *Criticks Censure* was, it wanted just *Decorum*; made it flag at last' is a recognition of this old-fashioned element.[23]

Gripe and Moneylove are 'city scriveners', financial brokers who offer investment services for rich clients. They are several rungs below those clients in social status, even if their wealth makes up some of the distance, and their wives' fondest aspirations are to ape the manners of their betters. Gripe and Moneylove desire each other's wife and are persuaded by the servants to offer enormous bribes to the women for their services—which puts them in thrall to the manipulative women. Above the servants but below the city couples on the play's social-evolutionary ladder are Mrs Amlet, itinerant trader in ladies' goods, and her son Dick, a young gentleman of mysterious means who is paying court to Corinna Gripe under the alias 'Colonel Shapely', with the assistance of his 'servant' Brass. Those two strike up a relationship of mutually assured destruction reminiscent of Ben Jonson's comic tricksters in *The Alchemist* and *Volpone*; and Jonson is called to mind also by the way in which a stage-prop, a diamond necklace, recurs to the extent that it takes on symbolic overtones. It begins life as a pledge pawned by Clarissa Gripe to Mrs Amlet to defray her debts, is stolen by Dick from his mother, is extorted from Dick by Brass through blackmail, surfaces when Brass offers to sell it to Gripe (its real owner) for money that would payroll an elopement between Dick and Gripe's own daughter, and provokes the play's denouement. The necklace is more than a prop; it is a metonymy of, and metaphor for, the material possessions that this society craves—to the extent that, as in Jonson, they are willing to pervert natural relationships. Dick insists on his mother denying her relationship to him to preserve his social pretence, and the men are willing to prostitute each other's wife while grimly trying to hang on to their equity in their own. It is fitting that Mrs Amlet, who can buy and sell the others with the fortune that she has amassed from her undistinguished trade, is able to match the irrepressible Dick with his inamorata Corinna, purchasing his passage into higher society. A very lively play without doubt, the caricatured nature of the central couples and the imparting of comic energy to the servants ensures that as an analysis of contemporary social reality, the play never gets far off the ground.

---

[23] John Downes, *Roscius Anglicanus, or An Historical View of the Stage* (1708), ed. Judith Milhous and Robert D. Hume (Bath: Society for Theatre Research, 1987), 101.

The Country House

The Country House earns its place in this selection by dint of being a farcical take on marital disharmony. Based on a one-act Comédie Française piece by Dancourt performed in 1688 that Vanbrugh might have seen while he was imprisoned in France (initially for travelling without a valid passport), it follows the French, so Dobrée puts it, 'as a happy dog accompanies his master on a walk'.[24] Barnard is a miserly squire whose meanness and lack of hospitality are an affront to the country-house ideal of open-handed generosity. His wife is of the opposite humour, generous to the point of ruinous prodigality. This Jack-Sprat-and-his-wife marriage is tested by a succession of visitors, hangers-on, and gatecrashers arriving at the house, until Barnard and his brother Griffard cook up the scheme of posing as innkeepers. If this device seems vaguely familiar, it is perhaps because something similar is deployed by Goldsmith in *She Stoops to Conquer* (1773). In this guise, they humiliate Barnard's son Dorant in front of his gentle-men friends, but they finally fall victim to a plot led by Mariane, Barnard's daughter, and her suitor Erast. He has caused one of the king's deer to be driven into Barnard's yard, where it was gleefully turned into venison by the servant Collin. Since this is a serious offence, Barnard is happy to offload both his daughter and his ill-fated house to Erast. Fast-moving and accretive as successful farces have to be, expanding until the clock tells us that a pin has to prick its bubble, the piece offers wonderful cameo roles: for servants, for a couple of valetudinarian country cousins who arrive demanding 'cock-broth' three times a day, for a marquis and baron, both total strangers to Barnard, who are quickly inviting one another and all their own house guests to enjoy his hospitality, and for Mariane's cousin Charly who compliments her on her pretty 'bubbies' and announces his need to 'touch 'em'. To say that it dramatizes yet another unsuccessful marriage between partners with opposite dispositions is true but is probably making heavy weather of an enjoyable theatrical piece.

Staging Vanbrugh in our Time

The Relapse's post-Second World War professional stage history begins with Anthony Quayle's highly successful 1948 production at the Phoenix Theatre, with Cyril Ritchard playing Foppington. The

[24] Bonamy Dobrée and Geoffrey Webb (eds.), *The Complete Works of Sir John Vanbrugh*, 4 vols. (London: Nonesuch Press, 1927), ii, 207.

actor's account of this makes clear that the pantomimic vivacity of his interpretation, set against the austerity and gloom of a country recovering from war, was the key to its success.[25] Pantomimic vivacity has, however, been a central issue in the critical reception of subsequent major productions. Certainly the most successful production of *The Relapse* until 2001, and possibly of any of this period's comedies, was the young Trevor Nunn's for the Royal Shakespeare Company, premièred on 17 August 1967, with Donald Sinden in the lead role. The mistake that this production did *not* make was to conceptualize Foppington as camp or gay. Foppington is heterosexual, but his narcissism prevents his sexuality from being other-directed: as the critic J. C. Trewin graphically put the point in the *Illustrated London News*:

This is a masculine Foppington. He may wear a fondant-pink periwig; his mouth may be a pink Cupid's bow; his features may be a work of art in rouge, glitter, eye-shadow; the voice may suddenly bubble like a hookah. But we realise that if Rugby football had been known in 1696, Foppington might have gone into the front row of the scrum: not, perhaps, that he would have done so unless the ball were made of pink and silver velvet with a touch of tangerine.[26]

A good analogy is Lindsay Posner's RSC production of Sheridan's *The Rivals* (Swan, 2000), where the country booby Bob Acres is played by Robert Portal as a ludicrously berouged and bewigged 'macaroni', who is in no way effeminate. He's simply persuaded that this is what town women go for. It is this conception of Foppington's gender that guarantees the eduction of the play's dark and serious side, ensuring that it does not become a camp romp, as did the RSC's 1995/6 production (Swan and Barbican) by Ian Judge, with Victor Spinetti as Foppington.

Foppington has been an actor's vehicle since Colley Cibber first created it (though John Nettles attracted very little critical attention in a 1981 Old Vic production after the actor playing Loveless ran away a week before opening), and there is a constant danger of the role overbalancing the play in which it occurs. Some critics thought that the ebullience of Simon Callow, in the 1983 Lyric Hammersmith production directed by William Gaskill, did create this difficulty: Michael Billington in the *Guardian* felt that Callow lacked the 'stricken sadness

---

[25] *The Relapse or Virtue in Danger by Sir John Vanbrugh* with an introduction by Cyril Ritchard illustrated with plates (London: Peter Nevill, 1948), 8.

[26] J. C. Trewin, *Illustrated London News* review of *The Relapse* at the Aldwych, premièred 17 Aug. 1967.

of Donald Sinden's corsetted beau',[27] but there is an amiability about Foppington that captures audience sympathy especially when he is impassively stoical in the face of his trials at Clumsy Hall. This quality was well presented by Callow. This was a homely production, sepia tinted and lacking the rich colour of other realizations, that David Nokes in the *Times Literary Supplement* wittily termed 'a Lely among Hogarths'.[28]

Another issue that we have seen was first raised by Jeremy Collier in 1698 recurs in critical reaction to recent productions: the town versus the country. Sir Tunbelly Clumsy and Hoyden are such powerful acting roles that they threaten to act the town lovers off the stage. The grotesques, not the lovers, occupy the imagination, set aside as the latter were by silver-grey costumes in the 1967 triumph. Frances de la Tour as Hoyden in 1967 is described by Harold Hobson in the *Sunday Times* as 'like a haunted maiden out of one of Mrs Radcliffe's romances; she suggests both Cinderella and Mrs Rochester';[29] and in the 1995/6 production, the team of Lorraine Ashbourne as a northern Hoyden and Sheila Steafel as a nurse with a mammary fixation were regularly selected for praise. Hilary Spurling, writing in the *Spectator*, provides a clear account of the 1967 production's visual impact, illustrating the effect that design can have in striking a more acceptable balance between the play's worlds:

This production by Trevor Nunn has a glinting brilliance, from the ravishing mock-pastoral beginning to the baroque extravagance of the final ball—swags of silver fruit and flowers against a wall of mirrors and a blasé infant Cupid singing worldly songs with vine leaves in his hair . . . A tall screen at the back of the stage—gleaming in translucent morning light or reversing to sombre mirror-glass—gives the severity of an abstract composition to a knot of country bumpkins, a pair of sedan chairs in silhouette for a scene of sordid back-street haggling, or clipped privet hedge and topiary bird for adulterous overtures in a formal garden . . . Mr Morley has built a country seat—stout oak battlements and drawbridge lowered on creaking chains—which perfectly embodies the restoration view of the hated countryside: dank, desolate and unwholesome but a necessary source of funds.[30]

[27] Michael Billington, *Guardian* review of *The Relapse*, Lyric Hammersmith, premièred 20 Oct. 1983.

[28] David Nokes, *Times Literary Supplement* review of *The Relapse*, Lyric Hammersmith, premièred 20 Oct. 1983.

[29] Harold Hobson, *Sunday Times* review of *The Relapse* at the Aldwych, premièred 15 Aug. 1968.

[30] Hilary Spurling, *Spectator*, 25 Aug. 1967.

Although Ian Judge's 1995 production was not a critical success, much can be learned from watching the video.[31] One is struck by the extent to which Coupler signifies as a horrid counterpoint to Foppington. Where the latter is a mincing ninny, the former deliberately parodies the cramped movement imposed upon Foppington by his dancing shoes—so restricted that when his feet are tied in Clumsy Hall, there is no appreciable difference! Coupler's crotch-grabbing, rutting antics are in hideous contrast with his rotting, putrid state, which in turn throws light on Foppington's ludicrous attempt to seduce Amanda. Coupler's movement is echoed in that of the Nurse, while Hoyden's hopping antics and forced, statuesque postures are in effective contrast to town languor. Lorraine Ashbourne's Hilda Baker-esque presentation took its texture from music hall. Scenically, the production is dominated by a vast bed, the headboard changed to represent different locations. Amanda and Loveless are discovered in bed at the opening, but in this production there is never the remotest chance that we, or Amanda, can believe Loveless's professions. Argu-ably, there has to be *some* dramatic tension here: Loveless does have to undergo some struggle with his conscience and the emptiness of his professions has to be sensed as subconscious rather than as open cyni-cism. Judge's production entered into constant interplay with the audience, and one is gratified at how much topical and period refer-ence was fully understood by them as a result. Many contemporary in-jokes were met by the 1995 audience with loud laughter. Despite successes, the main failure of Judge's production is the Amanda/ Worthy attempted seduction in 5.3. Amanda is a relatively thankless role, usually shaded by Berinthia, whom it is possible to provide with useful gimmick props: Janet Suzman in the 1967 production, for example, was a clay-pipe smoking, spinette-playing fascination. Jennifer Ehle played the part in 1995 with a coldhearted and dislikeable brassiness, and although in 5.3 she is actually on the bed bestridden by the urgent Worthy (a literal-minded extension of the script) and she has to resist him very physically, there is little sense that she is tempted. Her coldness lays a poor foundation for Worthy's conversion: Michael Gardiner's Worthy was always too melodramatic. In this production, he so clearly doesn't have Amanda's heart, that his final speech fails.

Given Trevor Nunn's early success with *The Relapse*, the National Theatre's announcement of the play to be directed again by Nunn, with Stephen Rayne, in summer 2001, was intensely intriguing. Were

---

[31] This can be consulted in the Shakespeare Institute Library, Stratford-upon-Avon.

there new things to be said about the play? How deeply entrenched would the 1967 production be in the minds of the directors? In a private interview given to me by Trevor Nunn and Stephen Rayne, they explained that on the occasion of the twenty-fifth anniversary of the National in its South Bank home, there was some expectation that a major English-language 'classic' should be staged to show that this aspect of the NT's tradition was alive and well. A vehicle was required to complete a season for the comic talents of Alex Jennings, and, in Nunn's view, Lord Foppington is the 'benchmark' role, the consummate acting part in the entire Restoration and eighteenth-century repertoire. This is not to say that the play is one dimensional. Both Nunn and Rayne stress the unpredictabililty of the action and the constantly varying surface texture: 'as it begins', says Nunn, 'there is no suspicion that it will take you on the journey that in fact it does'.[32] Conceptually, the production is unified by the understanding that London in 1696 is a highly *theatricalized* society: Foppington presents his life as a form of theatre, and the boundaries between on-stage and off-stage spectacle are peculiarly permeable. Hence the design takes the form of a reproduction of the London stage in 1696: footlights, a set of backdrops representing the three worlds of town, pastoral 'southern' country where Loveless and Amanda live in retreat, and the harsh, fortified, grimstone 'northern' country where live the Clumsys. In the early parts of the action there is an on-stage audience, to represent both the bantering and the collusion that defined the actor-audience 'contract' at this point. This is not wholly successful: Loveless's initial interplay with the audience makes it very difficult for us to accept the production's harsh verdict upon him at the end. Thematically, the production took the subtitle ('Virtue in Danger') very seriously, showing that sexual gratification is inseparable from our real emotions and that Loveless's decision to intrigue with Berinthia would have consequences. Amanda and Worthy, in this production, are very nearly abandoned to the moment, but her last-gasp pulling-away, and his violent reaction and equally violent acceptance, suggest that she could give him her heart but only if his affection is proved by time. An ending in which Amanda and Worthy dance together while Loveless is excluded from the final chaconne, departing from the stage almost as a Malvolio figure unfitted to share the comic resolution, is an unusually open-ended way to close the play. Imogen Stubbs and Claire Price as

---

[32] Interview given by Trevor Nunn and Stephen Rayne to Brean Hammond, 14 July 2001.

Amanda and Berinthia give perspicuous accounts of their characters' motivation in this production: Berinthia determined to react against the entrapment of her nightmare former marriage, but also to undercut the smugness of her cousin who has never experienced temptation and does not dare to think through her husband's contemptible behaviour. Berinthia's treacherous behaviour is designed to prove her thesis that women's characters are not formed by the inclinations of their nature, but by the company they keep.

Unlike Sinden, whose Foppington was that of 'an extravagant and ridiculous man of middle years', to quote Nunn, Alex Jennings was a much younger Foppington, close enough in age to Raymond Coulthard as Young Fashion to make rivalry credible. The contrast between Jennings's presentation of a human being who is entirely the creation of artifice and Coulthard's swashbuckling, Errol Flynnish action man was well drawn. Another wonderful contrast was that between Foppington and Sir Tunbelly Clumsy, played by Brian Blessed as a mélange of Henry VIII, Squire Western (in Fielding's *Tom Jones*), and Attila the Hun. When they meet first, there is a 'take me to your leader' moment at which neither seems able to conceive of the other as belonging to the same species. 'Civilization' and 'barbarism' meet head on. Foppington endures his tortures in Clumsy Hall, even when he appears in charivari as a begrimed, bedaubed self-parody, with contained poise, expressing reactions no stronger than a disgusted boredom. Ultimately, the audience is won over by his relatively unmalicious reaction to losing the game.

Directors of *The Provoked Wife* are faced with even more intransigent problems in mediating such an unresolved and hard-hitting play to audiences expecting Restoration froth. Peter Wood directed the play for the National Theatre in 1980, the year in which Howard Brenton's *Romans in Britain* created a censorship furore; and some commentators thought that Vanbrugh's play was actually the more provocative! The critics treated this as an example of designer's theatre: set by Carl Toms in an iced-over London, it was felt that surface glitter rather than the underlying unpleasantness of the text was conveyed. Partly responsible was the introverted playing of John Wood as Brute—so much so that his debauched night seemed to some to be undermotivated. Dorothy Tutin's Miss Piggyish posturing before the mirror as Lady Fancyfull was liked, as was Geraldine McEwan as Lady Brute with her Edinburgh-Morningside strangled vowels. One suspects that Lindsay Posner's 1997 production of the play at the Old Vic had as its main imperative a reaction to the design extravagance of its main predecessor: John Gunter's unvarnished sets with scarecrow-like hanging trees on a bare stage were probably intended to allow the text to speak more clearly for itself. Yet there are decisions still to be taken. The eighteenth-century theatre critic Arthur Murphy saw the famous production that starred David Garrick, reporting on it in the *London Chronicle* for 3 March 1757. In common with critics nowadays who cannot stomach this play's unresolved marriage dilemma and Brute's—well, brutality—Murphy rewrites his own more acceptable play and expresses his disgust at Lady Brute's 'endeavouring to outstrip her husband in a dereliction of morals'. Murphy provides, however, a wonderful account of Garrick in the role that sets the agenda for all subsequent interpretations:

A large uncouth figure, with a deep toned voice, is by no means necessary. On the contrary, perhaps the appearance of one worn out with excessive debauchery is the more natural of the two, and it is probable, if the ladies of quality were called upon as evidence, we should find that men of flimsy texture have . . . as much brutality as more robust constitutions. Mr Garrick is not morosely sullen but peevishly fractious with his wife. In his manner there is an appearance of acrimony rather than downright insensibility and rudeness . . . it appears that the knight is naturally of a lively turn, with an unmannerly vein of wit. He sees things in a pleasant light, that is to say a light that diverts others.[33]

Stressed here is the essential *gentility* of Brute, a paradox retained by Garrick but relinquished by Posner, who directed Michael Pennington playing Brute into a flesh-creepingly leering, self-pitying performance that calls Coupler to mind. Alison Steadman's Lady Fancyfull, called by one critic 'a twittering cockatoo with an infinitely irritating laugh, pirouetting centre stage', split the critics—and although this is a virtuosa role on a parallel with Lord Foppington's, it does not direct itself in quite the same way. Foppington, we might say, is a self-basting turkey; Fancyfull has to be basted. Nicholas de Jongh in the *Evening Standard* made the important point that Vanbrugh gets to the theme of hellish, claustrophobic marriage before Strindberg and Albee do; and one might add to that Peter Nichols's 1981 *Passion Play*, so successfully revived at the Donmar Warehouse in 2000, illustrating that the deceptions forced upon those who undertake the austerities of monogamous marriage is a still-current theme.

[33] Arthur Murphy, *The Theatre*, no. 19. *London Chronicle*, 3 Mar. 1757, p. 223. Quoted from David Thomas (ed.), *Theatre in Europe: A Documentary History. Restoration and Georgian England 1660–1788* (Cambridge: CUP, 1989), 423.

NOTE ON THE TEXT

The only authoritative editions of all the plays are the first quarto editions: *The Relapse* (1697); *The Provoked Wife* (1697); *The Confederacy* (1705); *The Country House* (1715); and *A Journey to London* (1728). I am indebted to Michael Cordner's 1989 Vanbrugh edition, which used the first quartos collated against subsequent quartos and the collected editions of 1719, 1735, and 1776, which I have taken as copytext. Where I have dissented from Cordner, for example by adopting a substantive reading from a first quarto that he has not adopted, I have indicated this in the explanatory notes.

Although the establishment of the texts is not difficult in Vanbrugh's case, the editing enterprise is not entirely unproblematic. In the first quarto printing of *The Relapse*—a careless and messy piece of work—there are three scenes (in this edition 1.1, 3.2, and 5.4—but see below for act and scene divisions) in which passages are presented typographically as blank verse but which do not scan regularly as iambic pentameter. There is no definitive answer to this problem. In the case of *The Provoked Wife*, two scenes, 4.1 and 4.3, exist in two different versions: in the first quarto, Sir John Brute dresses as a clergyman to go on the rampage, and in the revisions he dresses in his wife's clothes. The revised scenes were first published in a Dublin edition of 1743, which raises the question of when, and by whom, they were actually written and interpolated into the play. *The Provoked Wife* was advertised as having alterations or revisions on three occasions: in January 1706, December 1715, and January 1726. Colley Cibber played Sir John Brute on the third of those occasions and in his autobiography, *An Apology for the Life of Colley Cibber*, he implies that this was a Command performance and that it was deemed necessary to clean the play up. Vanbrugh was himself asked to do the rewriting, says Cibber, and provided 'a new-written Scene in the Place of one in the fourth Act, where the Wantonness of his Wit and Humour had (originally) made a Rake talk like a Rake in the borrow'd Habit of a Clergyman: To avoid which Offence, he clapt the same Debauchee into the Undress of a Woman of Quality' (ed. Lowe (1899), 2.233). It is possible, however, and some editors consider, that the new scenes may have been introduced as early as 1706. Despite this uncertainty, it seems likely that the early version represents Vanbrugh's intention for the text and the revisions a somewhat unwilling concession to popular taste; so that the solution of printing the revisions in an appendix seems sensible. *The Country House* is Vanbrugh's version of Florent-Carton Dancourt's *La Maison de campagne*, presented in January 1688 at the Comédie Française. Vanbrugh's version was acted in 1698 but not published until 1715. There is a later edition of the play published in 1740 that has substantial variations. However, this has no particular textual authority and I have used the first edition as copytext.

My edition is a modernized one: that is to say, spelling and punctuation accord with present-day orthographical, typographical, and grammatical standards. Semicolons and commas tend to be used where the original has colons and semicolons; and the capitalizations after dashes and semicolons have been emended to follow modern usage. Punctuation in playtexts, however, has a special importance because it relates to performance—to 'pointing'. Where one chooses to begin and end sentences has some relevance to an actor's breathing, phrasing, and delivery. Dashes form an important exception to what is said above about standards. Seventeenth-century playtexts are sprinkled with dashes, to an extent that might be considered 'inordinate', as Bernard Harris puts it in his 1971 New Mermaids edition of *The Relapse*. Dashes also relate, however, to performative aspects of the playtext. They frequently indicate that the speaker is gesturing, moving, or pausing in a semiotically significant way. Their use intensifies when a speaker is in a heightened emotional state. I have therefore tried to retain dashes whenever I believe that they might signify in this way, as well as when they are conjunctive and work as they would in modern written English. In the first quartos, the plays are divided into acts but not usually into scenes. Following modern practice, I have divided the plays further into scenes that change when characters exit and the location changes. Where I have interpolated stage directions not present in the original quarto, those are given in square brackets.

NOTE ON THE MUSIC IN
VANBRUGH'S PLAYS

Two plays reprinted here, *The Relapse* and *The Provoked Wife*, contain songs; a third, *The Confederacy*, contains a snatch of song. *The Relapse* contains the song 'I smile at love and all its arts' in Act 4 and the musical masque 'Dialogue between Cupid and Hymen' in Act 5. The lyrics for those musical items were separately published in a pamphlet called *Words for the Musick in* The Relapse: *or, Vertue in Danger* (?1708), suggesting continued interest. The only reference I have been able to locate to music in *The Relapse*, however, is to a song that does *not* appear in the published text. David Hunter, in his *Opera and Song Books published in England, 1703–1726: A Descriptive Bibliography* (London: Bibliographical Society, 1997), records that in *A Collection of Choicest Songs & Dialogues* (October 1703), there is a song listed entitled 'Long has Pastora rul'd the plain' composed by Jeremiah Clarke and sung by Mrs Campion, supposedly coming from *The Relapse*. Although the song is printed in this collection, and also occurs separately printed, it is not, as Hunter claims, associated with *The Relapse*.

The Provoked Wife has the following: 'Fly, fly, you happy shepherds, fly' in Act 1, a male/female duet called 'Ah lovely nymph, the world's on fire' in Act 2, and a further song 'Not an angel dwells above' in that act; Lord Rake's song 'What a pother of late' in Act 3; and 'When yielding first to Damon's flame' in Act 5. Settings for the first and last of these exist, composed by John Eccles. The first can be found in his *Collection of Songs for One, Two, and Three Voices* (London, 1704, BL G300, no. 94). *The British Union Catalogue of Early Music* supplies the detail that 'Fly ye happy shepherds' was sung by Mrs Hodgson.

'When yielding first to Damon's flame' survives in a separate printing as BL G316. n (3). The printed version says 'Sung by Jemy Laroche'. Eccles was appointed Master of the King's Musick in June 1700 at a fee of £250, composing music for New Year and Birthday odes. He composed music for Congreve's *The Judgement of Paris* in March 1701, but after 1705 he wrote music for court celebrations and less for the theatre. (See P. H. Highfill *et al.*, *A Biographical Dictionary of Actors . . .* (Carbondale: Southern Illinois University Press, 1973–93), v. 6.) James ('Jemmy') Laroch[e] was born around 1688, so was under 10 when he sang the song. He played Cupid in *The Loves of Mars and Venus* (*Biographical Dictionary*, ix. 155). Eccles may have composed all the music for *The Provoked Wife*.

Anthony Coleman, in his 1982 edition of *The Provoked Wife* (Appendix C, pp. 186–7), says that Lord Rake's song 'What a pother of late' 'borrows in content and versification' from 'The Claret-Drinker's Song; or the Good-Fellows Design' to be found in *Roxburghe Collection*, IV. 642–3. The tune is given as 'Let Coesar [*sic*] Live Long' which exists in two versions. He supplies further information about songs, four altogether, sung by the actor/singer playing Colonel Bully or in the 'tavern scene' in later revivals of the play. Dobrée prints a version of one of those, a 'Scotch Medley' commencing 'We're gaily yet', in his edition at 1.184.

SELECT BIBLIOGRAPHY

Editions

The only edition that contains anything like a complete Vanbrugh is Bonamy Dobrée and Geoffrey Webb (eds.), *The Complete Works of Sir John Vanbrugh*, 4 vols. (London: Nonesuch Press, 1927). This contains his plays and all of the extant prose, including the letters. The only other recent selection of Vanbrugh's plays is Michael Cordner (ed.), *Sir John Vanbrugh: Four Comedies* (Harmondsworth: Penguin, 1989), which has been of great value to the present editor.

Vanbrugh's most popular plays, *The Relapse* and *The Provoked Wife*, exist in several modern editions. Two recent anthologies of drama from the period include *The Relapse*. James E. Gill has edited it for J. Douglas Canfield (ed.), *The Broadview Anthology of Restoration and Early Eighteenth-Century Drama* (Ormskirk, Lancs: Broadview Press, 2001); and it is also included in David Womersley (ed.), *Restoration Drama: An Anthology* (Oxford: OUP, 2000). Prior to those, we have: Eugene Waith (1968); Curt A. Zimansky (Regents Restoration Drama Series. London: Edward Arnold, 1970); and Bernard Harris (The New Mermaids Series; London: Ernest Benn, 1971, repr. London: A&C Black, 1995). And of *The Provoked Wife*: Curt A. Zimansky (Regents Restoration Drama Series; London: Edward Arnold, 1970); James L. Smith (New Mermaids Series; London: Ernest Benn, 1974); Antony Coleman (The Revels Plays; Manchester: MUP, 1982).

The only other edition of a play by Vanbrugh is of *The Confederacy*: Thomas E. Lowderbaugh, 'A Critical Edition of Sir John Vanbrugh's *The Confederacy*'. University of Maryland dissertation, 1976.

Biographical Works

The major biography of Vanbrugh is Kerry Downes, *Sir John Vanbrugh: A Biography* (London: Sidgwick & Jackson, 1987), which does not entirely supercede an earlier study of his architecture, *Vanbrugh*, published by Zwemmer in 1977. Before that, there was Madeleine Bingham, *Masks And Façades: Sir John Vanbrugh, The Man in His Setting* (London: Allen & Unwin, 1984).

Criticism

Two general books on the period's drama deserve mention: Robert D. Hume, *The Development of English Drama in the Late Seventeenth Century* (Oxford: Clarendon Press, 1976) and Derek Hughes, *English Drama 1660–1700* (Oxford: Clarendon Press, 1996). Frank McCormick's *Sir John Vanbrugh: A Reference Guide* (New York: G. K. Hall, 1992) is a valuable sourcebook, covering all writing by and about Vanbrugh to 1990. One of the very few book-length studies of Vanbrugh is Gerald M. Berkowitz, *Sir John Vanbrugh and the End of Restoration Comedy* (Newark, NJ: Rodopi, 1981), though much can be gleaned from an earlier article listed below. Although there are no more recent book-length studies of Vanbrugh, John Bull's *Vanbrugh and Farquhar*, published by Macmillan/Palgrave in their English Dramatists series in 1998, has two central chapters on Vanbrugh in addition to an overview of contemporary staging conditions. Earlier short books on Vanbrugh include Bernard Harris's study for the Writers and Their Work series (Longman, 1967) and Arthur Huseboe's for Twayne's English Authors (Boston, 1976). The best single-chapter account of Vanbrugh and his context is now Michael Cordner, 'Playwright versus Priest: Profanity and The Wit of Restoration Comedy', in Deborah Payne Fisk (ed.), *Cambridge Companion to English Restoration Theatre* (Cambridge: CUP, 2000), 209–25. This article sets Vanbrugh against the context of the so-called 'Collier controversy'. Robert Hume's 'Jeremy Collier and the Future of the London Theater in 1698', *Studies in Philology*, 96.4 (1999), 480–511 is an authoritative consideration of this topic.

The critical inheritance on Vanbrugh has been constructed by a series of key articles, often in conversation with one another. Modern Vanbrugh criticism was initiated by Paul Mueschke and Jannette Fleischer in 'A Re-valuation of Vanbrugh', *PMLA*, 49 (1934), 848–89, a long article amongst the best critical writing ever produced on his plays. Alan Roper's 'Language and Action in *The Way of the World*, *Love's Last Shift*, and *The Relapse*', *English Literary History*, 40 (1973), 44–69 shows how Vanbrugh's language works by transferring pious religious formulae to the contexts of vicious practices. An article by Gerald M. Berkowitz based on his earlier thesis, 'Sir John Vanbrugh and the Conventions of Restoration Comedy', *Genre*, 6 (1973), 346–61, is a valuable treatment of the ways in which Vanbrugh does and does not obey generic rules. In a similar vein, Lincoln B. Faller's 'Between Jest and Earnest: The Comedy of Sir John Vanbrugh', *Modern Philology* (August 1974), 17–29 takes a phrase that Vanbrugh twice uses, 'between jest and earnest', and argues that exploitation of generic uncertainty is his distinctive contribution to the period's drama. Shirley Strum Kenny's 'Perennial Favorites: Congreve, Vanbrugh, Cibber, Farquhar, and Steele', *Modern Philology*, 73.4 Part 2 (May 1976), S4–11, shows how repeated performance of outstanding plays by this group of playwrights, by stable troupes of actors, established them in the repertory. She reminds us how important conditions of performance are to playwrights' reputations. 1984 was a good year for writing on Vanbrugh. Frank McCormick's piece on 'The Unity of Vanbrugh's *A Journey to London*', *Durham University Journal*, 76 (1984), 187–94 is the only article devoted to that play's structure and aesthetic integrity. The author speculates interestingly on how the play would have ended. A collection of essays edited by Robert Markley and Laurie Finke entitled *From Renaissance to Restoration: Metamorphoses of the Drama* (Cleveland, 1984) has an essay on women in Vanbrugh by Laurie Finke. In the following year, Frank McCormick's 'Vanbrugh's *Relapse* Reconsidered', in *Studia Neophilologica* (1985), 53–61, considers how it can be that Vanbrugh treats some of his characters 'romantically' and others 'realistically'. Derek Hughes's articles on Vanbrugh published in the 1980s are now incorporated into his book mentioned above. Michael Cordner, in 'Marriage Comedy after the 1688 Revolution: Southerne to Vanbrugh', *Modern Language Review*, 85.2 (April 1990), 273–89 takes an approach not dissimilar to that of Shirley Strum Kenny above. He conducts an analysis of a group of mid-1690s dramatists who take marital disharmony as a principal comic subject: from 1691 to 1697 Southerne, Crowne, Cibber, and Vanbrugh all wrote about a wife's reaction to her husband's infidelity and neglect in ways distinct from earlier treatments of the same theme. James E. Gill, 'Character, Plot, and the Language of Love in *The Relapse*: A Reappraisal', *Restoration: Studies in English Literary Culture, 1660–1700*, 16.2 (1992), 110–25 takes off from Alan Roper into a sensitive study of the moral fabric of *The Relapse*. Vanbrugh does not lend support to vice, but neither does he support the dead pieties of morally improving texts. His solution lies in the honest wit of the play's critical treatment of conventional language and its perversions. Of feminist-influenced approaches, Helga Drougge's ' "The Deep Reserves of Man": Anxiety in Vanbrugh's *The Relapse*', *Studies in English Literature*, 34 (1994), 507–22 is surely amongst the best. To her, Vanbrugh's prime concern is virility under threat. In 'The Fun Never Stops: Young Tom Fashion's Role in Sir John Vanbrugh's *The Relapse*', *Restoration and Eighteenth-Century Theatre Research*, 12.2

(1997), 1–14, Robert Eggleston contends that Young Fashion's character can be understood in terms of the Carnival Lord of Misrule figure and literature that draws upon it.

A CHRONOLOGY OF JOHN VANBRUGH

1664   John Vanbrugh born in the parish of St Nicolas Acons, London.
        Son of Giles Vanbrugh and Elizabeth, daughter of Sir Dudley
        Carleton. Grandfather was Gillis van Brugg of Ghent, who emi-
        grated to England in the reign of James I.

1666   Family moves to Chester, where Giles becomes a 'sugar baker'—a
        refiner, not a confectioner. V. probably educated at the grammar
        school in Chester.

1686   V. commissioned in the Earl of Huntington's regiment of foot
        soldiers.

1688–92 V. imprisoned in Calais for travelling without a passport. Served time
        in prison in Vincennes and, from January 1692, in the Bastille.
        Attempts made to exchange him for an important French agent,
        Bertelier, come to nothing. V. released November 1692. V.'s claims
        to have written a very early sketch of *The Provoked Wife* have given
        rise to the suggestion, no longer accepted, that it was written in the
        Bastille. It is now thought to predate his period of French exile.

1693   V. obtains a heraldic position as Auditor, Duchy of Lancaster,
        Southern Division.

1695   V. becomes Captain in Lord Berkeley's marine regiment. Known
        around town as 'Captain Vanbrugh'.

1696   *The Relapse*, probably written in the autumn, is premièred at Drury
        Lane, 21 November, and runs for six nights, very successfully. It is
        rapidly followed by *Aesop* in December. First quarto publications
        of both plays follow early in 1697, though *The Relapse* may have
        been out by the end of 1696.

1697   *Aesop Part II* is mounted at Drury Lane, probably in March; fol-
        lowed in mid-April by *The Provoked Wife* at Lincoln's Inn Fields,
        with almost simultaneous publication.

1698   Drury Lane mounts V.'s two-act version of Dancourt's *La Maison
        de campagne* (1688) as *The Country House* on 18 January. In
        response to the publication of Jeremy Collier's *A Short View of the
        Immorality and Profaneness of the English Stage*, which undertakes a
        detailed analysis of *The Relapse*, V. publishes his *A Short Vindica-
        tion of* The Relapse *and* The Provok'd Wife *from Immorality and
        Profaneness*.

1699   V. has commenced designs for Lord Carlisle's Castle Howard in
        Yorkshire, and is working in collaboration with Nicholas
        Hawksmoor.

1700   Drury Lane mounts V.'s version of John Fletcher's earlier play *The
        Pilgrim* on 29 April, with a prologue and epilogue by John Dryden.
        Debut performance of the famous actress Anne Oldfield as Alinda
        in the play.

1701   V. begins constructing his own residence on the site of the burned-
        out Palace of Whitehall, a house that Swift would compare to a
        goose pie due to its squat, square construction.

1702   An action for indecency is brought against the cast of *The Provoked
        Wife* in February. They are fined £5 each. *The False Friend*, based
        on Le Sage's *Le Traitre puni* (1700) and on a prior Spanish original,
        performed at Drury Lane and published in February. V. succeeds
        William Talman as Comptroller of the Board of Works in June.

1703   V. has negotiated purchase of the site for a new theatre to be
        called the Queen's in the Haymarket. Introduced into the College
        of Heralds as Carlisle Herald.

1704   V. appointed Clarenceux King-at-Arms, a very high office in the
        College of Heralds. A farce authored jointly with Congreve and
        Walsh, *Squire Trelooby*, is premièred at LIF on 30 March. Founda-
        tion stone for Haymarket Theatre laid in April. Society for the
        Reformation of Manners petitions Archbishop Tenison to prevent
        V. from becoming a theatre manager.

1705   Queen's Theatre in the Haymarket opens 9 April, with a per-
        formance of an Italian opera. V.'s own *The Confederacy* based on
        Dancourt's *Les Bourgeoises à la mode* opens in this theatre on 30
        October: a qualified success. *The Mistake*, based on Molière's *Le
        Dépit amoureux*, opens at Queen's, 27 December. V. and Hawksmoor
        are engaged to design and build Blenheim Palace for the Marlbor-
        oughs. Foundation stone laid 18 June. Beginning of a long and
        stormy business relationship with the Duchess of Marlborough.

1706   *The Provoked Wife* performed on 19 January 'with alterations'. It is
        unclear what those were, but it is possible that the revised scenes in
        which Sir John impersonates his own wife rather than a clergyman
        were introduced at this point. V. in Hanover, carrying out the
        Queen's instructions to convey the insignia of the Order of the
        Garter to the future King George I.

1707   Afterpiece *The Cuckold in Conceit* based on an original by Molière,
        performed at Queen's on 22 March. Lady Manchester asks V. and
        Hawksmoor to become involved in redesigning Kimbolton Castle
        in Huntingdonshire.

1708   V. designs staircase and screen in Audley End, Essex, for Lord
        Bindon.

1709   V. acquires Chargate Farm in Esher and commences building
        house for himself.

1710–14 V. doing redesign work on King's Weston, Gloucestershire, for MP Edward Southwell.

1712 Queen commands the abandoning of building on Blenheim after Duke of Marlborough is dismissed from his positions. V. saddled with enormous debts.

1713 V. loses position as Comptroller of Works after complaining about the Treasury's handling of the financing of Blenheim.

1714 V.'s fortunes improve on accession of George I. Knighted in September; Blenheim arrears to be considered as debts accruing to the late Queen Anne. Sells Chargate to Lord Clare in October who renames it 'Claremont'.

1715 V. reappointed Comptroller in January. V. employed by Lord Clare on substantial alterations to Claremont 1715–20.

1716 V. succeeds Wren as Surveyor for rebuilding of Greenwich Hospital. Begins the redesign of Eastbury, Dorset, for George 'Bubb' Dodington.

1718 V. builds Floors Castle, near Kelso, for the Duke of Roxburgh. Obtains land in Greenwich.

1719 V. proposes garden designs for buildings in Lord Cobham's garden at Stowe. Marries Henrietta Yarburgh of Heslington Hall, York. Begins building of 'Vanbrugh Castle' between Greenwich Park and Blackheath, as his principal residence. Publication of his collected plays.

1720 Architect on Seaton Delaval, Northumberland, for George Delaval.

1722 V. commences work on Grimsthorpe Castle, Lincolnshire, for various members of the Bertie family.

1724 Duchess of Marlborough completes work on Blenheim, executing V.'s designs. Lady V. is forbidden entrance to the park when she visits.

1726 V. dies of a quinsy in March. An uncompleted play entitled *A Journey to London* is found amongst his papers. Colley Cibber reworks the play as *The Provok'd Husband*, premièred at Drury Lane on 10 January 1728. V's uncompleted play was simultaneously published in 1728.

THE RELAPSE;
or,
Virtue in Danger

A Comedy°

THE PREFACE

To go about to excuse half the defects this abortive brat is come into the world with would be to provoke the town° with a long useless preface, when 'tis, I doubt, sufficiently soured already by a tedious play.

I do therefore, with all the humility of a repenting sinner, confess it wants everything—but length; and in that, I hope, the severest critic will be pleased to acknowledge I have not been wanting. But my modesty will sure atone for everything, when the world shall know it is so great, I am even to this day insensible of those two shining graces in the play which some part of the town is pleased to compliment me with, blasphemy and bawdy.°

For my part, I cannot find 'em out. If there was any obscene expressions upon the stage, here they are in the print; for I have dealt fairly. I have not sunk a syllable that could, though by racking of mysteries,° be ranged under that head; and yet I believe with a steady faith, there is not one woman of a real reputation in town, but when she has read it impartially over in her closet,° will find it so innocent, she'll think it no affront to her prayer-book to lay it upon the same shelf. So to them, with all manner of deference, I entirely refer my cause, and I'm confident they'll justify me against those pretenders to good manners, who at the same time have so little respect for the ladies, they would extract a bawdy jest from an ejaculation,° to put 'em out of countenance. But I expect to have these well-bred persons always my enemies, since I'm sure I shall never write anything lewd enough to make 'em my friends.

As for the Saints° (your thorough-paced ones I mean, with screwed faces and wry mouths) I despair of them, for they are friends to nobody. They love nothing but their altars and themselves. They have too much zeal to have any charity; they make debauches in piety, as sinners do in wine, and are as quarrelsome in their religion as other people are in their drink. So I hope nobody will mind what they say. But if any man with flat plod shoes, a little band, greasy hair, and a dirty face, who is wiser than I at the expense of being forty years older, happens to be offended at a story of a cock and a bull, and a priest and a bulldog, I beg his pardon with all my heart, which I hope I shall obtain by eating my words, and making this public recantation. I do

therefore for his satisfaction acknowledge I lied when I said, they
never quit their hold: for in that little time I have lived in the world, I
thank God I have seen 'em forced to it more than once; but next time
I'll speak with more caution and truth, and only say they have very   40
good teeth.

If I have offended any honest gentlemen of the town,° whose
friendship or good word is worth the having, I am very sorry for it; I
hope they'll correct me as gently as they can, when they consider I
have had no other design in running a very great risk than to divert (if   45
possible) some part of their spleen,° in spite of their wives and their
taxes.

One word more about the bawdy, and I have done. I own the first
night this thing was acted some indecencies had like to have happened,
but 'twas not my fault. The fine gentleman of the play° drinking his   50
mistress's health in Nantes brandy° from six in the morning to the
time he waddled on upon the stage in the evening, had toasted himself
up to such a pitch of vigour, I confess I once gave Amanda for gone,
and I am since (with all due respect to Mrs Rogers) very sorry she
escaped; for I am confident a certain lady (let no one take it to herself   55
that's handsome) who highly blames the play for the barrenness of the
conclusion, would then have allowed it a very natural close.

THE CHARACTERS OF THE PLAY

Sir Novelty Fashion,° newly created Lord Foppington	*Mr Cibber*
Young Fashion,° his brother	*Mrs Kent*
Loveless,° husband to Amanda	*Mr Verbruggen*
Worthy, a gentleman of the town	*Mr Powell*
Sir Tunbelly Clumsy,° a country gentleman	*Mr Bullock*
Sir John Friendly, his neighbour	*Mr Mills*
Coupler, a match-maker	*Mr Johnson*
Bull, chaplain to Sir Tunbelly	*Mr Simson*
Syringe, a surgeon	*Mr Haynes*
Lory,° servant to Young Fashion	*Mr Doggett*
[Waterman]	
[Page to Lord Foppington]	
[La Verole,° valet to Lord Foppington]	
Shoemaker	
Tailor	
[Mendlegs, a hosier]	
[Foretop, a periwig-maker]	
[Servant to Loveless]	
[Porter]	
[Clerk]	
[Constable]	
[Servants to Sir Tunbelly]	
Amanda, wife to Loveless	*Mrs Rogers*
Berinthia, her cousin, a young widow	*Mrs Verbruggen*
Miss Hoyden,° a great fortune, daughter to Sir Tunbelly	*Mrs Cross*
Nurse, her gouvernante	*Mrs Powell*
[Mrs Callicoe, a sempstress]	
[Abigail, maid to Berinthia]	
[Maid to Amanda]	

First Prologue
Spoken by Miss Cross°

Ladies, this play in too much haste was writ,
To be o'er-charged with either plot or wit;
'Twas got, conceived, and born in six weeks' space,°
And wit, you know, 's as slow in growth—as grace.
Sure it can ne'er be ripened to your taste.   5
I doubt 'twill prove our author bred too fast.
For mark 'em well, who with the muses marry,
They rarely do conceive, but they miscarry.
'Tis the hard fate of those wh' are big with rhyme,
Still to be brought to bed before their time.   10
Of our late poets, nature few has made;
The greatest part—are only so by trade.
Still want of something brings the scribbling fit;
For want of money, some of 'em have writ,
And others do't, you see—for want of wit.   15
Honour, they fancy, summons 'em to write,
So out they lug in resty nature's spite,°
As some of you spruce beaux do—when you fight.
Yet let the ebb of wit be ne'er so low,
Some glimpse of it a man may hope to show   20
Upon a theme so ample—as a beau.
So, howsoe'er true courage may decay,
Perhaps there's not one smock-face here today,
But's bold as Cæsar—to attack a play.
Nay, what's yet more, with an undaunted face   25
To do the thing with more heroic grace,
'Tis six to four y'attack the strongest place.
You are such Hotspurs in this kind of venture,°
Where there's no breach, just there you needs must enter.
But be advised.   30
E'en give the hero and the critic o'er,
For nature sent you on another score;
She formed her beau for nothing but her whore.

Prologue on the Third Day°
Spoken by Mrs Verbruggen

Apologies for plays, experience shows,
Are things almost as useless—as the beaux.
Whate'er we say, like them we neither move
Your friendship, pity, anger, nor your love.
'Tis interest turns the globe; let us but find°   5
The way to please you, and you'll soon be kind.
But to expect you'd for our sakes approve,
Is just as though you for their sakes should love;
And that, we do confess, we think a task
Which, though they may impose, we never ought to ask.   10
This is an age where all things we improve,
But most of all, the art of making love.
In former days, women were only won
By merit, truth, and constant service done;
But lovers now are much more expert grown.   15
They seldom wait t'approach by tedious form;°
They're for dispatch, for taking you by storm.
Quick are their sieges, furious are their fires,
Fierce their attacks, and boundless their desires.
Before the play's half ended, I'll engage   20
To show you beaux come crowding on the stage,°
Who with so little pains have always sped,°
They'll undertake to look a lady dead.
How I have shook, and trembling stood with awe,
When here, behind the scenes, I've seen 'em draw—   25
A comb, that dead-doing weapon to the heart,°
And turn each powdered hair into a dart.
When I have seen 'em sally on the stage,
Dressed to the war, and ready to engage,
I've mourned your destiny—yet more their fate,   30
To think, that after victories so great,
It should so often prove their hard mishap
To sneak into a lane—and get a clap.
But hush! they're here already. I'll retire,
And leave 'em to you ladies to admire.   35

They'll show you twenty thousand airs and graces,
They'll entertain you with their soft grimaces,°
Their snuff-box, awkward bows—and ugly faces.
In short, they're after all so much your friends
That lest the play should fail the author's ends,   40
They have resolved to make you some amends.
Between each act (performed by nicest rules)
They'll treat you—with an interlude of fools.°
Of which, that you may have the deeper sense,
The entertainment's—at their own expense.   45

1.1

Enter Loveless reading°

LOVELESS How true is that philosophy which says,
  Our heaven is seated in our minds?
  Through all the roving pleasures of my youth,
  Where nights and days seemed all consumed in joy,
  Where the false face of luxury°   5
  Displayed such charms
  As might have shaken the most holy hermit
  And made him totter at his altar,
  I never knew one moment's peace like this.
  Here—in this little soft retreat,   10
  My thoughts unbent from all the cares of life,
  Content with fortune,
  Eased from the grating duties of dependence,°
  From envy free, ambition under foot,
  The raging flame of wild destructive lust   15
  Reduced to a warm pleasing fire of lawful love,
  My life glides on, and all is well within.
    Enter Amanda
LOVELESS (*meeting her kindly*) How does the happy cause of my
    content,
  My dear Amanda?
  You find me musing on my happy state,   20
  And full of grateful thoughts to heaven, and you.
AMANDA Those grateful offerings heaven can't receive
  With more delight than I do.
  Would I could share with it as well
  The dispensations of its bliss,   25
  That I might search its choicest favours out,
  And shower 'em on your head for ever.
LOVELESS The largest boons that heaven thinks fit to grant
  To things it has decreed shall crawl on earth,
  Are in the gift of women formed like you.   30
  Perhaps, when time shall be no more,
  When the aspiring soul shall take its flight,
  And drop this ponderous lump of clay behind it,°

It may have appetites we know not of,°
And pleasures as refined as its desires.   35
But till that day of knowledge shall instruct me,
The utmost blessing that my thought can reach
        (*Taking her in his arms*)
Is folded in my arms, and rooted in my heart.

AMANDA There let it grow forever.

LOVELESS Well said, Amanda—let it be forever.   40
Would heaven grant that—

AMANDA 'Twere all the heaven I'd ask.
But we are clad in black mortality,
And the dark curtain of eternal night
At last must drop between us.   45

LOVELESS It must.
That mournful separation we must see.
A bitter pill it is to all; but doubles its ungrateful taste,
When lovers are to swallow it.

AMANDA Perhaps that pain may only be my lot.   50
You possibly may be exempted from it.
Men find out softer ways to quench their fires.

LOVELESS Can you then doubt my constancy, Amanda?
You'll find 'tis built upon a steady basis—
The rock of reason now supports my love,°   55
On which it stands so fixed,
The rudest hurricane of wild desire
Would, like the breath of a soft slumbering babe,
Pass by, and never shake it.

AMANDA Yet still 'tis safer to avoid the storm;   60
The strongest vessels, if they put to sea,
May possibly be lost.
Would I could keep you here, in this calm port, for ever!
Forgive the weakness of a woman.
I am uneasy at your going to stay so long in town.   65
I know its false insinuating pleasures;
I know the force of its delusions;
I know the strength of its attacks;
I know the weak defence of nature;
I know you are a man—and I—a wife.   70

LOVELESS You know then all that needs to give you rest,°
For wife's the strongest claim that you can urge
When you would plead your title to my heart.°

On this you may depend. Therefore be calm.
Banish your fears, for they are traitors to your peace;   75
Beware of 'em.
They are insinuating busy things
That gossip to and fro,°
And do a world of mischief where they come.
But you shall soon be mistress of 'em all;   80
I'll aid you with such arms for their destruction,
They never shall erect their heads again.°
You know the business is indispensable, that obliges me to go for
London; and you have no reason that I know of to believe I'm
Glad of the occasion. For my honest conscience is my witness: 85
I have found a due succession of such charms
In my retirement here with you,
I have never thrown one roving thought that way;
But since, against my will, I'm dragged once more
To that uneasy theatre of noise,   90
I am resolved to make such use on't
As shall convince you, 'tis an old cast mistress,
Who has been so lavish of her favours,
She's now grown bankrupt of her charms,
And has not one allurement left to move me.   95
AMANDA Her bow, I do believe, is grown so weak,
Her arrows, at this distance, cannot hurt you,
But in approaching 'em you give 'em strength.
The dart that has not far to fly will put
The best of armour to a dangerous trial.   100
LOVELESS That trial past, and y'are at ease forever.
When you have seen the helmet proved,°
You'll apprehend no more for him that wears it.
Therefore to put a lasting period to your fears,
I am resolved, this once, to launch into temptation.   105
I'll give you an essay of all my virtues.°
My former boon companions of the bottle
Shall fairly try what charms are left in wine:
I'll take my place amongst 'em,
They shall hem me in,   110
Sing praises to their god, and drink his glory,
Turn wild enthusiasts for his sake,°
And beasts to do him honour,
Whilst I, a stubborn atheist,°

Sullenly look on,   115
Without one reverend glass to his divinity.
That for my temperance.
Then for my constancy.—
AMANDA Ay, there take heed.
LOVELESS Indeed the danger's small.   120
AMANDA And yet my fears are great.
LOVELESS Why are you so timorous?
AMANDA Because you are so bold.
LOVELESS My courage should disperse your apprehensions.
AMANDA My apprehensions should alarm your courage.   125
LOVELESS Fie, fie, Amanda, it is not kind thus to distrust me.
AMANDA And yet my fears are founded on my love.
LOVELESS Your love then is not founded as it ought;
    For if you can believe 'tis possible
    I should again relapse to my past follies,   130
    I must appear to you a thing
    Of such an undigested composition,°
    That but to think of me with inclination
    Would be a weakness in your taste
    Your virtue scarce could answer.   135
AMANDA 'Twould be a weakness in my tongue
    My prudence could not answer
    If I should press you farther with my fears.
    I'll therefore trouble you no longer with 'em.
LOVELESS Nor shall they trouble you much longer.   140
    A little time shall show you they were groundless.
    This winter shall be the fiery trial of my virtue°
    Which when it once has passed,
    You'll be convinced 'twas of no false allay.°
    There all your cares will end.   145
AMANDA Pray heaven they may.
        Exeunt hand in hand

1.2

Whitehall°

Enter Young Fashion, Lory and Waterman
YOUNG FASHION Come, pay the waterman, and take the portmantle.

LORY Faith sir, I think the waterman had as good take the portmantle
and pay himself.

YOUNG FASHION Why sure there's something left in't!

LORY But a solitary old waistcoat, upon honour, sir.   5

YOUNG FASHION Why, what's become of the blue coat, sirrah?

LORY Sir, 'twas eaten at Gravesend,° the reckoning came to thirty
shillings, and your privy purse was worth but two half crowns.°

YOUNG FASHION 'Tis very well.

WATERMAN Pray master will you please to dispatch me?   10

YOUNG FASHION Ay, here, a—canst thou change me a guinea?°

LORY (aside) Good.

WATERMAN Change a guinea, master; ha, ha, your honour's pleased
to compliment.

YOUNG FASHION Egad, I don't know how I shall pay thee then, for I   15
have nothing but gold about me.

LORY (aside) Hum, hum.

YOUNG FASHION What dost thou expect, friend?

WATERMAN Why master, so far against wind and tide is richly worth
half a piece.°   20

YOUNG FASHION Why, faith, I think thou art a good conscionable
fellow. Egad, I begin to have so good an opinion of thy honesty, I
care not if I leave my portmantle with thee, till I send thee thy
money.

WATERMAN Ha! God bless your honour; I should be as willing to   25
trust you, master, but that you are, as a man may say, a stranger to
me, and these are nimble times. There are a great many sharpers
stirring. (Taking up the portmantle) Well master, when your worship
sends the money, your portmantle shall be forthcoming. My
name's Tug,° my wife keeps a brandy-shop in Drab Alley at   30
Wapping.°

YOUNG FASHION Very well; I'll send for't tomorrow.

      Exit Waterman

LORY So. Now sir, I hope you'll own yourself a happy man. You have
out-lived all your cares.

YOUNG FASHION How so, sir?   35

LORY Why, you have nothing left to take care of.

YOUNG FASHION Yes sirrah, I have myself and you to take care of
still.

LORY Sir, if you could but prevail with somebody else to do that for
you, I fancy we might both fare the better for't.   40

YOUNG FASHION Why if thou canst tell me where to apply myself. I

have at present so little money and so much humility about me, I
don't know but I may follow a fool's advice.

LORY Why then, sir, your fool advises you to lay aside all animosity,
and apply to Sir Novelty, your elder brother.   45

YOUNG FASHION Damn my elder brother.

LORY With all my heart, but get him to redeem your annuity°
however.

YOUNG FASHION My annuity? 'Sdeath he's such a dog, he would not
give his powder puff° to redeem my soul.   50

LORY Look you, sir, you must wheedle him, or you must starve.

YOUNG FASHION Look you, sir, I will neither wheedle him, nor
starve.

LORY Why, what will you do then?

YOUNG FASHION I'll go into the army.   55

LORY You can't take the oaths; you are a Jacobite.°

YOUNG FASHION Thou may'st as well say I can't take orders° because
I'm an atheist.

LORY Sir, I ask your pardon. I find I did not know the strength of your
conscience so well as I did the weakness of your purse.   60

YOUNG FASHION Methinks, sir, a person of your experience should
have known that the strength of the conscience proceeds from the
weakness of the purse.

LORY Sir, I am very glad to find you have a conscience able to take
care of us, let it proceed from what it will; but I desire you'll please   65
to consider, that the army alone will be but a scanty maintenance
for a person of your generosity,° at least as rents° now are paid. I
shall see you stand in damnable need of some auxiliary guineas, for
your *menus plaisirs.*° I will therefore turn fool once more for your
service, and advise you to go directly to your brother.   70

YOUNG FASHION Art thou then so impregnable a blockhead, to
believe he'll help me with a farthing?°

LORY Not if you treat him *de haut en bas*° as you use to do.

YOUNG FASHION Why, how wouldst have me treat him?

LORY Like a trout, tickle him.°   75

YOUNG FASHION I can't flatter.

LORY Can you starve?

YOUNG FASHION Yes.

LORY I can't. Goodbye t'ye sir. (*Going*)

YOUNG FASHION Stay, thou wilt distract me. What wouldst thou have   80
me say to him?

LORY Say nothing to him. Apply yourself to his favourites: speak to

his periwig, his cravat, his feather, his snuff-box, and when you are
well with them—desire him to lend you a thousand pounds. I'll
engage° you prosper.   85
YOUNG FASHION 'Sdeath and furies! Why was that coxcomb thrust
  into the world before me? O Fortune, Fortune—thou art a bitch by
  Gad!
        Exeunt

1.3

A dressing room [in Lord Foppington's house]
Enter Lord Foppington in his nightgown°
FOPPINGTON Page!
        Enter Page
PAGE Sir.
FOPPINGTON Sir! Pray sir, do me the favour to teach your tongue the
  title the king has thought fit to honour me with.
PAGE I ask your lordship's pardon: my lord.   5
FOPPINGTON O, you can pronounce the word then. I thought it
  would have choked you. D'ye hear?
PAGE My lord.
FOPPINGTON Call La Verole, I would dress.
        Exit Page
  (*Alone*) Well, 'tis an unspeakable pleasure to be a man of quality,   10
  strike me dumb! 'My lord!' 'Your lordship!' 'My Lord Fop-
  pington!' *Ah! C'est quelque chose de beau, que le diable m'emporte.*°
  Why, the ladies were ready to pewk° at me, whilst I had nothing but
  Sir Navelty to recommend me to 'em. Sure whilst I was but a
  knight, I was a very nauseous fellow. Well, 'tis ten thousand pawnd° 15
  well given, stap my vitals!°
        Enter La Verole
LA VEROLE Me lord, de shoemaker, de tailor, de hosier, de sempstress,
  de barber, be all ready, if your lordship please to be dress.°
FOPPINGTON 'Tis well, admit 'em.
LA VEROLE Hey, *messieurs, entrez.*   20
        *Enter Tailor, [Sempstress, Shoemaker, Hosier, Periwig-Maker,
        Page]*
FOPPINGTON So, gentlemen, I hope you have all taken pains to show
  yourselves masters in your professions.

TAILOR I think I may presume to say, sir—

LA VEROLE My lord! You clawn° you.

TAILOR [*aside*] Why, is he made a lord? [*Aloud*] My lord, I ask your   25
    lordship's pardon my lord; I hope, my lord, your lordship will
    please to own, I have brought your lordship as accomplished a suit
    of clothes as ever peer of England trod the stage in, my lord. Will
    your lordship please to try 'em now?

FOPPINGTON Ay, but let my people dispose the glasses so, that I may   30
    see myself before and behind, for I love to see myself all raund.

> [*La Verole and Page put looking-glasses all round Lord
> Foppington.*] *Whilst he puts on his clothes, enter Young Fashion
> and Lory*

YOUNG FASHION Hey-day, what the devil have we here? Sure my
    gentleman's grown a favourite at court, he has got so many people
    at his levee.°

LORY Sir, these people come in order to make him a favourite at court;   35
    they are to establish him with the ladies.

YOUNG FASHION Good God, to what an ebb of taste are women
    fallen, that it should be in the power of a laced coat to recommend a
    gallant to 'em.

LORY Sir, tailors and periwig-makers are now become the bawds of   40
    the nation; 'tis they debauch all the women.

YOUNG FASHION Thou say'st true; for there's that fop now, has not
    by nature wherewithal to move a cook-maid, and by the time these
    fellows have done with him, egad he shall melt down a countess.
    But now for my reception; I'll engage it shall be as cold a one as a   45
    courtier's to his friend, who comes to put him in mind of his
    promise.

FOPPINGTON (*to his tailor*) Death and eternal tartures, sir, I say the
    packet's too high by a foot.°

TAILOR My lord, if it had been an inch lower, it would not have held   50
    your lordship's pocket-handkerchief.

FOPPINGTON Rat° my pocket-handkerchief, have not I a page to
    carry it? You may make him a packet up to his chin a purpose for it,
    but I will not have mine come so near my face.

TAILOR 'Tis not for me to dispute your lordship's fancy.°   55

YOUNG FASHION (*to Lory*) His lordship! Lory, did you observe that?

LORY Yes sir, I always thought 'twould end there. Now I hope you'll
    have a little more respect for him.

YOUNG FASHION Respect! Damn him for a coxcomb; now has he
    ruined his estate to buy a title, that he may be a fool of the first rate.   60

But let's accost him. (*To Foppington*) Brother, I'm your humble servant.

FOPPINGTON O Lard, Tam, I did not expect you in England; brother, I am glad to see you. (*Turning to his tailor*) Look you sir, I shall never be reconciled to this nauseous packet, therefore pray get 65 me another suit with all manner of expedition, for this is my eternal aversion. Mrs Callicoe, are not you of my mind?

SEMPSTRESS O, directly my lord; it can never be too low.

FOPPINGTON You are positively in the right on't, for the packet becomes no part of the body but the knee. 70

  [*Exit Tailor*]

SEMPSTRESS I hope your Lordship is pleased with your Stinkirk.°

FOPPINGTON In love with it, stap my vitals. Bring your bill, you shall be paid tomarrow.

SEMPSTRESS I humbly thank your honour.

  Exit Sempstress

FOPPINGTON Hark thee, shoemaker, these shoes a'n't ugly but they 75 don't fit me.°

SHOEMAKER My lord, my thinks° they fit you very well.

FOPPINGTON They hurt me just below the instep.

SHOEMAKER (*feeling his foot*) My lord, they don't hurt you there.

FOPPINGTON I tell thee they pinch me execrably. 80

SHOEMAKER My lord, if they pinch you, I'll be bound to be hanged, that's all.

FOPPINGTON Why, wilt thou undertake to persuade me I cannot feel?

SHOEMAKER Your lordship may please to feel what you think fit; but that shoe does not hurt you. I think I understand my trade. 85

FOPPINGTON Now by all that's great and powerful, thou art an incomprehensible coxcomb; but thou makest good shoes, and so I'll bear with thee.

SHOEMAKER My lord, I have worked for half the people of quality in town these twenty years, and 'twere very hard I should not know 90 when a shoe hurts, and when it don't.

FOPPINGTON Well, prithee be gone about thy business.

  Exit Shoemaker

(*To the Hosier*) Mr Mendlegs, a word with you; the calves of these stockins° are thickened a little too much. They make my legs look like a chairman's.° 95

MENDLEGS My lord, my thinks they look mighty well.

FOPPINGTON Ay, but you are not so good judge of these things as I am; I have studied 'em all my life. Therefore pray let the next be the thickness of a crawn-piece° less. (*Aside*) If the town takes notice my legs are fallen away, 'twill be attributed to the violence of some new intrigue.

[*Exit Hosier*]

(*To the Periwig-Maker*) Come, Mr Foretop,° let me see what you have done, and then the fatigue of the marning will be over.

FORETOP My lord, I have done what I defy any prince in Europe t'outdo; I have made you a periwig° so long, and so full of hair, it will serve you for hat and cloak in all weathers.

FOPPINGTON Then thou hast made me thy friend to eternity. Come, comb it out.

YOUNG FASHION [*to Lory aside*] Well, Lory, what dost think on't? A very friendly reception from a brother after three years' absence.

LORY Why, sir, it's your own fault. We seldom care for those that don't love what we love. If you would creep into his heart, you must enter into his pleasures. Here have you stood ever since you came in, and have not commended any one thing that belongs to him.

YOUNG FASHION Nor never shall, whilst they belong to a coxcomb.

LORY Then, sir, you must be content to pick a hungry bone.

YOUNG FASHION No, sir, I'll crack it, and get to the marrow before I have done.

FOPPINGTON Gad's curse; Mr Foretop, you don't intend to put this upon me for a full periwig?

FORETOP Not a full one, my lord? I don't know what your lordship may please to call a full one, but I have crammed twenty ounces of hair into it.

FOPPINGTON What it may be by weight, sir, I shall not dispute, but by tale,° there are not nine hairs of a side.

FORETOP O Lord! O Lord! O Lord! Why, as Gad shall judge me, your honour's side-face is reduced to the tip of your nose.

FOPPINGTON My side-face may be in eclipse for aught I know; but I'm sure my full-face is like the full moon.

FORETOP Heavens bless my eyesight. (*Rubbing his eyes*) Sure I look through the wrong end of the perspective, for by my faith, an't please your honour, the broadest place I see in your face does not seem to me to be two inches diameter.

FOPPINGTON If it did, it would be just two inches too broad; far a periwig to a man should be like a mask to a woman: nothing should be seen but his eyes.

FORETOP My lord, I have done; if you please to have more hair in your wig, I'll put it in.

FOPPINGTON Pasitively, yes.

FORETOP Shall I take it back now, my lord?   140

FOPPINGTON No, I'll wear it today; though it show such a manstrous
pair of cheeks—stap my vitals, I shall be taken for a trumpeter.
Exit Foretop

YOUNG FASHION Now your people of business are gone, brother, I
hope I may obtain a quarter of an hour's audience of you.

FOPPINGTON Faith, Tam, I must beg you'll excuse me at this   145
time, for I must away to the House of Lards immediately; my
Lady Teaser's case° is to come on today, and I would not be
absent for the salvation of mankind. Hey page, is the coach at the
door?

PAGE Yes, my lord.   150

FOPPINGTON You'll excuse me, brother. (*Going*)

YOUNG FASHION Shall you be back at dinner?

FOPPINGTON As Gad shall jidge me, I can't tell; for 'tis passible I
may dine with some of aur House at Lacket's.°

YOUNG FASHION Shall I meet you there? For I must needs talk with   155
you.

FOPPINGTON That I'm afraid mayn't be so praper; far the lards I
commonly eat with, are people of a nice conversation,° and you
know, Tam, your education has been a little at large; but if you'll
stay here, you'll find a family dinner. [*Calls to servant*] Hey fellow!   160
what is there for dinner? There's beef; I suppose, my brother will
eat beef. Dear Tam, I'm glad to see thee in England, stap my vitals.
*Exeunt [Lord Foppington] with his equipage° [La Verole and
Page]*

YOUNG FASHION Hell and furies, is this to be borne?

LORY Faith, sir, I could almost have given him a knock o'th' pate
myself.   165

YOUNG FASHION 'Tis enough; I will now show thee the excess of my
passion by being very calm. Come, Lory, lay your loggerhead° to
mine, and in cool blood let us contrive his destruction.

LORY Here comes a head, sir, would contrive it better than us both, if
he would but join in the confederacy.   170
Enter Coupler

YOUNG FASHION By this light, old Coupler alive still! Why, how now,
match-maker, art thou here still to plague the world with matrimony? You old bawd, how have you the impudence to be hobbling
out of your grave twenty years after you are rotten?

COUPLER When you begin to rot, sirrah, you'll go off like a pippin.° 175
One winter will send you to the devil. What mischief brings you
home again? Ha! you young lascivious rogue, you. Let me put my
hand in your bosom, sirrah.

YOUNG FASHION Stand off, old Sodom.°

COUPLER Nay, prithee now don't be so coy. 180

YOUNG FASHION Keep your hands to yourself, you old dog you, or
I'll wring your nose off.

COUPLER Hast thou then been a year in Italy,° and brought home a
fool at last? By my conscience, the young fellows of this age profit
no more by their going abroad than they do by their going to 185
church. Sirrah, sirrah, if you are not hanged before you come to my
years, you'll know a cock from a hen. But come, I'm still a friend to
thy person, though I have a contempt of thy understanding; and
therefore I would willingly know thy condition, that I may see
whether thou stand'st in need of my assistance, for widows swarm, 190
my boy—the town's infected with 'em.

YOUNG FASHION I stand in need of anybody's assistance, that will
help me to cut my elder brother's throat without the risk of being
hanged for him.

COUPLER Egad sirrah, I could help thee to do him almost as good a 195
turn, without the danger of being burnt in the hand° for't.

YOUNG FASHION Sayest thou so, old Satan? Show me but that, and
my soul is thine.

COUPLER Pox o' thy soul, give me thy warm body, sirrah; I shall have
a substantial title to't when I tell thee my project. 200

YOUNG FASHION Out with it then, dear dad, and take possession as
soon as thou wilt.

COUPLER Say'st thou so, my Hephestion?° Why then thus lies the
scene. But hold, who's that? If we are heard we are undone.

YOUNG FASHION What, have you forgot Lory? 205

COUPLER Who? Trusty Lory, is it thee?

LORY At your service sir.

COUPLER Give me thy hand, old boy. Egad, I did not know thee
again, but I remember thy honesty, though I did not thy face; I
think thou hadst like to have been hanged once or twice for thy 210
master.

LORY Sir, I was very near once having that honour.

COUPLER Well, live and hope; don't be discouraged. Eat with him,
and drink with him, and do what he bids thee, and it may be thy
reward at last as well as another's. (*To Young Fashion*) Well sir, you 215

must know I have done you the kindness to make up a match for
your brother.

YOUNG FASHION Sir, I am very much beholding to you, truly.

COUPLER You may be, sirrah, before the wedding-day yet. The lady is
a great heiress; fifteen hundred pound a year, and a great bag of   220
money. The match is concluded, the writings° are drawn, and the
pipkin's to be cracked° in a fortnight. Now you must know, stripling—with respect to your mother—your brother's the son of a
whore.

YOUNG FASHION Good.   225

COUPLER He has given me a bond of a thousand pounds for helping
him to this fortune, and has promised me as much more in ready
money upon the day of marriage, which I understand by a friend,
he ne'er designs to pay me. If therefore you will be a generous
young dog, and secure me five thousand pounds, I'll be a covetous   230
old rogue and help you to the lady.

YOUNG FASHION Egad, if thou canst bring this about, I'll have thy
statue cast in brass. But don't you dote, you old pander you, when
you talk at this rate?

COUPLER That your youthful parts shall judge of. This plump par-   235
tridge that I tell you of lives in the country, fifty miles off,° with her
honoured parents,° in a lonely old house which nobody comes near;
she never goes abroad, nor sees company at home. To prevent all
misfortunes, she has her breeding within doors; the parson of the
parish teaches her to play upon the bass-viol, the clerk to sing, her   240
nurse to dress, and her father to dance. In short, nobody can give
you admittance there but I, nor can I do it any other way, than by
making you pass for your brother.

YOUNG FASHION And how the devil wilt thou do that?

COUPLER Without the devil's aid, I warrant thee. Thy brother's face,   245
not one of the family ever saw; the whole business has been managed by me, and all the letters go through my hands. The last that
was writ to Sir Tunbelly Clumsy (for that's the old gentleman's
name) was to tell him, his lordship would be down in a fortnight to
consummate. Now you shall go away immediately, pretend you writ   250
that letter only to have the romantic pleasure of surprising your
mistress, fall desperately in love as soon as you see her, make that
your plea for marrying her immediately, and when the fatigue of
the wedding-night's over, you shall send me a swingeing purse of
gold, you dog you.   255

YOUNG FASHION Egad, old dad, I'll put my hand in thy bosom now.

COUPLER Ah, you young hot lusty thief, let me muzzle° you—(*kissing*)—sirrah, let me muzzle you.

YOUNG FASHION (*aside*) Psha, the old lecher—

COUPLER Well, I'll warrant thou hast not a farthing of money in thy   260
pocket now; no, one may see it in thy face.

YOUNG FASHION Not a souse,° by Jupiter.

COUPLER Must I advance then? Well sirrah, be at my lodgings in half
an hour, and I'll see what may be done; we'll sign and seal, and eat a
pullet, and when I have given thee some farther instructions, thou   265
shalt hoist sail and be gone. (*Kissing*) T'other buss, and so adieu.

YOUNG FASHION Um, psha!

COUPLER Ah, you young warm dog you; what a delicious night will
the bride have on't.
          Exit Coupler

YOUNG FASHION So Lory, Providence thou seest at last takes care of   270
men of merit. We are in a fair way to be great people.

LORY Ay sir, if the devil don't step between the cup and the lip,° as he
uses to do.

YOUNG FASHION Why faith he has played me many a damned trick to
spoil my fortune, and egad, I'm almost afraid he's at work about it   275
again now; but if I should tell thee how, thou'dst wonder at me.

LORY Indeed sir, I should not.

YOUNG FASHION How dost know?

LORY Because, sir, I have wondered at you so often, I can wonder at
you no more.   280

YOUNG FASHION No? What wouldst thou say, if a qualm of
conscience should spoil my design?

LORY I would eat my words, and wonder more than ever.

YOUNG FASHION Why faith, Lory, though I am a young rakehell, and
have played many a roguish trick, this is so full grown a cheat, I find   285
I must take pains to come up to't. I have scruples—

LORY They are strong symptoms of death;° if you find they increase,
pray sir make your will.

YOUNG FASHION No, my conscience shan't starve me neither. But
thus far I will hearken to it before I execute this project. I'll try my   290
brother to the bottom. I'll speak to him with the temper of a philosopher; my reasons, though they press him home, shall yet be
clothed with so much modesty, not one of all the truths they urge
shall be so naked to offend his sight. If he has yet so much humanity about him as to assist me, though with a moderate aid, I'll drop   295
my project at his feet, and show him I can—do for him much more

21

than what I ask he'd do for me. This one conclusive trial of him I
resolve to make.

> Succeed or no, still victory's my lot,
> If I subdue his heart, 'tis well; if not,   300
> I shall subdue my conscience to my plot.

Exeunt

2.1

[*Loveless's lodgings in London*]

Enter Loveless and Amanda

LOVELESS How do you like these lodgings, my dear? For my part I am
so well pleased with 'em, I shall hardly remove whilst we stay in
town, if you are satisfied.

AMANDA I am satisfied with everything that pleases you; else I had
not come to town at all.   5

LOVELESS O, a little of the noise and bustle of the world sweetens the
pleasures of retreat. We shall find the charms of our retirement
doubled when we return to it.

AMANDA That pleasing prospect will be my chiefest entertainment,
whilst, much against my will, I am obliged to stand surrounded   10
with these empty pleasures which 'tis so much the fashion to be
fond of.

LOVELESS I own most of 'em are indeed but empty; nay, so empty
that one would wonder by what magic power they act, when they
induce us to be vicious for their sakes. Yet some there are we may   15
speak kindlier of. There are delights, of which a private life is
destitute, which may divert an honest man, and be a harmless
entertainment to a virtuous woman. The conversation of the town
is one; and truly, with some small allowances, the plays,° I think,
may be esteemed another.   20

AMANDA The plays, I must confess, have some small charms, and
would have more, would they restrain that loose obscene
encouragement to vice, which shocks, if not the virtue of some
women, at least the modesty of all.

LOVELESS But till that reformation can be made, I would not leave the   25
wholesome corn for some intruding tares° that grow amongst it.
Doubtless, the moral of a well-wrought scene is of prevailing
force—last night there happened one, that moved me strangely.

AMANDA Pray, what was that?

LOVELESS Why 'twas about—but 'tis not worth repeating.   30

AMANDA Yes, pray let me know it.

LOVELESS No, I think 'tis as well let alone.

AMANDA Nay, now you make me have a mind to know.

LOVELESS 'Twas a foolish thing: you'd perhaps grow jealous should I
tell it you, though without cause, heaven knows.   35

AMANDA I shall begin to think I have cause, if you persist in making it
a secret.

LOVELESS I'll then convince you you have none, by making it no
longer so. Know then, I happened in the play to find my very
character, only with the addition of a relapse;° which struck me so,   40
I put a sudden stop to a most harmless entertainment which till
then diverted me between the acts. 'Twas to admire the workman-
ship of nature in the face of a young lady that sate some distance
from me—she was so exquisitely handsome.

AMANDA So exquisitely handsome?   45

LOVELESS Why do you repeat my words, my dear?

AMANDA Because you seemed to speak 'em with such pleasure, I
thought I might oblige you with their echo.

LOVELESS Then you are alarmed, Amanda?

AMANDA It is my duty to be so, when you are in danger.   50

LOVELESS You are too quick in apprehending for me; all will be well
when you have heard me out. I do confess I gazed upon her; nay,
eagerly I gazed upon her.

AMANDA Eagerly? That's with desire.

LOVELESS No, I desired her not; I viewed her with a world of admir-   55
ation, but not one glance of love.

AMANDA Take heed of trusting to such nice distinctions.

LOVELESS I did take heed; for observing in the play that he who
seemed to represent me there was by an accident like this unwarily
surprised into a net, in which he lay a poor entangled slave, and   60
brought a train of mischiefs on his head, I snatched my eyes away.
They pleaded hard for leave to look again, but I grew absolute, and
they obeyed.

AMANDA Were they the only things that were inquisitive? Had I been
in your place, my tongue, I fancy, had been curious too; I should   65
have asked her name, and where she lived, yet still without design.
Who was she pray?

LOVELESS Indeed I cannot tell.

AMANDA You will not tell.

LOVELESS By all that's sacred then, I did not ask.   70

AMANDA Nor do you know what company was with her?

LOVELESS I do not.

AMANDA Then I am calm again.

LOVELESS Why were you disturbed?

AMANDA Had I then no cause?   75

LOVELESS None certainly.

24

AMANDA I thought I had.

LOVELESS But you thought wrong, Amanda. For turn the case, and let it be your story; should you come home and tell me you had seen a handsome man, should I grow jealous, because you had eyes?   80

AMANDA But should I tell you he were exquisitely so: that I had gazed on him with admiration; that I had looked with eager eyes upon him; should you not think 'twere possible I might go one step farther, and enquire his name?

LOVELESS (*aside*) She has reason on her side! I have talked too much;   85
but I must turn it off another way. (*To Amanda*) Will you then make no difference, Amanda, between the language of our sex and yours? There is a modesty restrains your tongues, which makes you speak by halves when you commend; but roving flattery gives a loose to ours, which makes us still speak double what we think. You should   90
not therefore in so strict a sense take what I said to her advantage.

AMANDA Those flights of flattery, sir, are to our faces only; when women once are out of hearing, you are as modest in your commendations as we are. But I shan't put you to the trouble of farther excuses; if you please this business shall rest here. Only give me   95
leave to wish both for your peace and mine, that you may never meet this miracle of beauty more.

LOVELESS I am content.

Enter Servant

SERVANT Madam, there's a young lady at the door in a chair, desires to know whether your ladyship sees company. I think her name is   100
Berinthia.

AMANDA O dear! 'Tis a relation I have not seen these five years. Pray her to walk in.

Exit Servant

(*To Loveless*). Here's another beauty for you. She was young when I saw her last; but I hear she's grown extremely handsome.   105

LOVELESS Don't you be jealous now; for I shall gaze upon her too.

Enter Berinthia

(*Aside*) Ha! By heavens the very woman.

BERINTHIA (*saluting Amanda*) Dear Amanda, I did not expect to meet with you in town.

AMANDA Sweet cousin, I'm overjoyed to see you. (*To Loveless*) Mr   110
Loveless, here's a relation and a friend of mine I desire you'll be better acquainted with.

LOVELESS (*saluting Berinthia*) If my wife never desires a harder thing, madam, her request will be easily granted.

BERINTHIA (*to Amanda*) I think, madam, I ought to wish you joy.°   115
AMANDA Joy! Upon what?
BERINTHIA Upon your marriage: you were a widow° when I saw you
last.
LOVELESS You ought rather, madam, to wish me joy upon that, since
I am the only gainer.   120
BERINTHIA If she has got so good a husband as the world reports,
she has gained enough to expect the compliments of her friends
upon it.
LOVELESS If the world is so favourable to me to allow I deserve that
title, I hope 'tis so just to my wife to own I derive it from her.   125
BERINTHIA Sir, it is so just to you both, to own you are, and deserve
to be, the happiest pair that live in it.
LOVELESS I'm afraid we shall lose that character, madam, whenever
you happen to change your condition.
          Enter Servant
SERVANT Sir, my lord Foppington presents his humble service to   130
you, and desires to know how you do. He but just now heard you
were in town. He's at the next door; and if it be not inconvenient,
he'll come and wait upon you.
LOVELESS Lord Foppington! I know him not.
BERINTHIA Not his dignity, perhaps, but you do his person. 'Tis Sir   135
Novelty; he has bought a barony in order to marry a great fortune.
His patent° has not been passed eight and forty hours, and he has
already sent how-do-ye's to all the town, to make 'em acquainted
with his title.
LOVELESS Give my service to his lordship, and let him know I am   140
proud of the honour he intends me.
          Exit [*Servant*]
Sure this addition of quality must have so improved his coxcomb,
he can't but be very good company for a quarter of an hour.
AMANDA Now it moves my pity more than my mirth, to see a man
whom nature has made no fool be so very industrious to pass for   145
an ass.
LOVELESS No, there you are wrong, Amanda; you should never
bestow your pity upon those who take pains for your contempt.
Pity those whom nature abuses, but never those who abuse
nature.   150
BERINTHIA Besides, the town would be robbed of one of its chief
diversions, if it should become a crime to laugh at a fool.
AMANDA I could never yet perceive the town inclined to part with any

of its diversions for the sake of their being crimes; but I have seen it
very fond of some I think had little else to recommend 'em.   155

BERINTHIA I doubt, Amanda, you are grown its enemy; you speak
with so much warmth against it.

AMANDA I must confess I am not much its friend.

BERINTHIA Then give me leave to make you mine, by not engaging in
its quarrel.   160

AMANDA You have many stronger claims than that, Berinthia,
whenever you think fit to plead your title.

LOVELESS You have done well to engage a second, my dear; for here
comes one will be apt to call you to an account° for your country
principles.   165

Enter Lord Foppington

FOPPINGTON (*to Loveless*) Sir, I am your most humble servant.

LOVELESS I wish you joy, my lord.

FOPPINGTON O Lard, sir! [*To Amanda*] Madam, your ladyship's
welcome to tawn.

AMANDA I wish your lordship joy.   170

FOPPINGTON O heavens, madam—

LOVELESS My lord, this young lady is a relation of my wife's.

FOPPINGTON (*saluting her*) The beautifull'st race of people upon
earth, rat me. Dear Loveless, I'm overjoyed to see you have braught
your family to tawn again; I am, stap my vitals—(*Aside*) Far I   175
design to lie with your wife. (*To Amanda*) Far Gad's sake, madam,
haw has your ladyship been able to subsist thus long, under the
fatigue of a country life?

AMANDA My life has been very far from that, my lord; it has been a
very quiet one.   180

FOPPINGTON Why, that's the fatigue I speak of madam: for 'tis
impossible to be quiet, without thinking. Now thinking is to me the
greatest fatigue in the world.

AMANDA Does not your lordship love reading then?

FOPPINGTON Oh, passionately, madam; but I never think of what I   185
read.

BERINTHIA Why, can your lordship read without thinking?

FOPPINGTON O Lard! Can your ladyship pray without devotion,
madam?

AMANDA Well, I must own I think books the best entertainment in the   190
world.

FOPPINGTON I am so much of your ladyship's mind, madam, that I
have a private gallery (where I walk sometimes) is furnished with

27

nothing but books and looking-glasses. Madam, I have gilded 'em,
and ranged 'em so prettily, before Gad, it is the most entertaining   195
thing in the world to walk and look upon 'em.

AMANDA Nay, I love a neat library too; but 'tis I think the inside of the
book should recommend it most to us.

FOPPINGTON That I must confess I am nat altogether so fand of. Far
to mind the inside of a book, is to entertain oneself with the forced   200
product of another man's brain. Naw I think a man of quality and
breeding may be much better diverted with the natural sprauts of
his own. But to say the truth, madam, let a man love reading never
so well, when once he comes to know this tawn, he finds so many
better ways of passing the four and twenty hours, that 'twere ten   205
thousand pities he should consume his time in that. Far example,
madam, my life: my life, madam, is a perpetual stream of pleasure,
that glides through such a variety of entertainments, I believe the
wisest of our ancestors never had the least conception of any of
'em. I rise, madam, about ten a' clock. I don't rise sooner, because   210
'tis the worst thing in the world for the complexion; nat that I
pretend to be a beau: but a man must endeavour to look wholesome,
lest he make so nauseous a figure in the side-bax, the ladies should
be compelled to turn their eyes upon the play. So at ten a' clack, I
say, I rise. Naw if I find 'tis a good day, I resalve to take a turn in the   215
park, and see the fine women: so huddle on my clothes, and get
dressed by one. If it be nasty weather, I take a turn in the chocolate-
hause; where, as you walk madam, you have the prettiest prospect
in the world; you have looking-glasses all round you. But I'm afraid
I tire the company?   220

BERINTHIA Not at all. Pray go on.

FOPPINGTON Why then, ladies, from thence I go to dinner at Lacket's, where you are so nicely and delicately served, that, stap my
vitals, they shall compose you a dish no bigger than a saucer, shall
come to fifty shillings. Between eating my dinner—and washing my   225
mauth, ladies—I spend my time, till I go to the play;° where, till
nine a' clack, I entertain myself with looking upon the company,
and usually dispose of one hour more in leading 'em aut.° So
there's twelve of the four and twenty pretty well over. The other
twelve, madam, are disposed of in two articles. In the first four, I   230
toast myself drunk, and in t'other eight, I sleep myself sober
again. Thus, ladies, you see my life is an eternal raund O° of
delights.

LOVELESS 'Tis a heavenly one, indeed.

28

AMANDA But I thought, my lord, you beaux spent a great deal of your 235
time in intrigues. You have given us no account of them yet.

FOPPINGTON (*aside*) So, she would enquire into my amours. That's
jealousy. She begins to be in love with me. (*To Amanda*) Why,
madam, as to time for my intrigues, I usually make detachments of
it from my other pleasures, according to the exigency. Far your 240
ladyship may please to take notice, that those who intrigue with
women of quality have rarely occasion far above half an hour at a
time; people of that rank being under those decorums, they can
seldom give you a langer view than will just serve to shoot 'em
flying.° So that the course of my other pleasures is not very much 245
interrupted by my amours.

LOVELESS But your lordship is now become a pillar of the state; you
must attend the weighty affairs of the nation.

FOPPINGTON Sir: as to weighty affairs, I leave them to weighty heads.
I never intend mine shall be a burden to my body. 250

LOVELESS O, but you'll find the House will expect your attendance.

FOPPINGTON Sir you'll find the House will compound for my
appearance.°

LOVELESS But your friends° will take it ill if you don't attend their
particular causes. 255

FOPPINGTON Not, sir, if I come time enough to give 'em my
particular vote.

BERINTHIA But pray, my lord, how do you dispose of yourself on
Sundays; for that, methinks, is a day should hang wretchedly upon
your hands? 260

FOPPINGTON Why faith, madam, Sunday is a vile day I must confess.
I intend to move for leave to bring in a bill, that the players may
work upon it, as well as the hackney coaches. Though this I must
say for the government, it leaves us the churches to entertain us.
But then again, they begin so abominable early, a man must rise by 265
candle-light to get dressed by the psalm.°

BERINTHIA Pray which church does your lordship most oblige with
your presence?

FOPPINGTON Oh, St James's,° madam—there's much the best
company. 270

AMANDA Is there good preaching too?

FOPPINGTON Why faith, madam, I can't tell. A man must have very
little to do there, that can give an account of the sermon.

BERINTHIA You can give us an account of the ladies at least?

FOPPINGTON Or I deserve to be excommunicated. There is my Lady 275

Tattle, my Lady Prate, my Lady Titter, my Lady Leer, my Lady
Giggle, and my Lady Grin. These sit in the front of the boxes, and
all church time are the prettiest company in the world, stap my
vitals. (*To Amanda*) Mayn't we hope for the honour to see your
ladyship added to our society, madam?   280

AMANDA Alas, my lord, I am the worst company in the world at
church: I'm apt to mind the prayers, or the sermon, or—

FOPPINGTON One is indeed strangely apt at church to mind what one
should not do. But I hope, madam, at one time or other, I shall have the
honour to lead your ladyship to your coach there. (*Aside*) Methinks   285
she seems strangely pleased with everything I say to her. 'Tis a vast
pleasure to receive encouragement from a woman before her husband's face—I have a good mind to pursue my conquest, and speak
the thing plainly to her at once—egad I'll do't, and that in so cavalier a
manner, she shall be surprised at it. Ladies I'll take my leave. I'm   290
afraid I begin to grow troublesome with the length of my visit.

AMANDA Your lordship's too entertaining to grow troublesome
anywhere.

FOPPINGTON (*aside*) That now was as much as if she had said, 'Pray
lie with me'. I'll let her see I'm quick of apprehension. (*To Amanda*)   295
O Lard, madam, I had like to have forgot a secret I must needs tell
your ladyship. (*To Loveless*) Ned, you must not be so jealous now as
to listen.

LOVELESS Not I, my lord. I am too fashionable a husband to pry into
the secrets of my wife.   300

FOPPINGTON (*to Amanda, squeezing her hand*) I am in love with you to
desperation, strike me speechless.

AMANDA (*giving him a box on the ear*) Then thus I return your
passion. An impudent fool!

FOPPINGTON Gad's curse madam, I'm a peer of the realm.   305

LOVELESS Hey, what the devil? Do you affront my wife sir? Nay
then—

> [*Foppington and Loveless*] *draw and fight. The women run*
> *shrieking for help*

AMANDA Ah! what has my folly done? Help! Murder, help! Part 'em
for heaven's sake.

FOPPINGTON (*falling back, and leaning upon his sword*) Ah—quite   310
through the body—stap my vitals.

> *Enter servants*

LOVELESS (*running to him*) I hope I han't killed the fool however. Bear
him up! Where's your wound?

FOPPINGTON Just through the guts.

LOVELESS Call a surgeon there. Unbutton him quickly.   315

FOPPINGTON Ay, pray make haste.

LOVELESS This mischief you may thank yourself for.

FOPPINGTON I may so. Love's the devil indeed, Ned.

    Enter Syringe° and Servant

SERVANT Here's Mr Syringe, sir, was just going by the door.

FOPPINGTON He's the welcom'st man alive.   320

SYRINGE Stand by, stand by, stand by. Pray gentlemen stand by. Lord
    have mercy upon us, did you never see a man run through the body
    before? Pray stand by.

FOPPINGTON Ah, Mr Syringe—I'm a dead man.

SYRINGE A dead man and I by; I should laugh to see that, egad.   325

LOVELESS Prithee don't stand prating, but look upon his wound.

SYRINGE Why, what if I won't look upon his wound this hour, sir?

LOVELESS Why, then he'll bleed to death, sir.

SYRINGE Why, then I'll fetch him to life again, sir.

LOVELESS 'Slife, he's run through the guts I tell thee.   330

SYRINGE Would he were run through the heart; I should get the more
    credit by his cure. Now I hope you're satisfied? Come, now let me
    come at him; now let me come at him. (*Viewing his wound*) Oons,
    what a gash is here! Why, sir, a man may drive a coach and six
    horses into your body.   335

FOPPINGTON Ho—

SYRINGE Why, what the devil! Have you run the gentleman through
    with a scythe? (*Aside*) A little prick, between the skin and the ribs,
    that's all.

LOVELESS Let me see his wound.   340

SYRINGE Then you shall dress it sir, for if anybody looks upon it, I
    won't.

LOVELESS Why, thou art the veriest coxcomb I ever saw.

SYRINGE Sir, I am not master of my trade for nothing.

FOPPINGTON Surgeon.   345

SYRINGE Well, sir.

FOPPINGTON Is there any hopes?

SYRINGE Hopes? I can't tell. What are you willing to give for your
    cure?

FOPPINGTON Five hundred paunds with pleasure.   350

SYRINGE Why then perhaps there may be hopes. But we must avoid
    farther delay. Here: help the gentleman into a chair, and carry him
    to my house presently, that's the properest place (*aside*) to bubble°

him out of his money. Come, a chair, a chair quickly. There, in with
him.   355

They put him into a chair

FOPPINGTON Dear Loveless—adieu. If I die—I forgive thee; and if I
live—I hope thou'lt do as much by me. I'm very sorry you and
I should quarrel; but I hope here's an end on't, for if you are
satisfied—I am.

LOVELESS I shall hardly think it worth my prosecuting any farther, so   360
you may be at rest, sir.

FOPPINGTON Thou art a generous fellow, strike me dumb. (*Aside*)
But thou hast an impertinent wife, stap my vitals.

SYRINGE So, carry him off, carry him off, we shall have him prate
himself into a fever by and by; carry him off.   365

Exeunt Syringe with Lord Foppington

AMANDA Now on my knees, my dear, let me ask your pardon for my
indiscretion; my own I never shall obtain.

LOVELESS O! there's no harm done. You served him well.

AMANDA He did indeed deserve it. But I tremble to think how dear
my indiscreet resentment might have cost you.   370

LOVELESS O no matter; never trouble yourself about that.

BERINTHIA For heaven's sake, what was't he did to you?

AMANDA O nothing; he only squeezed me kindly by the hand, and
frankly offered me a coxcomb's heart. I know I was to blame to
resent it as I did, since nothing but a quarrel could ensue. But the   375
fool so surprised me with his insolence, I was not mistress of my
fingers.

BERINTHIA Now I dare swear, he thinks you had 'em at great command; they obeyed you so readily.

Enter Worthy

WORTHY Save you,° save you good people. I'm glad to find you all   380
alive; I met a wounded peer carrying off. For heaven's sake what
was the matter?

LOVELESS O, a trifle. He would have lain with my wife before my face,
so she obliged him with a box o'th' ear, and I run him through the
body. That was all.   385

WORTHY Bagatelle° on all sides. But pray, madam, how long has this
noble lord been an humble servant of yours?

AMANDA This is the first I have heard on't. So I suppose 'tis his
quality more than his love has brought him into this adventure. He
thinks his title an authentic passport to every woman's heart, below   390
the degree of a peeress.

WORTHY He's coxcomb enough to think anything. But I would not have you brought into trouble° for him; I hope there's no danger of his life?

LOVELESS None at all. He's fallen into the hands of a roguish surgeon 395 I perceive designs to frighten a little money out of him. But I saw his wound. 'Tis nothing; he may go to the play tonight if he pleases.

WORTHY I am glad you have corrected him without farther mischief. And now, sir, if these ladies have no farther service for you, you'll oblige me if you can go to the place I spoke to you of t'other day. 400

LOVELESS With all my heart. (*Aside*) Though I could wish, methinks, to stay and gaze a little longer on that creature. Good gods! How beautiful she is—but what have I to do with beauty? I have already had my portion, and must not covet more. (*To Worthy*) Come, sir, when you please. 405

WORTHY Ladies, your servant.

AMANDA Mr Loveless, pray one word with you before you go.

LOVELESS (*to Worthy*) I'll overtake you, sir.

> *Exit Worthy*

What would my dear?

AMANDA Only a woman's foolish question. How do you like my 410 cousin here?

LOVELESS Jealous already, Amanda?

AMANDA Not at all; I ask you for another reason.

LOVELESS (*aside*) Whate'er her reason be, I must not tell her true. (*To Amanda*) Why, I confess she's handsome. But you must not think I 415 slight your kinswoman, if I own to you, of all the women who may claim that character, she is the last would triumph in my heart.

AMANDA I'm satisfied.

LOVELESS Now tell me why you asked?

AMANDA At night I will. Adieu. 420

LOVELESS (*kissing her*) I'm yours.

> *Exit Loveless*

AMANDA (*aside*) I'm glad to find he does not like her; for I have a great mind to persuade her to come and live with me. (*To Berinthia*) Now dear Berinthia, let me enquire a little into your affairs: for I do assure you I am enough your friend to interest myself in everything 425 that concerns you.

BERINTHIA You formerly have given me such proofs on't, I should be very much to blame to doubt it. I am sorry I have no secrets to trust you with, that I might convince you how entire a confidence I durst repose in you. 430

AMANDA Why, is it possible that one so young and beautiful as you
should live and have no secrets?

BERINTHIA What secrets do you mean?

AMANDA Lovers.

BERINTHIA O twenty; but not one secret one amongst 'em. Lovers in   435
this age have too much honour to do any thing underhand; they do
all above board.

AMANDA That now methinks would make me hate a man.

BERINTHIA But the women of the town are of another mind: for by
this means a lady may (with the expense of a few coquette glances)   440
lead twenty fools about in a string° for two or three years together;
whereas, if she should allow 'em greater favours, and oblige 'em to
secrecy, she would not keep one of 'em a fortnight.

AMANDA There's something indeed in that to satisfy the vanity of
a woman, but I can't comprehend how the men find their account   445
in it.°

BERINTHIA Their entertainment I must confess is a riddle to me. For
there's very few of 'em ever get farther than a bow and an ogle. I
have half a score for my share, who follow me all over the town; and
at the play, the park, and the church, do (with their eyes) say the   450
violent'st things to me. But I never hear any more of 'em.

AMANDA What can be the reason of that?

BERINTHIA One reason is, they don't know how to go farther. They
have had so little practice, they don't understand the trade. But
besides their ignorance, you must know there is not one of my half   455
score lovers but what follows half a score mistresses. Now their
affections being divided amongst so many, are not strong enough
for any one to make 'em pursue her to the purpose. Like a young
puppy in a warren, they have a flirt at all, and catch none.

AMANDA Yet they seem to have a torrent of love to dispose of.   460

BERINTHIA They have so; but 'tis like the rivers of a modern phil-
osopher° (whose works, though a woman, I have read): it sets out
with a violent stream, splits in a thousand branches, and is all lost in
the sands.

AMANDA But do you think this river of love runs all its course without   465
doing any mischief? Do you think it overflows nothing?

BERINTHIA O yes. 'Tis true it never breaks into anybody's ground
that has the least fence about it; but it overflows all the commons°
that lie in its way. And this is the utmost achievement of those
dreadful champions in the field of love—the beaux.   470

AMANDA But prithee, Berinthia, instruct me a little farther, for I'm so great a novice, I am almost ashamed on't. My husband's leaving me whilst I was young and fond threw me into that depth of discontent, that ever since I have led so private and recluse a life, my ignorance is scarce conceivable. I therefore fain would be instructed; not (heaven knows) that what you call intrigues° have any charms for me: my love and principles are too well fixed. The practic° part of all unlawful love is— 475

BERINTHIA O 'tis abominable! But for the speculative—that we must all confess is entertaining. The conversation of all the virtuous women in the town turns upon that and new clothes. 480

AMANDA Pray be so just then to me to believe, 'tis with a world of innocency I would enquire, whether you think those women we call women of reputation do really 'scape all other men, as they do those shadows of 'em, the beaux. 485

BERINTHIA O no, Amanda, there are a sort of men make dreadful work amongst 'em: men that may be called the beaux' antipathy, for they agree in nothing but walking upon two legs.
These have brains; the beau has none.
These are in love with their mistress; the beau with himself. 490
They take care of her reputation; he's industrious to destroy it.
They are decent; he's a fop.
They are sound; he's rotten.°
They are men; he's an ass.

AMANDA If this be their character, I fancy we had here e'en now a pattern of 'em both. 495

BERINTHIA His lordship and Mr Worthy?

AMANDA The same.

BERINTHIA As for the lord, he's eminently so: and for the other, I can assure you there's not a man in town who has a better interest with the women that are worth having an interest with. But 'tis all private. He's like a back-stair minister at court,° who, whilst the reputed favourites are sauntering in the bed-chamber, is ruling the roast° in the closet. 500

AMANDA He answers then the opinion I had ever of him. Heavens! what a difference there is between a man like him, and that vain nauseous fop Sir Novelty. (*Taking her hand*) I must acquaint you with a secret, cousin. 'Tis not that fool alone has talked to me of love. Worthy has been tampering too. 'Tis true, he has done't in vain; not all his charms or art have power to shake me. My love, my duty, and my virtue are such faithful guards, I need not fear my heart should e'er betray me. But what I wonder at is this: I find I 505 510 did not start at his proposal as when it came from one whom I contemned. I therefore mention his attempt, that I may learn from you whence it proceeds; that vice (which cannot change its nature) 515 should so far change at least its shape, as that the self-same crime proposed from one shall seem a monster gaping at your ruin— when from another it shall look so kind as though it were your friend and never meant to harm you. Whence, think you, can this difference proceed? For 'tis not love, heaven knows. 520

BERINTHIA O no! I would not for the world believe it were. But possibly, should there a dreadful sentence pass upon you, to undergo the rage of both their passions—the pain you'd apprehend from one might seem so trivial to the other, the danger would not quite so much alarm you. 525

AMANDA Fie, fie, Berinthia, you would indeed alarm me, could you incline me to a thought that all the merit of mankind combined could shake that tender love I bear my husband. No, he sits triumphant in my heart, and nothing can dethrone him.

BERINTHIA But should he abdicate again, do you think you should 530 preserve the vacant throne ten tedious winters more in hopes of his return?

AMANDA Indeed I think I should. Though I confess, after those obligations he has to me, should he abandon me once more, my heart would grow extremely urgent with me to root him thence, and cast 535 him out for ever.

BERINTHIA Were I that thing they call a slighted wife, somebody should run the risk of being that thing they call—a husband.°

AMANDA O fie Berinthia, no revenge should ever be taken against a husband; but to wrong his bed is a vengeance which of all 540 vengeance—

BERINTHIA Is the sweetest. Ha, ha, ha. Don't I talk madly?

AMANDA Madly indeed.

BERINTHIA Yet I'm very innocent.

AMANDA That I dare swear you are. I know how to make allowances 545 for your humour. You were always very entertaining company. But I find since marriage and widowhood have shown you the world a little, you are very much improved.

BERINTHIA (aside) Alack-a-day, there has gone more than that to improve me, if she knew all. 550

AMANDA For heavens sake, Berinthia, tell me what way I shall take to persuade you to come and live with me?

BERINTHIA Why, one way in the world there is—and but one.

AMANDA Pray which is that?

BERINTHIA It is, to assure me—I shall be very welcome.   555

AMANDA If that be all, you shall e'en lie here tonight.

BERINTHIA Tonight?

AMANDA Yes, tonight.

BERINTHIA Why, the people where I lodge will think me mad.

AMANDA Let 'em think what they please.   560

BERINTHIA Say you so Amanda? Why, then they shall think what
they please; for I'm a young widow, and I care not what anybody
thinks. Ah, Amanda, it's a delicious thing to be a young widow.

AMANDA You'll hardly make me think so.

BERINTHIA Phu, because you are in love with your husband; but that   565
is not every woman's case.

AMANDA I hope 'twas yours, at least.

BERINTHIA Mine, say ye? Now have I a great mind to tell you a lie,
but I should do it so awkwardly you'd find me out.

AMANDA Then e'en speak the truth.   570

BERINTHIA Shall I? Then after all I did love him, Amanda—as a nun
does penance.

AMANDA Why did not you refuse to marry him then?

BERINTHIA Because my mother would have whipped me.

AMANDA How did you live together?   575

BERINTHIA Like man and wife, asunder.
He loved the country; I the town.
He hawks and hounds; I coaches and equipage.
He eating and drinking; I carding and playing.°
He the sound of a horn; I the squeak of a fiddle.   580
We were dull company at table, worse abed. Whenever we met, we
gave one another the spleen.° And never agreed but once, which
was about lying alone.

AMANDA But tell me one thing, truly and sincerely.

BERINTHIA What's that?   585

AMANDA Notwithstanding all these jars, did not his death at last—
extremely trouble you?

BERINTHIA O yes. Not that my present pangs were so very violent,
but the after-pains were intolerable. I was forced to wear a beastly
widow's band° a twelvemonth for't.   590

AMANDA Women I find have different inclinations.

BERINTHIA Women I find keep different company. When your husband ran away from you, if you had fallen into some of my
acquaintance, 'twould have saved you many a tear. But you go and

live with a grandmother, a bishop, and an old nurse; which was   595
enough to make any woman break her heart for her husband. Pray,
Amanda, if ever you are a widow again, keep yourself so as I do.

AMANDA Why, do you then resolve you'll never marry?

BERINTHIA O no; I resolve I will.

AMANDA How so?   600

BERINTHIA That I never may.

AMANDA You banter me.

BERINTHIA Indeed I don't. But I consider I'm a woman, and form my
resolutions accordingly.

AMANDA Well, my opinion is, form what resolution you will,   605
matrimony will be the end on't.

BERINTHIA Faith it won't.

AMANDA How do you know?

BERINTHIA I'm sure on't.

AMANDA Why, do you think 'tis impossible for you to fall in love?   610

BERINTHIA No.

AMANDA Nay, but to grow so passionately fond, that nothing but the
man you love can give you rest?

BERINTHIA Well, what then?

AMANDA Why, then you'll marry him.   615

BERINTHIA How do you know that?

AMANDA Why, what can you do else?

BERINTHIA Nothing—but sit and cry.

AMANDA Psha!

BERINTHIA Ah, poor Amanda, you have led a country life: but if   620
you'll consult the widows of this town, they'll tell you you should
never take a lease of a house you can hire for a quarter's warning.°

Exeunt

3.1

[*Lord Foppington's house*]

Enter Lord Foppington and Servant

FOPPINGTON Hey, fellow, let the coach come to the door.

SERVANT Will your lordship venture so soon to expose yourself to the weather?

FOPPINGTON Sir, I will venture as soon as I can, to expose myself to the ladies. Though give me my cloak however; for in that side-box,° what between the air that comes in at the door on one side, and the intolerable warmth of the masks° on t'other, a man gets so many heats and colds, 'twould destroy the canstitution of a harse.

SERVANT (*putting on his cloak*) I wish your lordship would please to keep house a little longer. I'm afraid your honour does not well consider your wound.

FOPPINGTON My wound? I would not be in eclipse another day, though I had as many wounds in my guts as I have had in my heart.

[*Exit Servant*]

Enter Young Fashion

YOUNG FASHION Brother, your servant. How do you find yourself today?

FOPPINGTON So well, that I have arder'd my coach to the door; so there's no great danger of death this baut, Tam.

YOUNG FASHION I'm very glad of it.

FOPPINGTON (*aside*) That I believe's a lie. [*Aloud*] Prithee, Tam, tell me one thing: did nat your heart cut a caper° up to your mauth, when you heard I was run through the bady?

YOUNG FASHION Why do you think it should?

FOPPINGTON Because I remember mine did so, when I heard my father was shat through the head.

YOUNG FASHION It then did very ill.

FOPPINGTON Prithee, why so?

YOUNG FASHION Because he used you very well.

FOPPINGTON Well? Naw strike me dumb he starved me. He has let me want a thausand women for want of a thausand paund.

YOUNG FASHION Then he hindered you from making a great many ill bargains, for I think no woman is worth money that will take money.

FOPPINGTON If I were a younger brother, I should think so too.

YOUNG FASHION Why, is it possible you can value a woman that's to   35
be bought?

FOPPINGTON Prithee, why not as well as a pad nag?°

YOUNG FASHION Because a woman has a heart to dispose of; a horse
has none.

FOPPINGTON Look you Tam, of all things that belang to a woman, I   40
have an aversion to her heart; far when once a woman has given you
her heart—you can never get rid of the rest of her body.

YOUNG FASHION This is strange doctrine. But pray, in your amours
how is it with your own heart?

FOPPINGTON Why, my heart in my amours—is like my heart aut of   45
my amours: *à la glace*.° My bady, Tam, is a watch and my heart is
the pendulum to it; whilst the finger runs raund to every hour in
the circle, that still beats the same time.

YOUNG FASHION Then you are seldom much in love?

FOPPINGTON Never, stap my vitals.   50

YOUNG FASHION Why then did you make all this bustle about
Amanda?

FOPPINGTON Because she was a woman of an insolent virtue, and I
thought my self piqued in honour to debauch her.

YOUNG FASHION Very well. (*Aside*) Here's a rare fellow for you, to   55
have the spending of five thousand pounds a year. But now for my
business with him. (*To Foppington*) Brother, though I know to talk
to you of business (especially of money) is a theme not quite so
entertaining to you as that of the ladies, my necessities are such, I
hope you'll have patience to hear me.   60

FOPPINGTON The greatness of your necessities, Tam, is the worst
argument in the world for your being patiently heard. I do believe
you are going to make me a very good speech, but, strike me dumb, it
has the worst beginning of any speech I have heard this twelvemonth.

YOUNG FASHION I'm very sorry you think so.   65

FOPPINGTON I do believe thau art. But come, let's know thy affair
quickly, far 'tis a new play, and I shall be so rumpled and squeezed
with pressing through the crawd to get to my servant, the women
will think I have lain all night in my clothes.

YOUNG FASHION Why then (that I may not be the author of so great a   70
misfortune) my case in a word is this. The necessary expenses of
my travels have so much exceeded the wretched income of my
annuity, that I have been forced to mortgage it for five hundred
pounds, which is spent; so that unless you are so kind to assist me
in redeeming it, I know no remedy but to go take a purse.°   75

FOPPINGTON Why, faith, Tam—to give you my sense of the thing, I do think taking a purse the best remedy in the world: for if you succeed, you are relieved that way; if you are taken—you are relieved t'other.°

YOUNG FASHION I'm glad to see you are in so pleasant a humour; I   80
hope I shall find the effects on't.

FOPPINGTON Why, do you then really think it a reasonable thing I should give you five hundred paunds?

YOUNG FASHION I do not ask it as a due, brother; I am willing to receive it as a favour.   85

FOPPINGTON Thau art willing to receive it anyhaw, strike me speechless. But these are damned times to give money in; taxes are so great, repairs so exorbitant, tenants such rogues, and peri-wigs so dear, that the devil take me I am reduced to that extrem-ity in my cash, I have been forced to retrench in that one article   90
of sweet pawder,° till I have braught it dawn to five guineas a manth. Naw judge, Tam, whether I can spare you five hundred paunds.

YOUNG FASHION If you can't, I must starve, that's all. (*Aside*) Damn him.   95

FOPPINGTON All I can say is, you should have been a better husband.°

YOUNG FASHION Oons, if you can't live upon five thousand a year, how do you think I should do't upon two hundred?

FOPPINGTON Don't be in a passion Tam, far passion is the most   100
unbecoming thing in the world—to the face. Look you, I don't love to say anything to you to make you melancholy; but upon this occasion I must take leave to put you in mind, that a running horse° does require more attendance than a coach-horse. Nature has made some difference 'twixt you and I.   105

YOUNG FASHION Yes, she has made you older. (*Aside*) Pox take her.

FOPPINGTON That is nat all, Tam.

YOUNG FASHION Why, what is there else?

FOPPINGTON (*looking first upon himself, then upon his brother*) Ask the ladies.   110

YOUNG FASHION Why, thou essence-bottle, thou musk-cat,° dost thou then think thou hast any advantage over me, but what fortune has given thee?

FOPPINGTON I do, stap my vitals.

YOUNG FASHION Now, by all that's great and powerful, thou art the   115
prince of coxcombs.

FOPPINGTON Sir—I am praud of being at the head of so prevailing a
party.

YOUNG FASHION Will nothing then provoke thee? Draw, coward.

FOPPINGTON Look you, Tam, you know I have always taken you for a   120
mighty dull fellow, and here is one of the foolishest plats° broke out
that I have seen a long time. Your paverty makes your life so bur-
densome to you, you would provoke me to a quarrel, in hopes either
to slip through my lungs into my estate, or to get yourself run
through the guts, to put an end to your pain. But I will disappoint   125
you in both your designs; far with the temper of a philasapher, and
the discretion of a statesman—I will go to the play with my sword
in my scabbard.

    Exit Foppington

YOUNG FASHION So. Farewell, snuff-box. And now, conscience, I
defy thee. Lory!   130

    Enter Lory

LORY Sir.

YOUNG FASHION Here's rare news, Lory; his lordship has given me a
pill has purged off all my scruples.

LORY Then my heart's at ease again: for I have been in a lamentable
fright, sir, ever since your conscience had the impudence to intrude   135
into your company.

YOUNG FASHION Be at peace; it will come there no more. My brother
has given it a wring by the nose, and I have kicked it downstairs. So
run away to the inn; get the horses ready quickly, and bring 'em to
old Coupler's, without a moment's delay.   140

LORY Then, sir, you are going straight about the fortune?

YOUNG FASHION I am. Away! Fly, Lory!

LORY The happiest day I ever saw. I'm upon the wing already.

    Exeunt several° ways

3.2

    A garden [*in Loveless's house*]

    Enter Loveless and Servant

LOVELESS Is my wife within?

SERVANT No, sir, she has been gone out this half hour.

LOVELESS 'Tis well; leave me.

    [*Exit Servant*]

(*Alone*) Sure fate has yet some business to be done,
Before Amanda's heart and mine must rest.   5
Else why amongst those legions of her sex
Which throng the world
Should she pick out for her companion
The only one on earth
Whom nature has endowed for her undoing?   10
'Undoing' was't I said? Who shall undo her?
Is not her empire fixed? Am I not hers?
Did she not rescue me, a grovelling slave,
When chained and bound by that black tyrant vice,
I laboured in his vilest drudgery?°   15
Did she not ransome me, and set me free?
Nay more.
When by my follies sunk
To a poor tattered despicable beggar,
Did she not lift me up to envied fortune?   20
Give me herself, and all that she possessed,
Without a thought of more return
Than what a poor repenting heart might make her?
Han't she done this? And if she has,
Am I not strongly bound to love her for it?   25
To love her! Why, do I not love her then?
By earth and heaven I do.
Nay, I have demonstration that I do:
For I would sacrifice my life to serve her.
Yet hold—if laying down my life   30
Be demonstration of my love,
What is't I feel in favour of Berinthia?
For should she be in danger, methinks I could incline
To risk it for her service too; and yet I do not love her.
How then subsists my proof?   35
O, I have found it out.
What I would do for one is demonstration of my love; and if I'd do
as much for t'other, it there is demonstration of my friendship—
ay—it must be so. I find I'm very much her friend.
—Yet let me ask myself one puzzling question more.   40
Whence springs this mighty friendship all at once?
For our acquaintance is of later date.
Now friendship's said to be a plant of tedious growth:° its root
composed of tender fibres; nice in their taste, cautious in spreading,

checked with the least corruption in the soil; long ere it take,° and 45
longer still ere it appear to do so; whilst mine is in a moment shot so
high, and fixed so fast, it seems beyond the power of storms to
shake it. I doubt it thrives too fast. (*Musing*)
  Enter Berinthia
—Ha, she here! Nay, then take heed my heart, for there are dangers
towards. 50

BERINTHIA What makes you look so thoughtful, sir? I hope you are
not ill?

LOVELESS I was debating, madam, whether I was so or not; and that
was it which made me look so thoughtful.

BERINTHIA Is it then so hard a matter to decide? I thought all people 55
had been acquainted with their own bodies, though few people
know their own minds.

LOVELESS What if the distemper I suspect be in the mind?

BERINTHIA Why, then I'll undertake to prescribe you a cure.

LOVELESS Alas, you undertake you know not what. 60

BERINTHIA So far at least then allow me to be a physician.

LOVELESS Nay, I'll allow you so yet farther: for I have reason to
believe, should I put myself into your hands, you would increase
my distemper.

BERINTHIA Perhaps I might have reasons from the College° not to be 65
too quick in your cure; but 'tis possible I might find ways to give
you often ease, sir.

LOVELESS Were I but sure of that, I'd quickly lay my case before
you.

BERINTHIA Whether you are sure of it or no, what risk do you run in 70
trying?

LOVELESS O, a very great one.

BERINTHIA How?

LOVELESS You might betray my distemper to my wife.

BERINTHIA And so lose all my practice. 75

LOVELESS Will you then keep my secret?

BERINTHIA I will, if it don't burst me.

LOVELESS Swear.

BERINTHIA I do.

LOVELESS By what? 80

BERINTHIA By woman.

LOVELESS That's swearing by my deity. Do it by your own, or I shan't
believe you.

BERINTHIA By man, then.

LOVELESS I'm satisfied. Now hear my symptoms, and give me your 85
advice. The first were these:
When 'twas my chance to see you at the play,
A random glance you threw at first alarmed me;
I could not turn my eyes from whence the danger came.
I gazed upon you 'till you shot again, 90
And then my fears came on me.
My heart began to pant, my limbs to tremble,
My blood grew thin, my pulse beat quick,
My eyes grew hot and dim, and all the frame of nature
Shook with apprehension. 95
'Tis true, some small recruits of resolution
My manhood brought to my assistance,
And by their help I made a stand awhile,
But found at last your arrows flew so thick,
They could not fail to pierce me; 100
So left the field,
And fled for shelter to Amanda's arms.
What think you of these symptoms, pray?
BERINTHIA Feverish every one of 'em. But what relief pray did your
wife afford you? 105
LOVELESS Why, instantly she let me blood, which for the present
much assuaged my flame. But when I saw you, out it burst
again, and raged with greater fury than before. Nay, since you now
appear, 'tis so increased that in a moment if you do not help me, I
shall, whilst you look on, consume to ashes. (*Taking hold of her* 110
hand)
BERINTHIA (*breaking from him*) O Lard, let me go! 'Tis the plague,
and we shall all be infected.
LOVELESS (*catching her in his arms and kissing her*) Then we'll die
together,° my charming angel.
BERINTHIA O Ged—the Devil's in you. Lord, let me go, here's 115
somebody coming.
        Enter Servant
SERVANT Sir, my lady's come home, and desires to speak with you.
She's in her chamber.
LOVELESS Tell her I'm coming.
        Exit Servant
    (*To Berinthia*) But before I go, one glass of nectar more to drink her 120
    health.
BERINTHIA Stand off, or I shall hate you, by heavens.

LOVELESS (*kissing her*) In matters of love, a woman's oath is no more
to be minded than a man's.

BERINTHIA Um— 125

Enter Worthy

WORTHY Ha! What's here? My old mistress, and so close, i' faith? I
would not spoil her sport for the universe.

He retires

BERINTHIA O Ged! Now do I pray to heaven with all my heart and
soul, that the devil in hell may take me, if ever—(*exit Loveless running*)°—I was better pleased in my life! This man has bewitched 130
me, that's certain. (*Sighing*) Well, I am condemned; but thanks to
heaven I feel myself each moment more and more prepared for my
execution. Nay, to that degree, I don't perceive I have the least fear
of dying. No, I find, let the executioner be but a man, and there's
nothing will suffer with more resolution than a woman. Well, I 135
never had but one intrigue yet; but I confess I long to have another.
Pray heaven it end as the first did though, that we may both grow
weary at a time; for 'tis a melancholy thing for lovers to out-live one
another.

Enter Worthy

WORTHY (*aside*) This discovery's a lucky one. I hope to make a happy 140
use on't. That gentlewoman there is no fool; so I shall be able to
make her understand her interest. (*To Berinthia*) Your servant,
madam. I need not ask you how you do; you have got so good a
colour.

BERINTHIA No better than I used to have, I suppose? 145

WORTHY A little more blood in your cheeks.

BERINTHIA The weather's hot.

WORTHY If it were not, a woman may have a colour.

BERINTHIA What do you mean by that?

WORTHY Nothing. 150

BERINTHIA Why do you smile then?

WORTHY Because the weather's hot.

BERINTHIA You'll never leave roguing, I see that.

WORTHY (*putting his finger to his nose*) You'll never leave—I see that.

BERINTHIA Well, I can't imagine what you drive at. Pray tell me what 155
you mean?

WORTHY Do you tell me; it's the same thing.

BERINTHIA I can't.

WORTHY Guess!

BERINTHIA I shall guess wrong. 160

WORTHY Indeed you won't.

BERINTHIA Psha! either tell, or let it alone.

WORTHY Nay, rather than let it alone, I will tell. But first I must put
you in mind that after what has passed 'twixt you and I, very few
things ought to be secrets between us.   165

BERINTHIA Why, what secrets do we hide? I know of none.

WORTHY Yes, there are two; one I have hid from you, and t'other
you would hide from me. You are fond of Loveless, which I have
discovered. And I am fond of his wife—

BERINTHIA Which I have discovered.   170

WORTHY Very well, now I confess your discovery to be true. What do
you say to mine?

BERINTHIA Why, I confess—I would swear 'twere false, if I thought
you were fool enough to believe me.

WORTHY Now am I almost in love with you again. Nay, I don't know   175
but I might be quite so, had I made one short campaign with
Amanda. Therefore if you find 'twould tickle your vanity to bring
me down once more to your lure,° e'en help me quickly to dispatch
her business,° that I may have nothing else to do, but to apply
myself to yours.   180

BERINTHIA Do you then think, sir, I am old enough to be a bawd?

WORTHY No, but I think you are wise enough to—

BERINTHIA To do what?

WORTHY To hoodwink Amanda with a gallant, that she mayn't see
who is her husband's mistress.   185

BERINTHIA (aside) He has reason. The hint's a good one.

WORTHY Well, madam. What think you on't?

BERINTHIA I think you are so much a deeper politician in these
affairs than I am, that I ought to have a very great regard to your
advice.   190

WORTHY Then give me leave to put you in mind, that the most easy,
safe, and pleasant situation for your own amour, is the house in
which you now are, provided you keep Amanda from any sort of
suspicion; that the way to do that is to engage her in an intrigue of
her own, making yourself her confidant; and the way to bring her to   195
intrigue is to make her jealous of her husband in a wrong place,
which the more you foment, the less you'll be suspected. This is my
scheme, in short; which if you follow as you should do, my dear
Berinthia, we may all four pass the winter very pleasantly.

BERINTHIA Well, I could be glad to have nobody's sins to answer for   200
but my own. But where there is a necessity—

WORTHY Right as you say, where there is a necessity, a Christian is
bound to help his neighbour.° So, good Berinthia, lose no time, but
let us begin the dance as fast as we can.

BERINTHIA Not till the fiddles are in tune, pray, sir. Your lady's   205
strings will be very apt to fly, I can tell you that, if they are wound
up too hastily. But if you'll have patience to screw 'em to their
pitch by degrees, I don't doubt but she may endure to be played
upon.

WORTHY Ay, and will make admirable music too, or I'm mistaken;   210
but have you had no private closet discourse with her yet about
males and females, and so forth, which may give you hopes in her
constitution? For I know her morals are the devil against us.

BERINTHIA I have had so much discourse with her, that I believe were
she once cured of her fondness to her husband, the fortress of her   215
virtue would not be so impregnable as she fancies.

WORTHY What! She runs, I'll warrant you, into that common mistake
of fond° wives, who conclude themselves virtuous because they can
refuse a man they don't like, when they have got one they do.

BERINTHIA True, and therefore I think 'tis a presumptuous thing in a   220
woman to assume the name of virtuous, till she has heartily hated
her husband, and been soundly in love with somebody else; whom,
if she has withstood—then—much good may it do her.

WORTHY Well, so much for her virtue. Now, one word of her inclinations, and everyone to their post. What opinion do you find she   225
has of me?

BERINTHIA What you could wish; she thinks you handsome and
discreet.

WORTHY Good, that's thinking half-seas over.° One tide more brings
us into port.   230

BERINTHIA Perhaps it may, though still remember, there's a difficult
bar° to pass.

WORTHY I know there is, but I don't question I shall get well over it,
by the help of such a pilot.

BERINTHIA You may depend upon your pilot; she'll do the best she   235
can. So weigh anchor and be gone as soon as you please.

WORTHY I'm under sail already. Adieu.
        Exit Worthy

BERINTHIA Bon voyage.
    (*Alone*) So, here's fine work. What a business have I undertaken!
    I'm a very pretty gentlewoman truly. But there was no avoiding it: 240
    he'd have ruined me if I had refused him. Besides, faith, I begin to

48

fancy there may be as much pleasure in carrying on another body's intrigue as one's own. This at least is certain, it exercises almost all the entertaining faculties of a woman. For there's employment for hypocrisy, invention, deceit, flattery, mischief and lying.   245

Enter Amanda, her Woman following her

WOMAN If you please, madam, only to say, whither you'll have me buy 'em or not?

AMANDA Yes, no, go fiddle; I care not what you do. Prithee leave me.

WOMAN I have done.

Exit Woman

BERINTHIA What in the name of Jove's the matter with you?   250

AMANDA The matter Berinthia! I'm almost mad, I'm plagued to death.

BERINTHIA Who is it that plagues you?

AMANDA Who do you think should plague a wife, but her husband?

BERINTHIA O ho, is it come to that? We shall have you wish yourself a   255
widow by and by.

AMANDA Would I were any thing but what I am. A base ungrateful man, after what I have done for him, to use me thus!

BERINTHIA What, he has been ogling now, I'll warrant you?

AMANDA Yes, he has been ogling.   260

BERINTHIA And so you are jealous? Is that all?

AMANDA That all! Is jealousy then nothing?

BERINTHIA It should be nothing, if I were in your case.

AMANDA Why, what would you do?

BERINTHIA I'd cure myself.   265

AMANDA How?

BERINTHIA Let blood in the fond vein; care as little for my husband, as he did for me.

AMANDA That would not stop his course.

BERINTHIA Nor nothing else, when the wind's in the warm corner.   270
Look you, Amanda, you may build castles in the air, and fume, and fret, and grow thin and lean, and pale and ugly, if you please; but I tell you, no man worth having is true to his wife, or can be true to his wife, or ever was, or ever will be so.

AMANDA Do you then really think he's false to me? For I did but   275
suspect him.

BERINTHIA Think so? I know he's so.

AMANDA Is it possible? Pray tell me what you know?

BERINTHIA Don't press me then to name names; for that I have sworn I won't do.   280

AMANDA Well I won't; but let me know all you can without perjury.

BERINTHIA I'll let you know enough to prevent any wise woman's dying of the pip;° and I hope you'll pluck up your spirits, and show upon occasion, you can be as good a wife as the best of 'em.

AMANDA Well, what a woman can do I'll endeavour.   285

BERINTHIA O, a woman can do a great deal, if once she sets her mind to it. Therefore pray don't stand trifling any longer; and teasing yourself with this and that, and your love and your virtue, and I know not what. But resolve to hold up your head, get a-tiptoe, and look over 'em all; for to my certain knowledge your husband is   290 a-pickeering° elsewhere.

AMANDA You are sure on't?

BERINTHIA Positively; he fell in love at the play.

AMANDA Right, the very same; do you know the ugly thing?

BERINTHIA Yes, I know her well enough; but she's no such an ugly   295 thing, neither.

AMANDA Is she very handsome?

BERINTHIA Truly I think so.

AMANDA Hey ho.

BERINTHIA What do you sigh for now?   300

AMANDA Oh my heart.

BERINTHIA (aside) Only the pangs of nature; she's in labour of her love. Heaven send her a quick delivery; I'm sure she has a good midwife.

AMANDA I'm very ill; I must go to my chamber. Dear Berinthia, don't   305 leave me a moment.

BERINTHIA No, don't fear. (Aside) I'll see you safe brought to bed, I'll warrant you.

Exit Amanda leaning upon Berinthia

3.3

[Sir Tunbelly Clumsy's house in the country]

Enter Young Fashion and Lory

YOUNG FASHION So, here's our inheritance, Lory, if we can but get into possession. But methinks the seat of our family looks like Noah's ark,° as if the chief part on't were designed for the fowls of the air, and the beasts of the field.

LORY Pray sir, don't let your head run upon the orders of building°   5
here; get but the heiress, let the devil take the house.

YOUNG FASHION Get but the house, let the devil take the heiress, I
say; at least if she be as old Coupler describes her. But come, we
have no time to squander. Knock at the door.
Lory knocks two or three times
What the devil! Have they got no ears in this house? Knock harder.   10

LORY Egad, sir, this will prove some enchanted castle;° we shall have
the giant come out by and by with his club, and beat our brains out.
(*Knocks again*)

YOUNG FASHION Hush! They come.

[SERVANT] (*from within*) Who is there?   15

LORY Open the door and see. Is that your country breeding?

[SERVANT] (*within*) Ay, but two words to a bargain. Tummas, is the
blunderbuss° primed?

YOUNG FASHION Oons give 'em good words, Lory; we shall be shot
here a-fortune-catching.   20

LORY Egad, sir, I think y'are in the right on't. Ho, Mr What d'ye call
'um.
[Another] Servant appears at the window with a blunderbuss

[SERVANT] Weall, naw what's yare business?°

YOUNG FASHION Nothing, sir, but to wait upon Sir Tunbelly, with
your leave.   25

SERVANT To weat upon Sir Tunbelly? Why, you'll find that's just as
Sir Tunbelly pleases.

YOUNG FASHION But will you do me the favour, sir, to know whether
Sir Tunbelly pleases or not?

SERVANT Why, look you, do you see, with good words much may be   30
done. Ralph, go thy weas, and ask Sir Tunbelly if he pleases to be
waited upon. And dost hear? Call to Nurse, that she may lock up
Miss Hoyden, before the geats open.

YOUNG FASHION D'ye hear that, Lory?

LORY Ay sir, I'm afraid we shall find a difficult job on't. Pray heaven   35
that old rogue Coupler han't sent us to fetch milk out of the
gunroom.°

YOUNG FASHION I'll warrant thee all will go well. See, the door opens.
*Enter Sir Tunbelly, with his Servants, armed with guns, clubs,
pitchforks, scythes [and other rustic weapons]*

LORY (*running behind his master*) O Lord, O Lord, O Lord, we are
both dead men.   40

YOUNG FASHION Take heed, fool, thy fear will ruin us.

LORY My fear, sir! 'Sdeath, sir, I fear nothing. (*Aside*) Would I were
well up to the chin in a horse-pond.

SIR TUNBELLY Who is it here has any business with me?

YOUNG FASHION Sir, 'tis I, if your name be Sir Tunbelly Clumsy.   45

SIR TUNBELLY Sir, my name is Sir Tunbelly Clumsy, whither you
have any business with me or not. So you see I am not ashamed of
my name—nor my face neither.

YOUNG FASHION Sir, you have no cause, that I know of.

SIR TUNBELLY Sir, if you have no cause neither, I desire to know who   50
you are; for till I know your name, I shall not ask you to come into
my house; and when I know your name—'tis six to four I don't ask
you neither.

YOUNG FASHION (*giving him a letter*) Sir, I hope you'll find this letter
an authentic passport.   55

SIR TUNBELLY Cod's my life, I ask your lordship's pardon ten thousand times. (*To his servants*) Here, run in a-doors quickly: get a
Scotch-coal fire in the great parlour, set all the Turkey-work
chairs° in their places, get the great brass candlesticks out, and be
sure stick the sockets full of laurel°—run! (*Turning to Young*   60
Fashion) My Lord, I ask your lordship's pardon. (*To other servants*)
And do you hear, run away to Nurse, bid her let Miss Hoyden loose
again, and if it was not shifting-day,° let her put on a clean tucker°
quick.
      Exeunt Servants confusedly
(*To Young Fashion*) I hope your honour will excuse the disorder of   65
my family; we are not used to receive men of your lordship's great
quality every day. Pray where are your coaches and servants, my
lord?

YOUNG FASHION Sir, that I might give you and your fair daughter a
proof how impatient I am to be nearer akin to you, I left my   70
equipage to follow me, and came away post, with only one servant.

SIR TUNBELLY Your lordship does me too much honour. It was
exposing your person to too much fatigue and danger, I protest it
was; but my daughter shall endeavour to make you what amends
she can; and though I say it that should not say it—Hoyden has   75
charms.

YOUNG FASHION Sir, I am not a stranger to them, though I am to her.
Common fame has done her justice.

SIR TUNBELLY My Lord, I am common fame's very grateful humble
servant. My lord—my girl's young, Hoyden is young, my lord; but   80
this I must say for her, what she wants in art, she has by nature;

what she wants in experience, she has in breeding; and what's
wanting in her age is made good in her constitution. So pray, my
lord, walk in; pray my lord, walk in.

YOUNG FASHION Sir, I wait upon you.   85

    Exeunt

3.4

    [*A room in Sir Tunbelly's house*]

    Miss Hoyden alone

HOYDEN Sure never nobody was used as I am. I know well enough
what other girls do, for all they think to make a fool of me; it's well I
have a husband a-coming, or i'cod I'd marry the baker, I would so.
Nobody can knock at the gate, but presently I must be locked up,
and here's the young greyhound bitch can run loose about the   5
house all day long, she can. 'Tis very well.

NURSE (*without, opening the door*) Miss Hoyden, Miss, Miss, Miss!
Miss Hoyden!

    Enter Nurse

HOYDEN Well, what do you make such a noise for, ha? What do you
din a body's ears for? Can't one be at quiet for you?   10

NURSE What do I din your ears for? Here's one come will din your
ears for you.

HOYDEN What care I who's come? I care not a fig who comes, nor
who goes, as long as I must be locked up like the ale-cellar.

NURSE That, miss, is for fear you should be drank, before you are ripe. 15

HOYDEN O don't you trouble your head about that; I'm as ripe as you,
though not so mellow.

NURSE Very well; now have I a good mind to lock you up again, and
not let you see my lord tonight.

HOYDEN My lord? Why, is my husband come?   20

NURSE Yes marry is he, and a goodly person too.

HOYDEN (*hugging Nurse*) O my dear Nurse, forgive me this once, and
I'll never misuse you again; no, if I do, you shall give me three
thumps on the back, and a great pinch by the cheek.

NURSE Ah the poor thing, see how it melts, it's as full of good nature,   25
as an egg's full of meat.

HOYDEN But, my dear Nurse, don't lie now: is he come, by your
troth?

NURSE Yes, by my truly, is he.

HOYDEN O Lord! I'll go put on my laced smock, though I'm whipped   30
till the blood run down my heels for't.

    Exit [Hoyden] running

NURSE Eh! The Lord succour thee, how thou art delighted.

    Exit [Nurse] after her

3.5

    [*Another room in Sir Tunbelly's house*]

    Enter Sir Tunbelly, and Young Fashion [and a Servant with wine]

SIR TUNBELLY My lord, I am proud of the honour to see your lordship within my doors; and I humbly crave leave to bid you welcome,
in a cup of sack wine.°

YOUNG FASHION Sir, to your daughter's health. (*Drinks*)

SIR TUNBELLY Ah poor girl, she'll be scared out of her wits on her   5
wedding night; for, honestly speaking, she does not know a man
from a woman, but by his beard, and his breeches.

YOUNG FASHION Sir, I don't doubt but she has a virtuous education,
which with the rest of her merit, makes me long to see her mine. I
wish you would dispense with the canonical hour,° and let it be this   10
very night.

SIR TUNBELLY O not so soon neither, that's shooting my girl before
you bid her stand.° No, give her fair warning. We'll sign and seal
tonight, if you please; and this day sevennight—let the jade look to
her quarters.   15

YOUNG FASHION This day sennight! Why, what do you take me for—
a ghost, sir? 'Slife, sir, I'm made of flesh and blood, and bones and
sinews, and can no more live a week without your daughter—(*aside*)
than I can live a month with her.

SIR TUNBELLY Oh, I'll warrant you my hero; young men are hot I   20
know, but they don't boil over at that rate, neither. Besides, my
wench's wedding-gown is not come home yet.

YOUNG FASHION O, no matter, sir, I'll take her in her shift. (*Aside*) A
pox of this old fellow, he'll delay the business till my damned star°
finds me out, and discovers me. (*To Sir Tunbelly*) Pray, sir, let it be   25
done without ceremony, 'twill save money.

SIR TUNBELLY Money? Save money when Hoyden's to be married?

Udswoons, I'll give my wench a wedding-dinner, though I go to
grass with the king of Assyria° for't; and such a dinner it shall be, as
is not to be cooked in the poaching of an egg. Therefore, my noble   30
lord, have a little patience; we'll go and look over our deeds and
settlements immediately; and as for your bride, though you may be
sharp-set before she's quite ready, I'll engage for my girl, she stays
your stomach° at last.
     Exeunt

4.1

[Another room in Sir Tunbelly's house]

Enter Miss Hoyden and Nurse

NURSE Well miss, how do you like your husband that is to be?

HOYDEN O Lord, Nurse, I'm so overjoyed, I can scarce contain myself.

NURSE O but you must have a care of being too fond, for men nowadays hate a woman that loves 'em.   5

HOYDEN Love him? Why, do you think I love him, Nurse? I'cod I would not care if he were hanged, so I were but once married to him. No, that which pleases me is to think what work I'll make when I get to London; for when I am a wife and a lady both, Nurse, i'cod I'll flaunt it with the best of 'em.   10

NURSE Look, look, if his honour be not coming again to you; now if I were sure you would behave yourself handsomely, and not disgrace me that have brought you up, I'd leave you alone together.

HOYDEN That's my best Nurse, do as you would be done by.° Trust us together this once, and if I don't show my breeding   15 from the head to the foot of me, may I be twice married, and die a maid.

NURSE Well, this once I'll venture you, but if you disparage me—

HOYDEN Never fear, I'll show him my parts, I'll warrant him.

Exit Nurse

(*Alone*) These old women are so wise when they get a poor girl in   20 their clutches, but ere it be long I shall know what's what, as well as the best of 'em.

Enter Young Fashion

YOUNG FASHION Your servant, madam. I'm glad to find you alone, for I have something of importance to speak to you about.

HOYDEN Sir—my lord, I meant—you may speak to me about what   25 you please. I shall give you a civil answer.

YOUNG FASHION You give me so obliging a one, it encourages me to tell you in few words what I think both for your interest and mine. Your father, I suppose you know, has resolved to make me happy in being your husband, and I hope I may depend upon your consent   30 to perform what he desires.

HOYDEN Sir, I never disobey my father in anything but eating of green gooseberries.

56

YOUNG FASHION So good a daughter must needs make an admirable
wife. I am therefore impatient till you are mine; and hope you   35
will so far consider the violence of my love that you won't
have the cruelty to defer my happiness, so long as your father
designs it.

HOYDEN Pray, my lord, how long is that?

YOUNG FASHION Madam, a thousand year—a whole week.   40

HOYDEN A week! Why, I shall be an old woman by that time.

YOUNG FASHION And I an old man, which you'll find a greater
misfortune than t'other.

HOYDEN Why, I thought 'twas to be tomorrow morning, as soon as I
was up; I'm sure Nurse told me so.   45

YOUNG FASHION And it shall be tomorrow morning still, if you'll
consent.

HOYDEN If I'll consent? Why, I thought I was to obey you as my
husband?

YOUNG FASHION That's when we are married; till then, I am to obey   50
you.

HOYDEN Why then if we are to take it by turns, it's the same thing;
I'll obey you now, and when we are married, you shall obey me.

YOUNG FASHION With all my heart, but I doubt we must get Nurse
on our side, or we shall hardly prevail with the Chaplain.   55

HOYDEN No more we shan't indeed, for he loves her better than he
loves his pulpit, and would always be a-preaching to her, by his
good will.°

YOUNG FASHION Why then my dear little bedfellow, if you'll call her
hither, we'll try to persuade her presently.   60

HOYDEN O Lord, I can tell you a way how to persuade her to
anything.

YOUNG FASHION How's that?

HOYDEN Why, tell her she's a wholesome comely woman—and give
her half-a-crown.   65

YOUNG FASHION Nay, if that will do, she shall have half a score of
'em.

HOYDEN O gemini, for half that, she'd marry you herself. I'll run and
call her.
        Exit Hoyden

YOUNG FASHION (*alone*) So, matters go swimmingly. This is a rare   70
girl, i' faith. I shall have a fine time on't with her at London; I'm
much mistaken if she don't prove a March hare all the year round.
What a scampering chase will she make on't, when she finds the

whole kennel of beaux at her tail! Hey to the park and the play, and
the church, and the devil; she'll show 'em sport, I'll warrant 'em.   75
But no matter, she brings an estate will afford me a separate
maintenance.°

Enter Hoyden and Nurse

YOUNG FASHION How do you do, good mistress Nurse? I desired
your young lady would give me leave to see you, that I might thank
you for your extraordinary care and conduct in her education; pray   80
accept of this small acknowledgement for it at present, and depend
upon my farther kindness, when I shall be that happy thing her
husband. [*Handing over a guinea*]

NURSE (*aside*) Gold, by makings! Your honour's goodness is too great;
alas, all I can boast of is, I gave her pure good milk, and so your   85
honour would have said, an you had seen how the poor thing
sucked it. Eh, God's blessing on the sweet face on't, how it used to
hang at this poor teat, and suck and squeeze, and kick and sprawl it
would, 'till the belly on't was so full, it would drop off like a leech.°

HOYDEN (*to Nurse, taking her angrily aside*) Pray one word with you.   90
Prithee, Nurse, don't stand ripping up old stories, to make one
ashamed before one's love. Do you think such a fine proper°
gentleman as he cares for a fiddlecome tale of a draggle-tailed° girl?
If you have a mind to make him have a good opinion of a woman,
don't tell him what one did then, tell him what one can do now. (*To*   95
Young Fashion) I hope your honour will excuse my mismanners to
whisper before you; it was only to give some orders about the
family.

YOUNG FASHION O everything, madam, is to give way to business;
besides, good housewifery is a very commendable quality in a   100
young lady.

HOYDEN Pray sir, are the young ladies good housewives at London
town? Do they darn their own linen?

YOUNG FASHION O no, they study how to spend money, not to save
it.   105

HOYDEN I'cod, I don't know but that may be better sport than
t'other; ha, Nurse?

YOUNG FASHION Well, you shall have your choice when you come
there.

HOYDEN Shall I? Then by my troth I'll get there as fast as I can. (*To*   110
Nurse) His honour desires you'll be so kind as to let us be married
tomorrow.

NURSE Tomorrow, my dear madam?

YOUNG FASHION Yes, tomorrow, sweet Nurse, privately; young folks
  you know are impatient, and Sir Tunbelly would make us stay a   115
  week for a wedding-dinner. Now all things being signed, and
  sealed, and agreed, I fancy there could be no great harm in practis-
  ing a scene or two of matrimony in private, if it were only to give us
  the better assurance when we come to play it in public.

NURSE Nay, I must confess stolen pleasures are sweet; but if you   120
  should be married now, what will you do when Sir Tunbelly calls
  for you to be wed?

HOYDEN Why then we'll be married again.

NURSE What, twice my child?

HOYDEN I'cod I don't care how often I'm married, not I.   125

YOUNG FASHION Pray, Nurse, don't you be against your young
  lady's good, for by this means she'll have the pleasure of two
  wedding-days.

HOYDEN (to Nurse softly) And of two wedding-nights too, Nurse.

NURSE Well, I'm such a tender hearted fool, I find I can refuse   130
  nothing; so you shall e'en follow your own inventions.

HOYDEN Shall I? (Aside) O Lord, I could leap over the moon.

YOUNG FASHION Dear Nurse, this goodness of yours shan't go
  unrewarded; but now you must employ your power with Mr Bull
  the chaplain, that he may do us his friendly office too, and then we   135
  shall all be happy. Do you think you can prevail with him?

NURSE Prevail with him? Or he shall never prevail with me, I can tell
  him that.

HOYDEN My lord, she has had him upon the hip° this seven year.

YOUNG FASHION I'm glad to hear it; however, to strengthen your   140
  interest with him, you may let him know I have several fat livings°
  in my gift, and that the first that falls shall be in your disposal.

NURSE Nay, then I'll make him marry more folks than one, I'll
  promise him.

HOYDEN Faith do Nurse, make him marry you too. I'm sure he'll do't   145
  for a fat living, for he loves eating more than he loves his Bible; and
  I have often heard him say, a fat living was the best meat in the
  world.

NURSE Ay, and I'll make him commend the sauce too, or I'll bring his
  gown to a cassock,° I will so.   150

YOUNG FASHION Well Nurse, whilst you go and settle matters with
  him, then your lady and I will go take a walk in the garden.

NURSE I'll do your honour's business in the catching up of a garter.
  Exit Nurse

59

YOUNG FASHION (*giving her his hand*) Come, madam, dare you
    venture yourself alone with me?   155
HOYDEN O dear yes sir, I don't think you'll do anything to me I need
    be afraid on.
        Exeunt

4.2

[*Loveless's lodgings*]
Enter Amanda, and Berinthia

A SONG.°

1

      '*I smile at love, and all its arts*',
      The charming Cynthia cried;
      '*Take heed, for love has piercing darts*',
      A wounded swain replied.
      '*Once free and blest as you are now,*   5
      I trifled with his charms;
      I pointed at his little bow,
      And sported with his arms:
      Till urged too far, "*Revenge!*" *he cries,*
      A fatal shaft he drew,   10
      It took its passage through your eyes,
      And to my heart it flew.

2

      '*To tear it thence, I tried in vain,*
      To strive, I quickly found
      Was only to increase the pain,   15
      And to enlarge the wound.
      Ah! much too well I fear you know
      What pain I'm to endure,
      Since what your eyes alone could do,
      Your heart alone can cure.   20
      And that (grant heaven I may mistake)
      I doubt is doomed to bear
      A burden for another's sake,
      Who ill rewards its care.'

AMANDA Well now Berinthia, I'm at leisure to hear what 'twas you   25
had to say to me.

BERINTHIA What I had to say was only to echo the sighs and groans
of a dying lover.

AMANDA Phu, will you never learn to talk in earnest of anything?

BERINTHIA Why, this shall be in earnest, if you please. For my part, I   30
only tell you matter of fact—you may take it which way you like
best, but if you'll follow the women of the town, you'll take it both
ways; for when a man offers himself to one of them, first she takes
him in jest, and then she takes him in earnest.

AMANDA I'm sure there's so much jest and earnest in what you say to   35
me, I scarce know how to take it; but I think you have bewitched
me, for I don't find it possible to be angry with you, say what you
will.

BERINTHIA I'm very glad to hear it, for I have no mind to quarrel with
you, for more reasons than I'll brag of; but quarrel or not, smile or   40
frown, I must tell you what I have suffered upon your account.

AMANDA Upon my account?

BERINTHIA Yes, upon yours. I have been forced to sit still and hear
you commended for two hours together, without one compliment
to myself. Now don't you think a woman had a blessed time of that?   45

AMANDA Alas! I should have been unconcerned at it. I never knew
where the pleasure lay of being praised by the men. But pray who
was this that commended me so?

BERINTHIA One you have a mortal aversion to, Mr Worthy. He used
you like a text:° he took you all to pieces, but spoke so learnedly   50
upon every point, one might see the spirit of the church was in
him. If you are a woman, you'd have been in an ecstasy° to have
heard how feelingly he handled your hair, your eyes, your nose,
your mouth, your teeth, your tongue, your chin, your neck, and so
forth. Thus he preached for an hour, but when he came to use an   55
application,° he observed that all these without a gallant were nothing. Now consider of what has been said, and heaven give you grace
to put it in practice.°

AMANDA Alas! Berinthia, did I incline to a gallant (which you know I
do not) do you think a man so nice as he could have the least   60
concern for such a plain unpolished thing as I am? It is impossible!

BERINTHIA Now have you a great mind to put me upon commending
you.

AMANDA Indeed that was not my design.

BERINTHIA Nay, if it were, it's all one, for I won't do't. I'll leave that   65

to your looking-glass. But to show you I have some good nature left,
I'll commend him, and maybe that may do as well.

AMANDA You have a great mind to persuade me I am in love with
him.

BERINTHIA I have a great mind to persuade you, you don't know   70
what you are in love with.

AMANDA I am sure I am not in love with him, nor never shall be, so let
that pass; but you were saying something you would commend him
for.

BERINTHIA O you'd be glad to hear a good character of him, however.   75

AMANDA Psha!

BERINTHIA Psha? Well, 'tis a foolish undertaking for women in these
kind of matters, to pretend° to deceive one another. Have not I been
bred a woman as well as you?

AMANDA What then?   80

BERINTHIA Why then I understand my trade so well, that whenever I
am told of a man I like, I cry 'psha!' But that I may spare you the
pains of putting me a second time in mind to commend him, I'll
proceed, and give you this account of him: that though 'tis possible
he may have had women with as good faces as your ladyship's (no   85
discredit to it neither), yet you must know your cautious behaviour,
with that reserve in your humour, has given him his death's wound.
He mortally hates a coquette. He says 'tis impossible to love where
we cannot esteem; and that no woman can be esteemed by a man
who has sense if she makes herself cheap in the eye of a fool; that   90
pride to a woman is as necessary as humility to a divine; and that
far-fetched, and dear bought,° is meat for gentlemen as well as for
ladies; in short, that every woman who has beauty may set a price
upon herself, and that by underselling the market they ruin the
trade. This is his doctrine. How do you like it?   95

AMANDA So well, that since I never intend to have a gallant for myself,
if I were to recommend one to a friend, he should be the man.

Enter Worthy

Bless me! he's here; pray heaven he did not hear me.

BERINTHIA If he did, it won't hurt your reputation; your thoughts
are as safe in his heart, as in your own.   100

WORTHY I venture in at an unseasonable time of night, ladies; I hope,
if I'm troublesome, you'll use the same freedom in turning me out
again.

AMANDA I believe it can't be late, for Mr Loveless is not come home
yet, and he usually keeps good hours.   105

WORTHY Madam, I'm afraid he'll transgress a little tonight, for he told me about half an hour ago he was going to sup with some company he doubted would keep him out 'till three or four a-clock in the morning, and desired I would let my servant acquaint you with it, that you might not expect° him; but my fellow's a blunder-head, so lest he should make some mistake, I thought it my duty to deliver the message myself. 110

AMANDA I'm very sorry he should give you that trouble, sir. But—

BERINTHIA But since he has, will you give me leave, madam, to keep him to play at ombre° with us? 115

AMANDA Cousin, you know you command my house.

WORTHY (to Berinthia) And, madam, you know you command me, though I'm a very wretched gamester.

BERINTHIA O, you play well enough to lose your money, and that's all the ladies require; so without any more ceremony, let us go into the 120 next room, and call for the cards.

AMANDA With all my heart.

Exit Worthy, leading Amanda

BERINTHIA (alone) Well, how this business will end, heaven knows; but she seems to me to be in as fair a way—as a boy is to be a rogue, when he's put clerk to an attorney. 125

Exit Berinthia

4.3

Berinthia's chamber

Enter Loveless cautiously in the dark

LOVELESS So, thus far all's well. I'm got into her bed-chamber, and I think nobody has perceived me steal into the house. My wife don't expect me home till four a-clock, so if Berinthia comes to bed by eleven, I shall have a chase of five hours. Let me see, where shall I hide myself? Under her bed? No; we shall have her maid searching 5 there for something or other.° Her closet's a better place, and I have a master key will open it; I'll e'en in there, and attack her just when she comes to her prayers. That's the most likely to prove her critical minute, for then the devil will be there to assist me.°

He opens the closet, goes in, and shuts the door after him. Enter Berinthia with a candle in her hand

BERINTHIA Well, sure I am the best-natured woman in the world. I 10

that love cards so well (there is but one thing upon earth I love
better) have pretended letters to write, to give my friends—a *tête-à-
tête*. However, I'm innocent, for piquet° is the game I set 'em to; at
her own peril be it, if she ventures to play with him at any other.
But now what shall I do with myself? I don't know how in the   15
world to pass my time; would Loveless were here to *badiner°* a little.
Well, he's a charming fellow; I don't wonder his wife's so fond of
him. What if I should sit down and think of him till I fall asleep,
and dream of the lord knows what? O, but then if I should dream
we were married, I should be frightened out of my wits. (*Seeing a*   20
book) What's this book? I think I had best go read. O splénétique!°
It's a sermon. Well, I'll go into my closet, and read *The Plotting*
Sisters.°
>   *She opens the closet, sees Loveless, and shrieks out*
O Lord, a ghost, a ghost, a ghost, a ghost!
>   *Enter Loveless running to her*

LOVELESS Peace, my dear, it's no ghost; take it in your arms, you'll   25
find 'tis worth a hundred of 'em.

BERINTHIA Run in again, here's somebody coming.
>   [*Loveless retires*]
>   *Enter her Maid*

MAID Lord, madam, what's the matter?

BERINTHIA O heavens! I'm almost frighted out of my wits; I thought
verily I had seen a ghost, and 'twas nothing but the white curtain   30
with a black hood pinned up against it. You may be gone again; I
am the fearfull'st fool.
>   *Exit Maid*
>   *Re-enter Loveless*

LOVELESS Is the coast clear?

BERINTHIA The coast clear! I suppose you are clear; you'd never play
such a trick as this else.   35

LOVELESS I'm very well pleased with my trick° thus far, and shall
be so till I have played it out, if it ben't your fault. Where's my
wife?

BERINTHIA At cards.

LOVELESS With whom?   40

BERINTHIA With Worthy.

LOVELESS Then we are safe enough.

BERINTHIA Are you so? Some husbands would be of another mind, if
he were at cards with their wives.

LOVELESS And they'd be in the right on't too. But I dare trust mine.   45

Besides, I know he's in love in another place, and he's not one of
those who court half a dozen at a time.

BERINTHIA Nay, the truth on't is, you'd pity him if you saw how
uneasy he is at being engaged with us; but 'twas my malice. I
fancied he was to meet his mistress somewhere else, so did it to   50
have the pleasure of seeing him fret.

LOVELESS What says Amanda to my staying abroad so late?

BERINTHIA Why she's as much out of humour as he; I believe they
wish one another at the devil.

LOVELESS Then I'm afraid they'll quarrel at play, and soon throw up   55
the cards.

> *Offering to pull her into the closet*

Therefore my dear charming angel, let us make a good use of our
time.

BERINTHIA Heavens, what do you mean?

LOVELESS Pray what do you think I mean?   60

BERINTHIA I don't know.

LOVELESS I'll show you.

BERINTHIA You may as well tell me.

LOVELESS No, that would make you blush worse than t'other.

BERINTHIA Why, do you intend to make me blush?   65

LOVELESS Faith I can't tell that, but if I do, it shall be in the dark.

> *Pulling her*

BERINTHIA O heavens! I would not be in the dark with you for all the
world.

LOVELESS I'll try that.

> *Puts out the candles*

BERINTHIA O Lord! are you mad? What shall I do for light?   70

LOVELESS You'll do as well without it.

BERINTHIA Why, one can't find a chair to sit down.

LOVELESS Come into the closet, madam, there's moonshine upon the
couch.

BERINTHIA Nay, never pull, for I will not go.   75

LOVELESS Then you must be carried.

> *Carrying her*

BERINTHIA (*very softly*) Help, help, I'm ravished, ruined, undone. O
Lord, I shall never be able to bear it.

> [*Exeunt*]

4.4

Sir Tunbelly's house

Enter Miss Hoyden, Nurse, Young Fashion, and [Chaplain] Bull

YOUNG FASHION This quick dispatch of yours, Mr Bull, I take so
kindly, it shall give you a claim to my favour as long as I live, I do
assure you.

HOYDEN And to mine too, I promise you.

BULL I most humbly thank your honours, and I hope, since it has   5
been my lot to join you in the holy bands of wedlock, you will so
well cultivate the soil, which I have craved a blessing on, that your
children may swarm about you like bees about a honeycomb.

HOYDEN I'cod with all my heart, the more the merrier, I say; ha,
Nurse?   10

Enter Lory taking his master hastily aside

LORY One word with you for heaven's sake.

YOUNG FASHION What the devil's the matter?

LORY Sir, your fortune's ruined; and I don't think your life's worth a
quarter of an hour's purchase. Yonder's your brother arrived with
two coaches and six horses, twenty footmen and pages, a coat worth   15
fourscore pound, and a periwig down to his knees, so judge what
will become of your lady's heart.

YOUNG FASHION Death and furies, 'tis impossible.

LORY Fiends and spectres, sir, 'tis true.

YOUNG FASHION Is he in the house yet?   20

LORY No, they are capitulating° with him at the gate. The porter tells
him, he's come to run away with Miss Hoyden, and has cocked the
blunderbuss at him. Your brother swears Gad damme, they are a
parcel of clawns, and he has a good mind to break off the match.
But they have given the word for° Sir Tunbelly, so I doubt all will   25
come out presently. Pray sir resolve what you'll do this moment, for
egad they'll maul you.

YOUNG FASHION Stay a little. (*To Hoyden*) My dear, here's a troublesome business my man tells me of, but don't be frightened, we shall
be too hard for the rogue. Here's an impudent fellow at the gate   30
(not knowing I was come hither incognito) has taken my name upon
him, in hopes to run away with you.

HOYDEN O the brazen-faced varlet! It's well we are married, or
maybe we might never a been so.

YOUNG FASHION (*aside*) Egad, like enough. [*To Bull*] Prithee, dear   35

doctor, run to Sir Tunbelly, and stop him from going to the gate
before I speak with him.

BULL I fly, my good lord.

    Exit Bull

NURSE An't please your honour, my lady and I had best lock ourselves
up till the danger be over.

YOUNG FASHION Ay, by all means.

HOYDEN Not so fast, I won't be locked up any more. I'm married.

YOUNG FASHION Yes, pray my dear do, till we have seized this rascal.

HOYDEN Nay, if you pray me, I'll do anything.

    Exeunt Hoyden and Nurse

YOUNG FASHION O! here's Sir Tunbelly coming. (*To Lory*) Hark
you, sirrah, things are better than you imagine; the wedding's over.

LORY The devil it is, sir.

YOUNG FASHION Not a word, all's safe. But Sir Tunbelly don't know
it, nor must not yet; so I am resolved to brazen the business out,
and have the pleasure of turning the impostor upon his lordship,°
which I believe may easily be done.

    Enter Sir Tunbelly, Bull and servants armed

YOUNG FASHION Did you ever hear, sir, of so impudent an
undertaking?

SIR TUNBELLY Never, by the mass, but we'll tickle him I'll warrant
him.

YOUNG FASHION They tell me, sir, he has a great many people with
him disguised like servants.

SIR TUNBELLY Ay, ay, rogues enough; but I'll soon raise the posse°
upon 'em.

YOUNG FASHION Sir, if you'll take my advice, we'll go a shorter way
to work. I find whoever this spark is, he knows nothing of my being
privately here; so if you pretend to receive him civilly, he'll enter
without suspicion; and as soon as he is within the gate, we'll
whip up the drawbridge upon his back, let fly the blunderbuss to
disperse his crew, and so commit him to jail.

SIR TUNBELLY Egad, your lordship is an ingenious person, and a very
great general; but shall we kill any of 'em or not?

YOUNG FASHION No, no, fire over their heads only to fright 'em; I'll
warrant the regiment scours° when the colonel's a prisoner.

SIR TUNBELLY Then come along my boys, and let your courage be
great—for your danger is but small.

    Exeunt

4.5

The gate

Enter Lord Foppington and followers. [Porter at gate]

FOPPINGTON A pax of these bumkinly people; will they open the
gate, or do they desire I should grow at their moatside like a willow?
(*To the Porter*) Hey fellow—prithee do me the favour, in as few
words as thou canst find to express thyself, to tell me whether thy
master will admit me or not, that I may turn about my coach and be   5
gone?

PORTER Here's my master himself now at hand; he's of age, he'll give
you his answer.

Enter Sir Tunbelly, and servants

SIR TUNBELLY My most noble lord, I crave your pardon for making
your honour wait so long, but my orders to my servants have been   10
to admit nobody without my knowledge, for fear of some attempt
upon my daughter, the times being full of plots and roguery.°

FOPPINGTON Much caution, I must confess, is a sign of great wisdom; but, stop° my vitals, I have got a cold enough to destroy a
porter—he, hem.   15

SIR TUNBELLY I am very sorry for't, indeed, my lord; but if
your lordship please to walk in, we'll help you to some brown
sugar-candy.° My lord, I'll show you the way.

FOPPINGTON Sir, I follow you with pleasure.

Exeunt [Sir Tunbelly and Lord Foppington.] As Lord
Foppington's servants go to follow him in, they [Sir Tunbelly's
servants] clap the door against La Verole

SERVANTS (*within*) Nay, hold you me there, sir.   20

LA VEROLE *Jernie dieu, qu'est-ce que veut dire ça?*°

SIR TUNBELLY (*within*) Fire, porter.

PORTER (*fires*) Have among ye, my masters.

LA VEROLE *Ah je suis mort—*°

The servants all run off

PORTER Not one soldier left, by the mass.   25

[Exit Porter]

4.6

Scene changes to the Hall

Enter Sir Tunbelly, the Chaplain [Bull], and servants [including a Clerk and Constable], with Lord Foppington disarmed

SIR TUNBELLY Come, bring him along, bring him along.

FOPPINGTON What the pax do you mean, gentlemen? Is it fair time, that you are all drunk before dinner?

SIR TUNBELLY Drunk, sirrah? Here's an impudent rogue for you. Drunk or sober, bully, I'm a justice of the peace, and know how to deal with strollers.°   5

FOPPINGTON Strollers!

SIR TUNBELLY Ay, strollers. Come, give an account of yourself. What's your name, where do you live? Do you pay scot and lot?° Are you a Williamite, or a Jacobite?° Come.   10

FOPPINGTON And why dost thou ask me so many impertinent questions?

SIR TUNBELLY Because I'll make you answer 'em before I have done with you, you rascal you.

FOPPINGTON Before Gad, all the answer I can make thee to 'em is,   15
that thou art a very extraordinary old fellow, stop my vitals.

SIR TUNBELLY Nay, if you are for joking with deputy lieutenants, we'st know how to deal with you. Here, draw a warrant for him immediately.

FOPPINGTON A warrant—what the devil is't thou wouldst be at, old   20
gentleman?

SIR TUNBELLY I would be at you, sirrah, if my hands were not tied as a magistrate, and with these two double fists beat your teeth down your throat, you dog you.

FOPPINGTON And why wouldst thou spoil my face at that rate?   25

SIR TUNBELLY For your design to rob me of my daughter, villain.

FOPPINGTON Rab thee of thy daughter! Now do I begin to believe I am abed and asleep, and that all this is but a dream—if it be, 'twill be an agreeable surprise enough to waken by and by; and instead of the impertinent company of a nasty country justice, find my-   30
self, perhaps, in the arms of a woman of quality. (*To Sir Tunbelly*) Prithee, old father, wilt thou give me leave to ask thee one question?

SIR TUNBELLY I can't tell whether I will or not, till I know what it is.

FOPPINGTON Why, then it is, whether thou didst not write to my lord Foppington to come down and marry thy daughter?   35

SIR TUNBELLY Yes marry did I; and my lord Foppington is come
down, and shall marry my daughter before she's a day older.

FOPPINGTON Now give me thy hand, dear dad, I thought we should
understand one another at last.

SIR TUNBELLY This fellow's mad. Here, bind him hand and foot.   40
  They bind him down

FOPPINGTON Nay, prithee, knight, leave fooling, thy jest begins to
grow dull.

SIR TUNBELLY Bind him, I say, he's mad. Bread and water, a dark
room and a whip may bring him to his senses again.

FOPPINGTON (*aside*) Egad, if I don't waken quickly, by all I can see   45
this is like to prove one of the most impertinent dreams that ever I
dreamt in my life.
  Enter Hoyden and Nurse

HOYDEN (*going up to him*) Is this he that would have run away with
me? Fough, how he stinks of sweets! Pray, father, let him be
dragged through the horse pond.   50

FOPPINGTON (*aside*) This must be my wife by her natural inclination
to her husband.

HOYDEN Pray, father, what do you intend to do with him, hang him?

SIR TUNBELLY That at least, child.

NURSE Ay, and its e'en too good for him too.   55

FOPPINGTON (*aside*) *Madame la gouvernante,*° I presume. Hitherto
this appears to me to be one of the most extraordinary families that
ever man of quality matched into.

SIR TUNBELLY What's become of my lord, daughter?

HOYDEN He's just coming, sir.   60

FOPPINGTON (*aside*) My lord? What does he mean by that, now?
  Enter Young Fashion and Lory
(*Seeing him*) Stap my vitals, Tam! Now the dream's out.

YOUNG FASHION Is this the fellow, sir, that designed to trick me of
your daughter?

SIR TUNBELLY This is he, my lord; how do you like him? Is not he a   65
pretty fellow to get a fortune?

YOUNG FASHION I find by his dress he thought your daughter might
be taken with a beau.

HOYDEN O gimmeni!° Is this a beau? Let me see him again. Ha! I find
a beau's no such an ugly thing neither.   70

YOUNG FASHION [*aside*] I' gad, she'll be in love with him presently;
I'll e'en have him sent away to jail. (*To Lord Foppington*) Sir, though
your undertaking shows you are a person of no extraordinary mod-

esty, I suppose you han't confidence enough to expect much
favour from me?   75

FOPPINGTON Strike me dumb, Tam, thou art a very impudent fellow.

NURSE Look if the varlet has not the frontery° to call his lordship
plain Thomas.

BULL The business is, he would feign himself mad, to avoid going to
jail.   80

FOPPINGTON (*aside*) That must be the chaplain, by his unfolding of
mysteries.

SIR TUNBELLY Come, is the warrant writ?

CLERK Yes sir.

SIR TUNBELLY Give me the pen, I'll sign it. So now constable—away   85
with him.

FOPPINGTON Hold one moment, pray, gentlemen. My lord Foppington, shall I beg one word with your lordship?

NURSE O ho, it's my lord with him now; see how afflictions will
humble folks.   90

HOYDEN Pray, my lord, don't let him whisper too close, lest he bite
your ear off.

FOPPINGTON I am not altogether so hungry as your ladyship is
pleased to imagine. (*To Young Fashion*) Look you, Tam, I am
sensible I have not been so kind to you as I ought, but I hope   95
you'll forget what's past, and accept of the five thousand pounds
I offer; thou mayst live in extreme splendour with it, stap my
vitals.

YOUNG FASHION It's a much easier matter to prevent a disease than
to cure it. A quarter of that sum would have secured your mistress; 100
twice as much won't redeem her.

> *Leaving him*

SIR TUNBELLY Well, what says he?

YOUNG FASHION Only the rascal offered me a bribe to let him go.

SIR TUNBELLY Ay, he shall go with a pox to him. Lead on, constable.

FOPPINGTON One word more, and I have done.   105

SIR TUNBELLY Before Gad, thou art an impudent fellow, to trouble
the court at this rate after thou art condemned; but speak once for
all.

FOPPINGTON Why then once for all: I have at last luckily called to
mind, that there is a gentleman of this country,° who I believe   110
cannot live far from this place, if he were here would satisfy you I
am Navelty, baron of Foppington, with five thousand pounds a
year; and that fellow there, a rascal not worth a groat.

SIR TUNBELLY Very well; now who is this honest gentleman you are
so well acquainted with? (*To Young Fashion*) Come, sir, we shall   115
hamper him.

FOPPINGTON 'Tis Sir John Friendly.

SIR TUNBELLY So; he lives within half a mile, and came down into the
country but last night. This bold-faced fellow thought he had been
at London still, and so quoted him. Now we shall display him in his   120
colours; I'll send for Sir John immediately. Here fellow, away presently and desire my neighbour he'll do me the favour to step over,
upon an extraordinary occasion; and in the meanwhile you had best
secure this sharper in the gatehouse.

CONSTABLE An't please your worship, he may chance to give us the   125
slip thence. If I were worthy to advise, I think the dog-kennel's a
surer place.

SIR TUNBELLY With all my heart, anywhere.

FOPPINGTON Nay, for heaven's sake, sir, do me the favour to put me
in a clean room, that I mayn't daub my clothes.   130

SIR TUNBELLY O when you have married my daughter, her estate will
afford you new ones. Away with him.

FOPPINGTON A dirty country justice is a barbarous magistrate, stap
my vitals.

> *Exit Constable with Lord Foppington*

YOUNG FASHION (*aside*) Egad, I must prevent this knight's coming,   135
or the house will grow soon too hot to hold me. (*To Sir Tunbelly*)
Sir, I fancy 'tis not worthwhile to trouble Sir John upon this
impertinent fellow's desire; I'll send and call the messenger
back.

SIR TUNBELLY Nay, with all my heart; for to be sure he thought he   140
was far enough off, or the rogue would never have named him.

> *Enter Servant*

SERVANT Sir, I met Sir John just lighting at the gate; he's come to
wait upon you.

SIR TUNBELLY Nay, then it happens as one could wish.

YOUNG FASHION (*aside*) The devil it does. Lory, you see how things   145
are. Here will be a discovery presently, and we shall have our
brains beat out; for my brother will be sure to swear he don't
know me. Therefore run into the stable, take the two first horses
you can light on, I'll slip out at the back door, and we'll away
immediately.   150

LORY What, and leave your lady, sir?

YOUNG FASHION There's no danger in that as long as I have taken

possession; I shall know how to treat with 'em well enough, if once
I am out of their reach. Away, I'll steal after thee.

> *Exit Lory. His master follows him out at one door,° as Sir John*
> *[Friendly] enters at the other*

SIR TUNBELLY Sir John, you are the welcom'st man alive; I had   155
just sent a messenger to desire you'd step over, upon a very
extraordinary occasion. We are all in arms here.

SIR JOHN How so?

SIR TUNBELLY Why you must know, a finical sort of a tawdry fellow
here (I don't know who the devil he is, not I) hearing, I suppose,   160
that the match was concluded between my lord Foppington, and
my girl Hoyden, comes impudently to the gate, with a whole pack
of rogues in liveries, and would have passed upon me for his lordship. But what does I? I comes up to him boldly at the head of his
guards, takes him by the throat, strikes up his heels, binds him hand   165
and foot, dispatches a warrant, and commits him prisoner to the
dog-kennel.

SIR JOHN So, but how do you know but this was my lord? For I was
told he set out from London the day before me, with a very fine
retinue, and intended to come directly hither.   170

SIR TUNBELLY Why now, to show you how many lies people raise in
that damned town, he came two nights ago post, with only one
servant, and is now in the house with me. But you don't know the
cream of the jest yet. This same rogue (that lies yonder neck and
heels among the hounds), thinking you were out of the country,   175
quotes you for his acquaintance, and said if you were here, you'd
justify him to be Lord Foppington, and I know not what.

SIR JOHN Pray will you let me see him?

SIR TUNBELLY Ay, that you shall presently. Here, fetch the prisoner.

> *Exit Servant*

SIR JOHN I wish there ben't some mistake in this business. Where's   180
my lord? I know him very well.

SIR TUNBELLY He was here just now; see for him, doctor, tell him Sir
John is here to wait upon him.

> *Exit Chaplain [Bull]*

SIR JOHN I hope, Sir Tunbelly, the young lady is not married yet.

SIR TUNBELLY No, things won't be ready this week; but why do you   185
say you hope she is not married?

SIR JOHN Some foolish fancies only; perhaps I'm mistaken.

> *Re-enter Chaplain [Bull]*

BULL Sir, his lordship is just rid out to take the air.

SIR TUNBELLY To take the air! Is that his London breeding to go take
the air, when gentlemen come to visit him?   190

SIR JOHN 'Tis possible he might want it; he might not be well, some
sudden qualm° perhaps.

Enter Constable, etc., with Lord Foppington

FOPPINGTON Stap my vitals, I'll have satisfaction.

SIR JOHN (*running to him*) My dear Lord Foppington!

FOPPINGTON Dear Friendly thou art come in the critical minute,   195
strike me dumb.

SIR JOHN Why, I little thought I should have found you in fetters.

FOPPINGTON Why truly the world must do me the justice to confess
I do use to appear a little more *dégagé*;° but this old gentleman, not
liking the freedom of my air, has been pleased to skewer down my   200
arms like a rabbit.

SIR TUNBELLY Is it then possible that this should be the true Lord
Foppington at last?

FOPPINGTON Why, what do you see in his face to make you doubt of
it? Sir, without presuming to have any extraordinary opinion of my   205
figure, give me leave to tell you, if you had seen as many lords as I
have done, you would not think it impossible a person of a worse
taille° than mine might be a modern man of quality.

SIR TUNBELLY Unbind him, slaves. My lord, I'm struck dumb, I can
only beg pardon by signs; but if a sacrifice will appease you, you   210
shall have it. Here, pursue this tartar, bring him back. Away, I say!
A dog! Oons—I'll cut off his ears, and his tail, I'll draw out all his
teeth, pull his skin over his head—and—and what shall I do more?

SIR JOHN He does indeed deserve to be made an example of.

FOPPINGTON He does deserve to be *châtré*,° stap my vitals.   215

SIR TUNBELLY May I then hope I have your honour's pardon?

FOPPINGTON Sir, we courtiers do nothing without a bribe; that fair
young lady might do miracles.

SIR TUNBELLY Hoyden, come hither Hoyden.

FOPPINGTON Hoyden is her name, sir?   220

SIR TUNBELLY Yes, my lord.

FOPPINGTON The prettiest name for a song I ever heard.

SIR TUNBELLY My lord, here's my girl, she's yours; she has a wholesome body, and a virtuous mind, she's a woman complete, both in
flesh and in spirit; she has a bag of milled crowns,° as scarce as they   225
are, and fifteen hundred a year stitched fast to her tail.° So go thy
ways Hoyden.

FOPPINGTON Sir, I do receive her like a gentleman.

SIR TUNBELLY Then I'm a happy man, I bless heaven, and if your
    lordship will give me leave, I will like a good Christian at Christ-   230
    mas° be very drunk by way of thanksgiving. Come, my noble peer, I
    believe dinner's ready; if your honour pleases to follow me, I'll lead
    you on to the attack of a venison pasty.
        Exit Sir Tunbelly
FOPPINGTON Sir, I wait upon you. Will your ladyship do me the
    favour of your little finger, madam?   235
HOYDEN My lord, I'll follow you presently. I have a little business
    with my nurse.
FOPPINGTON Your ladyship's most humble servant. Come Sir John,
    the ladies have *des affaires*.°
        Exeunt Lord Foppington and Sir John
HOYDEN So Nurse, we are finely brought to bed; what shall we do   240
    now?
NURSE Ah dear miss, we are all undone; Mr Bull, you were used to
    help a woman to a remedy. (*Crying*)
BULL Alack-a-day, but it's past my skill now; I can do nothing.
NURSE Who would have thought that ever your invention should have   245
    been drained so dry?
HOYDEN Well, I have often thought old folks fools, and now I'm sure
    they are so; I have found a way myself to secure us all.
NURSE Dear lady, what's that?
HOYDEN Why, if you two will be sure to hold your tongues, and not   250
    say a word of what's past, I'll e'en marry this lord too.
NURSE What! Two husbands, my dear?
HOYDEN Why you have had three, good Nurse; you may hold your
    tongue.
NURSE Ay, but not altogether, sweet child.   255
HOYDEN Psha, if you had, you'd ne'er a thought much on't.
NURSE O but 'tis a sin, sweeting.
BULL Nay, that's my business to speak to, Nurse. I do confess, to take
    two husbands for the satisfaction of the flesh, is to commit the sin
    of exorbitancy; but to do it for the peace of the spirit, is no more   260
    than to be drunk by way of physic.° Besides, to prevent a parent's
    wrath is to avoid the sin of disobedience; for when the parent's
    angry, the child is froward. So that upon the whole matter, I do
    think, though miss should marry again, she may be saved.
HOYDEN I'cod and I will marry again then, and so there's an end of   265
    the story.
        [*Exeunt*]

5.1

London

Enter Coupler, Young Fashion, and Lory

COUPLER Well, and so Sir John coming in—

YOUNG FASHION And so Sir John coming in, I thought it might be manners in me to go out, which I did, and getting on horseback as fast as I could, rid away as if the devil had been at the rear of me. What has happened since, heaven knows. 5

COUPLER Egad sirrah, I know as well as heaven.

YOUNG FASHION What do you know?

COUPLER That you are a cuckold.

YOUNG FASHION The devil I am? By who?

COUPLER By your brother. 10

YOUNG FASHION My brother! Which way?

COUPLER The old way, he has lain with your wife.

YOUNG FASHION Hell and furies, what dost thou mean?

COUPLER I mean plainly, I speak no parable.

YOUNG FASHION Plainly! Thou dost not speak common sense; I cannot understand one word thou say'st. 15

COUPLER You will do soon, youngster. In short, you left your wife a widow, and she married again.

YOUNG FASHION It's a lie.

COUPLER I'cod, if I were a young fellow, I'd break your head, sirrah. 20

YOUNG FASHION Dear dad don't be angry, for I'm as mad as Tom of Bedlam.°

COUPLER When I had fitted you with a wife, you should have kept her.

YOUNG FASHION But is it possible the young strumpet could play me such a trick? 25

COUPLER A young strumpet, sir—can play twenty tricks.

YOUNG FASHION But prithee instruct me a little farther; whence comes thy intelligence?

COUPLER From your brother, in this letter; there you may read it. 30

YOUNG FASHION (*reads*) 'Dear Coupler, (*pulling off his hat*)° I have only time to tell thee in three lines, or thereabouts, that here has been the devil; that rascal Tam, having stole the letter thou hadst formerly writ for me to bring to Sir Tunbelly, formed a damnable design upon my mistress, and was in a fair way of success when I 35 arrived. But after having suffered some indignities, in which I have all daubed my embroidered coat, I put him to flight. I sent out a party of horse after him, in hopes to have made him my prisoner, which if I had done, I would have qualified him for the seraglio,° stap my vitals.   40

'The danger I have thus narrowly 'scaped, has made me fortify myself against further attempts, by entering immediately into an association with the young lady, by which we engage to stand by one another, as long as we both shall live.

'In short, the papers are sealed, and the contract is signed, so the   45
business of the lawyer is *achevé*,° but I defer the divine part of the thing till I arrive at London; not being willing to consummate in any other bed but my own.

'Postscript. 'Tis passible I may be in tawn as soon as this letter, far I find the lady is so violently in love with me, I have determined   50
to make her happy with all the dispatch that is practicable, without disardering my coach-harses.'

So, here's rare work, i' faith!

LORY Egad, Miss Hoyden has laid about her bravely.

COUPLER I think my country girl has played her part as well as if she   55
had been born and bred in St James's parish.

YOUNG FASHION That rogue the Chaplain.

LORY And then that jade the Nurse, sir.

YOUNG FASHION And then that drunken sot Lory,° sir, that could not keep himself sober to be a witness to the marriage.   60

LORY Sir, with respect, I know very few drunken sots that do keep themselves sober.

YOUNG FASHION Hold your prating sirrah, or I'll break your head. Dear Coupler, what's to be done?

COUPLER Nothing's to be done, till the bride and bridegroom come   65
to town.

YOUNG FASHION Bride, and bridegroom! Death and furies, I can't bear that thou shouldst call 'em so.

COUPLER Why, what shall I call 'em, dog and cat?

YOUNG FASHION Not for the world, that sounds more like man and   70
wife than t'other.

COUPLER Well, if you'll hear of 'em in no language, we'll leave 'em for the Nurse and the Chaplain.

YOUNG FASHION The devil and the witch.

COUPLER When they come to town—   75

LORY We shall have stormy weather.

COUPLER Will you hold your tongues, gentlemen, or not?

LORY Mum.

COUPLER I say when they come, we must find what stuff they are
made of; whether the churchman be chiefly composed of the flesh,   80
or the spirit. I presume the former, for as chaplains now go, 'tis
probable he eats three pound of beef to the reading of one chapter.
This gives him carnal desires: he wants money, preferment, wine, a
whore; therefore we must invite him to supper, give him fat capons,
sack and sugar, a purse of gold, and a plump sister.° Let this be   85
done, and I'll warrant thee, my boy, he speaks truth like an oracle.

YOUNG FASHION Thou art a profound statesman I allow it; but how
shall we gain the Nurse?

COUPLER O never fear the Nurse, if once you have got the priest, for
the devil always rides the hag.° Well, there's nothing more to be   90
said of the matter at this time, that I know of; so let us go and
enquire if there's any news of our people yet. Perhaps they may be
come. But let me tell you one thing by the way, sirrah. I doubt you
have been an idle fellow; if thou hadst behaved thyself as thou
shouldst have done, the girl would never have left thee.   95

    Exeunt

5.2

Berinthia's apartment

Enter her Maid passing the stage, followed by Worthy

WORTHY Hem, Mrs Abigail, is your mistress to be spoken with?

ABIGAIL By you, sir, I believe she may.

WORTHY Why 'tis by me I would have her spoken with.

ABIGAIL I'll acquaint her, sir.

    Exit Abigail

WORTHY (*alone*) One lift more I must persuade her to give me, and   5
then I'm mounted. Well, a young bawd and a handsome one for my
money, 'tis they do the execution; I'll never go to an old one, but
when I have occasion for a witch. Lewdness looks heavenly to a
woman when an angel appears in its cause; but when a hag is
advocate, she thinks it comes from the devil.° An old woman has   10
something so terrible in her looks that whilst she is persuading your
mistress to forget she has a soul, she stares hell and damnation full
in her face.

Enter Berinthia

BERINTHIA Well sir, what news bring you?

WORTHY No news, madam; there's a woman going to cuckold her   15
husband.

BERINTHIA Amanda?

WORTHY I hope so.

BERINTHIA Speed her well.

WORTHY Ay, but there must be more than a God-speed, or your   20
charity won't be worth a farthing.

BERINTHIA Why, han't I done enough already?

WORTHY Not quite.

BERINTHIA What's the matter?

WORTHY The lady has a scruple still, which you must remove.   25

BERINTHIA What's that?

WORTHY Her virtue—she says.

BERINTHIA And do you believe her?

WORTHY No, but I believe it's what she takes for her virtue; it's some
relics of lawful love. She is not yet fully satisfied her husband has   30
got another mistress, which unless I can convince her of, I have
opened the trenches in vain, for the breach must be wider before I
dare storm the town.

BERINTHIA And so I'm to be your engineer?°

WORTHY I'm sure you know best how to manage the battery.   35

BERINTHIA What think you of springing a mine? I have a thought just
now come into my head, how to blow her up at once.

WORTHY That would be a thought indeed.

BERINTHIA Faith, I'll do't, and thus the execution of it shall be. We
are all invited to my lord Foppington's tonight to supper; he's come   40
to town with his bride, and makes a ball with an entertainment of
music. Now you must know, my undoer here, Loveless, says he
must needs meet me about some private business (I don't know
what 'tis) before we go to the company. To which end he has told
his wife one lie, and I have told her another. But to make her   45
amends, I'll go immediately, and tell her a solemn truth.

WORTHY What's that?

BERINTHIA Why, I'll tell her that to my certain knowledge, her husband has a rendezvous with his mistress this afternoon; and that if
she'll give me her word she'll be satisfied with the discovery, with-   50
out making any violent inquiry after the woman, I'll direct her to a
place where she shall see 'em meet. Now friend, this I fancy may
help you to a critical minute. For home she must go again to dress.

You (with your good breeding) come to wait upon us to the ball, find her all alone, her spirit inflamed against her husband for his treason, and her flesh in a heat from some contemplations upon the treachery, her blood on a fire, her conscience in ice, a lover to draw, and the devil to drive°—ah, poor Amanda!   55

WORTHY (*kneeling*) Thou angel of light, let me fall down and adore thee!   60

BERINTHIA Thou minister of darkness, get up again, for I hate to see the devil at his devotions.

WORTHY Well, my incomparable Berinthia, how I shall requite you—

BERINTHIA O ne'er trouble yourself about that: virtue is its own   65
reward.° There's a pleasure in doing good, which sufficiently pays itself. Adieu.

WORTHY Farewell, thou best of women.
          Exeunt several ways
          Enter Amanda, meeting Berinthia

AMANDA Who was that went from you?

BERINTHIA A friend of yours.   70

AMANDA What does he want?

BERINTHIA Something you might spare him, and be ne'er the poorer.

AMANDA I can spare him nothing but my friendship. My love already's all disposed of: though, I confess, to one ungrateful to my bounty.   75

BERINTHIA Why there's the mystery. You have been so bountiful, you have cloyed him. Fond wives do by their husbands, as barren wives do by their lap-dogs: cram 'em with sweetmeats till they spoil their stomachs.

AMANDA Alas! Had you but seen how passionately fond he has been   80
since our last reconciliation, you would have thought it were impossible he ever should have breathed an hour without me.

BERINTHIA Ay, but there you thought wrong again Amanda; you should consider that in matters of love, men's eyes are always bigger than their bellies. They have violent appetites, 'tis true; but they   85
have soon dined.

AMANDA Well; there's nothing upon earth astonishes me more than men's inconstancy.

BERINTHIA Now there's nothing upon earth astonishes me less, when I consider what they and we are composed of. For nature has made   90
them children, and us babies. Now, Amanda, how we used our babies, you may remember. We were mad to have 'em as soon as we

saw 'em, kissed 'em to pieces as soon as we got 'em, then pulled off
their clothes, saw 'em naked, and so threw 'em away.

AMANDA But do you think all men are of this temper?   95

BERINTHIA All but one.

AMANDA Who is that?

BERINTHIA Worthy.

AMANDA Why he's weary of his wife too, you see.

BERINTHIA Ay, that's no proof.   100

AMANDA What can be a greater?

BERINTHIA Being weary of his mistress.

AMANDA Don't you think 'twere possible he might give you that too?

BERINTHIA Perhaps he might, if he were my gallant; not if he were
yours.   105

AMANDA Why do you think he should be more constant to me, than
he would to you? I'm sure I'm not so handsome.

BERINTHIA Kissing goes by favour,° he likes you best.

AMANDA Suppose he does? That's no demonstration he would be
constant to me.   110

BERINTHIA No, that I'll grant you: but there are other reasons to
expect it. For you must know after all, Amanda, the inconstancy we
commonly see in men of brains does not so much proceed from the
uncertainty of their temper, as from the misfortunes of their love. A
man sees perhaps a hundred women he likes well enough for an   115
intrigue, and away. But possibly, through the whole course of his
life, does not find above one, who is exactly what he could wish her.
Now her, 'tis a thousand to one, he never gets. Either she is not to
be had at all (though that seldom happens, you'll say) or he wants
those opportunities that are necessary to gain her. Either she likes   120
somebody else much better than him, or uses him like a dog,
because he likes nobody so well as her. Still something or other fate
claps in the way between them and the woman they are capable of
being fond of; and this makes them wander about from mistress to
mistress, like a pilgrim from town to town, who every night must   125
have a fresh lodging, and's in haste to be gone in the morning.

AMANDA 'Tis possible there may be something in what you say; but
what do you infer from it as to the man we were talking of?

BERINTHIA Why, I infer that you being the woman in the world the
most to his humour, 'tis not likely he would quit you for one that is   130
less.

AMANDA That is not to be depended upon, for you see Mr Loveless
does so.

BERINTHIA What does Mr Loveless do?

AMANDA Why, he runs after something for variety I'm sure he does   135
not like so well as he does me.

BERINTHIA That's more than you know, madam.

AMANDA No, I'm sure on't. I'm not very vain, Berinthia; and yet I'd
lay my life, if I could look into his heart, he thinks I deserve to be
preferred to a thousand of her.   140

BERINTHIA Don't be too positive in that neither; a million to one,
but she has the same opinion of you. What would you give to see
her?

AMANDA Hang her, dirty trull! Though I really believe she's so ugly,
she'd cure me of my jealousy.   145

BERINTHIA All the men of sense about town say she's handsome.

AMANDA They are as often out in those things as any people.

BERINTHIA Then I'll give you farther proof: all the women about
town say she's a fool. Now I hope you're convinced?

AMANDA Whate'er she be, I'm satisfied he does not like her well   150
enough to bestow anything more than a little outward gallantry
upon her.

BERINTHIA Outward gallantry? (*Aside*) I can't bear this. (*To Amanda*)
Don't you think she's a woman to be fobbed off so. Come, I'm too
much your friend to suffer you should be thus grossly imposed   155
upon by a man who does not deserve the least part about you unless
he knew how to set a greater value upon it. Therefore, in one word,
to my certain knowledge, he is to meet her now within a quarter of
an hour, somewhere about that Babylon of wickedness, Whitehall.°
And if you'll give me your word that you'll be content with seeing   160
her masked in his hand, without pulling her headclothes off, I'll
step immediately to the person from whom I have my intelligence,
and send you word whereabouts you may stand to see 'em meet.
My friend and I'll watch 'em from another place, and dodge 'em to
their private lodging; but don't you offer to follow 'em lest you do it   165
awkwardly, and spoil all. I'll come home to you again as soon as I
have earthed 'em, and give you an account in what corner of the
house the scene of their lewdness lies.

AMANDA If you can do this, Berinthia, he's a villain.

BERINTHIA I can't help that. Men will be so.   170

AMANDA Well! I'll follow your directions; for I shall never rest till I
know the worst of this matter.

BERINTHIA Pray, go immediately, and get yourself ready then. Put on
some of your woman's clothes, a great scarf and a mask, and you

shall presently receive orders. (*Calls within*) Here, who's there? Get   175
me a chair quickly.

SERVANT [*calls*] There are chairs at the door, madam.

BERINTHIA 'Tis well, I'm coming.

AMANDA But pray, Berinthia, before you go, tell me how I may know
this filthy thing, if she should be so forward (as I suppose she will)   180
to come to the rendezvous first, for methinks I would fain view her
a little.

BERINTHIA Why she's about my height; and very well shaped.

AMANDA I thought she had been a little crooked?

BERINTHIA O no, she's as straight as I am. But we lose time, come   185
away.

    Exeunt

5.3

[*Young Fashion's lodgings*]

Enter Young Fashion, meeting Lory

YOUNG FASHION Well, will the doctor come?

LORY Sir I sent a porter to him as you ordered me. He found him with
a pipe of tobacco and a great tankard of ale, which he said he would
dispatch while I could tell three, and be here.

YOUNG FASHION He does not suspect 'twas I that sent for him?   5

LORY Not a jot sir; he divines as little for himself, as he does for other
folks.

YOUNG FASHION Will he bring Nurse with him?

LORY Yes.

YOUNG FASHION That's well; where's Coupler?   10

LORY He's half way up the stairs taking breath; he must play his
bellows a little, before he can get to the top.

    Enter Coupler

YOUNG FASHION O here he is. Well, old phthisic?° The doctor's
coming.

COUPLER Would the pox had the doctor—I'm quite out of wind. (*To*   15
Lory) Set me a chair, sirrah. Ah—(*Sits down. To Young Fashion*)
Why the plague canst not thou lodge upon the ground floor?

YOUNG FASHION Because I love to lie as near heaven as I can.

COUPLER Prithee let heaven alone; ne'er affect tending that way. Thy
centre's downwards.   20

YOUNG FASHION That's impossible. I have too much ill luck in this world, to be damned in the next.

COUPLER Thou art out in thy logic. Thy major is true, but thy minor° is false; for thou art the luckiest fellow in the universe.

YOUNG FASHION Make out that.   25

COUPLER I'll do't. Last night the devil ran away with the parson of Fatgoose living.

YOUNG FASHION If he had run away with the parish too, what's that to me?

COUPLER I'll tell thee what it's to thee. This living is worth five   30
hundred pound a year, and the presentation of it is thine, if thou canst prove thyself a lawful husband to Miss Hoyden.

YOUNG FASHION Say'st thou so, my protector? Then i'cad I shall have a brace of evidences here presently.

COUPLER The nurse and the doctor?   35

YOUNG FASHION The same. The devil himself won't have interest enough to make 'em withstand it.

COUPLER That we shall see presently: here they come.

> Enter Nurse and Chaplain [*Bull*]. *They start back, seeing Young Fashion*

NURSE Ah goodness, Roger, we are betrayed.

YOUNG FASHION (*laying hold of them*) Nay, nay, ne'er flinch for the   40
matter; for I have you safe. Come, to your trials immediately: I have no time to give you copies of your indictment. There sits your judge.

BOTH (*kneeling*) Pray, sir, have compassion on us.

NURSE I hope, sir, my years will move your pity; I am an aged woman.   45

COUPLER That is a moving argument indeed.

BULL I hope, sir, my character will be considered; I am heaven's ambassador.

COUPLER (*to Bull*) Are not you a rogue of sanctity?°

BULL Sir, with respect to my function, I do wear a gown.   50

COUPLER Did not you marry this vigorous young fellow to a plump young buxom wench?

NURSE (*to Bull*) Don't confess, Roger, unless you are hard put to it indeed.

COUPLER Come, out with't. Now is he chewing the cud of his   55
roguery, and grinding a lie between his teeth.

BULL Sir—I cannot positively say—I say, sir—positively I cannot say—

COUPLER Come, no equivocations;° no Roman turns upon us.

Consider thou standest upon Protestant ground, which will slip   60
from under thee like a Tyburn cart;° for in this country, we have
always ten hangmen for one Jesuit.

BULL (*to Young Fashion*) Pray, sir, then will you but permit me to
speak one word in private with Nurse?

YOUNG FASHION Thou art always for doing something in private   65
with Nurse.

COUPLER But pray let his betters be served before him for once. I
would do something in private with her myself. Lory, take care of
this reverend gown-man° in the next room a little. Retire priest.
        Exit Lory with Bull
Now, virgin, I must put the matter home to you a little. Do you   70
think it might not be possible to make you speak truth.

NURSE Alas! Sir, I don't know what you mean by truth.

COUPLER Nay, 'tis possible thou mayst be a stranger to it.

YOUNG FASHION Come, Nurse, you and I were better friends when
we saw one another last; and I still believe, you are a very good   75
woman in the bottom. I did deceive you and your young lady, 'tis
true, but I always designed to make a very good husband to her, and
to be a very good friend to you. And 'tis possible in the end she
might have found herself happier, and you richer, than ever my
brother will make you.   80

NURSE Brother! Why is your worship then his lordship's brother?

YOUNG FASHION I am, which you should have known if I durst have
stayed to have told you; but I was forced to take horse a little in
haste you know.

NURSE You were indeed, sir; poor young man, how he was bound to   85
scour for't. Now won't your worship be angry, if I confess the truth
to you? When I found you were a cheat (with respect be it spoken),
I verily believed Miss had got some pitiful skip-jack varlet or other
to her husband; or I had ne'er let her think of marrying again.

COUPLER But where was your conscience all this while, woman? Did   90
not that stare in your face, with huge saucer eyes, and a great horn
upon the forehead? Did not you think you should be damned for
such a sin? Ha?

YOUNG FASHION Well said, divinity; pass that home upon her.

NURSE Why, in good truly sir, I had some fearful thoughts on't,   95
and could never be brought to consent, till Mr Bull said it was a
peckadilla, and he'd secure my soul for a tithe-pig.°

YOUNG FASHION There was a rogue for you.

COUPLER And he shall thrive accordingly. He shall have a good living.

Come, honest Nurse, I see you have butter in your compound; you   100
can melt. Some compassion you can have of this handsome young
fellow.

NURSE I have indeed, sir.

YOUNG FASHION Why then I'll tell you what you shall do for me. You
know what a warm living here is fallen; and that it must be in the   105
disposal of him who has the disposal of Miss. Now if you and the
doctor will agree to prove my marriage, I'll present him to it, upon
condition he makes you his bride.

NURSE Now the blessing of the Lord follow your good worship both
by night and by day. Let him be fetched in by the ears; I'll soon   110
bring his nose to the grind-stone.

COUPLER (aside) Well said, old white-leather.° Hey, bring in the prisoner there.

       Enter Lory with Bull

COUPLER Come, advance holy man. Here's your duck does not think
fit to retire with you into the chancel at this time: but she has a   115
proposal to make to you, in the face of the congregation. Come,
Nurse, speak for yourself; you are of age.

NURSE Roger, are not you a wicked man, Roger, to set your strength
against a weak woman; and persuade her it was no sin to conceal
Miss's nuptials? My conscience flies in my face for it, thou priest of   120
Baal;° and I find by woeful experience, thy absolution is not worth
an old cassock. Therefore I am resolved to confess the truth to the
whole world, though I die a beggar for it. But his worship overflows
with his mercy and his bounty. He is not only pleased to forgive us
our sins, but designs thou sha't squat thee down in Fatgoose living,   125
and which is more than all, has prevailed with me to become the
wife of thy bosom.

YOUNG FASHION All this I intend for you, doctor. What you are to do
for me, I need not tell you.

BULL Your worships' goodness is unspeakable. Yet there is one thing   130
seems a point of conscience; and conscience is a tender babe. If I
should bind myself, for the sake of this living, to marry nurse and
maintain her afterwards, I doubt it might be looked on as a kind of
simony.°

COUPLER (rising up) If it were sacrilege, the living's worth it; there-   135
fore no more words, good doctor. But with the parish—here—
(giving Nurse to him) take the parsonage house. 'Tis true, 'tis a little
out of repair; some dilapidations there are to be made good. The
windows are broke, the wainscot is warped, the ceilings are peeled,

86

and the walls are cracked; but a little glazing, painting, whitewash   140
and plaster will make it last thy time.

BULL Well, sir, if it must be so, I shan't contend. What providence
orders, I submit to.

NURSE And so do I, with all humility.

COUPLER Why, that now was spoke like good people. Come, my turtle   145
doves, let us go help this poor pigeon to his wandering mate again;
and after institution and induction,° you shall all go a-cooing
together.

Exeunt

5.4

[Loveless's lodgings]

*Enter Amanda in a scarf etc., as just returned, her Woman
following her*

AMANDA Prithee what care I who has been here?

WOMAN Madam, 'twas my Lady Bridle, and my Lady Tiptoe.

AMANDA My Lady Fiddle, and my Lady Faddle. What dost stand
troubling me with the visits of a parcel of impertinent women?
When they are well seamed with the smallpox, they won't be so   5
fond of showing their faces. There are more coquettes about this
town—

WOMAN Madam, I suppose they only came to return your ladyship's
visit, according to the custom of the world.

AMANDA Would the world were on fire, and you in the middle on't!   10
Begone; leave me.

Exit Woman
Amanda alone

At last I am convinced. My eyes are testimonies of his falsehood.
The base, ungrateful, perjured villain!
Good gods—what slippery stuff are men composed of?
Sure, the account of their creation's false,   15
And 'twas the woman's rib that they were formed of.°
But why am I thus angry?
This poor relapse should only move my scorn.
'Tis true, the roving flights of his unfinished youth
Had strong excuse, from the plea of nature;   20
Reason had thrown the reins loose on his neck

And slipped him to unlimited desire.°
If therefore he went wrong, he had a claim
To my forgiveness, and I did him right.
But since the years of manhood rein him in,   25
And reason well digested into thought
Has pointed out the course he ought to run,
If now he strays,
'Twould be as weak, and mean in me to pardon,
As it has been in him t'offend.   30
But hold:
'Tis an ill cause indeed, where nothing's to be said for't.
My beauty possibly is in the wane;
Perhaps sixteen has greater charms for him.
Yes, there's the secret. But let him know,   35
My quiver's not entirely emptied yet;
I still have darts, and I can shoot 'em too;
They're not so blunt, but they can enter still,
The wants not in my power, but in my will.
Virtue's his friend, or through another's heart,   40
I yet could find the way to make his smart.
        Going off, she meets Worthy
Ha! he here? Protect me heaven, for this looks ominous.

WORTHY You seem disordered, madam; I hope there's no misfortune
happened to you?

AMANDA None that will long disorder me, I hope.   45

WORTHY Whate'er it be disturbs you, I would to heaven 'twere in my
power to bear the pain, till I were able to remove the cause.

AMANDA I hope ere long it will remove itself. At least, I have given it
warning to be gone.

WORTHY Would I durst ask, where 'tis the thorn torments you? For-   50
give me if I grow inquisitive. 'Tis only with desire to give you ease.

AMANDA Alas! 'tis in a tender part. It can't be drawn without a world
of pain. Yet out it must; for it begins to fester in my heart.

WORTHY If 'tis the sting of unrequited love, remove it instantly: I
have a balm will quickly heal the wound.   55

AMANDA You'll find the undertaking difficult: the surgeon who
already has attempted it has much tormented me.

WORTHY I'll aid him with a gentler hand—if you will give me leave.

AMANDA How soft soe'er the hand may be, there still is terror in the
operation.°   60

WORTHY Some few preparatives would make it easy, could I persuade

you to apply 'em. Make home reflections,° madam, on your
slighted love. Weigh well the strength and beauty of your charms;
rouse up that spirit women ought to bear, and slight your god if he
neglects his angel. With arms of ice receive his cold embraces, and   65
keep your fire for those who come in flames. Behold a burning lover
at your feet, his fever raging in his veins. See how he trembles, how
he pants; see how he glows, how he consumes. Extend the arms of
mercy to his aid; his zeal may give him title to your pity, although
his merit cannot claim your love.   70

AMANDA Of all my feeble sex, sure I must be the weakest, should I
again presume to think on love. (*Sighing*) Alas! my heart has been
too roughly treated.

WORTHY 'Twill find the greater bliss in softer usage.

AMANDA But where's that usage to be found?   75

WORTHY 'Tis here, within this faithful breast; which if you doubt, I'll
rip it up before your eyes, lay all its secrets open to your view, and
then you'll see 'twas sound.

AMANDA With just such honest words as these the worst of men
deceived me.   80

WORTHY He therefore merits all revenge can do; his fault is such, the
extent and stretch of vengeance cannot reach it. O make me but
your instrument of justice. You'll find me execute it with such zeal
as shall convince you I abhor the crime.

AMANDA The rigour of an executioner has more the face of cruelty   85
than justice; and he who puts the cord about the wretch's neck is
seldom known to exceed him in his morals.

WORTHY What proof then can I give you of my truth?

AMANDA There is on earth but one.

WORTHY And is that in my power?   90

AMANDA It is. And one that would so thoroughly convince me, I
should be apt to rate your heart so high, I possibly might purchas't
with a part of mine.

WORTHY Then heaven thou art my friend, and I am blest; for if
'tis in my power, my will I'm sure will reach it. No matter what   95
the terms may be when such a recompense is offered. O tell me
quickly what this proof must be; what is it will convince you of my
love?

AMANDA I shall believe you love me as you ought, if, from this
moment, you forbear to ask whatever is unfit for me to grant—you   100
pause upon it, sir. I doubt, on such hard terms, a woman's heart is
scarcely worth the having.

WORTHY A heart like yours on any terms is worth it; 'twas not on that
I paused. But I was thinking (*drawing nearer to her*) whether some
things there may not be, which women cannot grant without a   105
blush, and yet which men may take without offence. (*Taking her
hand*) Your hand, I fancy, may be of the number. O pardon me if I
commit a rape upon it (*kissing it eagerly*) and thus devour it with my
kisses.

AMANDA O heavens! Let me go.   110

WORTHY Never, whilst I have strength to hold you here.
        Forcing her to sit down on a couch
My life, my soul, my goddess—O forgive me!

AMANDA O whither am I going? Help, heaven, or I am lost.

WORTHY Stand neuter, gods, this once I do invoke you.

AMANDA Then save me, virtue, and the glory's thine.   115

WORTHY Nay, never strive.

AMANDA I will, and conquer too. My forces rally bravely to my aid
(*breaking from him*) and thus I gain the day.

WORTHY Then mine as bravely double their attack (*seizing her again*)
and thus I wrest it from you. Nay, struggle not; for all's in vain. Or   120
death, or victory. I am determined.

AMANDA And so am I. (*Rushing from him*) Now keep your distance, or
we part for ever.

WORTHY (*offering again*) For heaven's sake—

AMANDA (*going*) Nay, then farewell.   125

WORTHY (*kneeling and holding her by her clothes*) O stay, and see the
magic force of love: behold this raging lion at your feet, struck dead
with fear, and tame as charms can make him. What must I do to be
forgiven by you?

AMANDA Repent, and never more offend.   130

WORTHY Repentance for past crimes is just and easy; but sin no
more's a task too hard for mortals.

AMANDA Yet those who hope for heaven must use their best
endeavours to perform it.

WORTHY Endeavours we may use, but flesh and blood are got in   135
t'other scale and they are ponderous things.

AMANDA Whate'er they are, there is a weight in resolution sufficient
for their balance. The soul, I do confess, is usually so careless of its
charge, so soft, and so indulgent to desire, it leaves the reins in the
wild hand of nature, who, like a Phaeton,° drives the fiery chariot,   140
and sets the world on flame. Yet still the sovereignty is in the mind,
whene'er it pleases to exert its force. Perhaps you may not think it

worth your while to take such mighty pains for my esteem, but that
I leave to you.

> You see the price I set upon my heart,   145
> Perhaps 'tis dear: but spite of all your art,
> You'll find on cheaper terms we ne'er shall part.

Exit Amanda

WORTHY (*alone*) Sure there's divinity about her; and she 'as dis-
pensed some portion on't to me. For what but now was the wild
flame of love, or (to dissect that specious term) the vile, the gross   150
desires of flesh and blood, is in a moment turned to adoration. The
coarser appetite of nature's gone, and 'tis methinks the food of
angels I require. How long this influence may last, heaven knows.
But in this moment of my purity, I could on her own terms accept
her heart. Yes, lovely woman; I can accept it. For now 'tis doubly   155
worth my care. Your charms are much increased, since thus
adorned. When truth's extorted from us, then we own the robe of
virtue is a graceful habit.

> Could women but our secret counsels scan,
> Could they but reach the deep reserves of man,   160
> They'd wear it on, that that of love might last,
> For when they throw off one, we soon the other cast.°
> Their sympathy is such—
> The fate of one, the other scarce can fly;
> They live together, and together die.   165

Exit [Worthy]

5.5

[*Lord Foppington's house*]

Enter Hoyden and Nurse

HOYDEN But is it sure and certain, say you, he's my lord's own
brother?

NURSE As sure as he's your lawful husband.

HOYDEN I'cod, if I had known that in time, I don't know but I might
have kept him; for between you and I, Nurse, he'd have made a   5
husband worth two of this I have. But which do you think you
should fancy most, Nurse?

NURSE Why truly, in my poor fancy, madam, your first husband is the
prettier gentleman.

HOYDEN I don't like my lord's shapes,° Nurse.   10

NURSE Why in good truly, as a body may say, he is but a slam.°

HOYDEN What do you think now he puts me in mind of? Don't you
remember a long, loose, shambling sort of a horse my father called
Washy?°

NURSE As like as two twin brothers.   15

HOYDEN I'cod, I have thought so a hundred times. Faith I'm tired of
him.

NURSE Indeed, madam, I think you had e'en as good stand to your
first bargain.

HOYDEN O but, Nurse, we han't considered the main thing yet. If I   20
leave my lord, I must leave my lady too; and when I rattle about the
streets in my coach, they'll only say, there goes Mistress—Mistress—
Mistress what? What's this man's name I have married, Nurse?

NURSE Squire Fashion.

HOYDEN Squire Fashion is it? Well, Squire, that's better than noth-   25
ing. Do you think one could not get him made a knight, Nurse?

NURSE I don't know but one might, madam, when the king's in a
good humour.

HOYDEN I'cod, that would do rarely. For then he'd be as good a man
as my father, you know.   30

NURSE By'r Lady, and that's as good as the best of 'em.

HOYDEN So 'tis, faith; for then I shall be my lady, and your ladyship at
every word, and that's all I have to care for. Ha, Nurse, but hark you
me; one thing more, and then I have done. I'm afraid, if I change my
husband again, I shan't have so much money to throw about, Nurse?   35

NURSE O, enough's as good as a feast. Besides, madam, one don't
know but as much may fall to your share with the younger brother as
with the elder. For though these lords have a power of wealth
indeed: yet, as I have heard say, they give it all to their sluts and their
trulls, who joggle it about in their coaches, with a murrain to 'em,   40
whilst poor madam sits sighing and wishing and knotting° and crying, and has not a spare half-crown to buy her a *Practice of Piety*.°

HOYDEN O, but for that, don't deceive yourself, Nurse. For this I
must say for my lord, and a—(*snapping her fingers*) for him. He's as
free as an open house at Christmas. For this very morning he told   45
me I should have two hundred a year to buy pins.° Now, Nurse, if he
gives me two hundred a year to buy pins, what do you think he'll
give me to buy fine petticoats?

NURSE Ah, my dearest, he deceives thee faully, and he's no better than
a rogue for his pains. These Londoners have got a gibberidge° with   50
'em would confound a gypsy. That which they call pin-money, is to
buy their wives everything in the varsal° world, dawn to their very
shoe-ties. Nay, I have heard folks say that some ladies, if they will
have gallants, as they call 'um, are forced to find them out of their
pin-money too.   55

HOYDEN Has he served me so, say ye? Then I'll be his wife no longer,
so that's fixed. Look, here he comes, with all the fine folk at's heels.
I'cod, Nurse, these London ladies will laugh till they crack again,
to see me slip my collar, and run away from my husband. But d'ye
hear? Pray take care of one thing: when the business comes to break   60
out, be sure you get between me and my father, for you know his
tricks. He'll knock me down.

NURSE I'll mind him, ne'er fear, madam.

     Enter Lord Foppington, Loveless, Worthy, Amanda, and
     Berinthia

FOPPINGTON Ladies and gentlemen, you are all welcome. (*To Love-*
less) Loveless, that's my wife: prithee do me the favour to salute her;   65
and dost hear (*aside to him*) if thau hast a mind to try thy fartune, to
be revenged of me, I won't take it ill, stap my vitals.

LOVELESS You need not fear, sir; I'm too fond of my own wife, to have
the least inclination to yours.

     All salute Hoyden

FOPPINGTON (*aside*) I'd give you a thausand paund he would make   70
love to her, that he may see she has sense enough to prefer me to
him, though his own wife has not. (*Viewing him*) He's a very beastly
fellow, in my opinion.

HOYDEN (*aside*) What a power of fine men there are in this London!
He that kissed me first is a goodly gentleman, I promise you. Sure   75
those wives have a rare time on't that live here always?

     Enter Sir Tunbelly with musicians and dancers

SIR TUNBELLY Come; come in, good people, come in; come tune your
fiddles, tune your fiddles. (*To the hautboys*)° Bagpipes, make ready
there. Come strike up. (*Sings*)

     For this is Hoyden's wedding-day,   80
     And therefore we keep holiday,
     And come to be merry.

Ha! there's my wench i' faith! Touch and take,° I'll warrant her:
she'll breed like a tame rabbit.

HOYDEN (*aside*) I'cod, I think my father's gotten drunk before supper.   85

SIR TUNBELLY (*to Loveless and Worthy*) Gentlemen, you are welcome. (*Saluting Amanda and Berinthia*) Ladies by your leave. Ha, they bill like turtles. Udsookers, they set my old blood afire; I shall cuckold somebody before morning.

FOPPINGTON (*to Sir Tunbelly*) Sir, you being master of the enter-   90 tainment, will you desire the company to sit?

SIR TUNBELLY Oons, sir—I'm the happiest man on this side the Ganges.°

FOPPINGTON (*aside*) This is a mighty unaccountable old fellow. (*To Sir Tunbelly*) I said, sir, it would be convenient to ask the company   95 to sit.

SIR TUNBELLY Sit! With all my heart. Come, take your places, ladies, take your places, gentlemen. Come sit down, sit down; a pox of ceremony, take your places.

　　　They sit, and the masque° begins

DIALOGUE BETWEEN CUPID AND HYMEN

I

CUPID　　　Thou bane to my empire, thou spring of contest,   100
　　　　　　Thou source of all discord, thou period to rest;
　　　　　　Instruct me, what wretches in bondage can see,
　　　　　　That the aim of their life is still pointed to thee.

2

HYMEN　　　Instruct me, thou little impertinent god,
　　　　　　From whence all thy subjects have taken the mode,   105
　　　　　　To grow fond of a change, to whatever it be
　　　　　　And I'll tell thee why those would be bound who are free.

CHORUS　　　For change, we're for change, to whatever it be,
　　　　　　We are neither contented with freedom, nor thee.
　　　　　　Constancy's an empty sound,   110
　　　　　　Heaven and earth, and all go round,
　　　　　　All the works of nature move,
　　　　　　And the joys of life and love
　　　　　　Are in variety.

3

CUPID　　　Were love the reward of a painstaking life,   115
　　　　　　Had a husband the art to be fond of his wife,
　　　　　　Were virtue so plenty, a wife could afford,

94

These very hard times, to be true to her lord,
Some specious account might be given of those,
Who are tied by the tail, to be led by the nose.   120

4

But since 'tis the fate of a man and his wife
To consume all their days in contention and strife;
Since whatever the bounty of heaven may create her,
He's morally sure he shall heartily hate her;
I think 'twere much wiser to ramble at large,   125
And the volleys of love on the herd to discharge.

5

HYMEN   Some colour of reason thy council might bear,
Could a man have no more than his wife to his share;
Or were I a monarch so cruelly just,
To oblige a poor wife to be true to her trust;   130
But I have not pretended, for many years past,
By marrying of people, to make 'em grow chaste.

6

I therefore advise thee to let me go on,
Thou'lt find I'm the strength and support of thy throne;
For hadst thou but eyes, thou woudst quickly perceive it,   135
How smoothly thy dart
Slips into the heart
Of a woman that's wed,
Whilst the shivering maid,
Stands trembling and wishing, but dare not receive it.   140

CHORUS   For change, etc.

The masque ended, enter Young Fashion, Coupler, and Bull

SIR TUNBELLY So, very fine, very fine i' faith, this is something like a
wedding. Now if supper were but ready, I'd say a short grace, and if
I had such a bedfellow as Hoyden tonight—I'd say as short prayers.
(*Seeing Young Fashion*) How now, what have we got here? A ghost?   145
Nay, it must be so, for his flesh and his blood could never have
dared to appear before me. (*To him*) Ah, rogue—

FOPPINGTON Stap my vitals, Tam again.

SIR TUNBELLY My lord, will you cut his throat? Or shall I?

FOPPINGTON Leave him to me, sir, if you please. Prithee Tam be so   150
ingenuous now as to tell me what thy business is here?

YOUNG FASHION 'Tis with your bride.

FOPPINGTON Thau art the impudent'st fellow that nature has yet spawned into the warld, strike me speechless.

YOUNG FASHION Why, you know my modesty would have starved me; I sent it a begging to you, and you would not give it a groat. 155

FOPPINGTON And dost thau expect by an excess of assurance, to extart a maintenance fram me?

YOUNG FASHION (*taking Hoyden by the hand*) I do intend to extort your mistress from you, and that I hope will prove one. 160

FOPPINGTON I ever thaught Newgate° or Bedlam would be his fartune, and naw his fate's decided. Prithee Loveless, dost know of ever a mad doctor° hard by?

YOUNG FASHION There's one at your elbow will cure you presently. (*To Bull*) Prithee doctor, take him in hand quickly. 165

FOPPINGTON Shall I beg the favour of you, sir, to pull your fingers out of my wife's hand?

YOUNG FASHION His wife! Look you there, now I hope you are all satisfied he's mad.

FOPPINGTON Naw is it nat possible far me to penetrate what species 170 of fally it is thau art driving at.

SIR TUNBELLY Here, here, here, let me beat out his brains, and that will decide all.

FOPPINGTON No, pray sir, hold, we'll destray him presently, according to law. 175

YOUNG FASHION (*to Bull*) Nay, then advance doctor. Come, you are a man of conscience, answer boldly to the questions I shall ask. Did not you marry me to this young lady, before ever that gentleman there saw her face?

BULL Since the truth must out, I did. 180

YOUNG FASHION Nurse, sweet Nurse, were not you a witness to it?

NURSE Since my conscience bids me speak—I was.

YOUNG FASHION (*to Hoyden*) Madam, am not I your lawful husband?

HOYDEN Truly I can't tell, but you married me first. 185

YOUNG FASHION Now I hope you are all satisfied?

SIR TUNBELLY (*offering to strike him, is held by Loveless and Worthy*) Oons and thunder, you lie.

FOPPINGTON Pray sir, be calm. The battle is in disarder, but requires more canduct than courage to rally our forces. Pray dactar, one 190 word with you. (*To Bull aside*) Look you, sir, though I will not presume to calculate your notions of damnation fram the descrip-

tion you give us of hell, yet since there is at least a passibility you
may have a pitchfork thrust in your backside, methinks it should
not be worth your while to risk your saul in the next warld, far the   195
sake of a beggarly yaunger brather, who is nat able to make your
bady happy in this.

BULL Alas! my lord, I have no worldly ends. I speak the truth, heaven
knows.

FOPPINGTON Nay prithee, never engage heaven in the matter, for by   200
all I can see, 'tis like to prove a business for the devil.

YOUNG FASHION Come, pray, sir, all above-board, no corrupting of
evidences, if you please. This young lady is my lawful wife, and I'll
justify it in all the courts of England; so your lordship (who always
had a passion for variety) may go seek a new mistress if you think   205
fit.

FOPPINGTON I am struck dumb with his impudence, and cannot
pasitively tell whether ever I shall speak again or not.

SIR TUNBELLY Then let me come and examine the business a little.
I'll jerk the truth out of 'em presently; here, give me my dog-whip.   210

YOUNG FASHION Look you, old gentleman, 'tis in vain to make a
noise. If you grow mutinous, I have some friends within call, have
swords by their sides above four foot long; therefore be calm, hear
the evidence patiently, and when the jury have given their verdict,
pass sentence according to law. Here's honest Coupler shall be   215
foreman, and ask as many questions as he pleases.

COUPLER All I have to ask is, whether Nurse persists in her evidence?
The parson I dare swear will never flinch from his.

NURSE (*to Sir Tunbelly kneeling*) I hope in heaven your worship will
pardon me. I have served you long and faithfully, but in this thing I   220
was overreached. Your worship, however, was deceived as well as I,
and if the wedding-dinner had been ready, you had put madam to
bed to him with your own hands.

SIR TUNBELLY But how durst you do this, without acquainting of
me?   225

NURSE Alas! if your worship had seen how the poor thing begged, and
prayed, and clung and twined about me, like ivy to an old wall, you
would say, I who had suckled it, and swaddled it, and nursed it both
wet and dry, must have had a heart of adamant° to refuse it.

SIR TUNBELLY Very well.   230

YOUNG FASHION Foreman, I expect your verdict.

COUPLER Ladies, and gentlemen, what's your opinions?

ALL A clear case, a clear case.

COUPLER   Then my young folks, I wish you joy.

SIR TUNBELLY (*to Young Fashion*)   Come hither, stripling; if it be true   235
then that thou hast married my daughter, prithee tell me who thou
art?

YOUNG FASHION   Sir, the best of my condition is, I am your son-in-
law; and the worst of it is, I am brother to that noble peer there.

SIR TUNBELLY   Art thou brother to that noble peer? Why then, that   240
noble peer, and thee, and thy wife, and the nurse, and the priest—
may all go and be damned together.
    Exit Sir Tunbelly

FOPPINGTON (*aside*)   Now for my part, I think the wisest thing a man
can do with an aching heart is to put on a serene countenance, for a
philosophical air is the most becoming thing in the world to the   245
face of a person of quality. I will therefore bear my disgrace like a
great man, and let the people see I am above an affront. (*To Young
Fashion*) Dear Tam, since things are thus fallen aut, prithee give me
leave to wish thee jay. I do it *de bon coeur*,° strike me dumb; you
have married a woman beautiful in her person, charming in her   250
airs, prudent in her canduct, canstant in her inclinations, and of a
nice marality, split my windpipe.

YOUNG FASHION   Your lordship may keep up your spirits with your
grimace° if you please; I shall support mine with this lady, and two
thousand pound a year. (*Taking Hoyden*) Come, madam.   255

> We once again you see are man and wife,
> And now perhaps the bargain's struck for life;
> If I mistake, and we should part again,
> At least you see you may have choice of men.
> Nay, should the war at length such havoc make°   260
> That lovers should grow scarce, yet for your sake
> Kind heaven always will preserve a beau—
> (*pointing to Lord Foppington*)
> You'll find his lordship ready to come to.°

FOPPINGTON   Her ladyship shall stap my vitals if I do.

Epilogue

Spoken by Lord Foppington.

Gentlemen and ladies:
These people have regaled you here today
(In my opinion) with a saucy play,
In which the author does presume to show
That coxcomb, *ab origine*—was beau.°   5
Truly, I think the thing of so much weight,
That if some smart chastisement ben't his fate,
Gad's curse, it may in time destroy the state.
I hold no-one its friend, I must confess,
Who would discauntenance your men of dress.   10
Far, give me leave t'abserve, good clothes are things
Have ever been of great support to kings.
All treasons come fram slovens, it is not
Within the reach of gentle beaux to plat;
They have no gall, no spleen, no teeth, no stings,   15
Of all Gad's creatures the most harmless things.
Through all recard, no prince was ever slain,
By one who had a feather in his brain.
They're men of too refined an education
To squabble with a court—for a vile dirty nation.   20
I'm very pasitive, you never saw
A through republican a finished beau;°
Nor truly shall you very often see
A Jacobite much better dressed than he.
In shart, through all the courts that I have been in,   25
Your men of mischief—still are in faul linen.
Did ever one yet dance the Tyburn jig°
With a free air, ar a well-pawdered wig?
Did ever highwayman yet bid you stand
With a sweet bawdy snuff-bax in his hand?°   30
Ar do you ever find they ask your purse
As men of breeding do? Ladies, Gad's curse,
This author is a dag, and 'tis not fit
You shou'd allow him ev'n one grain of wit.
To which, that his pretence may ne'er be named,   35
My humble motion is—he may be damned.

THE PROVOKED WIFE

A Comedy

THE CHARACTERS OF THE PLAY

Constant	*Mr Verbruggen*
Heartfree	*Mr Hudson*
Sir John Brute	*Mr Betterton*
Treble, a singing master	*Mr Bowman*
Rasor, valet de chambre to Sir John Brute	*Mr Bowen*
Justice of the Peace	*Mr Bright*

Lord Rake, companion to Sir John Brute
Colonel Bully, companion to Sir John Brute
Constable and Watch
[Jo, a porter]
[Tailor]
[Page]
[Footmen, servants and drinking companions to Lord Rake]

Lady Brute	*Mrs Barry*
Bellinda her niece	*Mrs Bracegirdle*
Lady Fancyfull	*Mrs Bowman*
Madamoiselle°	*Mrs Willis*

Cornet and Pipe, servants to Lady Fancyfull
[Lovewell, servant to Lady Brute]

Prologue

Spoken by Mrs Bracegirdle

Since 'tis the intent and business of the stage
To copy out the follies of the age;
To hold to every man a faithful glass°
And show him of what species he's an ass;
I hope the next that teaches in the school   5
Will show our author he's a scribbling fool.
And that the satire may be sure to bite,°
Kind heaven, inspire some venomed priest to write,°
And grant some ugly lady may indite.°
For I would have him lashed, by heavens! I would,   10
Till his presumption swam away in blood.
Three plays at once proclaims a face of brass,°
No matter what they are! That's not the case;
To write three plays, e'en that's to be an ass.
But what I least forgive, he knows it too,   15
For to his cost he lately has known you.°
Experience shows, to many a writer's smart,
You hold a court where mercy ne'er had part;
So much of the old serpent's sting you have,
You love to damn, as heaven delights to save.   20
In foreign parts, let a bold volunteer
For public good upon the stage appear,
He meets ten thousand smiles to dissipate his fear.
All tickle on th' adventuring young beginner,
And only scourge th' incorrigible sinner;   25
They touch indeed his faults, but with a hand
So gentle, that his merit still may stand;°
Kindly they buoy the follies of his pen,°
That he may shun 'em when he writes again.
But 'tis not so in this good-natured town;   30
All's one, an ox, a poet, or a crown,
Old England's play was always knocking down.

1.1

Sir John Brute's house

Enter Sir John°

SIR JOHN What cloying meat is love—when matrimony's° the sauce to it. Two years' marriage has debauched my five senses. Everything I see, everything I hear, everything I feel, everything I smell, and everything I taste—methinks has wife in't. No boy was ever so weary of his tutor, no girl of her bib, no nun of doing penance nor old maid of being chaste, as I am of being married. Sure there's a secret curse entailed upon the very name of wife. My lady is a young lady, a fine lady, a witty lady, a virtuous lady—and yet I hate her. There is but one thing on earth I loathe beyond her: that's fighting. Would my courage come up but to a fourth part of my ill nature, I'd stand buff to her relations, and thrust her out of doors. But marriage has sunk me down to such an ebb of resolution, I dare not draw my sword, though even to get rid of my wife. But here she comes.

Enter Lady Brute°

LADY BRUTE Do you dine at home today, Sir John?

SIR JOHN Why, do you expect I should tell you what I don't know myself?

LADY BRUTE I thought there was no harm in asking you.

SIR JOHN If thinking wrong were an excuse for impertinence, women might be justified in most things they say or do.

LADY BRUTE I'm sorry I have said anything to displease you.

SIR JOHN Sorrow for things past is of as little importance to me, as my dining at home or abroad ought to be to you.

LADY BRUTE My enquiry was only that I might have provided what you liked.

SIR JOHN Six to four you had been in the wrong there again, for what I liked yesterday I don't like today, and what I like today, 'tis odds I mayn't like tomorrow.

LADY BRUTE But if I had asked you what you liked?

SIR JOHN Why then there would have been more asking about it than the thing was worth.

LADY BRUTE I wish I did but know how I might please you.

SIR JOHN Ay, but that sort of knowledge is not a wife's talent.

LADY BRUTE Whate'er my talent is, I'm sure my will has ever been to make you easy.

SIR JOHN If women were to have their wills, the world would be finely   35
governed.

LADY BRUTE What reason have I given you to use me as you do of
late? It once was otherwise. You married me for love.

SIR JOHN And you me for money: so you have your reward, and I
have mine.   40

LADY BRUTE What is it that disturbs you?

SIR JOHN A parson.

LADY BRUTE Why, what has he done to you?

SIR JOHN He has married me.

      Exit Sir John

LADY BRUTE The devil's in the fellow I think. I was told before I   45
married him that thus 'twould be. But I thought I had charms
enough to govern him, and that where there was an estate, a woman
must needs be happy; so my vanity has deceived me, and my ambition has made me uneasy. But some comfort still: if one would be
revenged of him, these are good times. A woman may have a gal-   50
lant, and a separate maintenance° too. The surly puppy! Yet he's a
fool for't: for hitherto he has been no monster.° But who knows
how far he may provoke me? I never loved him, yet I have been ever
true to him; and that, in spite of all the attacks of art and nature
upon a poor weak woman's heart in favour of a tempting lover.   55
Methinks so noble a defence as I have made should be rewarded
with a better usage. Or who can tell? Perhaps a good part of what I
suffer from my husband may be a judgement° upon me for my
cruelty to my lover. Lord, with what pleasure could I indulge that
thought, were there but a possibility of finding arguments to make   60
it good. And how do I know but there may? Let me see. What
opposes? My matrimonial vow? Why, what did I vow? I think I
promised to be true to my husband. Well: and he promised to be
kind to me. But he han't kept his word. Why then I'm absolved
from mine—ay, that seems clear to me. The argument's good   65
between the king and the people, why not between the husband and
the wife?° O, but that condition was not expressed. No matter,
'twas understood. Well, by all I see, if I argue the matter a little
longer with myself, I shan't find so many bugbears in the way as I
thought I should. Lord what fine notions of virtue do we women   70
take up upon the credit of old foolish philosophers. Virtue's its own
reward,° virtue's this, virtue's that—virtue's an ass, and a gallant's
worth forty on't.

      Enter Bellinda

LADY BRUTE Good morrow, dear cousin.

BELLINDA Good morrow, madam; you look pleased this morning.   75

LADY BRUTE I am so.

BELLINDA With what, pray?

LADY BRUTE With my husband.

BELLINDA Drown husbands; for yours is a provoking fellow. As he
went out just now, I prayed him to tell me what time of day 'twas;   80
and he asked me if I took him for the church clock, that was obliged
to tell all the parish.

LADY BRUTE He has been saying some good obliging things to me too.
In short, Bellinda, he has used me so barbarously of late that I
could almost resolve to play the downright wife—and cuckold him.   85

BELLINDA That would be downright indeed.

LADY BRUTE Why, after all, there's more to be said for't than you'd
imagine, child. I know according to the strict statute law of religion,
I should do wrong; but if there were a Court of Chancery° in
heaven, I'm sure I should cast him.   90

BELLINDA If there were a House of Lords° you might.

LADY BRUTE In either I should infallibly carry my cause. Why, he is
the first aggressor, not I.

BELLINDA Ay, but you know, we must return good for evil.

LADY BRUTE That may be a mistake in the translation.° Prithee be of   95
my opinion, Bellinda, for I'm positive I'm in the right; and if you'll
keep up the prerogative° of a woman, you'll likewise be positive you
are in the right, whenever you do anything you have a mind to. But
I shall play the fool, and jest on till I make you begin to think I'm in
earnest.   100

BELLINDA I shan't take the liberty, madam, to think of anything that
you desire to keep a secret from me.

LADY BRUTE Alas, my dear, I have no secrets. My heart could never
yet confine my tongue.

BELLINDA Your eyes, you mean; for I am sure I have seen them gad-   105
ding, when your tongue has been locked up safe enough.

LADY BRUTE My eyes gadding? Prithee after who, child?

BELLINDA Why, after one that thinks you hate him, as much as I
know you love him.

LADY BRUTE Constant, you mean.   110

BELLINDA I do so.

LADY BRUTE Lord, what should put such a thing into your head?

BELLINDA That which puts things into most people's heads,
observation.

LADY BRUTE Why, what have you observed, in the name of wonder?   115

BELLINDA I have observed you blush when you meet him; force your-self away from him; and then be out of humour with everything about you. In a word, never was poor creature so spurred on by desire, and so reined in with fear.

LADY BRUTE How strong is fancy!   120

BELLINDA How weak is woman!

LADY BRUTE Prithee, niece, have a better opinion of your aunt's inclinations.

BELLINDA Dear aunt, have a better opinion of your niece's understanding.   125

LADY BRUTE You'll make me angry.

BELLINDA You'll make me laugh.

LADY BRUTE Then you are resolved to persist?

BELLINDA Positively.

LADY BRUTE And all I can say—   130

BELLINDA Will signify nothing.

LADY BRUTE Though I should swear 'twere false—

BELLINDA I should think it true.

LADY BRUTE Then let us both forgive (*kissing her*) for we have both offended—I in making a secret, you in discovering it.   135

BELLINDA Good nature may do much; but you have more reason to forgive one, than I have to pardon t'other.

LADY BRUTE 'Tis true, Bellinda, you have given me so many proofs of your friendship that my reserve has been indeed a crime. But that you may more easily forgive me—remember, child, that when our   140
nature prompts us to a thing our honour and religion have forbid us, we would (were't possible) conceal even from the soul itself the knowledge of the body's weakness.

BELLINDA Well, I hope, to make your friend amends, you'll hide nothing from her for the future, though the body should still grow   145
weaker and weaker.

LADY BRUTE No, from this moment I have no more reserve; and for a proof of my repentance, I own, Bellinda, I'm in danger. Merit and wit assault me from without, nature and love solicit me within, my husband's barbarous usage piques me to revenge, and Satan, catch-   150
ing at the fair occasion, throws in my way that vengeance which of all vengeance pleases women best.

BELLINDA 'Tis well Constant don't know the weakness of the fortifi-cations, for o' my conscience he'd soon come on to the assault.

LADY BRUTE Ay, and I'm afraid carry the town too. But whatever you   155

may have observed, I have dissembled so well as to keep him ignorant. So you see I'm no coquette, Bellinda; and if you'll follow my
advice you'll never be one neither. 'Tis true, coquetry is one of the
main ingredients in the natural composition of a woman, and I as
well as others could be well enough pleased to see a crowd of young   160
fellows ogling and glancing and watching all occasions to do forty
foolish officious things; nay, should some of 'em push on even to
hanging or drowning, why, faith, if I should let pure woman alone, I
should e'en be but too well pleased with't.

BELLINDA I'll swear 'twould tickle me strangely.   165

LADY BRUTE But after all, 'tis a vicious practice in us, to give the least
encouragement but where we design to come to a conclusion. For
'tis an unreasonable thing to engage a man in a disease which we
beforehand resolve we never will apply a cure to.

BELLINDA 'Tis true; but then a woman must abandon one of the   170
supreme blessings of her life. For I am fully convinced, no man has
half that pleasure in possessing a mistress, as a woman has in jilting
a gallant.

LADY BRUTE The happiest woman then on earth must be our
neighbour.   175

BELLINDA O the impertinent composition! She has vanity and affectation enough to make her a ridiculous original, in spite of all that
art and nature ever furnished to any of her sex before her.

LADY BRUTE She concludes all men her captives; and whatever
course they take, it serves to confirm her in that opinion.   180

BELLINDA If they shun her, she thinks 'tis modesty, and takes it for a
proof of their passion.

LADY BRUTE And if they are rude to her, 'tis conduct, and done to
prevent town talk.

BELLINDA When her folly makes 'em laugh, she thinks they are   185
pleased with her wit.

LADY BRUTE And when her impertinence makes 'em dull, concludes
they are jealous of her favours.

BELLINDA All their actions and their words, she takes for granted aim
at her.   190

LADY BRUTE And pities all other women, because she thinks they
envy her.

BELLINDA Pray, out of pity to ourselves, let us find a better subject,
for I am weary of this. Do you think your husband inclined to
jealousy?   195

LADY BRUTE O no; he does not love me well enough for that. Lord,

how wrong men's maxims are. They are seldom jealous of their
wives, unless they are very fond of 'em; whereas they ought to
consider the woman's inclinations, for there depends their fate.
Well, men may talk; but they are not so wise as we, that's certain.   200

BELLINDA At least in our affairs.

LADY BRUTE Nay, I believe we should outdo 'em in the business of
the state too; for methinks they do and undo, and make but mad
work on't.

BELLINDA Why then don't we get into the intrigues of government as   205
well as they?

LADY BRUTE Because we have intrigues of our own that make us more
sport, child. And so let's in and consider of 'em.
        Exeunt

1.2

A dressing room [*in Lady Fancyfull's house*]
Enter Lady Fancyfull, Madamoiselle, and Cornet

LADY FANCYFULL How do I look this morning?

CORNET Your ladyship looks very ill, truly.

LADY FANCYFULL Lard how ill-natured thou art, Cornet, to tell me
so, though the thing should be true. Don't you know that I have
humility enough to be but too easily out of conceit with myself?   5
Hold the glass; I dare swear that will have more manners than you
have. Madamoiselle, let me have your opinion too.

MADAMOISELLE My opinion pe, matam, dat your ladyship° never
look so well in your life.

LADY FANCYFULL Well, the French are the prettiest obliging people;   10
they say the most acceptable, well-mannered things—and never
flatter.

MADAMOISELLE Your ladyship say great justice inteed.

LADY FANCYFULL Nay everything's just in my house but Cornet.
The very looking-glass gives her the *démenti*.°   15
        Looking affectedly in the glass
But I'm almost afraid it flatters me, it makes me look so very engaging.

MADAMOISELLE Inteed, matam, your face pe hansomer den all de
looking-glass in tee world, *croyez-moi*.°

LADY FANCYFULL But is it possible my eyes can be so languishing—
and so very full of fire?   20

MADAMOISELLE Matam, if de glass was burning glass, I believe your
eyes set de fire in de house.

LADY FANCYFULL You may take that nightgown, Madamoiselle. Get
out of the room, Cornet; I can't endure you. This wench methinks
does look so unsufferably ugly.   25

    Exit Cornet

MADAMOISELLE Everyting look ugly, matam, dat stand by your
latiship.

LADY FANCYFULL No really, Madamoiselle, methinks you look
mighty pretty.

MADAMOISELLE Ah matam, de moon have no *éclat*° ven de sun   30
appear.

LADY FANCYFULL O pretty expression. Have you ever been in love,
Madamoiselle?

MADAMOISELLE (*sighing*) Oui matam.

LADY FANCYFULL And were you beloved again?°   35

MADAMOISELLE (*sighing*) No matam.

LADY FANCYFULL O ye gods, what an unfortunate creature should I
be in such a case. But nature has made me nice for my own defence.
I'm nice, strangely nice, Madamoiselle; I believe were the merit of
whole mankind bestowed upon one single person, I should still   40
think the fellow wanted something to make it worth my while to
take notice of him. And yet I could love—nay fondly love, were it
possible to have a thing made on purpose for me; for I'm not cruel,
Madamoiselle, I'm only nice.

MADAMOISELLE Ah matam, I wish I was fine gentleman for your   45
sake. I do all de ting in de world to get leetel way into your heart. I
make song, I make verse, I give you de serenade, I give great many
present to Madamoiselle, I no eat, I no sleep, I be lean, I be mad, I
hang myself, I drown myself. *Ah ma chère dame, que je vous aimerais.*° (*Embracing her*)   50

LADY FANCYFULL Well, the French have strange obliging ways with
'em; you may take those two pair of gloves, Madamoiselle.

MADAMOISELLE Me humbly tanke my sweet lady.

    Enter Cornet

CORNET Madam here's a letter for your ladyship by the penny-post.°

LADY FANCYFULL Some new conquest I'll warrant you. For without 55
vanity I looked extremely clear last night when I went to the park.
O agreeable! Here's a new song made of me. And ready set too. O
thou welcome thing. (*Kissing it*) Call Pipe hither, she shall sing it
instantly.

[*Exit Cornet*]
Enter Pipe
Here, sing me this new song, Pipe.   60

SONG

1

Fly, fly, you happy shepherds, fly,
Avoid Philira's charms;
The rigour of her heart denies
The heaven that's in her arms.
Ne'er hope to gaze and then retire,   65
Nor yielding, to be blest;
Nature who formed her eyes of fire
Of ice composed her breast.

2

Yet, lovely maid, this once believe
A slave, whose zeal you move;
The gods, alas, your youth deceive,   70
Their heaven consists in love.
In spite of all the thanks you owe,
You may reproach 'em this,
That where they did their form bestow   75
They have denied their bliss.

[*Exit Pipe*]

LADY FANCYFULL Well, there may be faults, Madamoiselle, but the
design is so very obliging, 'twould be a matchless ingratitude in me
to discover 'em.

MADAMOISELLE *Ma foi,*° matam, I tink de gentelman's song tell you   80
de trute. If you never love, you never be happy. *Ah, que j'aime
l'amour, moi!*°

Enter Servant [Cornet] with another letter

SERVANT Madam, here's another letter for your ladyship.

[*Exit Cornet*]

LADY FANCYFULL 'Tis thus I am importuned every morning, Madamoiselle. Pray how do the French ladies when they are thus   85
accablées?°

MADAMOISELLE Matam, dey never complain. *Au contraire.*° When
one Frense laty have got hundred lover, den she do all she can—to
get hundred more.

LADY FANCYFULL Well, strike me dead, I think they have *le goût bon.*° 90

For 'tis an unutterable pleasure to be adored by all the men, and
envied by all the women. Yet I'll swear I'm concerned at the torture
I give 'em. Lard, why was I formed to make the whole creation
uneasy? But let me read my letter. (*Reads*) 'If you have a mind to
hear of your faults, instead of being praised for your virtues, take   95
the pains to walk in the Green Walk in St James's° with your
woman an hour hence. You'll there meet one who hates you for
some things as he could love you for others, and therefore is willing
to endeavour your reformation. If you come to the place I mention,
you'll know who I am; if you don't, you never shall, so take your   100
choice.' This is strangely familiar, Madamoiselle; now have I a
provoking fancy to know who this impudent fellow is.

MADAMOISELLE Den take your scarf and your mask, and go to de
rendezvous. De Frense laty do *justement comme ça*.°

LADY FANCYFULL Rendezvous! What, rendezvous with a man,   105
Madamoiselle?

MADAMOISELLE *Eh, pourquoi non?*°

LADY FANCYFULL What, and a man perhaps I never saw in my life?

MADAMOISELLE *Tant mieux; c'est donc quelque chose de nouveau.*°

LADY FANCYFULL Why, how do I know what designs he may have?   110
He may intend to ravish me for ought I know.

MADAMOISELLE Ravish? *Bagatelle*.° I would fain see one impudent
rogue ravish Madamoiselle; *oui, je le voudrais*.°

LADY FANCYFULL O but my reputation, Madamoiselle, my reputation, *ah ma chère réputation*.°   115

MADAMOISELLE Matam, *quand on l'a une fois perdue—on n'en est plus
embarassée*.°

LADY FANCYFULL Fé Madamoiselle, fé! Reputation is a jewel.

MADAMOISELLE *Qui coute bien chère*,° matam.

LADY FANCYFULL Why sure you would not sacrifice your honour to   120
your pleasure?

MADAMOISELLE *Je suis philosophe*.°

LADY FANCYFULL Bless me how you talk! Why, what if honour be a
burden, Madamoiselle, must it not be borne?

MADAMOISELLE *Chaque un à sa façon. Quand quelque chose*   125
m'incommode, moi—je m'en défais, vite.°

LADY FANCYFULL Get you gone you little naughty French woman
you! I vow and swear I must turn you out of doors if you talk thus.

MADAMOISELLE Turn me out of doors? Turn yourself out of doors
and go see what de gentelman have to say to you. *Tenez*.°   130
    Giving her her things hastily

Voilà votre écharpe, voilà votre coiffe, voilà votre masque, voilà tout.
Hey, Mercure, Coquin!° Call one chair for matam, and one oder
(*calling within*) for me, *va t'en vite.*
    Turning to her lady and helping her on hastily with her things
Allons, matam; *dépêchez vous donc. Mon Dieu quelles scrupules.*°

LADY FANCYFULL Well, for once, Madamoiselle, I'll follow your   135
    advice, out of the intemperate desire I have to know who this ill-
    bred fellow is. But I have too much *délicatesse*° to make a practice
    on it.

MADAMOISELLE *Belle chose vraiment que la délicatesse, lors qu'il s'agit*
    de se devertir. Ah, ça! Vous voilà équipée, partons. Hé bien? Qu'avez   140
    vous donc?°

LADY FANCYFULL *J'ai peur.*°

MADAMOISELLE *Je n'en ai point, moi.*°

LADY FANCYFULL I dare not go.

MADAMOISELLE *Demeurez donc.*   145

LADY FANCYFULL *Je suis poltrone.*

MADAMOISELLE *Tant pis pour vous.*°

LADY FANCYFULL Curiosity's a wicked devil.

MADAMOISELLE *C'est une charmante sainte.*°

LADY FANCYFULL It ruined our first parents.   150

MADAMOISELLE *Elle a bien diverti leurs enfants.*

LADY FANCYFULL *L'honneur est contre.*

MADAMOISELLE *Le plaisir est pour.*°

LADY FANCYFULL Must I then go?

MADAMOISELLE Must you go? Must you eat, must you drink, must   155
    you sleep, must you live? De nature bid you do one, de nature bid
    you do t'oder. *Vous me ferez enrager.*°

LADY FANCYFULL But when reason corrects nature, Madamoiselle.

MADAMOISELLE *Elle est donc bien insolente. C'est sa soeur aînée.*°

LADY FANCYFULL Do you then prefer your nature to your reason,   160
    Madamoiselle?

MADAMOISELLE *Oui da.*

LADY FANCYFULL *Pourquoi?*°

MADAMOISELLE Because my nature make me merry, my reason make
    me mad.   165

LADY FANCYFULL *Ah la méchante Française!*

MADAMOISELLE (*forcing her lady off*) *Ah la belle Anglaise!*°
    [*Exeunt*]

2.1

St James's Park

Enter Lady Fancyfull and Madamoiselle

LADY FANCYFULL Well, I vow Madamoiselle, I'm strangely impatient to know who this confident fellow is.

Enter Heartfree

Look, there's Heartfree. But sure it can't be him, he's a professed woman-hater. Yet who knows what my wicked eyes may have done?

MADAMOISELLE *Il nous approche, madame.*°   5

LADY FANCYFULL Yes, 'tis he. Now will he be most intolerably cavalier, though he should be in love with me.

HEARTFREE Madam, I'm your humble servant; I perceive you have more humility and good nature than I thought you had.

LADY FANCYFULL What you attribute to humility and good-nature,   10
sir, may perhaps be only due to curiosity. I had a mind to know who
'twas had ill manners enough to write that letter.

Throwing [Heartfree] his letter

HEARTFREE Well, and now I hope you are satisfied.

LADY FANCYFULL I am so, sir; goodbye to ye.

HEARTFREE Nay, hold there; though you have done your business, I   15
han't done mine. By your ladyship's leave, we must have one
moment's prattle together. Have you a mind to be the prettiest
woman about town, or not? How she stares upon me! What! This
passes for an impertinent question with you now, because you think
you are so already?   20

LADY FANCYFULL Pray sir, let me ask you a question in my turn. By
what right do you pretend to examine me?

HEARTFREE By the same right that the strong govern the weak,
because I have you in my power; for you cannot get so quickly to
your coach, but I shall have time enough to make you hear every-   25
thing I have to say to you.

LADY FANCYFULL These are strange liberties you take, Mr
Heartfree.

HEARTFREE They are so, madam, but there's no help for it; for know
that I have a design upon you.   30

LADY FANCYFULL Upon me, sir!

HEARTFREE Yes; and one that will turn to your glory and my comfort,
if you will but be a little wiser than you use to be.

LADY FANCYFULL Very well, sir.

HEARTFREE Let me see. Your vanity, madam, I take to be about some   35
eight degrees higher than any woman's in the town, let t'other be
who she will; and my indifference is naturally about the same pitch.
Now, could you find the way to turn this indifference into fire
and flames, methinks your vanity ought to be satisfied; and this,
perhaps, you might bring about upon pretty reasonable terms.   40

LADY FANCYFULL And pray at what rate would this indifference be
bought off, if one should have so depraved an appetite to desire it?

HEARTFREE Why, madam, to drive a quaker's bargain,° and make but
one word with you, if I do part with it, you must lay me down—
your affection.   45

LADY FANCYFULL My affection, sir!

HEARTFREE Why, I ask you nothing but what you may very well
spare.

LADY FANCYFULL You grow rude, sir. Come, Madamoiselle, 'tis high
time to be gone.   50

MADAMOISELLE *Allons, allons, allons.*°

HEARTFREE (*stopping them*) Nay, you may as well stand still; for hear
me you shall, walk which way you please.

LADY FANCYFULL What mean you, sir?

HEARTFREE I mean to tell you that you are the most ungrateful   55
woman upon earth.

LADY FANCYFULL Ungrateful! To who?

HEARTFREE To nature.

LADY FANCYFULL Why, what has nature done for me?

HEARTFREE What you have undone by art. It made you handsome, it   60
gave you beauty to a miracle, a shape without a fault, wit enough to
make 'em relish, and so turned you loose to your own discretion;
which has made such work with you, that you are become the pity
of our sex, and the jest of your own. There is not a feature in your
face, but you have found the way to teach it some affected convul-   65
sion. Your feet, your hands, your very fingers' ends are directed
never to move without some ridiculous air or other; and your
language is a suitable trumpet, to draw people's eyes upon the
raree-show.°

MADAMOISELLE (*aside*) *Est-ce qu'on fais l'amour en Angleterre comme*   70
ça?°

LADY FANCYFULL (*aside*) Now could I cry for madness, but that I
know he'd laugh at me for it.

HEARTFREE Now do you hate me for telling you the truth; but that's

because you don't believe it is so: for were you once convinced of   75
that, you'd reform for your own sake. But 'tis as hard to persuade a
woman to quit anything that makes her ridiculous, as 'tis to prevail
with a poet to see a fault in his own play.

LADY FANCYFULL Every circumstance of nice breeding must needs
appear ridiculous to one who has so natural an antipathy to good   80
manners.

HEARTFREE But suppose I could find the means to convince you that
the whole world is of my opinion, and that those who flatter and
commend you do it to no other intent but to make you persevere in
your folly, that they may continue in their mirth?   85

LADY FANCYFULL Sir, though you and all that world you talk of
should be so impertinently officious as to think to persuade me I
don't know how to behave myself, I should still have charity enough
for my own understanding to believe myself in the right, and all
you in the wrong.   90

MADAMOISELLE *Le voilà mort.*°
    Exeunt Lady Fancyfull and Madamoiselle

HEARTFREE (*gazing after her*) There her single clapper° has published
the sense of the whole sex. Well, this once I have endeavoured to
wash the blackamoor white;° but henceforward I'll sooner undertake to teach sincerity to a courtier, generosity to an usurer, honesty   95
to a lawyer, nay, humility to a divine, than discretion to a woman I
see has once set her heart upon playing the fool.
    Enter Constant
Morrow, Constant.

CONSTANT Good morrow, Jack. What are you doing here this
morning?   100

HEARTFREE Doing! Guess if thou canst. Why, I have been endeavouring to persuade my Lady Fancyfull that she's the foolishest woman
about town.

CONSTANT A pretty endeavour truly.

HEARTFREE I have told her in as plain English as I could speak, both   105
what the town says of her, and what I think of her. In short, I have
used her as an absolute king would do Magna Carta.°

CONSTANT And how does she take it?

HEARTFREE As children do pills; bite 'em, but can't swallow 'em.

CONSTANT But, prithee, what has put it in your head, of all mankind,   110
to turn reformer?

HEARTFREE Why, one thing was, the morning hung upon my hands; I
did not know what to do with myself. And another was, that as little

as I care for women, I could not see with patience one that heaven
had taken such wondrous pains about, be so very industrious to   115
make herself the Jack Pudding° of the creation.

CONSTANT Well, now could I almost wish to see my cruel mistress
make the self-same use of what heaven has done for her, that so I
might be cured of a disease that makes me so very uneasy; for love,
love is the devil, Heartfree.   120

HEARTFREE And why do you let the devil govern you?

CONSTANT Because I have more flesh and blood than grace and self-
denial. My dear, dear mistress. 'Sdeath, that so genteel a woman
should be a saint, when religion's out of fashion!

HEARTFREE Nay, she's much in the wrong truly; but who knows how 125
far time and good example may prevail?

CONSTANT O! They have played their parts in vain already. 'Tis now
two years since that damned fellow her husband invited me to his
wedding; and there was the first time I saw that charming woman
whom I have loved ever since, more than e'er a martyr did his soul. 130
But she's cold, my friend, still cold as the northern star.

HEARTFREE So are all women by nature, which makes 'em so willing
to be warmed.

CONSTANT O, don't profane the sex! Prithee think 'em all angels for
her sake, for she's virtuous, even to a fault.   135

HEARTFREE A lover's head is a good accountable thing truly; he
adores his mistress for being virtuous, and yet is very angry with
her, because she won't be lewd.

CONSTANT Well, the only relief I expect in my misery is to see thee
some day or other as deeply engaged as myself, which will force me 140
to be merry in the midst of all my misfortunes.

HEARTFREE That day will never come, be assured, Ned. Not but that
I can pass a night with a woman, and for the time, perhaps, make
myself as good sport as you can do. Nay, I can court a woman too,
call her nymph, angel, goddess, what you please; but here's the   145
difference 'twixt you and I—I persuade a woman she's an angel;
she persuades you she's one. Prithee let me tell you how I avoid
falling in love; that which serves me for prevention may chance to
serve you for a cure.

CONSTANT Well, use the ladies moderately then, and I'll hear you. 150

HEARTFREE That using 'em moderately undoes us all; but I'll use 'em
justly, and that you ought to be satisfied with. I always consider a
woman, not as the tailor, the shoemaker, the tire-woman, the sempstress, (and which is more than all that) the poet makes her, but I

consider her as pure nature has contrived her, and that more   155
strictly than I should have done our old grandmother Eve, had I
seen her naked in the garden: for I consider her turned inside out.
Her heart well examined, I find there pride, vanity, covetousness,
indiscretion, but above all things, malice; plots eternally aforging to
destroy one another's reputations, and as honestly to charge the   160
levity of men's tongues with the scandal; hourly debates how to
make poor gentlemen in love with 'em, with no other intent but to
use 'em like dogs when they have done; a constant desire of doing
more mischief, and an everlasting war waged against truth and
good-nature.   165

CONSTANT Very well sir, an admirable composition truly.

HEARTFREE Then for her outside, I consider it merely as an outside;
she has a thin tiffany° covering over just such stuff as you and I are
made on. As for her motion, her mien, her airs, and all those tricks,
I know they affect you mightily. If you should see your mistress at a   170
coronation, dragging her peacock's train, with all her state and
insolence about her, 'twould strike you with all the awful thoughts
that heaven itself could pretend to from you; whereas I turn the
whole matter into a jest, and suppose her strutting in the self-same
stately manner, with nothing on but her stays and her under scanty   175
quilted petticoat.°

CONSTANT Hold thy profane tongue, for I'll hear no more.

HEARTFREE What, you'll love on then?

CONSTANT Yes, to eternity.

HEARTFREE Yet you have no hopes at all.   180

CONSTANT None.

HEARTFREE Nay, the resolution may be discreet enough; perhaps you
have found out some new philosophy, that love's like virtue—its
own reward. So you and your mistress will be as well content at a
distance, as others that have less learning are in coming together.   185

CONSTANT No; but if she should prove kind at last, my dear
Heartfree. (*Embracing him*)

HEARTFREE Nay, prithee don't take me for your mistress, for lovers
are very troublesome.

CONSTANT Well, who knows what time may do?   190

HEARTFREE And just now he was sure time could do nothing.

CONSTANT Yet not one kind glance in two years is somewhat strange.

HEARTFREE Not strange at all; she don't like you, that's all the
business.

CONSTANT Prithee don't distract me.   195

HEARTFREE Nay, you are a good handsome young fellow; she might use you better. Come, will you go see her? Perhaps she may have changed her mind; there's some hopes as long as she's a woman.

CONSTANT O, 'tis in vain to visit her; sometimes to get a sight of her, I visit that beast her husband, but she certainly finds some pretence to quit the room as soon as I enter.   200

HEARTFREE It's much she don't tell him you have made love to her too, for that's another good-natured thing usual amongst women, in which they have several ends. Sometimes 'tis to recommend their virtue, that they may be lewd with the greater security. Some-   205
times 'tis to make their husbands fight in hopes they may be killed, when their affairs require it should be so. But most commonly 'tis to engage two men in a quarrel, that they may have the credit of being fought for; and if the lover's killed in the business, they cry, 'Poor fellow! he had ill luck'—and so they go to cards.   210

CONSTANT Thy injuries to women are not to be forgiven. Look to't if ever thou dost fall into their hands—

HEARTFREE They can't use me worse than they do you, that speak well of 'em.

CONSTANT O ho! here comes the knight.   215

Enter Sir John Brute

HEARTFREE Your humble servant, Sir John.

SIR JOHN Servant, sir.

HEARTFREE How does all your family?

SIR JOHN Pox o' my family.

CONSTANT How does your lady? I han't seen her abroad a good while.   220

SIR JOHN Do! I don't know how she does, not I; she was well enough yesterday. I han't been at home tonight.

CONSTANT What! Were you out of town?

SIR JOHN Out of town! No, I was drinking.

CONSTANT You are a true Englishman; don't know your own happi-   225
ness. If I were married to such a woman, I would not be from her a night for all the wine in France.

SIR JOHN Not from her! Oons, what a time should a man have of that!

HEARTFREE Why, there's no division, I hope?

SIR JOHN No, but there's a conjunction,° and that's worse. A pox o'   230
the parson. Why the plague don't you two marry? I fancy I look like the devil to you.

HEARTFREE Why, you don't think you have horns, do you?

SIR JOHN No, I believe my wife's religion will keep her honest.

HEARTFREE And what will make her keep her religion?   235

SIR JOHN Persecution; and therefore she shall have it.

HEARTFREE Have a care knight; women are tender things.

SIR JOHN And yet, methinks, 'tis a hard matter to break their hearts.

CONSTANT Fie, fie; you have one of the best wives in the world, and
    yet you seem the most uneasy husband.   240

SIR JOHN Best wives! The woman's well enough, she has no vice that
    I know of, but she's a wife, and—damn a wife; if I were married to a
    hogshead of claret, matrimony would make me hate it.

HEARTFREE Why did you marry then? You were old enough to know
    your own mind.   245

SIR JOHN Why did I marry! I married because I had a mind to lie with
    her, and she would not let me.

HEARTFREE Why did not you ravish her?

SIR JOHN Yes, and so have hedged myself into forty quarrels with her
    relations, besides buying my pardon. But more than all that, you   250
    must know, I was afraid of being damned in those days, for I kept
    sneaking cowardly company, fellows that went to church, said grace
    to their meat, and had not the least tincture of quality about 'em.

HEARTFREE But I think you are got into a better gang now.

SIR JOHN Zoons, sir, my Lord Rake and I are hand and glove. I   255
    believe we may get our bones broke together tonight; have you a
    mind to share a frolic?

CONSTANT Not I truly, my talent lies to softer exercises.

SIR JOHN What? A down bed and a strumpet? A pox of venery, I say.
    Will you come and drink with me this afternoon?   260

CONSTANT I can't drink today, but we'll come and sit an hour with
    you if you will.

SIR JOHN Phugh, pox, sit an hour! Why can't you drink?

CONSTANT Because I'm to see my mistress.

SIR JOHN Who's that?   265

CONSTANT Why, do you use to tell?

SIR JOHN Yes.

CONSTANT So won't I.

SIR JOHN Why?

CONSTANT Because 'tis a secret.   270

SIR JOHN Would my wife knew it, 'twould be no secret long.

CONSTANT Why, do you think she can't keep a secret?

SIR JOHN No more than she can keep Lent.

HEARTFREE Prithee tell it her to try, Constant.

SIR JOHN No, prithee don't, that I mayn't be plagued with it.   275

CONSTANT I'll hold you a guinea you don't make her tell it you.

SIR JOHN I'll hold you a guinea I do.

CONSTANT Which way?

SIR JOHN Why I'll beg her not to tell it me.

HEARTFREE Nay, if anything does it, that will.   280

CONSTANT But do you think, sir—

SIR JOHN Oons, sir, I think a woman and a secret are the two imperti-
nentest themes in the universe. Therefore pray let's hear no more
of my wife nor your mistress. Damn 'em both with all my heart,
and everything else that daggles a petticoat, except four generous   285
whores, with Betty Sands° at the head of 'em, who were drunk with
my Lord Rake and I, ten times in a fortnight.

Exit Sir John

CONSTANT Here's a dainty fellow for you. And the veriest coward too.
But his usage of his wife makes me ready to stab the villain.

HEARTFREE Lovers are short-sighted. All their senses run into that of   290
feeling. This proceeding of his is the only thing on earth can make
your fortune. If anything can prevail with her to accept of a gallant,
'tis his ill usage of her; for women will do more for revenge than
they'll do for the gospel. Prithee take heart, I have great hopes for
you, and since I can't bring you quite off of her, I'll endeavour to   295
bring you quite on; for a whining lover° is the damned'st companion upon earth.

CONSTANT My dear friend, flatter me a little more with these hopes;
for whilst they prevail I have heaven within me, and could melt
with joy.   300

HEARTFREE Pray no melting yet; let things go farther first. This
afternoon perhaps we shall make some advance. In the meanwhile,
let's go dine at Locket's,° and let hope get you a stomach.

Exeunt

2.2

Lady Fancyfull's house

Enter Lady Fancyfull and Madamoiselle

LADY FANCYFULL Did you ever see anything so importune,
Madamoiselle?

MADAMOISELLE Inteed matam, to say de trute, he want leetel good
breeding.

LADY FANCYFULL Good breeding? He wants to be caned,   5

Madamoiselle; an insolent fellow. And yet let me expose my weakness; 'tis the only man on earth I could resolve to dispense my
favours on, were he but a fine gentleman. Well; did men but know
how deep an impression a fine gentleman makes in a lady's heart,
they would reduce all their studies to that of good breeding alone.   10

    Enter Cornet

CORNET Madam here's Mr Treble. He has brought home the verses
your ladyship made, and gave him to set.

LADY FANCYFULL O let him come in by all means. [*Exit Cornet*]
Now, Madamoiselle, am I going to be unspeakably happy.

    Enter Treble [*and Pipe*]

So Mr Treble, you have set my little dialogue?   15

TREBLE Yes madam, and I hope your ladyship will be pleased with it.

LADY FANCYFULL O, no doubt on't; for really Mr Treble, you set all
things to a wonder: but your music is in particular heavenly, when
you have my words to clothe in't.

TREBLE Your words themselves, madam, have so much music in 'em   20
they inspire me.

LADY FANCYFULL Nay, now you make me blush, Mr Treble; but pray
let's hear what you have done.

TREBLE You shall, madam.

    A song to be sung between a man and a woman.

MAN [TREBLE]	*Ah lovely nymph, the world's on fire;*	25
	Veil, veil those cruel eyes.	
WOMAN [PIPE]	*The world may then in flames expire,*	
	And boast that so it dies.	
MAN [TREBLE]	*But when all mortals are destroyed,*	
	Who then shall sing your praise?	30
WOMAN [PIPE]	*Those who are fit to be employed;*	
	The gods shall altars raise.	

TREBLE How does your ladyship like it, madam?

LADY FANCYFULL Rapture, rapture, Mr Treble, I'm all rapture. O
wit and art, what power you have when joined! I must needs   35
tell you the birth of this little dialogue, Mr Treble. Its father was
a dream, and its mother was the moon. I dreamed that by an
unanimous vote, I was chosen queen of that pale world. And that
the first time I appeared upon my throne—all my subjects fell in
love with me. Just then I waked: and seeing pen, ink and paper lie   40
idle upon the table, I slid into my morning gown, and writ this
impromptu.°

TREBLE So I guess the dialogue, madam, is supposed to be between
your majesty and your first minister of state.

LADY FANCYFULL Just. He as minister advises me to trouble my head   45
about the welfare of my subjects; which I as sovereign find a very
impertinent proposal. But is the town so dull, Mr Treble, it affords
us never another new song?

TREBLE Madam, I have one in my pocket came out but yesterday, if
your ladyship pleases to let Mrs Pipe sing it.   50

LADY FANCYFULL By all means. Here Pipe. Make what music you
can of this song here.

SONG

[1]

[PIPE]   *Not an angel dwells above*
Half so fair as her I love:
Heaven knows how she'll receive me.   55
If she smiles, I'm blest indeed;
If she frowns, I'm quickly freed;
Heaven knows, she ne'er can grieve me.

2

None can love her more than I,
Yet she ne'er shall make me die,   60
If my flame can never warm her.
Lasting beauty, I'll adore;
I shall never love her more,
Cruelty will so deform her.

LADY FANCYFULL Very well. This is Heartfree's poetry without   65
question.

TREBLE Won't your ladyship please to sing yourself this morning?

LADY FANCYFULL O Lord, Mr Treble, my cold is still so barbarous to
refuse me that pleasure; he he hem.

TREBLE I'm very sorry for it, madam; methinks all mankind should   70
turn physicians for the cure on't.

LADY FANCYFULL Why truly to give mankind their due, there's few
that know me, but have offered their remedy.

TREBLE They have reason, madam, for I know nobody sings so near a
cherubin as your ladyship.   75

LADY FANCYFULL What I do I owe chiefly to your skill and care, Mr
Treble. People do flatter me indeed, that I have a voice and a *je ne*

sais quoi° in the conduct of it, that will make music of anything.
And truly I begin to believe so, since what happened t'other night.
Would you think it, Mr Treble? Walking pretty late in the park (for   80
I often walk late in the park, Mr Treble) a whim took me to sing
'Chivy-Chase',° and—would you believe it?—next morning I had
three copies of verses, and six *billets-doux* at my levee upon it.

TREBLE And without all dispute you deserved as many more, madam.
Are there any further commands for your ladyship's humble servant?   85

LADY FANCYFULL Nothing more at this time, Mr Treble. But I shall
expect you here every morning for this month, to sing my little
matter there to me. I'll reward you for your pains.

TREBLE O Lord, madam—

LADY FANCYFULL Good morrow, sweet Mr Treble.   90

TREBLE Your ladyship's most obedient servant.
        Exit Treble [and Pipe]
        Enter Servant

SERVANT Will your ladyship please to dine yet?

LADY FANCYFULL Yes, let 'em serve.
        [*Exit Servant*]
Sure this Heartfree has bewitched me, Madamoiselle. You can't
imagine how oddly he mixed himself in my thoughts during my   95
rapture e'en now. I vow 'tis a thousand pities he is not more pol-
ished. Don't you think so?

MADAMOISELLE Matam, I tink it so great pity, dat if I was in your
ladyship place, I take him home in my house, I lock him up in my
closet, and I never let him go till I teach him everyting dat fine laty   100
expect from fine gentleman.

LADY FANCYFULL Why truly, I believe I should soon subdue his
brutality; for without doubt he has a strange *penchant*° to grow fond
of me, in spite of his aversion to the sex, else he would ne'er have
taken so much pains about me. Lord, how proud would some poor   105
creatures be of such a conquest? But I alas, I don't know how to
receive as a favour, what I take to be so infinitely my due. But what
shall I do to new-mould him, Madamoiselle? For till then he's my
utter aversion.

MADAMOISELLE Matam, you must laugh at him in all de place dat   110
you meet him, and turn into de ridicule all he say and all he do.

LADY FANCYFULL Why truly satire has been ever of wondrous use, to
reform ill manners. Besides 'tis my particular talent to ridicule
folks. I can be severe; strangely severe, when I will, Madamoiselle—Give me the pen and ink—I find myself whimsical—I'll   115

write to him (*sitting down to write*)—or I'll let it alone, and be severe
upon him that way. (*Rising up again. Sitting down*)—Yet active
severity is better than passive. (*Rising*)—'Tis as good let alone too,
for every lash I give him, perhaps he'll take for a favour. (*Sitting*)—
Yet 'tis a thousand pities so much—satire—should be lost. (*Rising*)   120
—But if it should have a wrong effect upon him 'twould distract
me. (*Sitting*)—Well I must write though after all. (*Rising*)—Or I'll
let it alone, which is the same thing.

MADAMOISELLE *La voilà determinée.*°
        Exeunt

3.1

[*Sir John Brute's house*]

Scene opens.° *Sir John, Lady Brute and Bellinda rising from the table*

[*Enter Rasor*]

SIR JOHN (*to* [*Rasor*])° Here, take away the things; I expect company. But first bring me a pipe. I'll smoke.

[*Exit Rasor*]

LADY BRUTE Lord, Sir John, I wonder you won't leave that nasty custom.

SIR JOHN Prithee don't be impertinent.   5

[*Rasor returns with pipe and clears table*]

BELLINDA (*to Lady Brute*) I wonder who those are he expects this afternoon.

LADY BRUTE I'd give the world to know. Perhaps 'tis Constant; he comes here sometimes. If it does prove him, I'm resolved I'll share the visit.   10

BELLINDA We'll send for our work and sit here.

LADY BRUTE He'll choke us with his tobacco.

BELLINDA Nothing will choke us, when we are doing what we have a mind to. Lovewell!

Enter Lovewell°   15

LOVEWELL Madam.

LADY BRUTE Here; bring my cousin's work and mine hither.

Exit Lovewell and re-enters with their work

SIR JOHN Whu, pox, can't you work somewhere else?

LADY BRUTE We shall be careful not to disturb you, sir.

[*Exit Lovewell*]

BELLINDA Your pipe would make you too thoughtful, uncle, if you were left alone; our prittle-prattle will cure your spleen.°   20

SIR JOHN (*sitting and smoking*) Will it so, Mrs Pert? Now I believe it will so increase it, I shall take my own house for a paper-mill.°

LADY BRUTE (*to Bellinda aside*) Don't let's mind him; let him say what he will.

SIR JOHN (*aside*) A woman's tongue a cure for the spleen! Oons! If   25
a man had got the headache, they'd be for applying the same remedy.

LADY BRUTE You have done a great deal, Bellinda, since yesterday.

BELLINDA Yes, I have worked very hard; how do you like it?

LADY BRUTE O, 'tis the prettiest fringe in the world. Well cousin, you   30
have the happiest fancy. Prithee, advise me about altering my
crimson petticoat.

SIR JOHN A pox o' your petticoat; here's such a prating, a man can't
digest his own thoughts for you.

LADY BRUTE (*aside*) Don't answer him. [*Aloud*] Well what do you   35
advise me?

BELLINDA Why really I would not alter it at all. Methinks 'tis very
pretty as it is.

LADY BRUTE Ay that's true; but you know one grows weary of the
prettiest things in the world, when one has had 'em long.   40

SIR JOHN Yes, I have taught her that.

BELLINDA Shall we provoke him a little?

LADY BRUTE With all my heart, Bellinda. Don't you long to be
married?

BELLINDA Why there are some things in't I could like well enough.   45

LADY BRUTE What do you think you should dislike?

BELLINDA My husband, a hundred to one else.

LADY BRUTE O ye wicked wretch; sure you don't speak as you think.

BELLINDA Yes I do; especially if he smoked tobacco.

          He looks earnestly at them

LADY BRUTE Why that many times takes off worse smells.   50

BELLINDA Then he must smell very ill indeed.

LADY BRUTE So some men will, to keep their wives from coming near
'em.

BELLINDA Then those wives should cuckold 'em at a distance.

          *He rises in a fury, throws his pipe at them and drives them out. As
          they run off, Constant and Heartfree enter. Lady Brute runs
          against Constant*

SIR JOHN Oons, get you gone upstairs, you confederating strumpets   55
you, or I'll cuckold you with a vengeance.

LADY BRUTE O Lord, he'll beat us, he'll beat us. Dear, dear Mr
Constant, save us.

          Exeunt [Lady Brute and Bellinda]

SIR JOHN I'll cuckold you with a pox.

CONSTANT Heavens, Sir John, what's the matter?   60

SIR JOHN Sure if woman had been ready created, the devil, instead of
being kicked down into hell, had been married.°

HEARTFREE Why what new plague have you found now?

SIR JOHN Why these two gentlewomen did but hear me say I expected

you here this afternoon; upon which, they presently resolved to   65
take up the room, o' purpose to plague me and my friends.

CONSTANT Was that all? Why, we should have been glad of their
company.

SIR JOHN Then I should have been weary of yours. For I can't relish
both together. They found fault with my smoking tobacco too; and   70
said men stunk. But I have a good mind—to say something.

CONSTANT No, nothing against the ladies, pray.

SIR JOHN Split the ladies. Come, will you sit down?
        [*Enter Rasor*]
    (*To* [*Rasor*]) Give us some wine, fellow. (*To Constant and Heartfree*)
    You won't smoke?   75

CONSTANT No nor drink neither at this time. I must ask your pardon.

SIR JOHN What, this mistress of yours runs in your head; I'll warrant
it's some such squeamish minx as my wife, that's grown so dainty
of late, she finds fault even with a dirty shirt.

HEARTFREE That a woman may do, and not be very dainty neither.   80

SIR JOHN Pox o' the women, let's drink. Come, you shall take one
glass, though I send for a box of lozenges to sweeten your mouth
after it.

CONSTANT Nay if one glass will satisfy you I'll drink it without
putting you to that expense.   85

SIR JOHN Why that's honest. [*To Rasor*] Fill some wine, sirrah.
        [*Exit Rasor*]
    [*To Constant and Heartfree*] So, here's to you gentlemen—a wife's the
    devil. To your being both married ([*Constant and Heartfree*] *drink*)

HEARTFREE O your most humble servant, sir.

SIR JOHN Well, how do you like my wine?   90

CONSTANT 'Tis very good indeed.

HEARTFREE 'Tis admirable.

SIR JOHN Then give us t'other glass.

CONSTANT No, pray excuse us now. We'll come another time, and
then we won't spare it.   95

SIR JOHN This one glass and no more. Come; it shall be your mistress's health, and that's a great compliment from me, I assure you.

CONSTANT And 'tis a very obliging one to me, so give us the glasses.

SIR JOHN So; let her live.

HEARTFREE And be kind.   100
        Sir John coughs in the glass

CONSTANT What's the matter? Does't go the wrong way?

SIR JOHN If I had love enough to be jealous, I should take this for an

ill omen. For I never drank my wife's health in my life, but I puked
in the glass.

CONSTANT O she's too virtuous to make a reasonable man jealous.   105

SIR JOHN Pox of her virtue. If I could but catch her adulterating I
might be divorced from her by law.

HEARTFREE And so pay her a yearly pension, to be a distinguished°
cuckold.

     Enter [Rasor]

[RASOR] Sir, there's my Lord Rake, Colonel Bully, and some other   110
gentlemen at the Blue Posts,° desire your company.

     [Exit Rasor]

SIR JOHN Cod's so, we are to consult about playing the devil tonight.

HEARTFREE Well, we won't hinder business.

SIR JOHN Methinks I don't know how to leave you though. But for
once I must make bold. Or look you, maybe the conference mayn't   115
last long, so if you'll wait here half an hour, or an hour, if I don't
come then—why then—I won't come at all.

HEARTFREE (*to Constant aside*) A good modest proposition, truly.

CONSTANT But let's accept on't, however. Who knows what may
happen?   120

HEARTFREE Well sir, to show you how fond we are of your company,
we'll expect your return as long as we can.

SIR JOHN Nay, maybe I mayn't stay at all; but business° you know
must be done. So, your servant. Or hark you; if you have a mind to
take a frisk with us, I have an interest with my lord. I can easily   125
introduce you.

CONSTANT We are much beholding to you, but for my part I'm
engaged another way.

SIR JOHN What? To your mistress I'll warrant. Prithee leave your
nasty punk to entertain herself with her own lewd thoughts, and   130
make one with us tonight.

CONSTANT Sir, 'tis business that is to employ me.

HEARTFREE And me; and business must be done you know.

SIR JOHN Ay, women's business, though the world were consumed
for't.   135

     Exit Sir John

CONSTANT Farewell beast. And now my dear friend, would my mistress be but as complaisant as some men's wives, who think it a
piece of good breeding to receive the visits of their husbands'
friends in his absence.

HEARTFREE Why for your sake I could forgive her, though she should   140

be so complaisant to receive something else in his absence. But
what way shall we invent to see her?

CONSTANT O ne'er hope it; invention will prove as vain as wishes.

Enter Lady Brute and Bellinda

HEARTFREE What do you think now, friend?

CONSTANT I think I shall swoon.   145

HEARTFREE I'll speak first then, whilst you fetch breath.

LADY BRUTE We think ourselves obliged gentlemen, to come and
return you thanks for your knight-errantry. We were just upon
being devoured by the fiery dragon.

BELLINDA Did not his fumes almost knock you down, gentlemen?   150

HEARTFREE Truly, ladies, we did undergo some hardships, and
should have done more, if some greater heroes than ourselves hard
by had not diverted him.

CONSTANT Though I'm glad of the service you are pleased to say we
have done you; yet I'm sorry we could do it no other way, than by   155
making ourselves privy to what you would perhaps have kept a
secret.

LADY BRUTE For Sir John's part, I suppose he designed it no secret
since he made so much noise. And for myself, truly I am not much
concerned, since 'tis fallen only into this gentleman's hands and   160
yours, who, I have many reasons to believe, will neither interpret
nor report any thing to my disadvantage.

CONSTANT Your good opinion, madam, was what I feared I never
could have merited.

LADY BRUTE Your fears were vain then, sir, for I am just to everybody. 165

HEARTFREE Prithee, Constant, what is't you do to get the ladies' good
opinions; for I'm a novice at it?

BELLINDA Sir, will you give me leave to instruct you?

HEARTFREE Yes, that I will with all my soul, madam.

BELLINDA Why then, you must never be slovenly, never be out of   170
humour, fare well and cry roast-meat,° smoke tobacco, nor drink
but when you are a-dry.

HEARTFREE That's hard.

CONSTANT Nay, if you take his bottle from him, you break his heart,
madam.   175

BELLINDA Why, is it possible the gentleman can love drinking?

HEARTFREE Only by way of antidote.

BELLINDA Against what, pray?

HEARTFREE Against love, madam.

LADY BRUTE Are you afraid of being in love, sir?   180

HEARTFREE I should, if there were any danger of it.

LADY BRUTE Pray why so?

HEARTFREE Because I always had an aversion to being used like a dog.

BELLINDA Why truly, men in love are seldom used better.

LADY BRUTE But was you never in love, sir? 185

HEARTFREE No, I thank heaven, madam.

BELLINDA Pray where got you your learning then?

HEARTFREE From other people's expense.

BELLINDA That's being a sponger, sir, which is scarce honest; if you'd buy some experience with your own money, as 'twould be fairlier 190 got, so 'twould stick longer by you.

Enter Footman

FOOTMAN Madam, here's my Lady Fancyfull, to wait upon your ladyship.

[Exit Footman]

LADY BRUTE Shield me, kind heaven; what an inundation of impertinence is here coming upon us! 195

Enter Lady Fancyfull, who runs first to Lady Brute, then to Bellinda, kissing them

LADY FANCYFULL My dear Lady Brute, and sweet Bellinda! Methinks 'tis an age since I saw you.

LADY BRUTE Yet 'tis but three days; sure you have passed your time very ill, it seems so long to you.

LADY FANCYFULL Why really, to confess the truth to you, I am so 200 everlastingly fatigued with the addresses of unfortunate gentlemen, that were it not for the extravagancy of the example, I should e'en tear out these wicked eyes with my own fingers, to make both myself and mankind easy. What think you on't, Mr Heartfree, for I take you to be my faithful adviser? 205

HEARTFREE Why truly, madam—I think—every project that is for the good of mankind ought to be encouraged.

LADY FANCYFULL Then I have your consent, sir.

HEARTFREE To do whatever you please, madam.

LADY FANCYFULL You had a much more limited complaisance this 210 morning, sir. Would you believe it, ladies? The gentleman has been so exceeding generous to tell me of above fifty faults, in less time than it was well possible for me to commit two of 'em.

CONSTANT Why truly, madam, my friend there is apt to be something familiar with the ladies. 215

LADY FANCYFULL He is indeed, sir; but he's wondrous charitable with it. He has had the goodness to design a reformation, even

down to my fingers' ends. 'Twas thus, I think, sir, you would have
had 'em stand.

Opening her fingers in an awkward manner

My eyes too he did not like. How was't you would have directed   220
'em? Thus, I think. (*Staring at him*) Then there was something
amiss in my gait too, I don't know well how 'twas; but as I take it, he
would have had me walk like him. Pray, sir, do me the favour to take
a turn or two about the room, that the company may see you—he's
sullen, ladies, and won't; but, to make short, and give you as true an   225
idea as I can of the matter, I think 'twas much about this figure in
general he would have moulded me to.

She walks awkwardly about, staring and looking ungainly,
then changes on a sudden to the extremity of her usual
affectation

But I was an obstinate woman, and could not resolve to make
myself mistress of his heart, by growing as awkward as his fancy.

Constant and Lady Brute talk together apart

HEARTFREE Just thus women do when they think we are in love with   230
'em, or when they are so with us.

LADY FANCYFULL 'Twould however be less vanity for me to conclude
the former than you the latter, sir.

HEARTFREE Madam, all I shall presume to conclude is that if I were
in love, you'd find the means to make me soon weary on't.   235

LADY FANCYFULL Not by over-fondness, upon my word sir. But pray
let's stop here, for you are so much governed by instinct, I know
you'll grow brutish at last.

BELLINDA (*aside*) Now am I sure she's fond of him; I'll try to make
her jealous. [*Aloud*] Well, for my part, I should be glad to find   240
somebody would be so free with me, that I might know my faults
and mend 'em.

LADY FANCYFULL Then pray let me recommend this gentleman to
you; I have known him some time, and will be surety for him, that
upon a very limited encouragement on your side, you shall find an   245
extended impudence on his.

HEARTFREE I thank you, madam, for your recommendation; but hat-
ing idleness, I'm unwilling to enter into a place where I believe
there would be nothing to do. I was fond of serving your ladyship,
because I knew you'd find me constant employment.   250

LADY FANCYFULL I told you he'd be rude, Bellinda.

BELLINDA O, a little bluntness is a sign of honesty, which makes me
always ready to pardon it. So, sir, if you have no other exceptions to

my service, but the fear of being idle in't, you may venture to list
yourself; I shall find you work, I warrant you.   255

HEARTFREE Upon those terms I engage, madam, and this (with your
leave) I take for earnest.° (*Offering to kiss her hand*)

BELLINDA Hold there, sir, I'm none of your earnest-givers. But if I'm
well served, I give good wages and pay punctually.

Heartfree and Bellinda seem to continue talking familiarly°

LADY FANCYFULL (*aside*) I don't like this jesting between 'em—   260
methinks the fool begins to look as if he were in earnest—but then
he must be a fool indeed.

Looking at Bellinda scornfully

Lard what a difference there is between me and her. How I should
despise such a thing if I were a man. What a nose she has! What a
chin! What a neck! Then her eyes—and the worst kissing lips in the   265
universe! No no, he can never like her, that's positive—yet I can't
suffer 'em together any longer. Mr Heartfree, do you know that you
and I must have no quarrel for all this? I can't forbear being a little
severe now and then; but women you know may be allowed
anything.   270

HEARTFREE Up to a certain age, madam.

LADY FANCYFULL Which I am not yet past, I hope.

HEARTFREE (*aside*) Nor never will, I dare swear.

LADY FANCYFULL (*to Lady Brute*) Come, madam; will your ladyship
be witness to our reconciliation?   275

LADY BRUTE You agree then at last.

HEARTFREE (*slightingly*) We forgive.

LADY FANCYFULL (*aside*) That was a cold ill-natured reply.

LADY BRUTE Then there's no challenges sent between you?

HEARTFREE Not from me I promise. (*Aside to Constant*) But that's   280
more than I'll do for her, for I know she can as well be damned as
forbear writing to me.

CONSTANT That I believe. But I think we had best be going lest she
should suspect something, and be malicious.

HEARTFREE With all my heart.   285

CONSTANT Ladies, we are your humble servants. I see Sir John is
quite engaged; 'twould be in vain to expect him. Come Heartfree.

Exit [Constant]

HEARTFREE Ladies, your servant. (*To Bellinda*) I hope, madam, you
won't forget our bargain; I'm to say what I please to you.

BELLINDA Liberty of speech entire, sir.   290

Exit Heartfree

LADY FANCYFULL (*aside*) Very pretty truly. But how the blockhead
went out—languishing at her; and not a look toward me. Well,
churchmen may talk, but miracles are not ceased.° For 'tis more
than natural such a rude fellow as he, and such a little impertinent
as she, should be capable of making a woman of my sphere uneasy.   295
But I can bear her sight no longer; methinks she's grown ten times
uglier than Cornet. I must go home and study revenge. (*To Lady
Brute*) Madam, your humble servant: I must take my leave.

LADY BRUTE What, going already madam?

LADY FANCYFULL I must beg you'll excuse me this once. For really I   300
have eighteen visits to return this afternoon so you see I'm importuned by the women as well as the men.

BELLINDA (*aside*) And she's quits with 'em both.

LADY FANCYFULL (*going*) Nay you shan't go one step out of the
room.   305

LADY BRUTE Indeed I'll wait upon you down.

LADY FANCYFULL No, sweet Lady Brute; you know I swoon at
ceremony.

LADY BRUTE Pray give me leave.

LADY FANCYFULL You know I won't.   310

LADY BRUTE Indeed I must.

LADY FANCYFULL Indeed you shan't.

LADY BRUTE Indeed I will.

LADY FANCYFULL Indeed you shan't.

LADY BRUTE Indeed I will.   315

LADY FANCYFULL Indeed you shan't. Indeed, indeed, indeed you
shan't.

> *Exit Lady Fancyfull running.*° [*Lady Brute and Bellinda*]
> *follow.* [*Bellinda remains offstage with Heartfree*]
> *Re-enter Lady Brute*

LADY BRUTE This impertinent woman has put me out of humour for
a fortnight. What an agreeable moment has her foolish visit interrupted! Lord, how like a torrent love flows into the heart when once   320
the sluice of desire is opened! Good gods, what a pleasure there is
in doing what we should not do!

> *Re-enter Constant*

Ha! Here again?

CONSTANT Though the renewing my visit may seem a little irregular,
I hope I shall obtain your pardon for it, madam, when you know I   325
only left the room lest the lady who was here should have been as
malicious in her remarks as she's foolish in her conduct.

LADY BRUTE He who has discretion enough to be tender of a wom-
    an's reputation carries a virtue about him may atone for a great
    many faults.   330
CONSTANT If it has a title to atone for any, its pretensions must needs
    be strongest where the crime is love. I therefore hope I shall
    be forgiven the attempt I have made upon your heart, since my
    enterprise has been a secret to all the world but yourself.
LADY BRUTE Secrecy indeed in sins of this kind is an argument of   335
    weight to lessen the punishment; but nothing's a plea for a pardon
    entire without a sincere repentance.
CONSTANT If sincerity in repentance consist in sorrow for offending,
    no cloister ever enclosed so true a penitent as I should be. But I
    hope it cannot be reckoned an offence to love, where 'tis a duty to   340
    adore.
LADY BRUTE 'Tis an offence, a great one, where it would rob a woman
    of all she ought to be adored for—her virtue.
CONSTANT Virtue? Virtue, alas, is no more like the thing that's called
    so, than 'tis like vice itself. Virtue consists in goodness, honour,   345
    gratitude, sincerity and pity, and not in peevish, snarling strait-
    laced chastity. True virtue, wheresoe'er it moves, still carries an
    intrinsic worth about it, and is in every place, and in each sex, of
    equal value. So is not continence, you see: that phantom of honour,
    which men in every age have so contemned, they have thrown it   350
    amongst the women to scrabble for.
LADY BRUTE If it be a thing of so very little value, why do you so
    earnestly recommend it to your wives and daughters?
CONSTANT We recommend it to our wives, madam, because we would
    keep 'em to ourselves. And to our daughters, because we would   355
    dispose of 'em to others.
LADY BRUTE 'Tis then of some importance it seems, since you can't
    dispose of 'em without it.
CONSTANT That importance, madam, lies in the humour of the coun-
    try, not in the nature of the thing.   360
LADY BRUTE How do you prove that, sir?
CONSTANT From the wisdom of a neighb'ring nation° in a contrary
    practice. In monarchies things go by whimsy, but commonwealths
    weigh all things in the scale of reason.
LADY BRUTE I hope we are not so very light a people to bring up°   365
    fashions without some ground.
CONSTANT Pray what does your ladyship think of a powdered coat°
    for deep mourning?

LADY BRUTE I think, sir, your sophistry has all the effect that you can reasonably expect it should have; it puzzles, but don't convince.   370

CONSTANT I'm sorry for it.

LADY BRUTE I'm sorry to hear you say so.

CONSTANT Pray why?

LADY BRUTE Because if you expected more from it, you have a worse opinion of my understanding than I desire you should have.   375

CONSTANT (*aside*) I comprehend her. She would have me set a value upon her chastity, that I may think myself the more obliged to her when she makes me a present of it. (*To her*) I beg you will believe I did but rally, madam; I know you judge too well of right and wrong to be deceived by arguments like those. I hope you'll have so   380 favourable an opinion of my understanding too, to believe the thing called virtue has worth enough with me to pass for an eternal obligation where'er 'tis sacrificed.

LADY BRUTE It is I think so great a one, as nothing can repay.

CONSTANT Yes; the making the man you love your everlasting debtor.   385

LADY BRUTE When debtors once have borrowed all we have to lend, they are very apt to grow very shy of their creditors' company.

CONSTANT That, madam, is only when they are forced to borrow of usurers, and not of a generous friend. Let us choose our creditors, and we are seldom so ungrateful to shun 'em.   390

LADY BRUTE What think you of Sir John, sir? I was his free choice.

CONSTANT I think he's married, madam.

LADY BRUTE Does marriage then exclude men from your rule of constancy?

CONSTANT It does. Constancy's a brave, free, haughty, generous   395 agent, that cannot buckle to the chains of wedlock. There's a poor sordid slavery in marriage, that turns the flowing tide of honour, and sinks us to the lowest ebb of infamy. 'Tis a corrupted soil; ill nature, avarice, sloth, cowardice and dirt are all its product.°

LADY BRUTE Have you no exceptions to this general rule as well as to   400 t'other?

CONSTANT Yes; I would (after all) be an exception to it myself if you were free in power and will to make me so.

LADY BRUTE Compliments are well placed where 'tis impossible to lay hold on 'em.   405

CONSTANT I would to heaven 'twere possible for you to lay hold on mine, that you might see it is no compliment at all. But since you are already disposed on beyond redemption to one who does not know the value of the jewel you have put into his hands, I hope you

would not think him greatly wronged though it should sometimes   410
be looked on by a friend who knows how to esteem it as he ought.

LADY BRUTE If looking on't alone would serve his turn, the wrong
perhaps might not be very great.

CONSTANT Why, what if he should wear it now and then a day, so he
gave good security to bring it home again at night?   415

LADY BRUTE Small security, I fancy, might serve for that. One might
venture to take his word.

CONSTANT Then where's the injury to the owner?

LADY BRUTE 'Tis an injury to him, if he think it one. For if happiness
be seated in the mind, unhappiness must be so too.   420

CONSTANT Here I close with you, madam, and draw my conclusive
argument from your own position; if the injury lie in the fancy,
there needs nothing but secrecy to prevent the wrong.

LADY BRUTE (*going*) A surer way to prevent it, is to hear no more
arguments in its behalf.   425

CONSTANT (*following her*) But, madam—

LADY BRUTE But, sir, 'tis my turn to be discreet now, and not suffer
too long a visit.

CONSTANT (*catching her hand*) By heaven, you shall not stir, till you
give me hopes that I shall see you again, at some more convenient   430
time and place.

LADY BRUTE I give you just hopes enough—(*breaking from him*)—to
get loose from you; and that's all I can afford you at this time.

    Exit [*Lady Brute*] *running*

CONSTANT (*alone*) Now by all that's great and good, she is a charming
woman. In what ecstasy of joy she has left me. For she gave me   435
hope; did she not say she gave me hope? Hope? Ay, what hope?
Enough to make me let her go. Why that's enough in conscience.
Or no matter how 'twas spoke; hope was the word. It came from
her, and it was said to me.

    Enter Heartfree

Ha, Heartfree: thou hast done me noble service in prattling to the   440
young gentlewoman without there. Come to my arms, thou vener-
able bawd, and let me squeeze thee (*embracing him eagerly*) as a new
pair of stays does a fat country girl, when she's carried to court to
stand for a maid of honour.

HEARTFREE Why what the devil's all this rapture for?   445

CONSTANT Rapture? There's ground for rapture, man; there's hopes,
my Heartfree, hopes, my friend.

HEARTFREE Hopes? Of what?

CONSTANT Why hopes that my lady and I together (for 'tis more than
one body's work) should make Sir John a cuckold.   450
HEARTFREE Prithee, what did she say to thee?
CONSTANT Say? What did she not say? She said that—says she—she
said—zoons, I don't know what she said, but she looked as if she
said everything I'd have her; and so if thou'lt go to the tavern, I'll
treat thee with anything that gold can buy. I'll give all my silver   455
amongst the drawers, make a bonfire before the door, say the plenipos have signed the peace,° and the Bank of England's° grown
honest.

> *Exeunt*

3.2

[The Blue Posts Tavern]

*Scene opens.° Lord Rake, Sir John, [and Colonel Bully] at a
table drinking [with a Page waiting on them]*

ALL Huzza.
LORD RAKE Come, boys. Charge again. So. Confusion to all order.
Here's liberty of conscience.°
ALL Huzza.
LORD RAKE I'll sing you a song I made this morning to this purpose.   5
SIR JOHN 'Tis wicked, I hope.
COLONEL BULLY Don't my lord tell you he made it?
SIR JOHN Well then, let's ha't.
LORD RAKE *(sings)*

1

> *What a pother of late°*
> *Have they kept in the state*   10
> *About setting our consciences free.*
> *A bottle has more*
> *Dispensation in store,°*
> *Than the king and the state can decree.*

2

> *When my head's full of wine,*   15
> *I o'erflow with design*
> *And know no penal laws that can curb me.°*

> *What e'er I devise,*
> *Seems good in my eyes,*
> *And religion ne'er dares to disturb me.*   20

3

> *No saucy remorse*
> *Intrudes in my course,*
> *Nor impertinent notions of evil.*
> *So there's claret in store,*
> *In peace I've my whore,*   25
> *And in peace I jog on to the devil.*

ALL (*sing*) *So there's claret, etc.*

LORD RAKE (*repeats*) *And in peace I jog on to the devil.* Well, how do you like it, gentlemen?

ALL O, admirable.   30

SIR JOHN I would not give a fig for a song that is not full of sin and impudence.

LORD RAKE Then my muse is to your taste. But drink away; the night steals upon us, we shall want time to be lewd in. Hey page, sally out, sirrah, and see what's doing in the camp; we'll beat up their   35
quarters° presently.

PAGE I'll bring your lordship an exact account.

> *Exit Page*

LORD RAKE Now let the spirit of clary° go round. Fill me a brimmer. Here's to our forlorn hope.° Courage, knight; victory attends you.

SIR JOHN And laurels shall crown me. Drink away and be damned.   40

LORD RAKE Again boys; t'other glass, and damn morality.

SIR JOHN (*drinks*) Ay—damn morality—and damn the watch. And let the constable be married.

ALL Huzza.

> *Re-enter Page*

LORD RAKE How are the streets inhabited, sirrah?   45

PAGE My lord, it's Sunday night; they are full of drunken citizens.

LORD RAKE Along then boys, we shall have a feast.

COLONEL BULLY Along, noble knight.

SIR JOHN Ay—along Bully; and he that says Sir John Brute is not as drunk and as religious as the drunkenest citizen of 'em all—is a liar,   50
and the son of a whore.

COLONEL BULLY Why that was bravely spoke, and like a free-born Englishman.

SIR JOHN What's that to you, sir, whether I am an Englishman or a
Frenchman?   55

COLONEL BULLY Zoons, you are not angry, sir?

SIR JOHN Zoons I am angry, sir—for if I am a free-born Englishman,
what have you to do, even to talk of my privileges?°

LORD RAKE Why prithee, knight, don't quarrel here; leave private
animosities to be decided by daylight; let the night be employed   60
against the public enemy.

SIR JOHN My lord I respect you, because you are a man of quality; but
I'll make that fellow know I am within a hair's breadth as absolute
by my privileges, as the King of France is by his prerogative. He by
his prerogative takes money where it is not his due; I, by my privil-   65
ege refuse paying it, where I owe it.° Liberty and property° and old
England, huzza!

ALL Huzza!

> *Exit Sir John reeling, [Lord Rake, Colonel Bully and Page]*
> *following him*

3.3

A bedchamber [in Sir John's house]

Enter Lady Brute and Bellinda

LADY BRUTE Sure it's late, Bellinda. I begin to be sleepy.

BELLINDA Yes 'tis near twelve. Will you go to bed?

LADY BRUTE To bed my dear? And by that time I'm fallen into a
sweet sleep (or perhaps a sweet dream which is better and better)
Sir John will come home, roaring drunk, and be overjoyed he finds   5
me in a condition to be disturbed.

BELLINDA O, you need not fear him, he's in for all night. The servants say he's gone to drink with my Lord Rake.

LADY BRUTE Nay 'tis not very likely indeed such suitable company
should part presently. What hogs men turn, Bellinda, when they   10
grow weary of women.

BELLINDA And what owls they are whilst they are fond of 'em.

LADY BRUTE But that we may forgive well enough, because they are
so upon our accounts.

BELLINDA We ought to do so indeed; but 'tis a hard matter. For when   15
a man is really in love he looks so unsufferably silly that though a
woman liked him well enough before, she has then much ado to

endure the sight of him. And this I take to be the reason why lovers
are so generally ill-used.

LADY BRUTE Well I own now, I'm well enough pleased to see a man 20
look like an ass for me.

BELLINDA Ay, I'm pleased he should look like an ass too—that is, I'm
pleased with myself for making him look so.

LADY BRUTE Nay truly, I think if he'd find some other way to express
his passion, 'twould be more to his advantage. 25

BELLINDA Yes, for then a woman might like his passion and him too.

LADY BRUTE Yet, Bellinda, after all, a woman's life would be but a
dull business, if 'twere not for men; and men that can look like asses
too. We should never blame fate for the shortness of our days; our
time would hang wretchedly upon our hands. 30

BELLINDA Why truly, they do help us off with a good share on't. For
were there no men in the world, o' my conscience I should be no
longer a-dressing than I'm a-saying my prayers; nay though it were
Sunday. For you know that one may go to church without stays on.

LADY BRUTE But don't you think emulation might do something? For 35
every woman you see desires to be finer than her neighbour.

BELLINDA That's only that the men may like her better than her
neighbour. No: if there were no men, adieu fine petticoats; we
should be weary of wearing 'em.

LADY BRUTE And adieu plays; we should be weary of seeing 'em. 40

BELLINDA Adieu Hyde Park; the dust° would choke us.

LADY BRUTE Adieu St James's; walking would tire us.

BELLINDA Adieu London; the smoke would stifle us.

LADY BRUTE And adieu going to church, for religion would ne'er
prevail with us. 45

BOTH Ha ha ha ha ha.

BELLINDA Our confession is so very hearty, sure we merit absolution.

LADY BRUTE Not unless we go through with't, and confess all. So
prithee, for the ease of our consciences, let's hide nothing.

BELLINDA Agreed. 50

LADY BRUTE Why then I confess, that I love to sit in the forefront of a
box, for if one sits behind, there's two acts gone perhaps before
one's found out. And when I am there, if I perceive the men whis-
pering and looking upon me, you must know I cannot for my life
forbear thinking they talk to my advantage. And that sets a 55
thousand little tickling vanities on foot—

BELLINDA Just my case for all the world; but go on.

LADY BRUTE I watch with impatience for the next jest in the play, that

I may laugh and show my white teeth. If the poet has been dull, and
the jest be long a-coming, I pretend to whisper one to my friend,   60
and from thence fall into a little short discourse, in which I take
occasion to show my face in all humours, brisk, pleased, serious,
melancholy, languishing. Not that what we say to one another
causes any of these alterations, but—

BELLINDA Don't trouble yourself to explain; for if I'm not mistaken,   65
you and I have had some of these necessary dialogues before now,
with the same intention.

LADY BRUTE Why I'll swear, Bellinda, some people do give strange
agreeable airs to their faces in speaking. Tell me true! Did you
never practise in the glass?°   70

BELLINDA Why, did you?

LADY BRUTE Yes faith, many a time.

BELLINDA And I too, I own it; both how to speak myself, and how to
look when others speak. But my glass and I could never yet agree
what face I should make when they come blurt out with a   75
nasty thing° in a play. For all the men presently look upon the
women, that's certain; so laugh we must not, though our stays burst
for't, because that's telling truth and owning we understand the
jest. And to look serious is so dull, when the whole house is
a-laughing.   80

LADY BRUTE Besides, that looking serious does really betray our
knowledge in the matter, as much as laughing with the company
would do. For if we did not understand the thing, we should
naturally do like other people.

BELLINDA For my part I always take that occasion to blow my nose.   85

LADY BRUTE You must blow your nose half off then at some plays.

BELLINDA Why don't some reformer or other° beat the poet for't?

LADY BRUTE Because he is not so sure of our private approbation as
of our public thanks. Well, sure there is not upon earth so impertinent a thing as women's modesty.   90

BELLINDA Yes; men's fantasque, that obliges us to it. If we quit our
modesty, they say we lose our charms, and yet they know that very
modesty is affectation, and rail at our hypocrisy.

LADY BRUTE Thus one would think 'twere a hard matter to please
'em, niece. Yet our kind mother nature has given us something that   95
makes amends for all. Let our weakness be what it will, mankind
will still be weaker, and whilst there is a world, 'tis woman that will
govern it. But prithee, one word of poor Constant before we go to
bed; if it be but to furnish matter for dreams. I dare swear he's

talking of me now, or thinking of me at least, though it be in the 100
middle of his prayers.

BELLINDA So he ought, I think; for you were pleased to make him a
good round advance today, madam.

LADY BRUTE Why, I have e'en plagued him enough to satisfy any
reasonable woman. He has besieged me these two years to no 105
purpose.

BELLINDA And if he besieged you two years more, he'd be well
enough paid, so he had the plundering of you at last.

LADY BRUTE That may be, but I'm afraid the town won't be able to
hold out much longer; for to confess the truth to you, Bellinda, the 110
garrison begins to grow mutinous.

BELLINDA Then the sooner you capitulate, the better.

LADY BRUTE Yet methinks I would fain stay a little longer, to see you
fixed too, that we might start together and see who could love
longest. What think you if Heartfree should have a month's mind° 115
to you?

BELLINDA Why faith I could almost be in love with him, for despising
that foolish affected Lady Fancyfull, but I'm afraid he's too cold
ever to warm himself by my fire.

LADY BRUTE Then he deserves to be froze to death. Would I were a 120
man for your sake, my dear rogue. (*Kissing her*)

BELLINDA You'd wish yourself a woman again for your own, or the
men are mistaken. But if I could make a conquest of this son of
Bacchus,° and rival his bottle, what should I do with him? He has
no fortune. I can't marry him; and sure you would not have me 125
commit fornication.

LADY BRUTE Why, if you did, child, 'twould be but a good friendly
part; if 'twere only to keep me in countenance whilst I commit—
you know what.

BELLINDA Well, if I can't resolve to serve you that way, I may perhaps 130
some other, as much to your satisfaction. But pray how shall we
contrive to see these blades again quickly?

LADY BRUTE We must e'en have recourse to the old way; make 'em an
appointment 'twixt jest and earnest. 'Twill look like a frolic, and
that you know's a very good thing to save a woman's blushes. 135

BELLINDA You advise well; but where shall it be?

LADY BRUTE In Spring Garden.° But they shan't know their women
till their women pull off their masks; for a surprise is the most
agreeable thing in the world. And I find myself in a very good
humour, ready to do 'em any good turn I can think on. 140

BELLINDA Then pray write 'em the necessary billet,° without farther delay.

LADY BRUTE Let's go into your chamber then, and whilst you say your prayers, I'll do it, child.

　　　　Exeunt

4.1

Covent Garden

Enter Lord Rake, Sir John [and Colonel Bully] with swords drawn

LORD RAKE Is the dog dead?

COLONEL BULLY No, damn him, I heard him wheeze.

LORD RAKE How the witch his wife howled!

COLONEL BULLY Ay, she'll alarm the watch presently.

LORD RAKE Appear, knight, then; come, you have a good cause to   5
fight for—there's a man murdered.

SIR JOHN Is there? Then let his ghost be satisfied; for I'll sacrifice
a constable to it presently, and burn his body upon his wooden
chair.

Enter a Tailor, with a bundle under his arm

COLONEL BULLY How now? What have we got here? A thief?   10

TAILOR No, an't please you; I'm no thief.

LORD RAKE That we'll see presently; here, let the general examine
him.

SIR JOHN Ay, ay, let me examine him; and I'll lay a hundred pound I
find him guilty, in spite of his teeth—for he looks—like a—   15
sneaking rascal. Come sirrah, without equivocation or mental reservation,° tell me of what opinion you are and what calling;° for by
them—I shall guess at your morals.

TAILOR An't please you, I'm a dissenting journeyman tailor.

SIR JOHN Then sirrah, you love lying by your religion, and theft by   20
your trade. And so, that your punishment may be suitable to your
crimes—I'll have you first gagged—and then hanged.

TAILOR Pray good worthy gentlemen, don't abuse me; indeed I'm an
honest man, and a good workman, though I say it that should not
say it.   25

SIR JOHN No words, sirrah, but attend your fate.

LORD RAKE Let me see what's in that bundle.

TAILOR An't please you, it's the doctor of the parish's° gown.

LORD RAKE The doctor's gown! Hark you, knight, you won't stick at
abusing the clergy, will you?   30

SIR JOHN No, I'm drunk, and I'll abuse anything—but my wife; and
her I name—with reverence.

LORD RAKE Then you shall wear this gown whilst you charge the

watch; that though the blows fall upon you, the scandal may light
upon the church.   35

SIR JOHN A generous design—by all the gods—give it me.
        Takes the gown and puts it on

TAILOR O dear gentlemen, I shall be quite undone if you take the
gown.

SIR JOHN Retire, sirrah; and since you carry off your skin—go home,
and be happy.   40

TAILOR (*pausing*) I think I had e'en as good follow the gentleman's
friendly advice. For if I dispute any longer, who knows but the
whim may take him to case me? These courtiers are fuller of tricks
than they are of money; they'll sooner cut a man's throat than pay
his bill.   45
        Exit Tailor

SIR JOHN So, how d'ye like my shapes now?

LORD RAKE This will do to a miracle; he looks like a bishop going to
the holy war. But to your arms, gentlemen, the enemy appears.
        Enter Constable and Watch

WATCHMAN Stand! Who goes there? Come before the constable.

SIR JOHN The constable's a rascal—and you are the son of a whore.   50

WATCHMAN A good civil answer for a parson, truly.

CONSTABLE Methinks, sir, a man of your coat might set a better
example.

SIR JOHN Sirrah, I'll make you know—there are men of my coat can
set as bad examples—as you can do, you dog you.   55
        *Sir John strikes the Constable. They knock him down, disarm
        him and seize him. Lord Rake [and Colonel Bully] run away*

CONSTABLE So, we have secured the parson however.

SIR JOHN Blood and blood—and blood.

WATCHMAN Lord have mercy upon us; how the wicked wretch raves
of blood. I'll warrant he has been murdering somebody tonight.

SIR JOHN Sirrah, there's nothing got by murder but a halter; my   60
talent lies towards drunkenness and simony.°

WATCHMAN Why that now was spoke like a man of parts, neighbours;
it's pity he should be so disguised.

SIR JOHN You lie—I am not disguised; for I am drunk barefaced.

WATCHMAN Look you there again. This is a mad parson, Mr   65
Constable; I'll lay a pot of ale upon's head, he's a good preacher.

CONSTABLE Come sir, out of respect to your calling, I shan't put you
into the round-house;° but we must secure you in our drawing-
room till morning, that you may do no mischief. So, come along.

SIR JOHN You may put me where you will, sirrah, now you have   70
overcome me—but if I can't do mischief, I'll think of mischief—in
spite of your teeth, you dog you.

Exeunt

4.2

A bedchamber [in Sir John's house]

Heartfree, alone

HEARTFREE What the plague ails me? Love? No, I thank you for that;
my heart's rock still. Yet 'tis Bellinda that disturbs me; that's positive. Well, what of all that? Must I love her for being troublesome?
At that rate, I might love all the women I meet, egad. But hold!
Though I don't love her for disturbing me, yet she may disturb me   5
because I love her. Ay, that may be, faith. I have dreamt of her,
that's certain. Well, so I have of my mother; therefore what's that to
the purpose? Ay, but Bellinda runs in my mind waking and so does
many a damned thing that I don't care a farthing for. Methinks,
though, I would fain be talking to her, and yet I have no business.   10
Well, am I the first man that has had a mind to do an impertinent
thing?

Enter Constant

CONSTANT How now, Heartfree? What makes you up and dressed so
soon? I thought none but lovers quarrelled with their beds; I
expected to have found you snoring, as I used to do.   15

HEARTFREE Why faith, friend, 'tis the care I have of your affairs that
makes me so thoughtful; I have been studying all night, how to
bring your matter about with Bellinda.

CONSTANT With Bellinda?

HEARTFREE With my lady, I mean; and faith, I have mighty hopes   20
on't. Sure you must be very well satisfied with her behaviour to you
yesterday?

CONSTANT So well, that nothing but a lover's fears can make me
doubt of success. But what can this sudden change proceed from?

HEARTFREE Why, you saw her husband beat her, did you not?   25

CONSTANT That's true. A husband is scarce to be borne upon any
terms, much less when he fights with his wife. Methinks she should
e'en have cuckolded him upon the very spot, to show that after the
battle, she was master of the field.

HEARTFREE A council of war of women would infallibly have advised   30
her to't. But, I confess, so agreeable a woman as Bellinda deserves a
better usage.

CONSTANT Bellinda again?

HEARTFREE My lady, I mean. What a pox makes me blunder so today?
(*Aside*) A plague of this treacherous tongue.   35

CONSTANT Prithee look upon me seriously, Heartfree. Now answer
me directly! Is it my lady, or Bellinda, employs your careful
thoughts thus?

HEARTFREE My lady, or Bellinda?

CONSTANT In love! By this light in love!   40

HEARTFREE In love?

CONSTANT Nay, ne'er deny it: for thou'lt do it so awkwardly, 'twill
but make the jest sit heavier about thee. My dear friend, I give thee
much joy.

HEARTFREE Why prithee, you won't persuade me to it, will you?   45

CONSTANT That she's mistress of your tongue, that's plain, and I
know you are so honest a fellow, your tongue and heart always go
together. But how, but how the devil? Pha, ha, ha, ha—

HEARTFREE Hey-day! Why sure you don't believe it in earnest?

CONSTANT Yes I do; because I see you deny it in jest.   50

HEARTFREE Nay, but look you Ned—a—deny in jest—a—gadzooks,
you know I say—a—when a man denies a thing in jest—a—

CONSTANT Pha, ha, ha, ha, ha.

HEARTFREE Nay, then we shall have it. What, because a man stumbles
at a word? Did you never make a blunder?   55

CONSTANT Yes, for I am in love, I own it.

HEARTFREE Then, so am I! (*Embracing him*) Now laugh till thy
soul's glutted with mirth; but, dear Constant, don't tell the town
on't.

CONSTANT Nay, then 'twere almost pity to laugh at thee, after so   60
honest a confession. But tell us a little, Jack. By what new-invented
arms has this mighty stroke been given?

HEARTFREE E'en by that unaccountable weapon called, *je ne sais
quoi*.° For everything that can come within the verge of beauty, I
have seen it with indifference.   65

CONSTANT So in few words then; the *je ne sais quoi* has been too hard
for the quilted petticoat.

HEARTFREE Egad, I think the *je ne sais quoi* is in the quilted petticoat;
at least, 'tis certain I ne'er think on't without—a—a *je ne sais quoi* in
every part about me.   70

CONSTANT Well, but have all your remedies lost their virtue? Have
you turned her inside out yet?

HEARTFREE I dare not so much as think on't.

CONSTANT But don't the two years' fatigue I have had discourage
you?   75

HEARTFREE Yes. I dread what I foresee, yet cannot quit the enterprise: like some soldiers whose courage dwells more in their honour
than their nature; on they go, though the body trembles at what the
soul makes it undertake.

CONSTANT Nay, if you expect your mistress will use you as your   80
profanations against her sex deserve, you tremble justly. But how
do you intend to proceed, friend?

HEARTFREE Thou know'st I'm but a novice; be friendly and advise
me.

CONSTANT Why look you then; I'd have you—serenade and a—write   85
a song—go to church—look like a fool—be very officious, ogle,
write and lead out°—and who knows, but in a year or two's time,
you may be—called a troublesome puppy and sent about your
business.

HEARTFREE That's hard.   90

CONSTANT Yet thus it oft falls out with lovers, sir.

HEARTFREE Pox on me for making one of the number.

CONSTANT Have a care: say no saucy things. 'Twill but augment your
crime, and if your mistress hears on't, increase your punishment.

HEARTFREE Prithee, say something then to encourage me; you know I   95
helped you in your distress.

CONSTANT Why then to encourage you to perseverance, that you may
be thoroughly ill used for your offences, I'll put you in mind that
even the coyest ladies of 'em all are made up of desires as well as we;
and though they do hold out a long time, they will capitulate at last.   100
For that thundering engineer, nature, does make such havoc in the
town, they must surrender at long run, or perish in their own
flames.

    Enter a Footman

FOOTMAN Sir, there's a porter without with a letter; he desires to give
it into your own hands.   105

CONSTANT Call him in.

    [*Exit Footman*]
    Enter Porter

CONSTANT What Jo; is it thee?

PORTER An't please you sir, I was ordered to deliver this into your

own hands, by two well-shaped ladies, at the New Exchange.° I was
at your honour's lodgings, and your servants sent me hither.   110

CONSTANT 'Tis well. Are you to carry any answer?

PORTER No, my noble master. They gave me my orders, and whip,
they were gone, like a maidenhead at fifteen.

CONSTANT Very well; there. (*Gives him money*)

PORTER God bless your Honour.   115

    Exit Porter

CONSTANT Now let's see what honest trusty Jo has brought us.
(*Reads*) 'If you and your playfellow can spare time from your business and devotions, don't fail to be at Spring Garden about eight in
the evening. You'll find nothing there but women, so you need
bring no other arms than what you usually carry about you.' So,   120
playfellow. Here's something to stay your stomach, till your
mistress's dish is ready for you.

HEARTFREE Some of our old battered acquaintance. I won't go,
not I.

CONSTANT Nay, that you can't avoid. There's honour in the case; 'tis   125
a challenge, and I want a second.

HEARTFREE I doubt I shall be but a very useless one to you; for I'm so
disheartened by this wound Bellinda has given me, I don't think I
shall have courage enough to draw my sword.

CONSTANT O, if that be all, come along; I'll warrant you find sword   130
enough for such enemies as we have to deal withal.

    Exeunt

4.3

    [*In the street*]

    Enter Constable [and Watch] with Sir John

CONSTABLE Come along, sir, I thought to have let you slip this morning, because you were a minister; but you are as drunk and as
abusive as ever. We'll see what the justice of the peace will say to
you.

SIR JOHN And you shall see what I'll say to the justice of the peace,   5
sirrah.

    They knock at the door
    Enter Servant

CONSTABLE Pray acquaint his worship, we have got an unruly parson

here; we are unwilling to expose him, but don't know what to do
with him.

SERVANT I'll acquaint my master.   10

    Exit Servant

SIR JOHN You—constable—what damned justice is this?

CONSTABLE One that will take care of you, I warrant you.

    Enter Justice

JUSTICE Well, Mr Constable, what's the disorder here?

CONSTABLE An't please your worship—

SIR JOHN Let me speak and be damned. I'm a divine, and can unfold   15
mysteries° better than you can do.

JUSTICE Sadness, sadness, a minister so overtaken. Pray sir, give the
constable leave to speak, and I'll hear you very patiently; I assure
you sir, I will.

SIR JOHN Sir—you are a very civil magistrate. Your most humble   20
servant.

CONSTABLE An't please your worship then, he has attempted to beat
the watch tonight, and swore—

SIR JOHN You lie.

JUSTICE Hold, pray sir, a little.   25

SIR JOHN Sir, your very humble servant.

CONSTABLE Indeed sir, he came at us without any provocation, called
us whores and rogues, and laid us on with a great quarter-staff. He
was in my Lord Rake's company. They have been playing the devil
tonight.   30

JUSTICE Hem, hem. Pray sir, may you be chaplain to my lord?

SIR JOHN Sir—I presume—I may if I will.

JUSTICE My meaning sir, is—are you so?

SIR JOHN Sir—you mean very well.

JUSTICE He hem, hem. Under favour, sir, pray answer me directly.   35

SIR JOHN Under favour, sir—do you use to answer directly when you
are drunk?

JUSTICE Good lack, good lack; here's nothing to be got from him.
Pray sir, may I crave your name?

SIR JOHN Sir—my name's—(*he hiccups*) Hiccup, sir.   40

JUSTICE Hiccup? Doctor Hiccup. I have known a great many country
parsons of that name, especially down in the Fens.° Pray where
do you live, sir?

SIR JOHN Here—and there, sir.

JUSTICE Why, what a strange man is this? Where do you preach, sir?   45
Have you any cure?°

SIR JOHN Sir—I have—a very good cure—for a clap, at your service.

JUSTICE Lord have mercy upon us.

SIR JOHN (*aside*) This fellow does ask so many impertinent questions, I believe, egad, 'tis the justice's wife in the justice's clothes. 50

JUSTICE Mr Constable, I vow and protest, I don't know what to do with him.

CONSTABLE Truly, he has been but a troublesome guest to us all night.

JUSTICE I think I had e'en best let him go about his business, for I'm unwilling to expose him. 55

CONSTABLE E'en what your worship thinks fit.

SIR JOHN Sir—not to interrupt Mr Constable—I have a small favour to ask.

JUSTICE Sir, I open both my ears to you. 60

SIR JOHN Sir, your very humble servant. I have a little urgent business calls upon me, and therefore I desire the favour of you to bring matters to a conclusion.

JUSTICE Sir, if I were sure that business were not to commit more disorders, I would release you. 65

SIR JOHN None—by my priesthood.

JUSTICE Then, Mr Constable, you may discharge him.

SIR JOHN Sir, your very humble servant. If you please to accept of a bottle—

JUSTICE I thank you kindly, sir; but I never drink in a morning. 70
Goodbye to ye, sir, goodbye to ye.

SIR JOHN Goodbye t'ye, good sir. (*Exit Justice*) So—now, Mr Constable, shall you and I go pick up a whore together?

CONSTABLE No thank you, sir; my wife's enough to satisfy any reasonable man. 75

SIR JOHN (*aside*) He, he, he, he, he—the fool is married then. (*To the Constable*) Well, you won't go?

CONSTABLE Not I, truly.

SIR JOHN Then I'll go by myself; and you and your wife may be damned. 80
Exit Sir John

CONSTABLE (*gazing after him*) Why God-a-mercy, parson!
Exeunt

4.4

Spring Garden

Constant and Heartfree cross the stage

CONSTANT So. I think we are about the time appointed. Let us walk up this way.

> *Exeunt. As they go off, enter Lady Fancyfull and Madamoiselle, masked and dogging them*°

LADY FANCYFULL Good. Thus far I have dogged 'em without being discovered. 'Tis infallibly some intrigue that brings them to Spring Garden. How my poor heart is torn and racked with fear and 5
jealousy. Yet let it be anything but that flirt Bellinda, and I'll try to bear it. But if it prove her, all that's woman in me shall be employed to destroy her.

> *Exeunt after Constant and Heartfree*
> *Re-enter Constant and Heartfree, Lady Fancyfull and*
> *Madamoiselle still following at a distance*

CONSTANT I see no females yet that have anything to say to us. I'm afraid we are bantered. 10

HEARTFREE I wish we were; for I'm in no humour to make either them or myself merry.

CONSTANT Nay, I'm sure you'll make them merry enough; if I tell 'em why you are dull. But prithee why so heavy and sad before you begin to be ill used? 15

HEARTFREE For the same reason, perhaps, that you are so brisk and well pleased; because both pains and pleasures are generally more considerable in prospect than when they come to pass.

> *Enter Lady Brute and Bellinda, masked and poorly dressed*

CONSTANT How now, who are these? Not our game,° I hope.

HEARTFREE If they are, we are e'en well enough served, to come 20
hunting here, when we had so much better game in chase elsewhere.

LADY FANCYFULL (*to Madamoiselle*) So: those are their ladies without doubt. But I'm afraid that doily° stuff is not worn for want of better clothes. They are the very shape and size of Bellinda and her 25
aunt.

MADAMOISELLE So day be inteed, matam.

LADY FANCYFULL We'll slip into this close arbour where we may hear all they say.

> *Exeunt Lady Fancyfull and Madamoiselle*

LADY BRUTE What, are you afraid of us, gentlemen?   30

HEARTFREE Why truly I think we may, if appearance don't lie.

BELLINDA Do you always find women what they appear to be, sir?

HEARTFREE No forsooth; but I seldom find 'em better than they appear to be.

BELLINDA Then the outside's best, you think?   35

HEARTFREE 'Tis the honestest.

CONSTANT Have a care, Heartfree; you are relapsing again.

LADY BRUTE Why, does the gentleman use to rail at women?

CONSTANT He has done formerly.

BELLINDA I suppose he had very good cause for't. They did not use   40
you so well as you thought you deserved, sir.

LADY BRUTE They made themselves merry at your expense, sir.

BELLINDA Laughed when you sighed.

LADY BRUTE Slept while you were waking.

BELLINDA Had your porter beat.   45

LADY BRUTE And threw your *billets-doux* in the fire.

HEARTFREE Hey-day, I shall do more than rail presently.

BELLINDA Why you won't beat us, will you?

HEARTFREE I don't know but I may.

CONSTANT What the devil's coming here? Sir John in a gown! And   50
drunk, i' faith.

Enter Sir John

SIR JOHN What a pox—here's Constant, Heartfree—and two whores
egad—o you covetous rogues; what, have you never a spare punk
for your friend? But I'll share with you.

He seizes both the women

HEARTFREE Why, what the plague have you been doing, knight?   55

SIR JOHN Why, I have been beating the watch, and scandalizing the
clergy.

HEARTFREE A very good account, truly.

SIR JOHN And what do you think I'll do next?

CONSTANT Nay, that no man can guess.   60

SIR JOHN Why, if you'll let me sup with you, I'll treat both your
strumpets.

LADY BRUTE (*aside*) O Lord, we are undone.

HEARTFREE No, we can't sup together, because we have some affairs
elsewhere. But if you'll accept of these two ladies, we'll be so com-   65
plaisant to you to resign our right in 'em.

BELLINDA (*aside*) Lord, what shall we do?

SIR JOHN Let me see, their clothes are such damned clothes, they won't pawn for the reckoning.

HEARTFREE Sir John, your servant. Rapture attend you.   70

CONSTANT Adieu ladies, make much of the gentleman.

LADY BRUTE Why sure, you won't leave us in the hands of a drunken fellow to abuse us.

SIR JOHN Who do you call a drunken fellow, you slut you? I'm a man of quality; the king has made me a knight.   75

Heartfree runs off

HEARTFREE Ay, ay, you are in good hands! Adieu, adieu.

LADY BRUTE The devil's hands. Let me go, or I'll—for heaven's sake protect us.

She breaks from him [and] runs to Constant, twitching off her mask and clapping it on again

SIR JOHN I'll devil you, you jade you. I'll demolish your ugly face.

CONSTANT Hold a little, knight, she swoons.   80

SIR JOHN I'll swoon her.

CONSTANT Hey, Heartfree.

Re-enter Heartfree. Bellinda runs to him and shows her face

HEARTFREE O heavens! My dear creature, stand there a little.

CONSTANT Pull him off, Jack.

HEARTFREE Hold, mighty man; look you, sir, we did but jest with   85
you. These are ladies of our acquaintance that we had a mind to frighten a little, but now you must leave us.

SIR JOHN Oons, I won't leave you, not I.

HEARTFREE Nay, but you must though; and therefore make no words on't.   90

SIR JOHN Then you are a couple of damned uncivil fellows. And I hope your punks will give you sauce to your mutton.°

Exit Sir John

LADY BRUTE Oh, I shall never come to myself again, I'm so frightened.

CONSTANT 'Twas a narrow 'scape, indeed.   95

BELLINDA Women must have frolics, you see, whatever they cost 'em.

HEARTFREE This might have proved a dear one though.

LADY BRUTE You are the more obliged to us for the risk we run upon your accounts.

CONSTANT And I hope you'll acknowledge something due to our   100
knight errantry, ladies. This is the second time we have delivered you.

LADY BRUTE 'Tis true; and since we see fate has designed you for our guardians, 'twill make us the more willing to trust ourselves in your hands. But you must not have the worse opinion of us for our innocent frolic. 105

HEARTFREE Ladies, you may command our opinions in everything that is to your advantage.

BELLINDA Then, sir, I command you to be of opinion that women are sometimes better than they appear to be. 110

Lady Brute and Constant talk apart

HEARTFREE Madam, you have made a convert of me in everything. I'm grown a fool: I could be fond of a woman.

BELLINDA I thank you, sir, in the name of the whole sex.

HEARTFREE Which sex nothing but yourself could ever have atoned for. 115

BELLINDA Now has my vanity a devilish itch to know in what my merit consists.

HEARTFREE In your humility, madam, that keeps you ignorant it consists at all.

BELLINDA One other compliment with that serious face, and I hate 120 you forever after.

HEARTFREE Some women love to be abused; is that it you would be at?

BELLINDA No, not that neither; but I'd have men talk plainly what's fit for women to hear, without putting 'em either to a real, or an affected blush. 125

HEARTFREE Why then, in as plain terms as I can find to express myself: I could love you even to—matrimony itself almost, egad.

BELLINDA Just as Sir John did her ladyship there. What think you? Don't you believe one month's time might bring you down to the same indifference, only clad in a little better manners, perhaps? 130 Well, you men are unaccountable things—mad till you have your mistresses, and then stark mad till you are rid of 'em again. Tell me honestly, is not your patience put to a much severer trial after possession than before?

HEARTFREE With a great many, I must confess, it is, to our eternal 135 scandal; but I—dear creature, do but try me.

BELLINDA That's the surest way indeed to know, but not the safest. (*To Lady Brute*) Madam, are not you for taking a turn in the great walk? It's almost dark, nobody will know us.

LADY BRUTE Really I find myself something idle, Bellinda; besides, I 140 dote upon this little odd private corner. But don't let my lazy fancy confine you.

CONSTANT (*aside*) So, she would be left alone with me, that's well.

BELLINDA Well, we'll take one turn, and come to you again. (*To Heartfree*) Come, sir, shall we go pry into the secrets of the garden? Who knows what discoveries we may make?

HEARTFREE Madam, I'm at your service.

CONSTANT (*to Heartfree aside*) Don't make too much haste back; for—d'ye hear—I may be busy.

HEARTFREE Enough.

Exeunt Bellinda and Heartfree

LADY BRUTE Sure you think me scandalously free, Mr Constant. I'm afraid I shall lose your good opinion of me.

CONSTANT My good opinion, madam, is like your cruelty, never to be removed.

LADY BRUTE But if I should remove my cruelty, then there's an end of your good opinion.

CONSTANT There is not so strict an alliance between 'em neither. 'Tis certain I should love you then better (if that be possible) than I do now; and where I love, I always esteem.

LADY BRUTE Indeed, I doubt you much. Why, suppose you had a wife, and she should entertain a gallant.

CONSTANT If I gave her just cause, how could I justly condemn her?

LADY BRUTE Ah; but you'd differ widely about just causes.

CONSTANT But blows can bear no dispute.

LADY BRUTE Nor ill manners much, truly.

CONSTANT Then no woman upon earth has so just a cause as you have.

LADY BRUTE O, but a faithful wife is a beautiful character.

CONSTANT To a deserving husband, I confess it is.

LADY BRUTE But can his faults release my duty?

CONSTANT In equity, without doubt. And where laws dispense with equity, equity should dispense with laws.°

LADY BRUTE Pray let's leave this dispute; for you men have as much witchcraft in your arguments as women have in their eyes.

CONSTANT But whilst you attack me with your charms, 'tis but reasonable I assault you with mine.

LADY BRUTE The case is not the same. What mischief we do, we can't help, and therefore are to be forgiven.

CONSTANT Beauty soon obtains pardon for the pain that it gives, when it applies the balm of compassion to the wound; but a fine face, and a hard heart, is almost as bad as an ugly face and a soft one—both very troublesome to many a poor gentleman.

LADY BRUTE Yes, and to many a poor gentlewoman too, I can assure
you. But pray which of 'em is it, that most afflicts you?

CONSTANT Your glass and conscience will inform you, madam. But   185
for heaven's sake (for now I must be serious) if pity or if gratitude
can move you; (*taking her hand*) if constancy and truth have
power to tempt you; if love, if adoration can affect you—give me
at least some hopes that time may do what you perhaps mean
never to perform. 'Twill ease my sufferings, though not quench   190
my flame.

LADY BRUTE Your sufferings eased, your flame would soon abate; and
that I would preserve, not quench it, sir.

CONSTANT Would you° preserve it, nourish it with favours; for that's
the food it naturally requires.   195

LADY BRUTE Yet on that natural food, 'twould surfeit soon, should I
resolve to grant all that you would ask.

CONSTANT And in refusing all, you starve it. Forgive me therefore,
since my hunger rages, if I at last grow wild, and in my frenzy force
at least this from you. (*Kissing her hand*) Or if you'd have my flame 200
soar higher still, (*kissing first her hand, then her neck*) then grant me
this, and this, and this, and thousands more. (*Aside*) For now's the
time; she melts into compassion.

LADY BRUTE (*aside*) Poor coward virtue, how it shuns the battle. O
heavens! Let me go.   205

CONSTANT Ay, go, ay; where shall we go, my charming angel? Into
this private arbour—nay, let's lose no time—moments are precious.

LADY BRUTE And lovers wild. Pray let us stop here; at least for this
time.

CONSTANT 'Tis impossible: he that has power over you, can have   210
none over himself.

LADY BRUTE Ah! I'm lost.

> As he is forcing her into the arbour, Lady Fancyfull and
> Madamoiselle bolt out upon them, and run over the stage

LADY FANCYFULL Fe, fe, fe, fe, fe.

MADAMOISELLE Fe, fe, fe, fe, fe.

CONSTANT Death and furies, who are these?   215

LADY BRUTE Oh heavens, I'm out of my wits; if they knew me, I'm
ruined.

CONSTANT Don't be frightened; ten thousand to one they are
strangers to you.

LADY BRUTE Whatever they are, I won't stay here a moment longer.   220

CONSTANT Whither will you go?

LADY BRUTE Home, as if the devil were in me. Lord where's this
  Bellinda now?
          Enter Bellinda and Heartfree
  O! it's well you are come: I'm so frightened my hair stands an° end.
  Let's be gone for heaven's sake.   225
BELLINDA Lord, what's the matter?
LADY BRUTE The devil's the matter; we are discovered. Here's a
  couple of women have done the most impertinent thing. Away,
  away, away, away, away.
          Exeunt [Lady Brute, Bellinda, and Heartfree] running. Re-enter
          Lady Fancyfull and Madamoiselle
LADY FANCYFULL Well Madamoiselle, 'tis a prodigious thing how   230
  women can suffer filthy fellows to grow so familiar with 'em.
MADAMOISELLE Ah matam, *il n'y a rien de si naturel.*°
LADY FANCYFULL Fe, fe, fe. But oh my heart! O jealousy, o torture,
  I'm upon the rack! What shall I do? My lover's lost; I ne'er shall see
  him mine. (*Pausing*) But I may be revenged; and that's the same   235
  thing. Ah sweet revenge. Thou welcome thought, thou healing bal-
  sam to my wounded soul. Be but propitious on this one occasion,
  I'll place my heaven in thee for all my life to come.

          To woman how indulgent nature's kind;
          No blast of fortune long disturbs her mind.   240
          Compliance to her fate supports her still;
          If love won't make her happy—mischief will.

          Exeunt

5.1

Lady Fancyfull's house

Enter Lady Fancyfull and Madamoiselle

LADY FANCYFULL Well, Madamoiselle, did you dog the filthy things?

MADAMOISELLE *O que oui,*° matam.

LADY FANCYFULL And where are they?

MADAMOISELLE *Au logis.*°

LADY FANCYFULL What? Men and all?   5

MADAMOISELLE *Tous ensemble.*°

LADY FANCYFULL O confidence! What, carry their fellows to their
  own house?

MADAMOISELLE *C'est que le mari n'y est pas.*°

LADY FANCYFULL No, so I believe, truly. But he shall be there, and   10
  quickly too, if I can find him out. Well, 'tis a prodigious thing, to
  see when men and women get together, how they fortify one
  another in their impudence. But if that drunken fool, her husband,
  be to be found in e'er a tavern in town, I'll send him amongst 'em.
  I'll spoil their sport.   15

MADAMOISELLE *En vérité* matam, *ce serait dommage.*°

LADY FANCYFULL 'Tis in vain to oppose it, Madamoiselle; therefore
  never go about it. For I am the steadiest creature in the world—
  when I have determined to do mischief. So, come along.

Exeunt

5.2

Sir John Brute's house

Enter Constant, Heartfree, Lady Brute, Bellinda, and Lovewell

LADY BRUTE But are you sure you don't mistake, Lovewell?

LOVEWELL Madam, I saw 'em all go into the tavern together, and my
  master was so drunk he could scarce stand.

  [Exit Lovewell]°

LADY BRUTE Then, gentlemen, I believe we may venture to let you
  stay and play at cards with us an hour or two; for they'll scarce part   5
  till morning.

BELLINDA I think 'tis pity they should ever part.

CONSTANT The company that's here, madam.

LADY BRUTE Then, sir, the company that's here must remember to part itself in time.

CONSTANT Madam, we don't intend to forfeit your future favours by an indiscreet usage of this. The moment you give us the signal, we shan't fail to make our retreat.

LADY BRUTE Upon those conditions then, let us sit down to cards.

Enter Lovewell

LOVEWELL O Lord, madam, here's my master just staggering in upon you; he has been quarrelsome yonder, and they have kicked him out of the company.

LADY BRUTE Into the closet, gentlemen, for heaven's sake; I'll wheedle him to bed, if possible.

Constant and Heartfree run into the closet
Enter Sir John, all dirt and bloody

LADY BRUTE Ah—ah—he's all over blood.

SIR JOHN What the plague does the woman—squall for? Did you never see a man in pickle before?

LADY BRUTE Lord, where have you been?

SIR JOHN I have been at—cuffs.

LADY BRUTE I fear that is not all. I hope you are not wounded.

SIR JOHN Sound as a roach,° wife.

LADY BRUTE I'm mighty glad to hear it.

SIR JOHN You know—I think you lie.

LADY BRUTE I know you do me wrong to think so then. For heaven's my witness, I had rather see my own blood trickle down than yours.

SIR JOHN Then will I be crucified.

LADY BRUTE 'Tis a hard fate I should not be believed.

SIR JOHN 'Tis a damned atheistical age, wife.

LADY BRUTE I am sure I have given you a thousand tender proofs how great my care is of you. Nay, spite of all your cruel thoughts, I'll still persist and at this moment, if I can, persuade you to lie down and sleep a little.

SIR JOHN Why—do you think I am drunk—you slut, you?

LADY BRUTE Heaven forbid I should! But I'm afraid you are feverish. Pray let me feel your pulse.

SIR JOHN Stand off and be damned.

LADY BRUTE Why, I see your distemper in your very eyes. You are all on fire. Pray go to bed; let me entreat you.

SIR JOHN Come kiss me then.

LADY BRUTE (*kissing him*) There: now go. (*Aside*) He stinks like poison.

SIR JOHN I see it goes damnably against your stomach—and therefore—kiss me again.

LADY BRUTE Nay, now you fool me.   50

SIR JOHN Do't, I say.

LADY BRUTE (*aside*) Ah Lord have mercy upon me. [*Kisses him*] Well, there: now will you go?

SIR JOHN Now, wife, you shall see my gratitude. You give me two kisses. I'll give you—two hundred.   55
    (*Kisses and tumbles° her*)

LADY BRUTE O Lord! Pray, Sir John, be quiet. Heavens, what a pickle am I in.

BELLINDA (*aside*) If I were in her pickle, I'd call my gallant out of the closet, and he should cudgel him soundly.

SIR JOHN So, now, you being as dirty and as nasty as myself, we may   60
go pig together.° But first, I must have a cup of your cold tea,° wife.
    Going to the closet

LADY BRUTE [*aside*] O, I'm ruined. [*To Sir John*] There's none there, my dear.

SIR JOHN I'll warrant you I'll find some, my dear.

LADY BRUTE You can't open the door, the lock's spoiled. I have been   65
turning and turning the key this half hour to no purpose. I'll send for the smith tomorrow.

SIR JOHN There's ne'er a smith in Europe can open a door with more expedition than I can do. As for example—pou!
    He bursts open the door with his foot
How now? What the devil have we got here? Constant—Heart-   70
free—and two whores again, egad! This is the worst cold tea—that ever I met with in my life.
    Enter Constant and Heartfree

LADY BRUTE (*aside*) O Lord, what will become of us?

SIR JOHN Gentlemen—I am your very humble Servant—I give you many thanks—I see you take care of my family— I shall do all I can   75
to return the obligation.

CONSTANT Sir, how oddly soever this business may appear to you, you would have no cause to be uneasy if you knew the truth of all things; your lady is the most virtuous woman in the world, and nothing has passed but an innocent frolic.   80

HEARTFREE Nothing else, upon my honour sir.

SIR JOHN You are both very civil° gentlemen—and my wife, there, is

a very civil gentlewoman; therefore I don't doubt but many civil
things have passed between you. Your very humble servant.

LADY BRUTE (*aside to Constant*) Pray be gone; he's so drunk he can't   85
hurt us tonight, and tomorrow morning you shall hear from us.

CONSTANT I'll obey you, madam. Sir, when you are cool, you'll
understand reason better. So then I shall take the pains to inform
you. If not—I wear a sword, sir, and so goodbye to you. Come
along, Heartfree.   90

SIR JOHN Wear a sword, sir! And what of all that, sir? He comes to my
house; eats my meat; lies with my wife; dishonours my family; gets
a bastard to inherit my estate—and when I ask a civil account of all
this—'Sir,' says he, 'I wear a sword.' 'Wear a sword, sir?' 'Yes sir,'
says he, 'I wear a sword.' It may be a good answer at cross-   95
purposes°; but 'tis a damned one to a man in my whimsical circumstance—'Sir,' says he, 'I wear a sword.' (*To Lady Brute*) And what
do you wear now? Ha? Tell me.

> *Sitting down in a great chair*

What? you are modest and can't? Why then I'll tell you, you slut
you. You wear—an impudent lewd face—a damned designing   100
heart—and a tail—and a tail full of—

> *He falls fast asleep, snoring*

LADY BRUTE So; thanks to kind heaven, he's fast for some hours.

BELLINDA 'Tis well he is so, that we may have time to lay our story
handsomely; for we must lie like the devil to bring ourselves off.

LADY BRUTE What shall we say, Bellinda?   105

BELLINDA (*musing*) I'll tell you. It must all light upon Heartfree and I.
We'll say he has courted me some time, but for reasons unknown to
us, has ever been very earnest the thing might be kept from Sir
John. That therefore hearing him upon the stairs, he run into the
closet, though against our will, and Constant with him, to prevent   110
jealousy. And to give this a good impudent face of truth (that I may
deliver you from the trouble you are in) I'll e'en, if he pleases,
marry him.

LADY BRUTE I'm beholding to you, cousin; but that would be carrying the jest a little too far for your own sake. You know he's a   115
younger brother, and has nothing.

BELLINDA 'Tis true; but I like him, and have fortune enough to keep
above extremity. I can't say I would live with him in a cell upon love
and bread and butter. But I had rather have the man I love, and a
middle state of life, than that gentleman in the chair there, and   120
twice your ladyship's splendour.

LADY BRUTE In truth, niece, you are in the right on't: for I am very
uneasy with my ambition. But perhaps, had I married as you'll do, I
might have been as ill-used.

BELLINDA Some risk, I do confess, there always is; but if a man has   125
the least spark, either of honour or good nature, he can never use a
woman ill that loves him and makes his fortune both. Yet I must
own to you, some little struggling I still have with this teasing
ambition of ours. For pride, you know, is as natural to a woman, as
'tis to a saint. I can't help being fond of this rogue; and yet it goes to   130
my heart to think I must never whisk to Hyde Park with above a
pair of horses; have no coronet upon my coach, nor a page to carry
up my train. But above all, that business of place°—well, taking
place is a noble prerogative.

LADY BRUTE Especially after a quarrel.   135

BELLINDA Or of a rival. But pray say no more on't, for fear I change
my mind. For o' my conscience, were't not for your affair in the
balance, I should go near to pick up some odious man of quality yet,
and only take poor Heartfree for a gallant.

LADY BRUTE Then him you must have, however things go?   140

BELLINDA Yes.

LADY BRUTE Why, we may pretend what we will; but 'tis a hard
matter to live without the man we love.

BELLINDA Especially when we are married to the man we hate. Pray
tell me, do the men of the town ever believe us virtuous, when they   145
see us do so?

LADY BRUTE O, no: nor indeed hardly, let us do what we will. They
most of 'em think, there is no such thing as virtue considered in the
strictest notions of it; and therefore when you hear 'em say, such a
one is a woman of reputation, they only mean she's a woman of   150
discretion. For they consider we have no more religion than they
have, nor so much morality; and between you and I, Bellinda, I'm
afraid the want of inclination seldom protects any of us.

BELLINDA But what think you of the fear of being found out?

LADY BRUTE I think that never kept any woman virtuous long. We are   155
not such cowards neither. No: let us once pass fifteen, and we have
too good an opinion of our own cunning to believe the world can
penetrate into what we would keep a secret. And so in short, we
cannot reasonably blame the men for judging of us by themselves.

BELLINDA But sure we are not so wicked as they are, after all.   160

LADY BRUTE We are as wicked, child, but our vice lies another
way. Men have more courage than we, so they commit more bold,

impudent sins. They quarrel, fight, swear, drink, blaspheme, and
the like. Whereas we, being cowards, only backbite, tell lies, cheat at
cards and so forth. But 'tis late. Let's end our discourse for tonight,   165
and out of an excess of charity, take a small care of that nasty
drunken thing there. Do but look at him, Bellinda.

BELLINDA Ah, 'tis a savoury dish.

LADY BRUTE As savoury as 'tis, I'm cloyed with't. Prithee, call the
butler to take away.   170

BELLINDA Call the butler? Call the scavenger.° (*To a servant within*)
Who's there? Call Rasor! Let him take away his master, scour him
clean with a little soap and sand, and so put him to bed.

LADY BRUTE Come Bellinda, I'll e'en lie with you tonight; and in the
morning we'll send for our gentlemen to set this matter even.   175

BELLINDA With all my heart.

LADY BRUTE (*making a low curtsey [to Sir John]*) Good night, my dear.

BOTH Ha, ha, ha.
       Exeunt
       Enter Rasor

RASOR My lady there's a wag—my master there's a cuckold. Marriage is a slippery thing—women have depraved appetites. My   180
lady's a wag. I have heard all, I have seen all, I understand all, and
I'll tell all; for my little Frenchwoman loves news dearly. This
story'll gain her heart or nothing will. (*To his master*) Come sir, your
head's too full of fumes at present to make room for your jealousy;
but I reckon we shall have rare work with you when your pate's   185
empty. Come; to your kennel, you cuckoldly drunken sot you.
       Carries him out upon his back

5.3

Lady Fancyfull's house

Enter Lady Fancyfull and Madamoiselle

LADY FANCYFULL But why did not you tell me before, Madamoiselle,
that Rasor and you were fond?

MADAMOISELLE De modesty hinder me, madam.

LADY FANCYFULL Why truly modesty does often hinder us from
doing things we have an extravagant mind to. But does he love you   5
well enough yet to do anything you bid him? Do you think to oblige
you he would speak scandal?

MADAMOISELLE Madam, to oblige your ladyship, he shall speak
blasphemy.

LADY FANCYFULL Why then, Madamoiselle, I'll tell you what you   10
shall do. You shall engage him to tell his master all that passed at
Spring Garden. I have a mind he should know what a wife and a
niece he has got.

MADAMOISELLE *Il le fera,*° madam.

 Enter a Footman, who speaks to Madamoiselle apart

FOOTMAN Madamoiselle, yonder's Mr Rasor desires to speak with   15
you.

MADAMOISELLE Tell him I come presently.

 Exit Footman

Rasor be dare, matam.

LADY FANCYFULL That's fortunate: well, I'll leave you together. And
if you find him stubborn, Madamoiselle—hark you—don't refuse   20
him a few little reasonable liberties, to put him into humour.

MADAMOISELLE *Laissez-moi faire.*°

 Exit Lady Fancyfull

 Rasor peeps in; and seeing Lady Fancyfull gone, runs to
 Madamoiselle, takes her about the neck and kisses her

MADAMOISELLE How now, confidence!

RASOR How now, modesty!

MADAMOISELLE Who make you so familiar, sirrah?   25

RASOR My impudence, hussy.

MADAMOISELLE Stand off, rogue-face.

RASOR Ah, Madamoiselle, great news at our house.

MADAMOISELLE Wy wat be de matter?

RASOR The matter? Why, uptails-all's° the matter.   30

MADAMOISELLE *Tu te moques de moi.*°

RASOR Now do you long to know the particulars—the time when, the
place where, the manner how;° but I won't tell you a word more.

MADAMOISELLE Nay, den dou kill me, Rasor.

RASOR (*clapping his hands behind him*) Come, kiss me then.   35

MADAMOISELLE Nay, pridee tell me.

RASOR (*going*) Goodbye to ye.

MADAMOISELLE Hold, hold; I will kiss dee.

 Kissing him.

RASOR So, that's civil. Why now, my pretty poll,° my goldfinch, my
little waterwagtail°—you must know that—come, kiss me again.   40

MADAMOISELLE I won't kiss dee no more.

RASOR Goodbye to ye.

MADAMOISELLE *Doucement.* (*Kissing him*) Dare: *es-tu content?*°

RASOR So: now I'll tell thee all. Why the news is, that cuckoldom in folio, is newly printed; and matrimony in quarto is just going into   45
the press. Will you buy any books, Madamoiselle?

MADAMOISELLE *Tu parles comme un libraire;*° de devil no understand dee.

RASOR Why then, that I may make myself intelligible to a waiting-woman, I'll speak like a *valet de chambre.*° My lady has cuckolded   50
my master.

MADAMOISELLE *Bon.*°

RASOR Which we take very ill from her hands, I can tell her that. We can't yet prove matter of fact° upon her.

MADAMOISELLE *N'importe.*°   55

RASOR But we can prove, that matter of fact had like to have been upon her.

MADAMOISELLE *Oui da.*°

RASOR For we have such bloody circumstances.

MADAMOISELLE *Sans doute.*°   60

RASOR That any man of parts may draw tickling° conclusions from 'em.

MADAMOISELLE *Fort bien.*°

RASOR We have found a couple of tight well-built gentlemen stuffed into her ladyship's closet.   65

MADAMOISELLE *Le diable!*°

RASOR And I, in my particular person, have discovered a most damnable plot, how to persuade my poor master that all this hide and seek, this will in the wisp, has no other meaning than a Christian marriage for sweet Mrs Bellinda.   70

MADAMOISELLE *Un mariage? Ah les drôlesses.*°

RASOR Don't you interrupt me, hussy; 'tis agreed, I say. And my innocent lady, to wriggle herself out at the back-door of the business, turns marriage-bawd to her niece, and resolves to deliver up her fair body to be tumbled and mumbled, by that young liquorish   75
whipster,° Heartfree. Now are you satisfied?

MADAMOISELLE No.

RASOR Right woman; always gaping for more.

MADAMOISELLE Dis be all den, dat dou know?

RASOR All? Ay, and a great deal too, I think.   80

MADAMOISELLE Dou be fool, dou know noting. *Écoute, mon pauvre Rasor.*° Dou see des two eyes? Des two eyes have see de devil.

RASOR The woman's mad.

MADAMOISELLE In Spring Garden, dat rogue Constant meet dy lady.

RASOR *Bon.*   85

MADAMOISELLE I'll tell dee no more.

RASOR Nay, prithee, my swan.

MADAMOISELLE (*clapping her hands behind her, as he had done before*) Come, kiss me den.

RASOR I won't kiss you, not I.

MADAMOISELLE Adieu.   90

RASOR Hold—(*gives her a hearty kiss*) Now proceed.

MADAMOISELLE *A ça*°—I hide my self in one cunning place, where I hear all, and see all. First dy drunken master come *mal à propos*;° but de sot no know his own dear wife, so he leave her to her sport—den de game begin.   95

    As she speaks, Rasor still acts the man and she the woman

De lover say soft ting. De lady look upon de ground. He take her by de hand. She turn her head one oder way. Den he squeeze very hard. Den she pull—very softly. Den he take her in his arm. Den she give him leetel pat. Den he kiss her *tétons.*° Den she say 'Pish, nay fie.' Den he tremble, den she—sigh. Den he pull her into de 100 arbour, den she pinch him.

RASOR Ay, but not so hard, you baggage you.

MADAMOISELLE Den he grow bold. She grow weak. He tro her down. *Il tombe dessus, le diable assiste, il emporte tout.*°

    Rasor struggles with her, as if he would throw her down

Stand off, sirrah.   105

RASOR You have set me afire, you jade you.

MADAMOISELLE Den go to de river and quench dyself.

RASOR What an unnatural harlot 'tis.

MADAMOISELLE (*looking languishingly on him*) Rasor.

RASOR Madamoiselle.   110

MADAMOISELLE Dou no love me.

RASOR Not love thee! More than a Frenchman does soup.

MADAMOISELLE Den dou will refuse noting dat I bid dee?

RASOR Don't bid me be damned then.

MADAMOISELLE No, only tell dy master all I have tell dee of dy laty. 115

RASOR Why you little malicious strumpet, you! Should you like to be served so?

MADAMOISELLE Dou dispute den? Adieu.

RASOR Hold! But why wilt thou make me be such a rogue, my dear?

MADAMOISELLE *Voilà un vrai Anglais! Il est amoureux, et cependant il* 120 *veut raisonner. Va t'en au diable!*°

RASOR Hold once more. In hopes thou'lt give me up thy body, I resign thee up my soul.

MADAMOISELLE *Bon. Écoute donc*: if dou fail me, I never see dee more—if dou obey me—*je m'abandonne à toi.*° 125
She takes him about the neck and gives him a smacking kiss
Exit Madamoiselle

RASOR (*licking his lips*) Not be a rogue? *Amor vincit omnia.*°
Exit Rasor
Enter Lady Fancyfull and Madamoiselle

LADY FANCYFULL Marry, say ye? Will the two things marry?

MADAMOISELLE *On le va faire,*° matam.

LADY FANCYFULL Look you, Madamoiselle: in short, I can't bear it—no, I find I can't. If once I see 'em abed together, I shall have ten 130 thousand thoughts in my head will make me run distracted. Therefore run and call Rasor back immediately, for something must be done to stop this impertinent wedding. If I can but defer it four and twenty hours, I'll make such work about town with that little pert slut's reputation, he shall as soon marry a witch. 135

MADAMOISELLE (*aside*) *La voilà bien intentionnée.*°
Exeunt

5.4

Constant's lodgings

Enter Constant and Heartfree

CONSTANT But what dost think will come of this business?

HEARTFREE 'Tis easier to think what will not come on't.

CONSTANT What's that?

HEARTFREE A challenge. I know the knight too well for that. His dear body will always prevail upon his noble soul to be quiet. 5

CONSTANT But though he dare not challenge me, perhaps he may venture to challenge his wife.

HEARTFREE Not if you whisper him in the ear you won't have him do't, and there's no other way left that I see. For as drunk as he was, he'll remember you and I were where we should not be; and I don't 10 think him quite blockhead enough yet to be persuaded we were got into his wife's closet only to peep in her prayer-book.
Enter Servant with a letter

SERVANT Sir, here's a letter; a porter brought it.
        [*Exit Servant*]
CONSTANT O ho, here's instructions for us. (*Reads*) 'The accident
    that has happened has touched our invention to the quick. We   15
    would fain come off without your help; but find that's impossible.
    In a word, the whole business must be thrown upon a matrimonial
    intrigue between your friend and mine. But if the parties are not
    fond enough to go quite through with the matter, 'tis sufficient for
    our turn they own the design. We'll find pretences enough to break   20
    the match. Adieu.' Well, woman for invention. How long would my
    blockhead have been a-producing this. Hey, Heartfree! What, mus-
    ing, man? Prithee be cheerful. What say'st thou, friend, to this
    matrimonial remedy?
HEARTFREE Why, I say it's worse than the disease.   25
CONSTANT Here's a fellow for you! There's beauty and money on her
    side, and love up to the ears on his; and yet—
HEARTFREE And yet, I think I may reasonably be allowed to boggle at
    marrying the niece in the very moment that you are a-debauching
    the aunt.   30
CONSTANT Why truly, there may be something in that. But have not
    you a good opinion enough of your own parts to believe you could
    keep a wife to yourself?
HEARTFREE I should have, if I had a good opinion enough of hers, to
    believe she could do as much by me. For to do 'em right after all,   35
    the wife seldom rambles till the husband shows her the way.
CONSTANT 'Tis true; a man of real worth scarce ever is a cuckold but
    by his own fault. Women are not naturally lewd; there must be
    something to urge 'em to it. They'll cuckold a churl out of revenge;
    a fool, because they despise him; a beast because they loath him.   40
    But when they make bold with a man they once had a well-
    grounded value for, 'tis because they first see themselves neglected
    by him.
HEARTFREE Nay, were I well assured that I should never grow Sir
    John, I ne'er should fear Bellinda'd play my lady. But our weakness, 45
    thou know'st, my friend, consists in that very change we so impu-
    dently throw upon (indeed) a steadier and more generous sex.
CONSTANT Why faith, we are a little impudent in that matter, that's
    the truth on't. But this is wonderful: to see you grown so warm an
    advocate for those, but t'other day, you took so much pains to abuse. 50
HEARTFREE All revolutions run into extremes; the bigot makes the
    boldest atheist, and the coyest saint the most extravagant strumpet.

But prithee advise me in this good and evil, this life and death, this
blessing and cursing, that is set before me. Shall I marry—or die a
maid? 55

CONSTANT Why faith, Heartfree, matrimony is like an army going to
engage. Love's the forlorn hope, which is soon cut off; the mar-
riage-knot is the main body,° which may stand buff° a long long
time; and repentance is the rear-guard, which rarely gives ground
as long as the main battle has a being. 60

HEARTFREE Conclusion then: you advise me to whore on, as you do.

CONSTANT That's not concluded yet. For though marriage be a lot-
tery in which there are a wondrous many blanks, yet there is one
inestimable lot in which the only heaven on earth is written. Would
your kind fate but guide your hand to that, though I were wrapped 65
in all that luxury itself could clothe me with, I still should envy you.

HEARTFREE And justly too: for to be capable of loving one doubtless
is better than to possess a thousand. But how far that capacity's in
me, alas I know not.

CONSTANT But you would know? 70

HEARTFREE I would so.

CONSTANT Matrimony will inform you. Come, one flight of resolution carries you to the land of experience; where, in a very moderate time, you'll know the capacity of your soul, and your body
both, or I'm mistaken. 75

Exeunt

5.5

Sir John Brute's house

Enter Lady Brute and Bellinda

BELLINDA Well, madam, what answer have you from 'em?

LADY BRUTE That they'll be here this moment. I fancy 'twill end in a
wedding. I'm sure he's a fool if it don't. Ten thousand pound, and
such a lass as you are, is no contemptible offer to a younger brother.
But are not you under strange agitations? Prithee how does your 5
pulse beat?

BELLINDA High and low; I have much ado to be valiant. Sure, it must
feel very strange to go to bed to a man?°

LADY BRUTE Um—it does feel a little odd at first, but it will soon
grow easy to you. 10

Enter Constant and Heartfree

LADY BRUTE Good morrow, gentlemen; how have you slept after your adventure?

HEARTFREE Some careful thoughts, ladies, on your accounts have kept us waking.

BELLINDA And some careful thoughts on your own, I believe, have   15
hindered you from sleeping. Pray how does this matrimonial
project relish with you?

HEARTFREE Why faith, e'en as storming towns does with soldiers,
where the hopes of delicious plunder banishes the fear of being
knocked on the head.   20

BELLINDA Is it then possible after all, that you dare think of downright lawful wedlock?

HEARTFREE Madam, you have made me so foolhardy I dare do
anything.

BELLINDA Then sir, I challenge you; and matrimony's the spot where   25
I expect you.

HEARTFREE 'Tis enough; I'll not fail. (*Aside*) So, now I am in for
Hobbes's voyage; a great leap in the dark.°

LADY BRUTE Well gentlemen, this matter being concluded then, have
you got your lessons ready? For Sir John is grown such an atheist of   30
late, he'll believe nothing upon easy terms.

CONSTANT We'll find ways to extend his faith, madam. But pray how
do you find him this morning?

LADY BRUTE Most lamentably morose, chewing the cud after last
night's discovery; of which however he had but a confused notion   35
e'en now. But I'm afraid his *valet de chambre* has told him all, for
they are very busy together at this moment. When I told him of
Bellinda's marriage, I had no other answer but a grunt; from which
you may draw what conclusions you think fit. But to your notes,°
gentlemen; he's here.   40

Enter Sir John and Rasor°

CONSTANT Good morrow, sir.

HEARTFREE Good morrow, Sir John. I'm very sorry my indiscretion
should cause so much disorder in your family.

SIR JOHN Disorders generally come from indiscretions, sir; 'tis no
strange thing at all.   45

LADY BRUTE I hope, my dear, you are satisfied there was no wrong
intended you.

SIR JOHN None, my dove.

BELLINDA If not, I hope my consent to marry Mr Heartfree will

convince you. For as little as I know of amours, sir, I can assure you,   50
one intrigue is enough to bring four people together, without
further mischief.

SIR JOHN And I know too, that intrigues tend to procreation of more
kinds than one. One intrigue will beget another as soon as beget a
son or a daughter.   55

CONSTANT I am very sorry, sir, to see you still seem unsatisfied with a
lady whose more than common virtue, I am sure, were she my wife,
should meet a better usage.

SIR JOHN Sir, if her conduct has put a trick upon her virtue, her
virtue's the bubble, but her husband's the loser.   60

CONSTANT Sir, you have received a sufficient answer already to justify
both her conduct and mine. You'll pardon me for meddling in your
family affairs; but I perceive I am the man you are jealous of, and
therefore it concerns me.

SIR JOHN Would it did not concern me, and then I should not care   65
who it concerned.

CONSTANT Well, sir, if truth and reason won't content you, I know
but one way more,° which, if you think fit, you may take.

SIR JOHN Lord, sir, you are very hasty. If I had been found at prayers
in your wife's closet, I should have allowed you twice as much time   70
to come to yourself in.

CONSTANT Nay, sir, if time be all you want, we have no quarrel.

HEARTFREE [*to Constant, aside*] I told you how the sword would work
upon him.

    Sir John muses

CONSTANT Let him muse; however, I'll lay fifty pound our foreman   75
brings us in not guilty.

SIR JOHN (*aside*) 'Tis well—'tis very well—in spite of that young
jade's matrimonial intrigue, I am a downright stinking cuckold—
here they are—boo—

    Putting his hand to his forehead

Methinks I could butt with a bull. What the plague did I marry   80
her for? I knew she did not like me; if she had, she would have
lain with me; for I would have done so because I liked her. But
that's past, and I have her. And now, what shall I do with her? If I
put my horns in my pocket, she'll grow insolent. If I don't, that
goat there, that stallion, is ready to whip me through the guts.   85
The debate then is reduced to this; shall I die a hero, or live a
rascal? Why, wiser men than I have long since concluded that a
living dog is better than a dead lion.° (*To Constant and Heartfree*)

Gentlemen, now my wine and my passion are governable, I must
own I have never observed anything in my wife's course of life to   90
back me in my jealousy of her: but jealousy's a mark of love; so
she need not trouble her head about it, as long as I make no more
words on't.

Lady Fancyfull enters disguised, and addresses Bellinda apart

CONSTANT I am glad to see your reason rule at last. Give me your
hand; I hope you'll look upon me as you are wont.   95

SIR JOHN Your humble servant. (*Aside*) A wheedling son of a whore.

HEARTFREE And that I may be sure you are friends with me too, pray
give me your consent to wed your niece.

SIR JOHN Sir, you have it with all my heart: damn me if you han't.
(*Aside*) 'Tis time to get rid of her: a young pert pimp; she'll make an   100
incomparable bawd in a little time.

Enter a Servant, who gives Heartfree a letter
[*Exit Servant*]

BELLINDA Heartfree your husband, say you? 'Tis impossible.

LADY FANCYFULL Would to kind heaven it were: but 'tis too true;
and in the world there lives not such a wretch. I'm young; and
either I have been flattered by my friends as well as glass, or nature   105
has been kind and generous to me. I had a fortune too, was greater
far than he could ever hope for. But with my heart, I am robbed of
all the rest. I'm slighted and I'm beggared both at once. I have
scarce a bare subsistence from the villain, yet dare complain to
none; for he has sworn, if e'er 'tis known I am his wife, he'll murder   110
me. (*Weeping*)

BELLINDA The traitor!

LADY FANCYFULL I accidentally was told he courted you. Charity
soon prevailed upon me to prevent your misery; and as you see, I'm
still so generous, even to him, as not to suffer he should do a thing   115
for which the law might take away his life.°

(*Weeping*)

BELLINDA [*aside*] Poor creature; how I pity her!

[*Bellinda and Lady Fancyfull*] *continue talking aside*

HEARTFREE (*aside*) Death and damnation! Let me read it again.
(*Reads*) 'Though I have a particular reason not to let you know who
I am till I see you, yet you'll easily believe 'tis a faithful friend that 120
gives you this advice. I have lain with Bellinda.' Good. 'I have a
child by her,'—better and better—'which is now at nurse'—heaven
be praised—'and I think the foundation laid for another.'—Ha! Old
truepenny! 'No rack could have tortured this story from me; but

friendship has done it. I heard of your design to marry her, and 125
could not see you abused. Make use of my advice, but keep my
secret till I ask you for't again. Adieu.'

Exit Lady Fancyfull

CONSTANT (*to Bellinda*) Come, madam; shall we send for the parson?
I doubt here's no business for the lawyer. Younger brothers have
nothing to settle but their hearts, and that I believe my friend here 130
has already done, very faithfully.

BELLINDA (*scornfully*) Are you sure, sir, there are no old mortgages
upon it?

HEARTFREE (*coldly*) If you think there are, madam, it mayn't be amiss
to defer the marriage till you are sure they are paid off. 135

BELLINDA (*aside*) How the galled horse kicks! (*To Heartfree*) We'll
defer it as long as you please, sir.

HEARTFREE The more time we take to consider on't, madam, the less
apt we shall be to commit oversights; therefore, if you please, we'll
put it off for just nine months. 140

BELLINDA Guilty consciences make men cowards: I don't wonder
you want time to resolve.

HEARTFREE And they make women desperate: I don't wonder you
were so quickly determined.

BELLINDA What does the fellow mean? 145

HEARTFREE What does the lady mean?

SIR JOHN Zoons, what do you both mean?

Heartfree and Bellinda walk chafing about

RASOR (*aside*) Here is so much sport going to be spoiled, it makes me
ready to weep again. A pox o' this impertinent Lady Fancyfull, and
her plots, and her Frenchwoman too. She's a whimsical, ill-natured 150
bitch, and when I have got my bones broke in her service, 'tis ten to
one but my recompense is a clap; I hear 'em tittering without still.
I'cod I'll e'en go lug 'em both in by the ears, and discover the plot,
to secure my pardon.

Exit Rasor

CONSTANT Prithee explain, Heartfree. 155

HEARTFREE A fair deliverance; thank my stars and my friend.

BELLINDA 'Tis well it went no farther. A base fellow.

LADY BRUTE What can be the meaning of all this?

BELLINDA What's his meaning, I don't know. But mine is, that if I
had married him—I had had no husband. 160

HEARTFREE And what's her meaning, I don't know. But mine is, that
if I had married her—I had had wife enough.

SIR JOHN Your people of wit have got such cramp ways of expressing
themselves, they seldom comprehend one another. Pox take you
both, will you speak that you may be understood?   165

>   *Enter Rasor in sackcloth,° pulling in Lady Fancyfull and*
>   *Madamoiselle*

RASOR If they won't, here comes an interpreter.

LADY BRUTE Heavens, what have we here?

RASOR A villain, but a repenting villain—stuff which saints in all ages
have been made of.

ALL Rasor!   170

LADY BRUTE What means this sudden metamorphose?

RASOR Nothing, without my pardon.

LADY BRUTE What pardon do you want?

RASOR *Imprimis*, your ladyship's, for a damnable lie made upon your
spotless virtue, and set to the tune of Spring Garden. (*To Sir John*)   175
Next, at my generous master's feet I bend, for interrupting his
more noble thoughts with phantoms of disgraceful cuckoldom. (*To
Constant*) Thirdly, I to this gentleman apply, for making him the
hero of my romance. (*To Heartfree*) Fourthly, your pardon, noble
sir, I ask, for clandestinely marrying you without either bidding of   180
banns, bishop's license, friends' consent—or your own knowledge.
(*To Bellinda*) And lastly, to my good young lady's clemency I come,
for pretending the corn was sowed in the ground before ever the
plough had been in the field.

SIR JOHN (*aside*) So that after all, 'tis a moot point whether I am a   185
cuckold or not.

BELLINDA Well sir, upon condition you confess all, I'll pardon you
myself, and try to obtain as much from the rest of the company. But
I must know then who 'tis has put you upon all this mischief?

RASOR Satan, and his equipage. Woman tempted me, lust weakened   190
me—and so the devil overcame me. As fell Adam, so fell I.

BELLINDA Then pray, Mr Adam, will you make us acquainted with
your Eve.

RASOR (*to Madamoiselle*) Unmask, for the honour of France.

ALL Madamoiselle?   195

MADAMOISELLE Me ask ten tousand pardon of all de good company.

SIR JOHN Why, this mystery thickens instead of clearing up. (*To
Rasor*) You son of a whore you, put us out of our pain.

RASOR One moment brings sunshine. (*Showing Madamoiselle*) 'Tis
true; this is the woman that tempted me. But this is the serpent that   200
tempted the woman; and if my prayers might be heard, her pun-

ishment for so doing should be like the serpent's of old. (*Pulls off Lady Fancyfull's mask*) She should lie upon her face all the days of her life.°

ALL Lady Fancyfull.

BELLINDA Impertinent. 205

LADY BRUTE Ridiculous.

ALL Ha, ha, ha, ha, ha.

BELLINDA I hope your ladyship will give me leave to wish you joy, since you have owned your marriage yourself. Mr Heartfree, I vow 'twas strangely wicked in you to think of another wife when you 210 had one already so charming as her ladyship.

ALL Ha, ha, ha, ha, ha.

LADY FANCYFULL (*aside*) Confusion seize 'em as it seizes me.

MADAMOISELLE *Que le diable étouffe ce maraut de Rasor.°*

BELLINDA Your ladyship seems disordered; a breeding qualm, per- 215 haps. Mr Heartfree, your bottle of Hungary water° to your lady. Why madam, he stands as unconcerned as if he were your husband in earnest.

LADY FANCYFULL Your mirth's as nauseous as yourself, Bellinda. You think you triumph o'er a rival now. *Hélas ma pauvre fille.°* 220 Where'er I'm rival, there's no cause for mirth. No, my poor wretch, 'tis from another principle I have acted. I knew that thing there would make so perverse a husband, and you so impertinent a wife, that lest your mutual plagues should make you both run mad, I charitably would have broke the match. He, 225 he, he, he, he.

> *Exit* [*Lady Fancyfull*] *laughing affectedly, Madamoiselle following her*

MADAMOISELLE He, he, he, he, he.

ALL Ha, ha, ha, ha, ha.

SIR JOHN (*aside*) Why now this woman will be married to somebody too. 230

BELLINDA Poor creature, what a passion she's in; but I forgive her.

HEARTFREE Since you have so much goodness for her, I hope you'll pardon my offence too, madam.

BELLINDA There will be no great difficulty in that, since I am guilty of an equal fault. 235

HEARTFREE Then pardons being passed on all sides, pray let's to church to conclude the day's work.

CONSTANT But before you go, let me treat you, pray, with a song a new-married lady made within this week; it may be of use to you both. 240

SONG°

1

When yielding first to Damon's flame
I sunk into his arms,
He swore he'd ever be the same,
Then rifled all my charms.
But fond of what h'ad long desired,   245
Too greedy of his prey,
My shepherd's flame, alas, expired
Before the verge of day.

2

My innocence in lovers' wars,
Reproached his quick defeat;   250
Confused, ashamed, and bathed in tears,
I mourned his cold retreat.
At length, 'Ah shepherdess,' cried he,
'Would you my fire renew,
Alas you must retreat like me,   255
I'm lost if you pursue.'

HEARTFREE So madam; now had the parson but done his business—
BELLINDA You'd be half weary of your bargain.
HEARTFREE No, sure, I might dispense with° one night's lodging.
BELLINDA I'm ready to try, sir.   260
HEARTFREE   Then let's to church. And if it be our chance,
                to disagree—
BELLINDA   Take heed—the surly husband's fate you see.

Epilogue

By another hand
Spoken by Lady Brute and Bellinda

LADY BRUTE	No epilogue?
BELLINDA	I swear I know of none.
LADY BRUTE	Lord! How shall we excuse it to the town?
BELLINDA	Why, we must e'en say something of our own.
LADY BRUTE	Our own! Ay, that must needs be precious stuff.
BELLINDA	I'll lay my life they'll like it well enough. Come faith, begin—
LADY BRUTE	Excuse me, after you.
BELLINDA	Nay, pardon me for that, I know my cue.
LADY BRUTE	O for the world, I would not have precedence.
BELLINDA	O Lord!
LADY BRUTE	I swear—
BELLINDA	O fie!
LADY BRUTE	I'm all obedience. First then, know all, before our doom is fixed, The third day is for us°—
BELLINDA	Nay, and the sixth.
LADY BRUTE	We speak not from the poet now, nor is it His cause—I want a rhyme—
BELLINDA	That we solicit.
LADY BRUTE	Then sure you cannot have the hearts to be severe And damn us—
BELLINDA	Damn us! Let 'em if they dare.
LADY BRUTE	Why, if they should, what punishment remains?
BELLINDA	Eternal exile from behind our scenes.°
LADY BRUTE	But if they're kind, that sentence we'll recall. We can be grateful—
BELLINDA	And have wherewithal.
LADY BRUTE	But at grand treaties hope not to be trusted, Before preliminaries are adjusted.°
BELLINDA	You know the time, and we appoint the place, Where, if you please, we'll meet and sign the peace.

5

10

15

20

25

30

REVISED SCENES°

4.1

Covent Garden

Enter Lord Rake, Sir John [and Colonel Bully] with swords drawn

LORD RAKE Is the dog dead?

COLONEL BULLY No, damn him, I heard him wheeze.

LORD RAKE How the witch his wife howled!

COLONEL BULLY Ay, she'll alarm the watch presently.

LORD RAKE Appear, knight, then; come, you have a good cause to   5
fight for—there's a man murdered.

SIR JOHN Is there? Then let his ghost be satisfied; for I'll sacrifice a
constable to it presently; and burn his body upon his wooden chair.

Enter a Tailor, with a bundle under his arm

COLONEL BULLY How now? What have we got here? A thief?

TAILOR No, an't please you; I'm no thief.   10

LORD RAKE That we'll see presently; here, let the general examine
him.

SIR JOHN Ay, ay, let me examine him; and I'll lay a hundred pound I
find him guilty, in spite of his teeth—for he looks—like a—
sneaking rascal. Come sirrah, without equivocation or mental res-   15
ervation, tell me of what opinion you are and what calling; for by
them—I shall guess at your morals.

TAILOR An't please you, I'm a dissenting journeyman tailor.

SIR JOHN Then sirrah, you love lying by your religion, and theft by
your trade. And so, that your punishment may be suitable to your   20
crimes—I'll have you first gagged—and then hanged.

TAILOR Pray good worthy gentlemen, don't abuse me; indeed I'm an
honest man, and a good workman, though I say it that should not
say it.

SIR JOHN No words, sirrah, but attend your fate.   25

LORD RAKE Let me see what's in that bundle.

TAILOR An't please you, it is my lady's short cloak and wrapping-
gown.

SIR JOHN What lady, you reptile you?

TAILOR My Lady Brute, your honour.   30

SIR JOHN My Lady Brute! My wife! The robe of my wife—with
reverence let me approach it! The dear angel is always taking care
of me in danger, and has sent me this suit of armour to protect me
in this day of battle. On they go.

OMNES O brave knight!   35

LORD RAKE Live Don Quixote the second.

SIR JOHN Sancho,° my squire, help me on with my armour.

TAILOR O dear gentlemen, I shall be quite undone if you take the
gown.

SIR JOHN Retire, sirrah; and since you carry off your skin, go home   40
and be happy.

TAILOR I think I'd e'en as good follow the gentleman's advice, for if I
dispute any longer, who knows but the whim may take 'em to case
me? These courtiers are fuller of tricks than they are of money;
they'll sooner break a man's bones than pay his bill.   45
        Exit Tailor

SIR JOHN So, how do you like my shapes now?

LORD RAKE To a miracle! He looks like a Queen of the Amazons.°
But to your arms, gentlemen. The enemy's upon their march;
here's the watch.

SIR JOHN Oons, if it were Alexander the Great at the head of his   50
army, I would drive him into a horse-pond.

OMNES Huzza! O brave knight!
        Enter Watch

SIR JOHN See, here he comes with all his Greeks about him. Follow
me, boys!

FIRST WATCH Hey-day! Who have we got here? Stand.   55

SIR JOHN Mayhap not!

FIRST WATCH What are you all doing here in the street at this time of
night? And who are you, madam, that seem to be at the head of this
noble crew?

SIR JOHN Sirrah, I am Bonduca, Queen of the Welshmen,° and with a   60
leek as long as my pedigree° I will destroy your Roman legion in an
instant. Britons, strike home.
        *Fights. [The Watch disarm Sir John. Lord Rake and Colonel
        Bully run away]*

FIRST WATCH So! We have got the queen,° however! We'll make her
pay well for her ransom. Come, madam, will your majesty please to
walk before the constable?   65

SIR JOHN The constable's a rascal, and you are a son of a whore!

FIRST WATCH A most princely reply, truly! If this be her royal style,

I'll warrant her maids of honour prattle prettily; but we'll teach you
a little of our court dialect before we part with you, princess. Away
with her to the round-house.   70

SIR JOHN Hands off, you ruffians! My honour's dearer to me than my
life. I hope you won't be uncivil.

FIRST WATCH Away with her.

SIR JOHN O! My honour, my honour!

    Exeunt

4.3

    [*In the street*]

    Enter Constable and Watch with Sir John

CONSTABLE Come, forsooth, come along if you please! I once in
compassion thought to have seen you safe home this morning; but
you have been so rampant and abusive all night, I shall see what the
justice of peace will say to you.

SIR JOHN And you shall see what I'll say to the justice of peace.   5

    [*First*] *Watch knocks*

    A Servant enters

CONSTABLE Is Mr Justice at home?

SERVANT Yes.

CONSTABLE Pray acquaint his worship we have got an unruly woman
here, and desire to know what he'll please to have done with her.

SERVANT I'll acquaint my master.   10

    Exit [*Servant*]

SIR JOHN Hark you, constable, what cuckoldy justice is that?

CONSTABLE One that will know how to deal with such romps as you
are, I'll warrant you.

    Enter Justice

JUSTICE Well, Mr Constable, what's the matter here?

CONSTABLE An't please your worship, this here comical sort of a   15
gentlewoman has committed great outrages tonight. She has been
frolicking with my Lord Rake and his gang; they attacked the
watch, and I hear there has been a gentleman killed. I believe 'tis
they have done it.

SIR JOHN There may have been murder for aught I know, and 'tis a   20
great mercy there has not been a rape too; for this fellow would
have ravished me.

FIRST WATCH Ravish! I ravish! O Lud! O Lud! O Lud! I ravish her!
Why, please your honour, I heard Mr Constable say he believed she
was little better than a mophrodite.°   25
JUSTICE Why truly, she does seem to be a little masculine about the
mouth.
FIRST WATCH Yes, and about the hands too, an't please your worship.
I did but offer in mere civility to help her up the steps into our
apartment; and with her gripen° fist—(*Sir John knocks him down*)—
ay, just so, sir.   30
SIR JOHN I felled him to the ground like an ox.
JUSTICE Out upon this boisterous woman! Out upon her!
SIR JOHN Mr Justice, he would have been uncivil! It was in defence of
my honour, and I demand satisfaction.   35
FIRST WATCH I hope your worship will satisfy her honour in
Bridewell;° that fist of hers will make an admirable hemp-
beater.
SIR JOHN Sir, I hope you will protect me against that libidinous ras-
cal. I am a woman of quality, and virtue too, for all I am in a sort of   40
an undress this morning.
JUSTICE Why, she really has the air of a sort of a woman a little
somethingish out of the common. Madam, if you expect I should
be favourable to you, I desire I may know who you are.
SIR JOHN Sir, I am anybody, at your service.   45
JUSTICE Lady, I desire to know your name.
SIR JOHN Sir, my name's Mary.
JUSTICE Ay, but your surname, madam?
SIR JOHN Sir, my surname's the very same with my husband's.
JUSTICE A strange woman this! Who is your husband, pray?   50
SIR JOHN Why, Sir John.
JUSTICE Sir John who?
SIR JOHN Why, Sir John Brute.
JUSTICE Is it possible, madam, you can be my Lady Brute?
SIR JOHN That happy woman, sir, am I! Only a little in my merriment   55
tonight.
JUSTICE I'm concerned for Sir John.
SIR JOHN Truly, so am I.
JUSTICE I've heard he's an honest gentleman.
SIR JOHN As ever drank.   60
JUSTICE Good lack! Indeed, lady, I am sorry he should have such a
wife.
SIR JOHN Sir, I am sorry he has any wife at all.

JUSTICE And so perhaps may he. I doubt you have not given him a
very good taste of matrimony.   65

SIR JOHN Taste, sir! I have scorned to stint him to a taste. I have given
him a full meal of it.

JUSTICE Indeed, I believe so! But pray, fair lady, may he have given
you any occasion for this extraordinary conduct? Does he not use
you well?   70

SIR JOHN A little upon the rough, sometimes.

JUSTICE Ay, any man may be out of humour now and then.

SIR JOHN Sir, I love peace and quiet, and when a woman don't find
that at home, she's apt sometimes to comfort herself with a few
innocent diversions abroad.   75

JUSTICE I doubt he uses you but too well. Pray, how does he as to
that weighty thing, money? Does he allow you what's proper of
that?

SIR JOHN Sir, I have generally enough to pay the reckoning, if this
son of a whore the drawer would bring his bill.   80

JUSTICE A strange woman this. Does he spend a reasonable portion of
his time at home, to the comfort of his wife and children?

SIR JOHN Never gave his wife cause to repine at his being abroad in
his life.

JUSTICE Pray, madam, how may he be in the grand matrimonial   85
point: is he true to your bed?

SIR JOHN Chaste! Oons, this fellow asks so many impertinent questions, egad, I believe it is the justice's wife in the justice's clothes.

JUSTICE 'Tis a great pity he should have been thus disposed of.
Pray, madam, and then I have done, what may be your ladyship's   90
common method of life, if I may presume so far?

SIR JOHN Why, sir, much like that of a woman of quality.

JUSTICE Pray how may you generally pass your time, madam? Your
morning, for example?

SIR JOHN Sir, like a woman of quality. I wake about two a' clock in the 95
afternoon. I stretch, and then—make a sign for my chocolate.
When I have drank three cups, I slide down again upon my back,
with my arms over my head, while two maids put on my stockings.
Then, hanging upon their shoulders, I am trailed to my great chair,
where I sit, and yawn for my breakfast. If it don't come presently, I 100
lie down upon my couch, to say my prayers, while my maid reads
me the playbills.

JUSTICE Very well, madam.

SIR JOHN When the tea is brought in, I drink twelve regular dishes,

with eight slices of bread and butter; and half an hour after, I send   105
to the cook to know if the dinner is almost ready.

JUSTICE So, madam.

SIR JOHN By that time my head's half-dressed,° I hear my
husband swearing himself into a state of perdition that the meat's
all cold upon the table; to mend which, I come down in an hour   110
more, and have it sent back to the kitchen to be all dressed over
again.

JUSTICE Poor man!

SIR JOHN When I have dined, and my idle servants are presumptu-
ously set down at their ease to do so too, I call for my coach, go to   115
visit fifty dear friends, of whom, I hope, I never shall find one at
home while I shall live.

JUSTICE So; there's the morning and the afternoon pretty well disposed of. Pray, madam, how do you pass your evenings?

SIR JOHN Like a woman of spirit, sir, a great spirit; give me a box and   120
dice. Seven's the main,° oons, sir, I set you a hundred pounds! Why,
do you think women are married nowadays to sit at home and mend
napkins? Sir, we have nobler ways of passing time.

JUSTICE Mercy upon us, Mr Constable, what will this age come
to!   125

CONSTABLE What will it come to indeed, if such women as these are
not set in the stocks?

SIR JOHN I have a little urgent business calls upon me; and therefore I
desire the favour of you to bring matters to a conclusion.

JUSTICE Madam, if I were sure that business were not to commit   130
more disorders, I would release you.

SIR JOHN None—by my virtue.

JUSTICE Then, Mr Constable, you may discharge her.

SIR JOHN Sir, your very humble servant. If you please to accept of a
bottle—   135

JUSTICE I thank you kindly, madam; but I never drink in a morning.
Goodbye, madam, goodbye to ye.

SIR JOHN Goodbye t'ye, good sir.
          Exit Justice
So. Now, Mr Constable, shall you and I go pick up a whore together?

CONSTABLE No, thank you, madam, my wife's enough to satisfy any   140
reasonable man.

SIR JOHN (*aside*) He, he, he, he, he, the fool is married then. [*Aloud*]
Well, you won't go?

CONSTABLE Not I, truly.

SIR JOHN Then I'll go by myself; and you and your wife may be   145
damned.
    Exit Sir John
CONSTABLE (*gazing after him*) Why, God-a-mercy, my lady.
    Exeunt

THE CONFEDERACY

A Comedy

THE CHARACTERS OF THE PLAY

Gripe, a rich money scrivener°   *Mr Leigh*
Moneytrap, a rich money scrivener   *Mr Dogget*
Dick, a gamester, son to Mrs Amlet   *Mr Booth*
Brass,° his companion, passes for his valet   *Mr Pack*
   de chambre
Clip,° a goldsmith   *Mr Mimes*
Jessamin, footboy to Clarissa
[Constable]

Clarissa, wife to Gripe, an expensive luxurious°
   woman, a great admirer of quality   *Mrs Barry*
Araminta, wife to Moneytrap, very intimate with
   Clarissa, of the same humour   *Mrs Porter*
Corinna, daughter to Gripe by a former wife, a good
   fortune, young, and kept very close by her father   *Mrs Bradshaw*
Flippanta,° Clarissa's maid   *Mrs Bracegirdle*
Mrs Amlet, a seller of all sorts of private affairs to the
   ladies   *Mrs Willis*
Mrs Cloggit, her neighbour   *Mrs Baker*

SCENE: IN LONDON

Prologue

Spoken by a shabby poet°

Ye gods! What crime had my poor father done,
That you should make a poet of his son?
Or is't for some great services of his,
Y'are pleased to compliment his boy—with this?
    Showing his crown of laurel°
The honour, I must needs confess, is great,   5
If, with his crown, you'd tell him where to eat.
'Tis well—but I have more complaints—look here!
    Showing his ragged coat
Hark ye! D'ye think this suit good winter wear?
In a cold morning; whu! At a lord's gate,
How you have let the porter let me wait!   10
You'll say, perhaps, you knew I'd get no harm,
You'd given me fire enough to keep me warm.
Ah—
A world of blessings to that fire we owe;
Without it I'd ne'er made this princely show.   15
I have a brother too, now in my sight,°
    Looking behind the scenes
A busy man amongst us here tonight.
Your fire has made him play a thousand pranks,
For which, no doubt, you've had his daily thanks.
He's thanked you first for all his decent plays,   20
Where he so nicked it, when he writ for praise.°
Next, for his meddling with some folks in black,°
And bringing—souse—a priest upon his back;°
For building houses here t'oblige the peers,°
And fetching all their House about his ears;   25
For a new play, he's now thought fit to write,
To soothe the town—which they—will damn tonight.
These benefits are such, no man can doubt
But he'll go on, and set your fancy out,°
Till, for reward of all his noble deeds,   30

At last like other sprightly folks he speeds:
Has this great recompense fixed on his brow°
At fam'd Parnassus; has your leave to bow,
And walk about the streets—equipped—as I am now.°

1.1

Covent Garden

Enter Mrs Amlet and Mrs Cloggit, meeting

MRS AMLET Good morrow, neighbour, good morrow, neighbour Cloggit; how does all at your house this morning?

MRS CLOGGIT Thank you kindly, Mrs Amlet, thank you kindly; how do you do, I pray?

MRS AMLET At the old rate, neighbour, poor and honest; these are 5
hard times, good lack.

MRS CLOGGIT If they are hard with you, what are they with us? You have a good trade going. All the great folks in town help you off with your merchandise.

MRS AMLET Yes, they do help us off with 'em indeed; they buy all. 10

MRS CLOGGIT And pay?

MRS AMLET For some.

MRS CLOGGIT Well, 'tis a thousand pities, Mrs Amlet, they are not as ready at one, as they are at t'other; for, not to wrong 'em, they give very good rates. 15

MRS AMLET O for that, let us do 'em justice, neighbour. They never make two words upon the price; all they haggle about is the day of payment.

MRS CLOGGIT There's all the dispute, as you say.

MRS AMLET But that's a wicked one. For my part, neighbour, I'm just 20
tired off my legs with trotting after 'em; besides, it eats out all our profit. Would you believe it, Mrs Cloggit, I have worn out four pair of pattens° with following my old lady Youthful for one set of false teeth and but three pots of paint.

MRS CLOGGIT Look you there now. 25

MRS AMLET If they would but once let me get enough by 'em, to keep a coach to carry me a-dunning° after 'em, there would be some conscience in it.

MRS CLOGGIT Ay, that were something. But now you talk of con-science, Mrs Amlet, how do you speed amongst your city 30
customers?

MRS AMLET My city customers? Now by my truth, neighbour, between the city and the court (with reverence be it spoken) there's not a—

[*She makes a gesture with her fingers*]

to choose; my ladies in the city, in times past, were as full of gold as   35
they were of religion, and as punctual in their payments as they
were in their prayers; but since they have set their minds upon
quality, adieu one, adieu t'other—their money and their consciences are gone, heaven knows where. There is not a goldsmith's
wife to be found in town, but's as hard-hearted as an ancient judge,   40
and as poor as a towering duchess.

MRS CLOGGIT But what the murrain have they to do with quality!
Why don't their husbands make 'em mind their shops?

MRS AMLET Their husbands! Their husbands, sayst thou, woman?
Alack, alack, they mind their husbands, neighbour, no more than   45
they do a sermon.

MRS CLOGGIT Good lack-a-day, that women born of sober parents
should be prone to follow ill examples. But now we talk of quality,
when did you hear of your son Richard, Mrs Amlet? My daughter
Flipp says she met him t'other day in a laced coat, with three fine   50
ladies, his footman at his heels, and as gay as a bridegroom.

MRS AMLET Is it possible? Ah the rogue! Well neighbour, all's well
that ends well; but Dick will be hanged.

MRS CLOGGIT That were pity.

MRS AMLET Pity indeed; for he's a hopeful young man to look on; but   55
he leads a life—well—where he has it heaven knows; but they say,
he pays his club° with the best of 'em. I have seen him but once
these three months, neighbour, and then the varlet wanted money.
But I bid him march, and march he did to some purpose; for in less
than an hour back comes my gentleman into the house, walks to and   60
fro in the room, with his wig over his shoulder, his hat on one side,
whistling a minuet, and tossing a purse of gold from one hand to
t'other, with no more respect (heaven bless us!) than if it had been
an orange. 'Sirrah', says I, 'where have you got that?' He answers
me never a word, but sets his arms akimbo, cocks his saucy hat in   65
my face, turns about upon his ungracious heel, as much as to say
kiss—and I've never set eye on him since.

MRS CLOGGIT Look you there now; to see what the youth of this age
are come to!

MRS AMLET See what they will come to, neighbour. Heaven shield, I   70
say; but Dick's upon the gallop. Well, I must bid you good morrow;
I'm going where I doubt I shall meet but a sorry welcome.

MRS CLOGGIT To get in some old debt, I'll warrant you?

MRS AMLET Neither better nor worse.

MRS CLOGGIT From a lady of quality?   75

MRS AMLET No, she's but a scrivener's wife; but she lives as well, and
pays as ill, as the stateliest countess of 'em all.
    Exeunt several ways

1.2

[*The street outside Gripe's house*]
    Enter Brass, alone

BRASS Well, surely through the world's wide extent there never
appeared so impudent a fellow as my schoolfellow Dick; pass himself upon the town for a gentleman, drop into all the best company
with an easy air, as if his natural element were in the sphere of
quality; when the rogue had a kettle-drum° to his father, who was   5
hanged for robbing a church, and has a pedlar to his mother, who
carries her shop under her arm. But here he comes.
    Enter Dick

DICK Well, Brass, what news? Hast thou given my letter to Flippanta?
BRASS I'm but just come; I han't knocked at the door yet. But I have a
damned piece of news for you.   10
DICK As how?
BRASS We must quit this country.
DICK We'll be hanged first.
BRASS So you will if you stay.
DICK Why, what's the matter?   15
BRASS There's a storm a-coming.
DICK From whence?
BRASS From the worst point in the compass; the law.
DICK The law! Why, what have I to do with the law?
BRASS Nothing; and therefore it has something to do with you.   20
DICK Explain.
BRASS You know you cheated a young fellow at piquet t'other day, of
the money he had to raise his company.°
DICK Well, what then?
BRASS Why, he's sorry he lost it.   25
DICK Who doubts that?
BRASS Ay, but that is not all. He's such a fool to think of complaining
on't.
DICK Then I must be so wise to stop his mouth.
BRASS How?   30

DICK Give him a little back; if that won't do, strangle him.

BRASS You are very quick in your methods.

DICK Men must be so that will dispatch business.

BRASS Hark you, Colonel, your father died in's bed?

DICK He might have done, if he had not been a fool.   35

BRASS Why, he robbed a church.

DICK Ay, but he forgot to make sure of the sexton.

BRASS Are not you a great rogue?

DICK Or I should wear worse clothes.

BRASS Hark you, I would advise you to change your life.   40

DICK And turn ballad-singer.°

BRASS Not so neither.

DICK What then?

BRASS Why, if you can get this young wench, reform and live honest.

DICK That's the way to be starved.   45

BRASS No, she has money enough to buy you a good place,° and pay
me into the bargain for helping her to so good a match. You have
but this throw left to save you, for you are not ignorant, youngster,
that your morals begin to be pretty well known about town. Have a
care your noble birth and your honourable relations are not dis-   50
covered too; there needs but that to have you tossed in a blanket, for
the entertainment of the first company of ladies you intrude into;
and then, like a dutiful son, you may daggle about with your
mother, and sell paint. She's old and weak, and wants somebody to
carry her goods after her. How like a dog will you look, with a pair   55
of plod shoes, your hair cropped up to your ears, and a band-box
under your arm?

DICK Why faith, Brass, I think thou art in the right on't; I must fix my
affairs quickly, or madam Fortune will be playing some of her bitch
tricks with me. Therefore I'll tell thee what we'll do. We'll pursue   60
this old rogue's daughter heartily; we'll cheat his family to purpose,
and they shall atone for the rest of mankind.

BRASS Have at her then; I'll about your business presently.

DICK One kiss—and success attend thee.

        Exit Dick

BRASS A great rogue. Well, I say nothing. But when I have got the   65
thing into a good posture, he shall sign and seal, or I'll have him
tumbled out of the house like a cheese. Now for Flippanta. (*[Brass]
knocks*)

        Enter Flippanta

FLIPPANTA Who's that, Brass?

BRASS Flippanta!

FLIPPANTA What want you, rogue's face?   70

BRASS Is your mistress dressed?

FLIPPANTA What, already? Is the fellow drunk?

BRASS Why, with respect to her looking-glass, it's almost two.

FLIPPANTA What then, fool?

BRASS Why then it's time for the mistress of the house to come down   75
and look after her family.

FLIPPANTA Prithee don't be an owl. Those that go to bed at night
may rise in the morning; we that go to bed in the morning rise in
the afternoon.

BRASS When does she make her visits then?   80

FLIPPANTA By candle-light; it helps off a muddy complexion. We
women hate inquisitive sunshine. But do you know that my lady is
going to turn good housewife?

BRASS What, is she going to die?

FLIPPANTA Die?   85

BRASS Why, that's the only way to save money for her family.

FLIPPANTA No; but she has thought of a project to save chair-hire.

BRASS As how?

FLIPPANTA Why all the company she used to keep abroad, she now
intends shall meet at her own house. Your master has advised her to   90
set up a basset-table.°

BRASS Nay, if he advised her to't, it's right; but has she acquainted her
husband with it yet?

FLIPPANTA What to do? When the company meet he'll see 'em.

BRASS Nay, that's true, as you say; he'll know it soon enough.   95

FLIPPANTA Well, I must be gone. Have you any business with my
lady?

BRASS Yes, as ambassador from Araminta. I have a letter for her.

FLIPPANTA Give it me.

BRASS Hold! And as first minister of state to the Colonel, I have an   100
affair to communicate to thee.

FLIPPANTA What is't? Quick.

BRASS Why—he's in love.

FLIPPANTA With what?

BRASS A woman—and her money together.   105

FLIPPANTA Who is she?

BRASS Corinna.

FLIPPANTA What would he be at?

BRASS At her—if she's at leisure.

FLIPPANTA Which way?   110

BRASS Honourably. He has ordered me to demand her of thee in
marriage.

FLIPPANTA Of me?

BRASS Why, when a man of quality has a mind to a city fortune,
wouldst have him apply to her father and mother?   115

FLIPPANTA No.

BRASS No, so I think. Men of our end of the town are better bred than
to use ceremony. With a long periwig we strike the lady, with a you-
know-what we soften the maid, and when the parson has done his
job, we open the affair to the family. Will you slip this letter into her   120
prayer-book, my little queen? It's a very passionate one. It's sealed
with a heart and a dagger; you may see by that what he intends to
do with himself.

FLIPPANTA Are there any verses in it? If not, I won't touch it.

BRASS Not one word in prose—it's dated in rhyme.   125

[*Flippanta*] *takes it*

FLIPPANTA Well, but—have you brought nothing else?

BRASS Gad forgive me, I'm the forgetfullest dog—I have a letter for
you too. Here: 'tis in a purse. [*Offers a purse*] But it's in prose; you
won't touch it. [*Withdrawing purse*]

FLIPPANTA Yes, hang it, it is not good to be too dainty.   130

BRASS How useful a virtue is humility! Well, child, we shall have an
answer tomorrow, shan't we?

FLIPPANTA I can't promise you that. For our young gentlewoman is
not so often in my way as she would be. Her father (who is a citizen
from the foot to the forehead of him) lets her seldom converse with   135
her mother-in-law° and me, for fear she should learn the airs of a
woman of quality. But I'll take the first occasion: see there's my
lady—go in and deliver your letter to her.

Exeunt

1.3

A parlour [*in Gripe's house*]

Enter Clarissa, followed by Flippanta and Brass

CLARISSA No messages this morning from anybody, Flippanta? Lard,
how dull that is! O, there's Brass; I did not see thee, Brass. What
news dost thou bring?

BRASS Only a letter from Araminta, madam.

CLARISSA Give it me—open it for me, Flippanta, I am so lazy today.   5
    Sitting down
    [*Flippanta opens the letter and gives it to Clarissa, who reads it*]

BRASS (*to Flippanta*) Be sure now you deliver my master's as carefully as I do this.

FLIPPANTA Don't trouble thyself, I'm no novice.

CLARISSA (*to Brass*) 'Tis well; there needs no answer, since she'll be here so soon.   10

BRASS Your ladyship has no farther commands then?

CLARISSA Not at this time, honest Brass.
    Exit Brass
  Flippanta!

FLIPPANTA Madam.

CLARISSA My husband's in love.   15

FLIPPANTA In love?

CLARISSA With Araminta.

FLIPPANTA Impossible.

CLARISSA This letter from her is to give me an account of it.

FLIPPANTA Methinks you are not very much alarmed.   20

CLARISSA No; thou know'st I'm not much tortured with jealousy.

FLIPPANTA Nay, you are much in the right on't, madam, for jealousy's a city passion; 'tis a thing unknown amongst people of quality.

CLARISSA Fey.° A woman must indeed be of a mechanic mould,° who   25
is either troubled or pleased with anything her husband can do to her. Prithee mention him no more; 'tis the dullest theme.

FLIPPANTA 'Tis splenetic° indeed. But when once you open your basset-table, I hope that will put him out of your head.

CLARISSA Alas, Flippanta, I begin to grow weary even of the thoughts   30
of that too.

FLIPPANTA How so?

CLARISSA Why I have thought on't a day and a night already, and four and twenty hours, thou know'st, is enough to make one weary of anything.   35

FLIPPANTA Now by my conscience, you have more woman in you than all your sex together. You never know what you would have.

CLARISSA Thou mistak'st the thing quite. I always know what I lack, but I am never pleased with what I have. The want of a thing is   40
perplexing enough, but the possession of it is intolerable.

FLIPPANTA Well, I don't know what you are made of, but other
women would think themselves blessed in your case; handsome,
witty, loved by everybody, and of so happy a composure to care a fig
for nobody. You have no one passion, but that of your pleasures;   45
and you have in me a servant devoted to all your desires, let 'em be
as extravagant as they will. Yet all this is nothing; you can still be
out of humour.

CLARISSA Alas, I have but too much cause.

FLIPPANTA Why, what have you to complain of?   50

CLARISSA Alas, I have more subjects for spleen than one. Is it not a
most horrible thing that I should be but a scrivener's wife? Come,
don't flatter me, don't you think nature designed me for something
plus elevée.°

FLIPPANTA Nay, that's certain; but on t'other side, methinks you   55
ought to be in some measure content, since you live like a woman of
quality, though you are none.

CLARISSA O fey; the very quintessence° of it is wanting.

FLIPPANTA What's that?

CLARISSA Why, I dare abuse nobody. I'm afraid to affront people,   60
though I don't like their faces; or to ruin their reputations, though
they pique me to it, by taking ever so much pains to preserve 'em. I
dare not raise a lie of a man, though he neglects to love me; nor
report a woman to be a fool, though she's handsomer than I am. In
short, I dare not so much as bid my footman kick the people° out of   65
doors, though they come to ask me for what I owe 'em.

FLIPPANTA All this is very hard indeed.

CLARISSA Ah, Flippanta, the perquisites of quality are of an unspeakable value.

FLIPPANTA They are of some use, I must confess; but we must not   70
expect to have everything. You have wit and beauty, and a fool to
your husband; come, come madam, that's a good portion for one.

CLARISSA Alas, what signifies beauty and wit, when one dares neither
jilt the men, nor abuse the women? 'Tis a sad thing, Flippanta,
when wit's confined; 'tis worse than the rising of the lights.° I have   75
been sometimes almost choked with scandal, and durst not cough it
up, for want of being a countess.

FLIPPANTA Poor lady!

CLARISSA O! Liberty is a fine thing, Flippanta; it's a great help in
conversation to have leave to say what one will. I have seen a woman   80
of quality, who has not had one grain of wit, entertain a whole
company the most agreeably in the world, only with her malice. But

'tis in vain to repine. I can't mend my condition till my husband dies; so I'll say no more on't, but think of making the most of the state I am in.

85

FLIPPANTA That's your best way, madam; and in order to it, pray consider how you'll get some ready money to set your basset-table a-going, for that's necessary.

CLARISSA Thou say'st true; but what trick I shall play my husband to get some, I don't know. For my pretence of losing my diamond necklace has put the man into such a passion, I'm afraid he won't hear reason.

90

FLIPPANTA No matter. He begins to think 'tis lost in earnest, so I fancy you may venture to sell it, and raise money that way.

95

CLARISSA That can't be, for he has left odious notes with all the goldsmiths in town.

FLIPPANTA Well, we must pawn it then.

CLARISSA I'm quite tired with dealing with those pawnbrokers.

FLIPPANTA (aside) I'm afraid you'll continue the trade a great while, for all that.

100

Enter Jessamin

JESSAMIN Madam, there's the woman below that sells paint and patches,° iron-bodice,° false teeth, and all sorts of things to the ladies; I can't think of her name.

[Exit Jessamin]

FLIPPANTA 'Tis Mrs Amlet; she wants money.

105

CLARISSA Well, I han't enough for myself; it's an unreasonable thing she should think I have any for her.

FLIPPANTA She's a troublesome jade.

CLARISSA So are all people that come a-dunning.

FLIPPANTA What will you do with her?

110

CLARISSA I have just now thought on't. She's very rich, the woman is, Flippanta. I'll borrow some money of her.

FLIPPANTA Borrow? Sure you jest, madam.

CLARISSA No, I'm in earnest; I give thee commission to do it for me.

FLIPPANTA Me?

115

CLARISSA Why dost thou stare, and look so ungainly? Don't I speak to be understood?

FLIPPANTA Yes, I understand you well enough; but Mrs Amlet—

CLARISSA But Mrs Amlet must lend me some money. Where shall I have any to pay her else?

120

FLIPPANTA That's true; I never thought of that truly. But here she is.

Enter Mrs Amlet

CLARISSA How d'you do? How d'you do, Mrs Amlet? I han't seen you
these thousand years, and yet I believe I'm down in your books.

MRS AMLET O madam, I don't come for that, alack.

FLIPPANTA Good morrow, Mrs Amlet.   125

MRS AMLET Good morrow, Mrs Flippanta.

CLARISSA How much am I indebted to you, Mrs Amlet?

MRS AMLET Nay, if your ladyship desires to see your bill, I believe I
may have it about me—there madam, if it ben't too much fatigue to
you to look it over.   130

CLARISSA Let me see it, for I hate to be in debt, (aside) where I am
obliged to pay. (Reads) 'Imprimis, for bolstering out the Countess of
Crump's left hip.' O fie, this does not belong to me.

MRS AMLET I beg your ladyship's pardon; I mistook indeed. 'Tis a
countess's bill I have writ out to little purpose. I furnished her two 135
years ago with three pair of hips, and am not paid for 'em yet. But
some are better customers than some. There's your ladyship's bill,
madam.

CLARISSA 'For the idea of a new invented commode'°—ay, this may
be mine, but 'tis of a preposterous length. Do you think I can   140
waste time to read every article, Mrs Amlet? I'd as lief read a
sermon.

MRS AMLET Alack-a-day, there's no need of fatiguing yourself at that
rate; cast an eye only, if your honour pleases, upon the sum total.

CLARISSA Total: fifty six pound—and odd things.   145

FLIPPANTA But six and fifty pound?

MRS AMLET Nay, another body would have made it twice as much,
but there's a blessing goes along with a moderate profit.

CLARISSA Flippanta, go to my cashier; let him give you six and fifty
pound. Make haste; don't you hear me? Six and fifty pound. Is it so 150
difficult to be comprehended?

FLIPPANTA No, madam, I—I comprehend six and fifty pound, but—

CLARISSA But go and fetch it then.

FLIPPANTA (aside) What she means I don't know, but I shall, I
suppose, before I bring her the money.   155

    Exit Flippanta

CLARISSA (setting her hair in a pocket-glass) The trade you follow gives
you a great deal of trouble, Mrs Amlet.

MRS AMLET Alack-a-day, a world of pain, madam, and yet there's
small profit, as your honour sees by your bill.

CLARISSA Poor woman! Sometimes you make great losses, Mrs   160
Amlet?

MRS AMLET I have two thousand pounds owing me, of which I shall never get ten shillings.

CLARISSA Poor woman! You have a great charge of children, Mrs Amlet? 165

MRS AMLET Only one wicked rogue, madam, who I think will break my heart.

CLARISSA Poor woman!

MRS AMLET He'll be hanged, madam—that will be the end of him. Where he gets it heaven knows, but he's always shaking his heels 170 with the ladies, and his elbows with the lords. He's as fine as a prince, and as gim as the best of 'em; but the ungracious rogue tells all he comes near that his mother is dead, and I am but his nurse.

CLARISSA Poor woman!

MRS AMLET Alas, madam, he's like the rest of the world; everybody's 175 for appearing to be more than they are, and that ruins all.

CLARISSA Well, Mrs Amlet, you'll excuse me; I have a little business. Flippanta will bring you your money presently. Adieu, Mrs Amlet.
        Exit Clarissa

MRS AMLET I return your honour many thanks. (*Alone*) Ah, there's my good lady, not so much as read her bill; if the rest were like her, I 180 should soon have money enough to go as fine as Dick himself.
        Enter Dick

DICK (*aside*) Sure Flippanta must have given my letter by this time; I long to know how it has been received.

MRS AMLET Misericord! What do I see?

DICK Fiends and hags—the witch my mother! 185

MRS AMLET Nay, 'tis he; ay my poor Dick, what art thou doing here?

DICK (*aside*) What a misfortune!

MRS AMLET Good Lard! how thou art bravely° decked. But it's all one, I am thy mother still; and though thou art a wicked child, nature will speak. I love thee still; ah Dick, my poor Dick. 190 (*Embracing him*)

DICK Blood and thunder! Will you ruin me? (*Breaking from her*)

MRS AMLET Ah, the blasphemous rogue, how he swears!

DICK You destroy all my hopes.

MRS AMLET Will your mother's kiss destroy you, varlet? Thou art an ungracious bird; kneel down, and ask me blessing, sirrah. 195

DICK Death and furies!

MRS AMLET Ah, he's a proper young man, see what a shape he has; ah poor child!
        Running to embrace him, he still avoiding her

DICK Oons, keep off, the woman's mad. If anybody comes, my fortune's lost.   200

MRS AMLET What fortune? Ha? Speak, graceless. Ah Dick, thou'lt be
hanged, Dick.

DICK Good dear mother now, don't call me Dick here.

MRS AMLET Not call thee Dick! Is it not thy name? What shall I call
thee? Mr Amlet? Ha! Art not thou a presumptuous rascal? Hark   205
you, sirrah, I hear of your tricks; you disown me for your mother,
and say I am but your nurse. Is not this true?

DICK No, I love you; I respect you. (*Taking her hand*) I am all duty.
But if you discover me here, you ruin the fairest prospect that man
ever had.   210

MRS AMLET What prospect? Ha! Come, this is a lie now.

DICK No, my honoured parent, what I say is true, I'm about a great
fortune. I'll bring you home a daughter-in-law, in a coach and six
horses, if you'll but be quiet. I can't tell you more now.

MRS AMLET Is it possible?   215

DICK 'Tis true, by Jupiter.

MRS AMLET My dear lad—

DICK For heaven's sake—

MRS AMLET But tell me, Dick—

DICK I'll follow you home in a moment, and tell you all.   220

MRS AMLET What a shape is there—

DICK Pray mother, go.

MRS AMLET I must receive some money here first, which shall go for
thy wedding dinner.

DICK Here's somebody coming; 'sdeath, she'll betray me.   225
     Enter Flippanta
     He makes signs to his mother

DICK Good morrow, dear Flippanta; how do all the ladies within?

FLIPPANTA At your service, Colonel; as far at least as my interest
goes.

MRS AMLET (*aside*) Colonel? Law you now, how Dick's respected.

DICK Waiting for thee, Flippanta, I was making acquaintance with   230
this old gentlewoman here.

MRS AMLET (*aside*) The pretty lad; he's as impudent as a page.

DICK Who is this good woman, Flippanta?

FLIPPANTA A gin of all trades,° an old daggling cheat, that hobbles
about from house to house to bubble the ladies of their money. I   235
have a small business of yours in my pocket, Colonel.

DICK An answer to my letter?

FLIPPANTA So quick indeed? No, it's your letter itself.

DICK Hast thou not given it then yet?

FLIPPANTA I han't had an opportunity; but 't won't be long first.   240
Won't you go in and see my lady?

DICK Yes, I'll go make her a short visit. But, dear Flippanta, don't
forget—my life and fortune are in your hands.

FLIPPANTA Ne'er fear, I'll take care of 'em.

MRS AMLET (*aside*) How he traps 'em; let Dick alone.°   245

DICK (*to his mother*) Your servant, good madam.

   Exit Dick

MRS AMLET Your honour's most devoted—a pretty, civil, well-bred
gentleman this, Mrs Flippanta. Pray who may he be?

FLIPPANTA A man of great note; Colonel Shapely.

MRS AMLET Is it possible? I have heard much of him indeed, but   250
never saw him before. One may see quality in every limb of him;
he's a fine man truly.

FLIPPANTA I think you are in love with him, Mrs Amlet.

MRS AMLET Alas, those days are done with me; but if I were as fair as
I was once, and had as much money as some folks, Colonel Shapely   255
should not catch cold for want of a bedfellow. I love your men of
rank; they have something in their air does so distinguish 'em from
the rascality.

FLIPPANTA People of quality are fine things indeed, Mrs Amlet, if
they had but a little more money; but for want of that, they are   260
forced to do things their great souls are ashamed of. For example—
here's my lady—she owes you but six and fifty pounds—

MRS AMLET Well?

FLIPPANTA Well, and she has it not by her to pay you.

MRS AMLET How can that be?   265

FLIPPANTA I don't know. Her cashkeeper's out of humour; he says he
has no money.

MRS AMLET What a presumptuous piece of vermin is a cashkeeper?
Tell his lady he has no money? Now, Mrs Flippanta, you may see
his bags are full by his being so saucy.   270

FLIPPANTA If they are, there's no help for't. He'll do what he pleases,
till he comes to make up his yearly accounts.

MRS AMLET But madam plays sometimes, so when she has good
fortune, she may pay me out of her winnings.

FLIPPANTA O ne'er think of that, Mrs Amlet; if she had won a thou-   275
sand pounds, she'd rather die in a jail than pay off a farthing with
it. Play-money, Mrs Amlet, amongst people of quality, is a sacred

thing, and not to be profaned. The deuce!° 'Tis consecrated to their pleasures; 'twould be sacrilege to pay their debts with it.

MRS AMLET Why what shall we do then? For I han't one penny to buy   280
bread.

FLIPPANTA I'll tell you—it just now comes in my head. I know my lady has a little occasion for money at this time; so—if you'll lend her—a hundred pound—do you see—then she may pay you your six and fifty out of it.   285

MRS AMLET Sure, Mrs Flippanta, you think to make a fool of me.

FLIPPANTA No, the devil fetch me if I do. You shall have a diamond necklace in pawn.

MRS AMLET Oho, a pawn! That's another case. And when must she have this money?   290

FLIPPANTA In a quarter of an hour.

MRS AMLET Say no more. Bring the necklace to my house; it shall be ready for you.

FLIPPANTA I'll be with you in a moment.

MRS AMLET Adieu, Mrs Flippanta.   295

FLIPPANTA Adieu, Mrs Amlet.

Exit Mrs Amlet

FLIPPANTA (*alone*) So—this ready money will make us all happy. This spring will set our basset going, and that's a wheel will turn twenty others. My lady's young and handsome; she'll have a dozen intrigues upon her hands before she has been twice at her prayers.   300
So much the better; the more the grist, the richer the miller. Sure never wench got into so hopeful a place; here's a fortune to be sold, a mistress to be debauched, and a master to be ruined. If I don't feather my nest, and get a good husband, I deserve to die both a maid and a beggar.   305

[*Exit Flippanta*]

2.1

Mr Gripe's house

Enter Clarissa and Dick

CLARISSA What in the name of dulness is the matter with you, Colonel? You are as studious as a cracked chemist.°

DICK My head, madam, is full of your husband.

CLARISSA The worst furniture for a head in the universe.

DICK I am thinking of his passion for your friend Araminta.   5

CLARISSA Passion! Dear Colonel, give it a less violent name.

Enter Brass

DICK Well, sir, what want you?

BRASS The affair I told you of goes ill. (*To Dick aside*) There's an action out.

DICK The devil there is.   10

CLARISSA What news brings Brass?

DICK Before Gad I can't tell, madam; the dog will never speak out. My Lord What-d'ye-call-him waits for me at my lodging; is not that it?

BRASS Yes sir.   15

DICK Madam, I ask your pardon.

CLARISSA Your servant, sir.

Exeunt Dick and Brass

Jessamin!

She sits down

Enter Jessamin

JESSAMIN Madam.

CLARISSA Where's Corinna? Call her to me, if her father han't locked   20
her up; I want her company.

JESSAMIN Madam, her guitar master° is with her.

[*Exit Jessamin*]

CLARISSA Psha, she's taken up with her impertinent guitar man. Flippanta stays an age with that old fool, Mrs Amlet. And Araminta, before she can come abroad, is so long a-placing her   25
coquette-patch,° that I must be a year without company. How insupportable is a moment's uneasiness to a woman of spirit and pleasure.

Enter Flippanta

O, art thou come at last? Prithee, Flippanta, learn to move a little quicker; thou know'st how impatient I am.   30

FLIPPANTA Yes, when you expect money: if you had sent me to buy a
prayer-book, you'd have thought I had flown.

CLARISSA Well, hast thou brought me any, after all?

FLIPPANTA Yes, I have brought some. There (*giving her a purse*), the
old hag has struck off her bill; the rest is in that purse.   35

CLARISSA 'Tis well; but take care, Flippanta, my husband don't suspect anything of this. 'Twould vex him, and I don't love to make
him uneasy; so I would spare him these little sort of troubles, by
keeping 'em from his knowledge.

FLIPPANTA See the tenderness she has for him, and yet he's always   40
complaining of you.

CLARISSA 'Tis the nature of 'em, Flippanta. A husband is a growling
animal.

FLIPPANTA How exactly you define 'em!

CLARISSA O! I know 'em, Flippanta; though I confess my poor wretch   45
diverts me sometimes with his ill humours. I wish he would quarrel
with me today a little, to pass away the time, for I find myself in a
violent spleen.

FLIPPANTA Why, if you please to drop yourself in his way, six to four
but he scolds one rubbers° with you.   50

CLARISSA Ay, but thou know'st he's as uncertain as the wind, and if
instead of quarrelling with me, he should chance to be fond, he'd
make me as sick as a dog.

FLIPPANTA If he's kind, you must provoke him; if he kisses you, spit
in's face.   55

CLARISSA Alas! when men are in the kissing fit, like lap-dogs they
take that for a favour.

FLIPPANTA Nay, then I don't know what you'll do with him.

CLARISSA (*yawning*) I'll e'en do nothing at all with him. Flippanta!

FLIPPANTA Madam.   60

CLARISSA My hoods and scarf, and a coach to the door.

FLIPPANTA Why, whither are you going?

CLARISSA I can't tell yet, but I would go spend some money since I
have it.

FLIPPANTA Why, you want nothing that I know of.   65

CLARISSA How awkward an objection now is that, as if a woman of
education bought things because she wanted 'em. Quality always
distinguishes itself; and therefore, as the mechanic people buy
things because they have occasion for 'em, you see women of rank
always buy things because they have not occasion for 'em. Now   70
there, Flippanta, you see the difference between a woman that has

breeding, and one that has none. O ho, here's Araminta come at
last.
    Enter Araminta
Lard, what a tedious while you have let me expect you. I was afraid
you were not well; how d'ye do today?   75

ARAMINTA As well as a woman can do, that has not slept all
night.

FLIPPANTA Methinks, madam, you are pretty well awake however.

ARAMINTA O, 'tis not a little thing will make a woman of my vigour
look drowsy.   80

CLARISSA But prithee what was't disturbed you?

ARAMINTA Not your husband, don't trouble yourself; at least, I am
not in love with him yet.

CLARISSA Well remembered, I had quite forgot that matter. I wish
you much joy; you have made a noble conquest indeed.   85

ARAMINTA But now I have subdued the country, pray is it worth my
keeping? You know the ground; you have tried it.

CLARISSA A barren soil, heaven can tell.

ARAMINTA Yet if it were well cultivated, it would produce something,
to my knowledge. Do you know 'tis in my power to ruin this   90
poor thing of yours? His whole estate is at my service.

FLIPPANTA Cods-fish, strike him, madam, and let my lady go your
halves. There's no sin in plundering a husband, so his wife has
share of the booty.

ARAMINTA Whenever she gives me her orders, I shall be very ready to   95
obey 'em.

CLARISSA Why, as odd a thing as such a project may seem, Araminta,
I believe I shall have a little serious discourse with you about it. But
prithee tell me how you have passed the night? For I am sure your
mind has been roving upon some pretty thing or other.   100

ARAMINTA Why, I have been studying all the ways my brain could
produce to plague my husband.

CLARISSA No wonder indeed you look so fresh this morning, after the
satisfaction of such pleasing ideas all night.

ARAMINTA Why, can a woman do less than study mischief, when she   105
has tumbled and tossed herself into a burning fever for want of
sleep, and sees a fellow lie snoring by her, stock-still, in a fine
breathing sweat?

CLARISSA Now see the difference of women's tempers. If my dear
would make but one nap of his whole life, and only waken to make   110
his will, I should be the happiest wife in the universe. But we'll

discourse more of these matters as we go, for I must make a tour among the shops.

ARAMINTA I have a coach waits at the door; we'll talk of 'em as we rattle along.   115

CLARISSA The best place in nature, for you know a hackney-coach is a natural enemy to a husband.

    Exeunt Clarissa and Araminta
    Flippanta alone

FLIPPANTA What a pretty little pair of amiable persons are there gone to hold a council of war together! Poor birds! What would they do with their time, if the plaguing their husbands did not help 'em to   120
employment? Well, if idleness be the root of all evil, then matrimony's good for something, for it sets many a poor woman to work. But here comes miss. I hope I shall help her into the holy state too ere long. And when she's once there, if she don't play her part as well as the best of 'em, I'm mistaken. Han't I lost the letter I'm to   125
give her? No, here 'tis; so, now we shall see how pure nature will work with her, for art she knows none yet.

    Enter Corinna

CORINNA What does my mother-in-law want with me, Flippanta? They tell me she was asking for me.

FLIPPANTA She's just gone out, so I suppose 'twas no great business.   130

CORINNA Then I'll go into my chamber again.

FLIPPANTA Nay, hold a little if you please. I have some business with you myself, of more concern than what she had to say to you.

CORINNA Make haste then, for you know my father won't let me keep you company. He says you'll spoil me.   135

FLIPPANTA I spoil you? He's an unworthy man to give you such ill impressions of a woman of my honour.

CORINNA Nay, never take it to heart, Flippanta, for I don't believe a word he says. But he does so plague me with his continual scolding, I'm almost weary of my life.   140

FLIPPANTA Why, what is't he finds fault with?

CORINNA Nay, I don't know, for I never mind him; when he has babbled for two hours together, methinks I have heard a mill going, that's all. It does not at all change my opinion, Flippanta. It only makes my head ache.   145

FLIPPANTA Nay, if you can bear it so, you are not to be pitied so much as I thought.

CORINNA Not pitied? Why, is it not a miserable thing such a young creature as I am should be kept in perpetual solitude, with no other

company but a parcel of old fumbling masters, to teach me geog- 150
raphy, arithmetic, philosophy, and a thousand useless things. Fine
entertainment, indeed, for a young maid at sixteen; methinks one's
time might be better employed.

FLIPPANTA Those things will improve your wit.

CORINNA Fiddle faddle; han't I wit enough already? My mother-in- 155
law has learned none of this trumpery, and is not she as happy as
the day's long?

FLIPPANTA Then you envy her, I find?

CORINNA And well I may. Does she not do what she has a mind to, in
spite of her husband's teeth? 160

FLIPPANTA (*aside*) Look you there now if she has not already conceived that as the supreme blessing of life.

CORINNA I'll tell you what, Flippanta, if my mother-in-law would but
stand by me a little, and encourage me, and let me keep her company, I'd rebel against my father tomorrow, and throw all my books 165
in the fire. Why, he can't touch a groat of my portion, do you know
that Flippanta?

FLIPPANTA (*aside*) So—I shall spoil her? Pray heaven the girl don't
debauch me!

CORINNA Look you: in short, he may think what he pleases; he may 170
think himself wise, but thoughts are free, and I may think in my
turn. I'm but a girl, 'tis true, and a fool too, if you'll believe him;
but let him know, a foolish girl may make a wise man's heart ache;
so he had as good be quiet. Now it's out—

FLIPPANTA Very well. I love to see a young woman have spirit. It's a 175
sign she'll come to something.

CORINNA Ah, Flippanta, if you would but encourage me, you'd find
me quite another thing. I'm a devilish girl in the bottom; I wish
you'd but let me make one amongst you.

FLIPPANTA That never can be, till you are married. Come, examine 180
your strength a little. Do you think you durst venture upon a
husband?

CORINNA A husband! Why, a—if you would but encourage me.
Come, Flippanta, be a true friend now. I'll give you advice, when I
have got a little more experience. Do you in your very conscience 185
and soul, think I am old enough to be married?

FLIPPANTA Old enough! Why, you are sixteen, are you not?

CORINNA Sixteen! I am sixteen, two months, and odd days, woman. I
keep an exact account.

FLIPPANTA The deuce you are! 190

CORINNA Why, do you then truly and sincerely think I am old
enough?

FLIPPANTA I do upon my faith, child.

CORINNA Why then to deal as fairly with you, Flippanta, as you do
with me, I have thought so any time these three years.°   195

FLIPPANTA Now I find you have more wit than ever I thought you
had, and to show you what an opinion I have of your discretion, I'll
show you a thing I thought to have thrown in the fire.

CORINNA What is it for Jupiter's sake?

FLIPPANTA Something will make your heart chuck within you.   200

CORINNA My dear Flippanta.

FLIPPANTA What do you think it is?

CORINNA I don't know, nor I don't care, but I'm mad to have it.

FLIPPANTA It's a four-cornered thing.

CORINNA What, like a cardinal's cap?   205

FLIPPANTA No, 'tis worth a whole conclave° of 'em. How do you like
it? (*Showing the letter*)

CORINNA O Lard, a letter! Is there ever a token in it?

FLIPPANTA Yes, and a precious one too. There's a handsome young
gentleman's heart.   210

CORINNA A handsome young gentleman's heart! (*Aside*) Nay then it's
time to look grave.

FLIPPANTA There.

CORINNA I shan't touch it.

FLIPPANTA What's the matter now?   215

CORINNA I shan't receive it.

FLIPPANTA Sure you jest.

CORINNA You'll find I don't. I understand myself better than to take
letters when I don't know who they are from.

FLIPPANTA I'm afraid I commended your wit too soon.   220

CORINNA 'Tis all one; I shan't touch it, unless I know who it comes
from.

FLIPPANTA Hey day! Open it and you'll see.

CORINNA Indeed I shall not.

FLIPPANTA Well—then I must return it where I had it.   225

CORINNA That won't serve your turn, madam. My father must have
an account of this.

FLIPPANTA Sure you are not in earnest?

CORINNA You'll find I am.

FLIPPANTA So, here's fine work. This 'tis to deal with girls before   230
they come to know the distinction of sexes.

CORINNA Confess who you had it from, and perhaps, for this once, I mayn't tell my father.

FLIPPANTA Why then since it must out, 'twas the Colonel. But why are you so scrupulous, madam?   235

CORINNA Because if it had come from anybody else, I would not have given a farthing for it.

     Twitching it eagerly out of her hand

FLIPPANTA Ah, my dear little rogue! (*Kissing her*) You frightened me out of my wits.

CORINNA Let me read it, let me read it, let me read it, let me read it, I   240
say. Um, um, um, 'cupid's', um, um, um, 'darts', um, um, um,
'beauty', um 'charms', um, um, um, 'angel', um 'goddess', um—
(*kissing the letter*) um, um, um, 'truest lover', hum, um, 'eternal
constancy', um, um, um, 'cruel', um, um, um, 'racks', um, um,
'tortures', um, um, 'fifty daggers', um, um, 'bleeding heart', um,   245
um, 'dead man'. Very well, a mighty civil letter I promise you; not
one smutty word in it: I'll go lock it up in my comb-box.

FLIPPANTA Well—but what does he say to you?

CORINNA Not a word of news, Flippanta; 'tis all about business.

FLIPPANTA Does he not tell you he's in love with you?   250

CORINNA Ay, but he told me that before.

FLIPPANTA How so? He never spoke to you.

CORINNA He sent me word by his eyes.

FLIPPANTA Did he so? Mighty well. I thought you had been to learn
that language.   255

CORINNA O, but you thought wrong, Flippanta. What, because I
don't go a-visiting, and see the world, you think I know nothing.
But you should consider, Flippanta, that the more one's alone, the
more one thinks; and 'tis thinking that improves a girl. I'll have you
to know, when I was younger than I am now by more than I'll boast   260
of, I thought of things would have made you stare again.

FLIPPANTA Well, since you are so well-versed in your business, I
suppose I need not inform you that if you don't write your gallant
an answer—he'll die.

CORINNA Nay, now, Flippanta, I confess you tell me something I did   265
not know before. Do you speak in serious sadness? Are men given
to die if their mistresses are sour to 'em?

FLIPPANTA Um—I can't say they all die—no, I can't say they all do,
but truly, I believe it would go very hard with the Colonel.

CORINNA Lard, I would not have my hands in blood for thousands;   270
and therefore Flippanta—if you'll encourage me—

FLIPPANTA O, by all means an answer.

CORINNA Well, since you say it then, I'll e'en in and do it, though I
protest to you (lest you should think me too forward now) he's the
only man that wears a beard, I'd ink my fingers for. (*Aside*) Maybe   275
if I marry him, in a year or two's time I mayn't be so nice.

> *Exit Corinna*

FLIPPANTA (*alone*) Now heaven give him joy; he's like to have a rare
wife o' thee. But where there's money, a man has a plaster to his
sore. They have a blessed time on't, who marry for love. See! Here
comes an example—Araminta's dread lord.   280

> *Enter Moneytrap*

MONEYTRAP Ah, Flippanta! How do you do, good Flippanta? How
do you do?

FLIPPANTA Thank you, sir, well—at your service.

MONEYTRAP And how does the good family, your master and your
fair mistress? Are they at home?   285

FLIPPANTA Neither of 'em. My master has been gone out these two
hours, and my lady is just gone with your wife.

MONEYTRAP Well, I won't say I have lost my labour, however, as long
as I have met with you, Flippanta. For I have wished a great while
for an opportunity to talk with you a little. You won't take it amiss if   290
I should ask you a few questions?

FLIPPANTA Provided you leave me to my liberty in my answers.
(*Aside*) What's this cotquean going to pry into now?

MONEYTRAP Prithee, good Flippanta, how do your master and mistress live together?   295

FLIPPANTA Live! Why—like man and wife: generally out of humour,
quarrel often, seldom agree, complain of one another; and perhaps
have both reason. In short, 'tis much as 'tis at your house.

MONEYTRAP Good-lack! But whose side are you generally of?

FLIPPANTA O' the right side always, my lady's. And if you'll have me   300
give you my opinion of these matters, sir, I do not think a husband
can ever be in the right.

MONEYTRAP Ha!

FLIPPANTA Little, peeking, creeping, sneaking, stingy, covetous, cowardly, dirty, cuckoldly things.   305

MONEYTRAP Ha!

FLIPPANTA Fit for nothing but tailors and dry-nurses.

MONEYTRAP Ha!

FLIPPANTA A dog in a manger, snarling and biting, to starve gentlemen with good stomachs.   310

MONEYTRAP Ha!

FLIPPANTA A sentry upon pleasure, set to be a plague upon lovers and damn poor women before their time.

MONEYTRAP A husband is indeed—

FLIPPANTA Sir, I say, he is nothing—a beetle without wings, a wind- 315
mill without sails, a ship in a calm.

MONEYTRAP Ha!

FLIPPANTA A bag without money—an empty bottle—dead small-beer.

MONEYTRAP Ha!

FLIPPANTA A quack without drugs. 320

MONEYTRAP Ha!

FLIPPANTA A lawyer without knavery.

MONEYTRAP Ha!

FLIPPANTA A courtier without flattery.

MONEYTRAP Ha! 325

FLIPPANTA A king without an army, or a people with one. Have I drawn him, sir?

MONEYTRAP Why truly, Flippanta, I can't deny, but there are some general lines of resemblance. But you know there may be exceptions. 330

FLIPPANTA Hark you, sir, shall I deal plainly with you? Had I got a husband, I would put him in mind, that he was married as well as I. (*Sings*)

> For were I the thing called a wife,
> And my fool grew too fond of his power, 335
> He should look like an ass all his life,
> For a prank that I'd play him in an hour.

Tol lol la ra tol lol, etc.—Do you observe that, sir?

MONEYTRAP I do; and think you would be in the right on't. But, prithee, why dost not give this advice to thy mistress? 340

FLIPPANTA For fear it should go round to your wife, sir, for you know they are playfellows.

MONEYTRAP O, there's no danger of my wife; she knows I'm none of those husbands.

FLIPPANTA Are you sure she knows that, sir? 345

MONEYTRAP I'm sure she ought to know it, Flippanta, for really I have but four faults in the world.

FLIPPANTA And, pray, what may they be?

MONEYTRAP Why, I'm a little slovenly, I shift but once a week.

FLIPPANTA Fough! 350

MONEYTRAP I am sometimes out of humour.

FLIPPANTA Provoking.

MONEYTRAP I don't give her so much money as she'd have.

FLIPPANTA Insolent.

MONEYTRAP And a—perhaps I mayn't be quite so young as I was.   355

FLIPPANTA The devil.

MONEYTRAP O, but then consider how 'tis on her side, Flippanta. She ruins me with washing, is always out of humour, ever wanting money, and will never be older.

FLIPPANTA That last article, I must confess, is a little hard upon you.   360

MONEYTRAP Ah, Flippanta, didst thou but know the daily provocations I have, thou'dst be the first to excuse my faults. But now I think on't—thou art none of my friend, thou dost not love me at all; no, not at all.

FLIPPANTA And whither is this little reproach going to lead us now?   365

MONEYTRAP You have power over your fair mistress, Flippanta.

FLIPPANTA Sir.

MONEYTRAP But what then? You hate me.

FLIPPANTA I understand you not.

MONEYTRAP There's not a moment's trouble her naughty husband   370
gives her, but I feel it too.

FLIPPANTA I don't know what you mean.

MONEYTRAP If she did but know what part I take in her sufferings.

FLIPPANTA Mighty obscure.

MONEYTRAP Well, I'll say no more; but—   375

FLIPPANTA All Hebrew.

MONEYTRAP If thou wouldst but tell her on't.

FLIPPANTA Still darker and darker.

MONEYTRAP I should not be ungrateful.

FLIPPANTA Ah, now I begin to understand you.   380

MONEYTRAP Flippanta—there's my purse.

[*Moneytrap gives Flippanta a purse*]

FLIPPANTA Say no more; now you explain indeed. You are in love?

MONEYTRAP Bitterly; and I do swear by all the Gods—

FLIPPANTA Hold! Spare 'em for another time, you stand in no need of 'em now. A usurer that parts with his purse gives sufficient proof of   385
his sincerity.

MONEYTRAP I hate my wife, Flippanta.

FLIPPANTA That we'll take upon your bare word.

MONEYTRAP She's the devil, Flippanta.

FLIPPANTA You like your neighbour's better.   390

214

MONEYTRAP Oh—an angel!

FLIPPANTA What pity it is the law don't allow trucking.°

MONEYTRAP If it did, Flippanta!

FLIPPANTA But since it don't, sir—keep the reins upon your passion; don't let your flame rage too high, lest my lady should be cruel, and it should dry you up to a mummy.

MONEYTRAP 'Tis impossible she can be so barbarous, to let me die. Alas, Flippanta, a very small matter would save my life.

FLIPPANTA Then y'are dead—for we women never grant anything to a man who will be satisfied with a little.

MONEYTRAP Dear Flippanta, that was only my modesty; but since you'll have it out—I am a very dragon. And so your lady'll find, if ever she thinks fit to be—now I hope you'll stand my friend.

FLIPPANTA Well sir, as far as my credit goes, it shall be employed in your service.

MONEYTRAP My best Flippanta—tell her—I'm all hers—tell her—my body's hers—tell her—my soul's hers—tell her—my estate's hers. Lard have mercy upon me, how I'm in love!

FLIPPANTA Poor man! What a sweat he's in! But hark! I hear my master; for heaven's sake compose yourself a little. You are in such a fit, o' my conscience he'll smell you out.

MONEYTRAP Ah, dear, I'm in such an emotion, I dare not be seen; put me in this closet for a moment.

FLIPPANTA Closet, man! It's too little, your love would stifle you. Go air yourself in the garden a little—you have need on't, i'faith.

She puts him out

Flippanta alone

A rare adventure by my troth. This will be curious news to the wives. Fortune has now put their husbands into their hands, and I think they are too sharp to neglect its favours.

Enter Gripe

GRIPE O, here's the right hand; the rest of the body can't be far off. Where's my wife, huswife?

FLIPPANTA An admirable question! Why, she's gone abroad sir.

GRIPE Abroad, abroad, abroad already? Why, she uses to be stewing in her bed three hours after this time, as late as 'tis; what makes her gadding so soon?

FLIPPANTA Business, I suppose.

GRIPE Business! She has a pretty head for business truly. Oho, let her change her way of living, or I'll make her change a light heart for a heavy one.

FLIPPANTA And why would you have her change her way of living, sir? You see it agrees with her. She never looked better in her life. 430

GRIPE Don't tell me of her looks. I have done with her looks long since. But I'll make her change her life, or—

FLIPPANTA Indeed, sir, you won't.

GRIPE Why, what shall hinder me, insolence?

FLIPPANTA That which hinders most husbands: contradiction. 435

GRIPE Suppose I resolve I won't be contradicted?

FLIPPANTA Suppose she resolves you shall.

GRIPE A wife's resolution is not good by law.

FLIPPANTA Nor a husband's by custom.

GRIPE I tell thee, I will not bear it. 440

FLIPPANTA I tell you, sir, you will bear it.

GRIPE Oons, I have borne it three years already.

FLIPPANTA By that you see 'tis but giving your mind to it.

GRIPE My mind to it! Death and the devil! My mind to it!

FLIPPANTA Look ye sir, you may swear and damn, and call the furies 445 to assist you, but till you apply the remedy to the right place, you'll never cure the disease. You fancy you have got an extravagant° wife, is't not so?

GRIPE Prithee change me that word 'fancy', and it is so.

FLIPPANTA Why there's it. Men are strangely troubled with the 450 vapours of late. You'll wonder now, if I tell you you have the most reasonable wife in town; and that all the disorders you think you see in her, are only here, here, here (*thumping his forehead*) in your own head.

GRIPE She is then, in thy opinion, a reasonable woman. 455

FLIPPANTA By my faith I think so.

GRIPE I shall run mad! Name me an extravagance in the world she is not guilty of.

FLIPPANTA Name me an extravagance in the world she is guilty of.

GRIPE Come then, does not she put the whole house in disorder? 460

FLIPPANTA Not that I know of, for she never comes into it but to sleep.

GRIPE 'Tis very well. Does she employ any one moment of her life in the government of her family?

FLIPPANTA She is so submissive a wife, she leaves it entirely to you. 465

GRIPE Admirable! Does she not spend more money in coach-hire, and chair-hire, than would maintain six children?

FLIPPANTA She's too nice of your credit to be seen daggling in the streets.

GRIPE Good. Do I set eye on her sometimes in a week together?   470

FLIPPANTA That, sir, is because you are never stirring at the same time. You keep odd hours; you are always going to bed when she's rising, and rising just when she's coming to bed.

GRIPE Yes truly, night into day, and day into night; bawdy-house play, that's her trade. But these are trifles. Has she not lost her diamond   475
necklace? Answer me to that, trapes.

FLIPPANTA Yes; and has sent as many tears after it, as if it had been her husband.

GRIPE Ah!—the pox take her; but enough. 'Tis resolved, and I will put a stop to the course of her life, or I will put a stop to the course   480
of her blood, and so she shall know the first time I meet with her; (*aside*) which though we are man and wife, and lie under one roof, 'tis very possible may not be this fortnight.

Exit Gripe

FLIPPANTA (*alone*) Nay, thou hast a blessed time on't, that must be confessed. What a miserable devil is a husband? Insupportable to   485
himself, and a plague to everything about him. Their wives do by them as children do by dogs, tease and provoke 'em till they make 'em so curst, they snarl and bite at everything that comes in their reach. This wretch here is grown perverse to that degree, he's for his wife's keeping home and making hell of his house, so he may be   490
the devil in it, to torment her. How niggardly soever he is of all things he possesses, he is willing to purchase her misery at the expense of his own peace. But he had as good be still, for he'll miss of his aim. If I know her (which I think I do) she'll set his blood in such a ferment, it shall bubble out at every pore of him; whilst hers   495
is so quiet in her veins, her pulse shall go like a pendulum.

[*Exit Flippanta*]

3.1

Mrs Amlet's house

Enter Dick

DICK Where's this old woman? A-hey. What the devil? Nobody at home? Ha! Her strong box! And the key in't! 'Tis so. Now fortune be my friend. What the deuce—not a penny of money in cash—nor a chequer-note°—nor a bank-bill° (*searching the strong box*)—nor a crooked stick!° Nor a—mum—here's something—a diamond 5
necklace by all the gods! Oons! The old woman! (*Enter Mrs Amlet*) Zest!°

       Claps the necklace in his pocket, then runs and asks her blessing
Pray, mother, pray to, etc.
    [*Kneels to Mrs Amlet*]

MRS AMLET Is it possible? Dick upon his humble knee! Ah my dear child! May heaven be good unto thee. 10

DICK I'm come, my dear mother, to pay my duty to you, and to ask your consent to—

MRS AMLET What a shape is there!

DICK To ask your consent, I say, to marry a great fortune; for what is riches in this world without a blessing, and how can there be a 15
blessing without respect and duty to parents?

MRS AMLET What a nose he has!

DICK And therefore, it being the duty of every good child not to dispose of himself in marriage, without the—

MRS AMLET Now the lord love thee (*kissing him*) for thou art a goodly 20
young man. Well Dick—and how goes it with the lady? Are her eyes open to thy charms? Does she see what's for her own good? Is she sensible of the blessings thou hast in store for her? Ha! Is all sure? Hast thou broke a piece of money° with her? Speak bird, do; don't be modest, and hide thy love from thy mother, for I'm an 25
indulgent parent.

DICK Nothing under heaven can prevent my good fortune but its being discovered I am your son—

MRS AMLET Then thou art still ashamed of thy natural mother. Graceless! Why, I'm no whore, sirrah. 30

DICK I know you are not—a whore! Bless us all—

MRS AMLET No. My reputation's as good as the best of 'em; and though I'm old, I'm chaste, you rascal you.

DICK Lord, that is not the thing we talk of, mother, but—

MRS AMLET I think as the world goes, they may be proud of marrying 35
their daughter into a vartuous° family.

DICK Oons, vartue is not the case—

MRS AMLET Where she may have a good example before her eyes.

DICK O Lord! O Lord! O Lord!

MRS AMLET I'm a woman that don't so much as encourage an in- 40
continent look towards me.

DICK I tell you, 'sdeath, I tell you—

MRS AMLET If a man should make an uncivil motion to me, I'd spit in
his lascivious face: and all this you may tell 'em, sirrah.

DICK Death and furies! The woman's out of her— 45

MRS AMLET Don't you swear, you rascal you, don't you swear; we
shall have thee damned at last, and then I shall be disgraced.

DICK Why then in cool blood hear me speak to you. I tell you it's a
city-fortune I'm about. She cares not a fig for your vartue; she'll
hear of nothing but quality. She has quarrelled with one of her 50
friends for having a better complexion, and is resolved she'll marry
to take place of her.

MRS AMLET What a cherry-lip is there!

DICK Therefore, good dear mother now, have a care and don't discover me; for if you do, all's lost. 55

MRS AMLET Dear, dear, how thy fair bride will be delighted! Go, get
thee gone, go. Go fetch her home, go fetch her home; I'll give her a
sack-posset, and a pillow of down she shall lay her head upon. Go,
fetch her home, I say.

DICK Take care then of the main chance, my dear mother; remember, 60
if you discover me—

MRS AMLET Go, fetch her home, I say.

DICK You promise me then—

MRS AMLET March.

DICK But swear to me— 65

MRS AMLET Begone, sirrah.

DICK Well, I'll rely upon you—but one kiss before I go.
Kisses her heartily and runs off

MRS AMLET Now the Lord love thee; for thou art a comfortable
young man.
Exit Mrs Amlet

3.2

Gripe's house

Enter Corinna and Flippanta

CORINNA But hark you, Flippanta, if you don't think he loves me dearly, don't give him my letter, after all.

FLIPPANTA Let me alone.

CORINNA When he has read it, let him give it you again.

FLIPPANTA Don't trouble yourself.   5

CORINNA And not a word of the pudding° to my mother-in-law.

FLIPPANTA Enough.

CORINNA When we come to love one another to the purpose, she shall know all.

FLIPPANTA Ay, then 'twill be time.   10

CORINNA But remember 'tis you make me do all this now, so if any mischief comes on't, 'tis you must answer for't.

FLIPPANTA I'll be your security.

CORINNA I'm young, and know nothing of the matter; but you have experience, so it's your business to conduct me safe.   15

FLIPPANTA Poor innocence!

CORINNA But tell me in serious sadness, Flippanta, does he love me with the very soul of him?

FLIPPANTA I have told you so a hundred times, and yet you are not satisfied.   20

CORINNA But, methinks I'd fain have him tell me so himself.

FLIPPANTA Have patience, and it shall be done.

CORINNA Why, patience is a virtue; that we must all confess. But I fancy, the sooner it's done the better, Flippanta.

Enter Jessamin

JESSAMIN Madam, yonder's your geography-master waiting for you.   25

Exit [Jessamin]

CORINNA Ah! How I am tired with these old fumbling fellows, Flippanta.

FLIPPANTA Well, don't let 'em break your heart; you shall be rid of 'em all ere long.

CORINNA Nay, 'tis not the study I'm so weary of, Flippanta, 'tis   30
the odious thing that teaches me. Were the Colonel my master I fancy I could take pleasure in learning everything he could show me.

FLIPPANTA And he can show you a great deal, I can tell you that. But

get you gone in, here's somebody coming, we must not be seen   35
together.

CORINNA I will, I will, I will. O! The dear Colonel.

Running off
Enter Mrs Amlet

FLIPPANTA O ho, it's Mrs Amlet. What brings you so soon to us
again, Mrs Amlet?

MRS AMLET Ah! My dear Mrs Flippanta, I'm in a furious fright.   40

FLIPPANTA Why, what's come to you?

MRS AMLET Ah! Mercy on us all. Madam's diamond necklace—

FLIPPANTA What of that?

MRS AMLET Are you sure you left it at my house?

FLIPPANTA Sure I left it? A very pretty question truly.   45

MRS AMLET Nay, don't be angry; say nothing to madam of it, I
beseech you. It will be found again, if it be heaven's good will. At
least 'tis I must bear the loss on't. 'Tis my rogue of a son has laid
his bird-lime° fingers on't.

FLIPPANTA Your son, Mrs Amlet? Do you breed your children up to   50
such tricks as these then?

MRS AMLET What shall I say to you, Mrs Flippanta? Can I help it? He
has been a rogue from his cradle, Dick has. But he has his desarts
too. And now it comes in my head, mayhap he may have no ill
design in this neither.   55

FLIPPANTA No ill design, woman? He's a pretty fellow if he can steal
a diamond necklace with a good one.

MRS AMLET You don't know him, Mrs Flippanta, so well as I that
bore him. Dick's a rogue, 'tis true, but—mum—

FLIPPANTA What does the woman mean?   60

MRS AMLET Hark you, Mrs Flippanta, is not here a young gentlewoman in your house, that wants a husband?

FLIPPANTA Why do you ask?

MRS AMLET By way of conversation only, it does not concern me; but
when she marries I may chance to dance at the wedding. Remember   65
I tell you so; I who am but Mrs Amlet.

FLIPPANTA You dance at her wedding! You!

MRS AMLET Yes, I, I, but don't trouble madam about her necklace;
perhaps it mayn't go out of the family. Adieu, Mrs Flippanta.

Exit Mrs Amlet

FLIPPANTA What—what—what does the woman mean? Mad! What   70
a capilotade of a story's here? The necklace lost; and her son Dick;
and a fortune to marry; and she shall dance at the wedding; and—

she does not intend, I hope, to propose a match between her son
Dick and Corinna? By my conscience I believe she does. An old
beldam!   75

    Enter Brass

BRASS Well, hussy, how stand our affairs? Has Miss writ us an answer
yet? My master's very impatient yonder.

FLIPPANTA And why the deuce does not he come himself? What does
he send such idle fellows as thee of his errands? Here I had her
alone just now. He won't have such an opportunity again this   80
month, I can tell him that.

BRASS So much the worse for him; 'tis his business. But now, my dear,
let thee and I talk a little of our own. I grow most damnably in love
with thee, dost hear that?

FLIPPANTA Phu! Thou art always timing things wrong; my head is   85
full, at present, of more important things than love.

BRASS Then it's full of important things indeed. Dost want a privy-
counsellor?

FLIPPANTA I want an assistant.

BRASS To do what?   90

FLIPPANTA Mischief.

BRASS I'm thy man—touch.

FLIPPANTA But before I venture to let thee into my project, prithee
tell me whether thou find'st a natural disposition to ruin a husband
to oblige his wife?   95

BRASS Is she handsome?

FLIPPANTA Yes.

BRASS Why then my disposition's at her service.

FLIPPANTA She's beholding to thee.

BRASS Not she alone neither, therefore don't let her grow vain upon't; 100
for I have three or four affairs of that kind going at this time.

FLIPPANTA Well, go carry this epistle from Miss to thy master, and
when thou com'st back I'll tell thee thy business.

BRASS I'll know it before I go, if you please.

FLIPPANTA Thy master waits for an answer.   105

BRASS I'd rather he should wait than I.

FLIPPANTA Why then, in short, Araminta's husband is in love with
my lady.

BRASS Very well, child, we have a Roland for her Oliver:° thy lady's
husband is in love with Araminta.   110

FLIPPANTA Who told you that, sirrah?

BRASS 'Tis a negotiation I am charged with, pert. Did not I tell thee I

did business for half the town? I have managed Master Gripe's
little affairs for him these ten years, you slut you.

FLIPPANTA Hark thee, Brass, the game's in our hands, if we can but   115
play the cards.

BRASS Pique and repique,° you jade you; if the wives will fall into a
good intelligence.

FLIPPANTA Let them alone; I'll answer for 'em they don't slip the
occasion. See: here they come. They little think what a piece of   120
good news we have for 'em.

   Enter Clarissa and Araminta [with packages, followed by
   Jessamin]

CLARISSA Jessamin! Here boy, carry up these things into my dressing-
room, and break as many of 'em by the way as you can, be sure.

   [*Exit Jessamin with packages*]

  O! art thou there, Brass? What news?

BRASS Madam, I only called in as I was going by. But some little   125
propositions Mrs Flippanta has been starting has kept me here to
offer your ladyship my humble service.

CLARISSA What propositions?

BRASS She'll acquaint you, madam.

ARAMINTA Is there anything new, Flippanta?   130

FLIPPANTA Yes, and pretty° too.

CLARISSA That follows of course, but let's have it quick.

FLIPPANTA Why, madam, you have made a conquest.

CLARISSA Huzza!° But of who? Quick!

FLIPPANTA Of Mr Moneytrap, that's all.   135

ARAMINTA My husband?

FLIPPANTA Yes, your husband, madam. You thought fit to corrupt
ours, so now we are even with you.

ARAMINTA Sure thou art in jest, Flippanta.

FLIPPANTA Serious as my devotions.   140

BRASS And the cross intrigue, ladies, is what our brains have been at
work about.

ARAMINTA (*to Clarissa*) My dear.

CLARISSA My life.

ARAMINTA My angel.   145

CLARISSA My soul.

   Hugging one another

ARAMINTA The stars have done this.

CLARISSA The pretty little twinklers.

FLIPPANTA And what will you do for them now?

CLARISSA What grateful creatures ought; show 'em we don't despise   150
their favours.

ARAMINTA But is not this a wager between these two blockheads?

CLARISSA I would not give a shilling to go the winner's halves.

ARAMINTA Then 'tis the most fortunate thing that ever could have
happened.   155

CLARISSA All your last night's ideas, Araminta, were trifles to it.

ARAMINTA Brass, my dear, will be useful to us.

BRASS At your service, madam.

CLARISSA Flippanta will be necessary, my life.

FLIPPANTA She waits your commands, madam.   160

ARAMINTA For my part then, I recommend my husband to thee,
Flippanta, and make it my earnest request thou won't leave him
one half-crown.

FLIPPANTA I'll do all I can to obey you, madam.

BRASS (to Clarissa) If your ladyship would give me the same kind   165
orders for yours.

CLARISSA O—if thou spar'st him, Brass, I'm thy enemy till I die.

BRASS 'Tis enough, madam. I'll be sure to give you a reasonable
account of him. But how do you intend we shall proceed, ladies?
Must we storm the purse at once, or break ground in form,° and   170
carry it by little and little?

CLARISSA Storm, dear Brass, storm; ever whilst you live, storm.

ARAMINTA O by all means; must it not be so, Flippanta?

FLIPPANTA In four and twenty hours, two hundred pounds apiece,
that's my sentence.   175

BRASS Very well. But, ladies, you'll give me leave to put you in mind
of some little expense in favours, 'twill be necessary you are at, to
these honest gentlemen.

ARAMINTA Favours, Brass?

BRASS Um—a—some small matters, madam, I doubt must be.   180

CLARISSA Now that's a vile article, Araminta; for that thing your
husband is so like mine—

FLIPPANTA Phu, there's a scruple indeed. Pray, madam, don't be so
squeamish; though the meat be a little flat, we'll find you savoury
sauce to it.   185

CLARISSA This wench is so mad.

FLIPPANTA Why what, in the name of Lucifer, is it you have to do,
that's so terrible?

BRASS A civil look only.

ARAMINTA There's no great harm in that.   190

FLIPPANTA An obliging word.

CLARISSA That one may afford 'em.

BRASS A little smile, *à propos.*°

ARAMINTA That's but giving oneself an air.

FLIPPANTA Receive a little letter, perhaps. 195

CLARISSA Women of quality do that from fifty odious fellows.

BRASS Suffer (maybe) a squeeze by the hand.

ARAMINTA One's so used to that one does not feel it.

FLIPPANTA Or if a kiss would do't?

CLARISSA I'd die first. 200

BRASS Indeed, ladies, I doubt 'twill be necessary to—

CLARISSA Get their wretched money without paying so dear for it.

FLIPPANTA Well, just as you please for that, my ladies: but I suppose you'll play upon the square° with your favours, and not pique yourselves upon being one more grateful than another. 205

BRASS And state a fair account of receipts and disbursements.

ARAMINTA That I think should be indeed.

CLARISSA With all my heart, and Brass shall be our bookkeeper. So get thee to work, man, as fast as thou canst. But not a word of all this to thy master! 210

BRASS I'll observe my orders, madam.

    Exit Brass

CLARISSA I'll have the pleasure of telling him myself; he'll be violently delighted with it. 'Tis the best man in the world, Araminta. He'll bring us rare company tomorrow—all sorts of gamesters; and thou shalt see, my husband will be such a beast to be out of humour at it. 215

ARAMINTA The monster—but hush, here's my dear approaching; prithee let's leave him to Flippanta.

FLIPPANTA Ay, pray do. I'll bring you a good account of him I'll warrant you. 220

CLARISSA Dispatch then for the basset-tables in haste.

    Exeunt Clarissa and Araminta
    Flippanta alone

FLIPPANTA So, now have at him; here he comes. We'll try if we can pillage the usurer, as he does other folks.

    Enter Moneytrap

MONEYTRAP Well, my pretty Flippanta, is thy mistress come home?

FLIPPANTA Yes sir. 225

MONEYTRAP And where is she, prithee?

FLIPPANTA Gone abroad sir.

MONEYTRAP How dost mean?

FLIPPANTA I mean right, sir; my lady'll come home and go abroad ten
    times in an hour, when she's either in very good humour, or very   230
    bad.

MONEYTRAP Good lack! But I'll warrant, in general, 'tis her naughty
    husband that makes her house uneasy to her. But hast thou said a
    little something to her, chicken, for an expiring lover? Ha?

FLIPPANTA Said! Yes, I have said, much good may it do me.   235

MONEYTRAP Well? And how?

FLIPPANTA And how? And how do you think? You would have
    me do't. And you have such a way with you, one can refuse you
    nothing. But I have brought myself into a fine business° by it.

MONEYTRAP Good lack! But I hope, Flippanta—   240

FLIPPANTA Yes, your hopes will do much when I am turned out of
    doors.

MONEYTRAP Was she then terrible angry?

FLIPPANTA Oh! had you seen how she flew, when she saw where I was
    pointing; for you must know I went round the bush, and round the   245
    bush, before I came to the matter.

MONEYTRAP Nay, 'tis a ticklish point, that must be owned.

FLIPPANTA On my word is it—I mean where a lady's truly virtuous,
    for that's our case you must know.

MONEYTRAP A very dangerous case indeed.   250

FLIPPANTA But I can tell you one thing—she has an inclination to
    you.

MONEYTRAP Is it possible?

FLIPPANTA Yes, and I told her so at last.

MONEYTRAP Well, and what did she answer thee?   255

FLIPPANTA Slap—and bid me bring it you for a token.
        Giving him a slap on the face

MONEYTRAP (*aside*) And you have lost none on't by the way, with a
    pox t'ye.

FLIPPANTA Now this, I think, looks the best in the world.

MONEYTRAP Yes, but really it feels a little oddly.   260

FLIPPANTA Why, you must know, ladies have different ways of
    expressing their kindness, according to the humour they are in. If
    she had been in a good one, it had been a kiss; but as long as she
    sent you something, your affairs go well.

MONEYTRAP Why, truly, I am a little ignorant in the mysterious paths   265
    of love, so I must be guided by thee. But, prithee, take her in a good
    humour, next token she sends me.

FLIPPANTA Ah—good humour?

MONEYTRAP What's the matter?

FLIPPANTA Poor lady!   270

MONEYTRAP Ha.

FLIPPANTA If I durst tell you all—

MONEYTRAP What then?

FLIPPANTA You would not expect to see her in one a good while.

MONEYTRAP Why, I pray?   275

FLIPPANTA I must own I did take an unseasonable time to talk of love
matters to her.

MONEYTRAP Why, what's the matter?

FLIPPANTA Nothing.

MONEYTRAP Nay, prithee tell me.   280

FLIPPANTA I dare not.

MONEYTRAP You must indeed.

FLIPPANTA Why, when women are in difficulties, how can they think
of pleasure?

MONEYTRAP Why, what difficulties can she be in?   285

FLIPPANTA Nay, I do but guess after all; for she has that grandeur of
soul, she'd die before she'd tell.

MONEYTRAP But what dost thou suspect?

FLIPPANTA Why, what should one suspect where a husband loves
nothing but getting of money, and a wife nothing but spending   290
on't?

MONEYTRAP So she wants that same then?

FLIPPANTA I say no such thing; I know nothing of the matter. Pray
make no wrong interpretation of what I say; my lady wants nothing
that I know of. 'Tis true she has had ill luck at cards of late; I   295
believe she has not won once this month. But what of that?

MONEYTRAP Ha?

FLIPPANTA 'Tis true, I know her spirit's that, she'd see her husband
hanged before she'd ask him for a farthing.

MONEYTRAP Ha?   300

FLIPPANTA And then I know him again, he'd see her drowned before
he'd give her a farthing; but that's a help to your affair you know.

MONEYTRAP 'Tis so indeed.

FLIPPANTA Ah—well, I'll say nothing; but if she had none of these
things to fret her—   305

MONEYTRAP Why really, Flippanta.

FLIPPANTA I know what you are going to say now: you are going to
offer your service, but 'twon't do; you have a mind to play the

gallant now, but it must not be; you want to be showing your liberality, but 'twon't be allowed. You'll be pressing me to offer it, and she'll be in a rage. We shall have the devil to do.   310

MONEYTRAP You mistake me, Flippanta; I was only going to say—

FLIPPANTA Ay, I know what you were going to say well enough; but I tell you it will never do so. If one could find out some way now— ay—let me see—   315

MONEYTRAP Indeed I hope—

FLIPPANTA Pray be quiet—no—but I'm thinking—hum—she'll smoke that though—let us consider—if one could find a way to— 'tis the nicest point in the world to bring about; she'll never touch it if she knows from whence it comes.   320

MONEYTRAP Shall I try if I can reason her husband out of twenty pounds, to make her easy the rest of her life?

FLIPPANTA Twenty pound, man—why you shall see her set that upon a card! O—she has a great soul. Besides, if her husband should oblige her, it might, in time, take off her aversion to him, and by   325 consequence, her inclination to you. No, no, it must never come that way.

MONEYTRAP What shall we do then?

FLIPPANTA Hold still—I have it. I'll tell you what you shall do.

MONEYTRAP Ay.   330

FLIPPANTA You shall make her—a restitution—of two hundred pounds.

MONEYTRAP Ha—a restitution?

FLIPPANTA Yes, yes, 'tis the luckiest thought in the world; madam often plays, you know, and folks who do so meet now and then with   335 sharpers. Now, you shall be a sharper.

MONEYTRAP A sharper?

FLIPPANTA Ay, ay, a sharper; and having cheated her of two hundred pounds, shall be troubled in mind, and send it her back again. You comprehend me?   340

MONEYTRAP Yes, I, I comprehend, but a—won't she suspect if it be so much?

FLIPPANTA No, no, the more the better.

MONEYTRAP Two hundred pound?

FLIPPANTA Yes, two hundred pound—o, let me see—so even a sum   345 may look a little suspicious—ay—let it be two hundred and thirty; that odd thirty will make it look so natural, the devil won't find it out.

MONEYTRAP Ha?

FLIPPANTA Pounds too look—I don't know how, guineas I fancy were   350
better—ay, guineas, it shall be guineas. You are of that mind, are
you not?

MONEYTRAP Um—a guinea you know, Flippanta is—

FLIPPANTA A thousand times genteeler, you are certainly in the right
on't; it shall be as you say, two hundred and thirty guineas.   355

MONEYTRAP Ho—well, if it must be guineas, let's see, two hundred
guineas.

FLIPPANTA And thirty; two hundred and thirty. If you mistake the
sum, you spoil all. So go put 'em in a purse, while it's fresh in your
head, and send 'em to me with a penitential letter, desiring I'll do   360
you the favour to restore 'em to her.

MONEYTRAP Two hundred and thirty pounds in a bag?

FLIPPANTA Guineas I say, guineas.

MONEYTRAP Ay, guineas; that's true. But Flippanta, if she don't
know they come from me, then I give my money for nothing, you   365
know.

FLIPPANTA Phu, leave that to me, I'll manage the stock for you; I'll
make it produce something I'll warrant you.

MONEYTRAP Well Flippanta, 'tis a great sum indeed; but I'll go
try what I can do for her. You say, two hundred guineas in a   370
purse?

FLIPPANTA And thirty; if the man's in his senses.

MONEYTRAP And thirty, 'tis true, I always forget that thirty.
       Exit Moneytrap

FLIPPANTA So, get thee gone; thou art a rare fellow, i' faith. Brass! It's
thee, is't not?   375
       Enter Brass

BRASS It is, huswife. How go matters? I stayed till thy gentleman was
gone. Hast done anything towards our common purse?

FLIPPANTA I think I have; he's going to make us a restitution of two
or three hundred pounds.

BRASS A restitution! Good.   380

FLIPPANTA A new way, sirrah, to make a lady take a present without
putting her to the blush.

BRASS 'Tis very well, mighty well indeed. Prithee where's thy master?
Let me try if I can persuade him to be troubled in mind too.

FLIPPANTA Not so hasty; he's gone into his closet to prepare himself   385
for a quarrel. I have advised him to be° with his wife.

BRASS What to do?

FLIPPANTA Why, to make her stay at home, now she has resolved to

do it beforehand. You must know, sirrah, we intend to make a merit
of our basset-table, and get a good pretence for the merry com-   390
panions we intend to fill his house with.

BRASS Very nicely spun truly; thy husband will be a happy man.

FLIPPANTA Hold your tongue, you fool you. See, here comes your
master.

BRASS He's welcome.   395

Enter Dick

DICK My dear Flippanta! How many thanks have I to pay thee?

FLIPPANTA Do you like her style?

DICK The kindest little rogue! There's nothing but she gives me leave
to hope. I am the happiest man the world has in its care.

FLIPPANTA Not so happy as you think for neither, perhaps; you have   400
a rival, sir, I can tell you that.

DICK A rival!

FLIPPANTA Yes, and a dangerous one too.

DICK Who, in the name of terror?

FLIPPANTA A devilish fellow, one Mr Amlet.   405

DICK Amlet? I know no such man.

FLIPPANTA You know the man's mother though; you met her here,
and are in her favour, I can tell you. If he worsts you in your
mistress, you shall e'en marry her, and disinherit him.

DICK If I have no other rival but Mr Amlet, I believe I shan't be much   410
disturbed in my amour. But can't I see Corinna?

FLIPPANTA I don't know; she has always some of her masters with
her. But I'll go see if she can spare you a moment, and bring you
word.

Exit Flippanta

DICK I wish my old hobbling mother han't been blabbing something   415
here she should not do.

BRASS Fear nothing, all's safe on that side yet. But how speaks young
mistress' epistle? Soft and tender?

DICK As pen can write.

BRASS So you think all goes well there?   420

DICK As my heart can wish.

BRASS You are sure on't?

DICK Sure on't.

BRASS Why then, ceremony aside (*putting on his hat*) you and I must
have a little talk, Mr Amlet.   425

DICK Ah, Brass, what art thou going to do? Won't ruin me?

BRASS Look you, Dick, few words; you are in a smooth way of making

your fortune. I hope all will roll on. But how do you intend matters
shall pass 'twixt you and me in this business?

DICK Death and furies! What a time dost take to talk on't? 430

BRASS Good words, or I betray you; they have already heard of one
Mr Amlet in the house.

DICK (*aside*) Here's a son of a whore.

BRASS In short, look smooth, and be a good prince.° I am your valet,
'tis true: your footman sometimes, which I'm enraged at; but you 435
have always had the ascendant, I confess. When we were schoolfellows, you made me carry your books, make your exercise, own
your rogueries, and sometimes take a whipping for you; when we
were fellow-prentices, though I was your senior, you made me open
the shop, clean my master's shoes, cut last at dinner, and eat all the 440
crust. In our sins too, I must own you still kept me under. You
soared up to adultery with our mistress, while I was at humble
fornication with the maid. Nay, in our punishments, you still made
good your post; for when once upon a time I was sentenced but to
be whipped, I cannot deny but you were condemned to be hanged. 445
So that in all times, I must confess, your inclinations have been
greater and nobler than mine. However, I cannot consent that you
should at once fix fortune for life, and I dwell in my humilities for
the rest of my days.

DICK Hark thee, Brass, if I do not most nobly by thee I'm a dog. 450

BRASS And when?

DICK As soon as ever I am married.

BRASS Ah, the pox take thee.

DICK Then you mistrust me?

BRASS I do, by my faith. Look you, sir, some folks we mistrust because 455
we don't know 'em; others we mistrust because we do know 'em.
And for one of these reasons I desire there may be a bargain
beforehand. If not (*raising his voice*), look ye, Dick Amlet—

DICK Soft, my dear friend and companion. (*Aside*) The dog will ruin
me. Say, what is't will content thee? 460

BRASS O ho.

DICK But how can'st thou be such a barbarian?

BRASS I learnt it at Algier.°

DICK Come, make thy Turkish demand° then.

BRASS You know you gave me a bank-bill this morning to receive for 465
you.

DICK I did so, of fifty pounds, 'tis thine. So, now thou art satisfied;
all's fixed.

BRASS It is not indeed. There's a diamond necklace you robbed your
mother of e'en now.   470

DICK Ah you Jew.

BRASS No words.

DICK My dear Brass!

BRASS I insist.

DICK My old friend.   475

BRASS (*raising his voice*) Dick Amlet, I insist.

DICK Ah the cormorant!° Well, 'tis thine. But thou'lt never thrive
with't.

BRASS When I find it begins to do me mischief, I'll give it you again.
But I must have a wedding-suit.   480

DICK Well.

BRASS Some good lace.

DICK Thou sha't.

BRASS A stock of linen.

DICK Enough.   485

BRASS Not yet—a silver sword.

DICK Well, thou sha't have that too. Now thou hast everything.

BRASS Gad forgive me, I forgot a ring of remembrance.° I would not
forget all these favours for the world; a sparkling diamond will be
always playing in my eye, and put me in mind of 'em.   490

DICK (*aside*) This unconscionable rogue! [*Aloud*] Well, I'll bespeak
one for thee.

BRASS Brillant.°

DICK It shall. But if the thing don't succeed after all?

BRASS I'm a man of honour, and restore. And so the treaty being   495
finished I strike my flag of defiance, and fall into my respects again.
(*Taking off his hat*)
        Enter Flippanta

FLIPPANTA I have made you wait a little, but I could not help it; her
master is but just gone. He has been showing her Prince Eugene's
march into Italy.°

DICK Prithee let me come to her. I'll show her a part of the world he   500
has never shown her yet.

FLIPPANTA So I told her, you must know; and she said she could like
to travel in good company. So if you'll slip up those back stairs you
shall try if you can agree upon the journey.

DICK My dear Flippanta!   505

FLIPPANTA None of your dear acknowledgements I beseech you, but
upstairs as hard as you can drive.

DICK I'm gone.
>
> *Exit Dick*

FLIPPANTA And do you follow him, Jackadandy, and see he is not surprised. 510

BRASS I thought that was your post, Mrs Useful. But if you'll come and keep me in humour, I don't care if I share the duty with you.

FLIPPANTA No words, sirrah, but follow him. I have somewhat else to do.

BRASS The jade's so absolute there's no contesting with her. One kiss 515 though to keep the sentinel warm (*gives her a long kiss*)—so.
>
> *Exit Brass*

FLIPPANTA (*alone*) A nasty rogue. (*Wiping her mouth*) But let me see, what have I to do now? This restitution will be here quickly, I suppose. In the meantime I'll go know if my lady's ready for the quarrel yet. Master, yonder, is so full on't he's ready to burst; but 520 we'll give him vent by and by, with a witness.°
>
> *Exit Flippanta*

4.1

Gripe's house

Enter Corinna, Dick, and Brass

BRASS Don't fear, I'll give timely notice.

Goes to the door

DICK Come, you must consent, you shall consent. How can you leave me thus upon the rack—a man who loves you to that excess that I do?

CORINNA Nay, that you love me, sir, that I'm satisfied in, for you have sworn you do. And I'm so pleased with it, I'd fain have you do so as long as you live, so we must never marry. 5

DICK Not marry, my dear! Why, what's our love good for, if we don't marry?

CORINNA Ah, I'm afraid 'twill be good for little if we do. 10

DICK Why do you think so?

CORINNA Because I hear my father and mother, and my uncle and aunt, and Araminta and her husband; and twenty other married folks say so from morning to night.

DICK O, that's because they are bad husbands and bad wives, but in our case, there will be a good husband and a good wife, and so we shall love forever. 15

CORINNA Why, there may be something in that truly; and I'm always willing to hear reason, as a reasonable young woman ought to do. But are you sure, sir, though we are very good now, we shall be so when we come to be better acquainted? 20

DICK I can answer for myself at least.

CORINNA I wish you could answer for me too. You see I'm a plain dealer, sir; I hope you don't like me the worse for it.

DICK O, by no means. 'Tis a sign of admirable morals; and I hope, since you practise it yourself, you'll approve of it in your lover. In one word, therefore, for 'tis in vain to mince the matter, my resolution's fixed, and the world can't stagger me; I marry—or I die. 25

CORINNA Indeed, sir, I have much ado to believe you; the disease of love is seldom so violent. 30

DICK Madam, I have two diseases to end my miseries. If the first don't do't, the latter shall. (*Drawing his sword*) One's in my heart, the t'other's in my scabbard.

CORINNA Not for a diadem. (*Catching hold of him*) Ah, put it up, put   35
it up.

DICK How absolute is your command! (*Dropping his sword*) A word,
you see, disarms me.

CORINNA (*aside*) What a power I have over him, the wondrous deeds
of love! [*Aloud*] Pray, sir, let me have no more of these rash doings   40
though; perhaps I mayn't be always in the saving humour. (*Aside*)
I'm sure if I had let him stick himself, I should have been envied by
all the great ladies in the town.

DICK Well, madam, have I then your promise? You'll make me the
happiest of mankind.   45

CORINNA I don't know what to say to you; but I believe I had as good
promise, for I find I shall certainly do't.

DICK Then let us seal the contract thus.
        Kisses her

CORINNA (*aside*) Um—he has almost taken away my breath. He kisses
purely.   50

DICK Hark—somebody comes!

BRASS (*peeping in*) Gar there,° the enemy—no, hold, y'are safe; 'tis
Flippanta.
        Enter Flippanta

FLIPPANTA Come, have you agreed the matter? If not, you must
end it another time, for your father's in motion, so pray kiss and   55
part.

CORINNA That's sweet and sour. (*They kiss*) Adieu t'ye, sir.
        Exeunt Dick and Corinna
        Enter Clarissa

CLARISSA Have you told him I'm at home, Flippanta?

FLIPPANTA Yes, madam.

CLARISSA And that I'll see him?   60

FLIPPANTA Yes, that too; but here's news for you. I have just now
received the restitution.

CLARISSA That's killing pleasure;° and how much has he restored
me?

FLIPPANTA Two hundred and thirty.   65

CLARISSA Wretched rogue! But retreat, your master's coming to
quarrel.

FLIPPANTA I'll be within call if things run high.
        Exit Flippanta
        Enter Gripe

GRIPE Oho—are you there i' faith? Madam, your humble servant. I'm

very glad to see you at home; I thought I should never have had that   70
honour again.

CLARISSA Good morrow, my dear, how d'ye do? Flippanta says you
are out of humour, and that you have a mind to quarrel with me. Is
it true, ha? I have a terrible pain in my head; I give you notice on't
beforehand.   75

GRIPE And how the pox should it be otherwise? It's a wonder you are
not dead—(*aside*) as a' would you were [*aloud*] with the life you
lead. Are you not ashamed? And do you not blush to—

CLARISSA My dear child, you crack my brain; soften the harshness of
your voice. Say what thou would, but let it be in an agreeable tone.   80

GRIPE Tone, madam? Don't tell me of a tone—

CLARISSA O, if you will quarrel, do it with temperance. Let it be all in
cool blood—even and smooth, as if you were not moved with what
you said—and then I'll hear you, as if I were not moved with it
neither.   85

GRIPE Had ever man such need of patience? Madam, madam, I must
tell you, madam—

CLARISSA Another key, or I walk off.

GRIPE Don't provoke me.

CLARISSA Shall you be long, my dear, in your remonstrances?   90

GRIPE Yes, madam; and very long.

CLARISSA If you would quarrel in *abregée*,° I should have a world of
obligation to you.

GRIPE What I have to say, forsooth, is not to be expressed in *abregée*;
my complaints are too numerous.   95

CLARISSA Complaints! Of what, my dear? Have I ever given you
subject of complaint, my life?

GRIPE O pox, my dear and my life; I desire none of your *tendresse*.°

CLARISSA How, find fault with my kindness, and my expressions of
affection and respect? The world will guess by this what the rest of   100
your complaints may be. I must tell you, I'm scandalized at your
procedure.

GRIPE I must tell you, I am running mad with yours.

CLARISSA Ah, how insupportable are the humours of some husbands;
so full of fancies, and so ungovernable! What have you in the world   105
to disturb you?

GRIPE What have I to disturb me? I have you, death and the devil.

CLARISSA Ay, merciful heaven, how he swears! You should never
accustom yourself to such words as these; indeed my dear you
should not. Your mouth's always full of 'em.   110

GRIPE Blood and thunder! Madam—

CLARISSA Ah, he'll fetch the house down. Do you know you make me tremble for you? Flippanta! Who's there? Flippanta!

GRIPE Here's a provoking devil for you!

Enter Flippanta

FLIPPANTA What in the name of Jove's the matter? You raise the neighbourhood.   115

CLARISSA Why, here's your master in a most violent fuss, and no mortal soul can tell for what.

GRIPE Not tell for what!

CLARISSA No, my life. I have begged him to tell me his griefs,   120
Flippanta, and then he swears. Good Lord, how he does swear!

GRIPE Ah, you wicked jade! Ah, you wicked jade!

CLARISSA Do you hear him, Flippanta? Do you hear him?

FLIPPANTA Pray, sir, let's know a little what puts you in all this fury?

CLARISSA Prithee stand near me, Flippanta. There's an odd froth   125
about his mouth, looks as if his poor head were going wrong. I'm afraid he'll bite.

GRIPE The wicked woman, Flippanta, the wicked woman.

CLARISSA Can anybody wonder I shun my own house, when he treats me at this rate in it?   130

GRIPE At this rate? Why in the devil's name—

CLARISSA Do you hear him again?

FLIPPANTA Come, a little moderation, sir, and try what that will produce.

GRIPE Hang her, 'tis all a pretence to justify her going abroad.   135

CLARISSA A pretence! A pretence! Do you hear how black a charge he loads me with? Charges me with a pretence? Is this the return for all my downright open actions? You know, my dear, I scorn pretences; whene'er I go abroad, it is without pretence.

GRIPE Give me patience.   140

FLIPPANTA You have a great deal, sir.

CLARISSA And yet he's never content, Flippanta.

GRIPE What shall I do?

CLARISSA What a reasonable man would do; own yourself in the wrong, and be quiet. Here's Flippanta has understanding, and I   145
have moderation; I'm willing to make her judge of our differences.

FLIPPANTA You do me a great deal of honour, madam; but I tell you beforehand, I shall be a little on master's side.

GRIPE Right; Flippanta has sense. Come, let her decide. Have I not reason to be in a passion? Tell me that.   150

237

CLARISSA You must tell her for what, my life.

GRIPE Why, for the trade you drive,° my soul.

FLIPPANTA Look you, sir, pray take things right. I know madam does
fret you a little now and then, that's true; but in the fund° she is the
softest, sweetest, gentlest lady breathing. Let her but live entirely to   155
her own fancy, and she'll never say a word to you from morning to
night.

GRIPE Oons, let her but stay at home, and she shall do what she will:
in reason that is.

FLIPPANTA D'ye hear that, madam? Nay, now I must be on master's   160
side; you see how he loves you, he desires only your company. Pray
give him that satisfaction, or I must pronounce against you.

CLARISSA Well, I agree. Thou know'st I don't love to grieve him. Let
him be always in good humour, and I'll be always at home.

FLIPPANTA Look you there, sir, what would you have more?   165

GRIPE Well, let her keep her word, and I'll have done quarrelling.

CLARISSA I must not, however, so far lose the merit of my consent, as
to let you think I'm weary of going abroad, my dear. What I do is
purely to oblige you; which, that I may be able to perform without a
relapse, I'll invent what ways I can to make my prison supportable   170
to me.

FLIPPANTA Her prison! Pretty bird! Her prison! Don't that word
melt you, sir?

GRIPE I must confess I did not expect to find her so reasonable.

FLIPPANTA O, sir, soon or late wives come into good humour;   175
husbands must only have a little patience to wait for it.

CLARISSA The innocent little diversions, dear, that I shall content
myself with, will be chiefly play and company.

GRIPE O, I'll find you employment. Your time shan't lie upon your
hands; though if you have a mind now for such a companion as a—   180
let me see—Araminta, for example, why I shan't be against her
being with you from morning till night.

CLARISSA You can't oblige me more; 'tis the best woman in the world.

GRIPE Is not she?

FLIPPANTA (aside) Ah, the old satyr.°   185

GRIPE Then we'll have, besides her, maybe sometimes—her husband;
and we shall see my niece that writes verses, and my sister Fidget,
with her husband's brother that's always merry; and his little
cousin, that's to marry the fat curate; and my uncle the apothecary,
with his wife and all his children. O, we shall divert ourselves rarely.   190

FLIPPANTA (aside) Good.

CLARISSA O, for that, my dear child, I must be plain with you, I'll see none of 'em but Araminta, who has the manners of the court; for I'll converse with none but women of quality.

GRIPE Ay, ay, they shall all have one quality or other.   195

CLARISSA Then, my dear, to make our home pleasant, we'll have consorts° of music sometimes.

GRIPE Music in my house?

CLARISSA Yes, my child, we must have music, or the house will be so dull I shall get the spleen, and be going abroad again.   200

FLIPPANTA Nay, she has so much complaisance for you, sir, you can't dispute such things with her.

GRIPE Ay, but if I have music—

CLARISSA Ay, but, sir, I must have music—

FLIPPANTA Not every day, madam don't mean.   205

CLARISSA No, bless me, no; but three consorts a week. Three days more we'll play after dinner, at ombre, picquet, basset, and so forth, and close the evening with a handsome supper and a ball.

GRIPE A ball?

CLARISSA Then my love you know there is but one day more upon   210
our hands, and that shall be the day of conversation. We'll read verses, talk of books, invent modes,° tell lies, scandalize our friends, be pert upon religion; and in short, employ every moment of it in some pretty witty exercise or other.

FLIPPANTA What order you see 'tis she proposes to live in; a most   215
wonderful regularity.

GRIPE (aside) Regularity with a pox!

CLARISSA And as this kind of life, so soft, so smooth, so agreeable, must needs invite a vast deal of company to partake of it, 'twill be necessary to have the decency of a porter° at our door, you   220
know.

GRIPE A porter! A scrivener have a porter, madam?

CLARISSA Positively, a porter.

GRIPE Why, no scrivener since Adam ever had a porter, woman!

CLARISSA You will therefore be renowned in story for having the first,   225
my life.

GRIPE Flippanta.

FLIPPANTA (aside to Gripe) Hang it, sir, never dispute a trifle; if you vex her, perhaps she'll insist upon a Swiss.°

GRIPE But madam—   230

CLARISSA But, sir, a porter, positively a porter; without that, treaty null, and I go abroad this moment.

FLIPPANTA Come, sir, never lose so advantageous a peace for a pitiful
porter.

GRIPE Why, I shall be hooted at; the boys will throw stones at my   235
porter. Besides, where shall I have money for all this expense?

CLARISSA My dear, who asks you for any? Don't be in a fright,
chicken.

GRIPE Don't be in a fright, madam. But where, I say?

FLIPPANTA Madam plays, sir, think on that; women that play have   240
inexhaustible mines, and wives who receive least money from their
husbands, are many times those who spend the most.

CLARISSA So, my dear, let what Flippanta says content you. Go, my
life, trouble yourself with nothing, but let me do just as I please,
and all will be well. I'm going into my closet, to consider of   245
some more things to enable me to give you the pleasure of my
company at home, without making it too great a misery to a
yielding wife.
       Exit Clarissa

FLIPPANTA Mirror of goodness! Pattern to all wives! Well sure, sir,
you are the happiest of all husbands.   250

GRIPE Yes—and a miserable dog for all that too, perhaps.

FLIPPANTA Why, what can you ask more than this matchless
complaisance?

GRIPE I don't know what I can ask, and yet I'm not satisfied with what
I have neither; the devil mixes in it all, I think—complaisant or   255
perverse, it feels just as't did.

FLIPPANTA Why, then your uneasiness is only a disease, sir; perhaps a
little bleeding and purging would relieve you.

CLARISSA (*calls within*) Flippanta!

FLIPPANTA Madam calls. I come, madam. Come, be merry, be merry,   260
sir, you have cause, take my word for't. (*Aside*) Poor devil!
       Exit Flippanta

GRIPE I don't know that, I don't know that; but this I do know, that an
honest man who has married a jade, whether she's pleased to spend
her time at home or abroad, had better have lived a bachelor.
       Enter Brass

BRASS O, sir, I'm mighty glad I've found you.   265

GRIPE Why, what's the matter, prithee?

BRASS Can nobody hear us?

GRIPE No, no, speak quickly.

BRASS You han't seen Araminta since the last letter I carried her from
you?   270

GRIPE Not I, I go prudently; I don't press things like your young firebrand lovers.

BRASS But seriously, sir, are you very much in love with her?

GRIPE As mortal man has been.

BRASS I'm sorry for't. 275

GRIPE Why so, dear Brass?

BRASS If you were never to see her more now? Suppose such a thing, d'you think 'twould break your heart?

GRIPE Oh!

BRASS Nay, now I see you love her; would you did not. 280

GRIPE My dear friend.

BRASS I'm in your interest deep; you see it.

GRIPE I do; but speak, what miserable story hast thou for me?

BRASS I had rather the devil had—phu—flown away with you quick, than to see you so much in love as I perceive you are, since— 285

GRIPE Since what? Ho!

BRASS Araminta, sir—

GRIPE Dead?

BRASS No.

GRIPE How then? 290

BRASS Worse.

GRIPE Out with't.

BRASS Broke.

GRIPE Broke?

BRASS She is, poor lady, in the most unfortunate situation of affairs. 295 But I have said too much.

GRIPE No, no, 'tis very sad, but let's hear it.

BRASS Sir, she charged me on my life never to mention it to you of all men living.

GRIPE Why, who shoudst thou tell it to, but to the best of her 300 friends?

BRASS Ay, why there's it now, it's going just as I fancied. Now will I be hanged if you are not enough in love to be engaging in this matter. But I must tell you, sir, that as much concern as I have for that most excellent, beautiful, agreeable, distressed, unfortunate lady, I'm too 305 much your friend and servant ever to let it be said 'twas the means of your being ruined for a woman—by letting you know, she esteemed you more than any other man upon earth.

GRIPE Ruined! What dost thou mean?

BRASS Mean? Why I mean that women always ruin those that love 310 'em—that's the rule.

GRIPE The rule?

BRASS Yes, the rule; why, would you have 'em ruin those that don't? How shall they bring that about?

GRIPE But is there a necessity then, they should ruin somebody?   315

BRASS Yes, marry is there; how would you have 'em support their expense else? Why, sir, you can't conceive now—you can't conceive what Araminta's privy-purse requires. Only her privy-purse, sir! Why, what do you imagine now she gave me for the last letter I carried her from you? 'Tis true, 'twas from a man she liked, else,   320 perhaps, I had had my bones broke. But what do you think she gave me?

GRIPE Why, mayhap—a shilling.

BRASS A guinea, sir, a guinea. You see by that how fond she was on't, by the by. But then, sir, her coach-hire, her chair-hire, her pin-   325 money, her play-money, her china, and her charity—would consume peers. A great soul, a very great soul; but what's the end of all this?

GRIPE Ha?

BRASS Why, I'll tell you what the end is—a nunnery.   330

GRIPE A nunnery!

BRASS A nunnery. In short, she is at last reduced to that extremity, and attacked with such a battalion of duns, that rather than tell her husband (who you know is such a dog, he'd let her go if she did), she has e'en determined to turn papist, and bid the world adieu for   335 life.

GRIPE O terrible! A papist?

BRASS Yes, when a handsome woman has brought herself into dif-ficulties the devil can't help her out of—to a nunnery, that's another rule, sir.   340

GRIPE But, but, but, prithee Brass, but—

BRASS But all the buts in the world, sir, won't stop her; she's a woman of a noble resolution. So, sir, your humble servant. I pity her, I pity you, turtle° and mate; but the fates will have it so. All's packed up, and I am now going to call her a coach; for she resolves to slip off   345 without saying a word, and the next visit she receives from her friends will be through a melancholy grate, with a veil instead of a top-knot.° (*Going*)

GRIPE It must not be, by the powers it must not; she was made for the world, and the world was made for her.   350

BRASS And yet you see, sir, how small a share she has on't.

GRIPE Poor woman! Is there no way to save her?

BRASS Save her! No, how can she be saved? Why she owes above five
hundred pound.

GRIPE Oh! 355

BRASS Five hundred pound, sir, she's like to be saved indeed. Not but
that I know them in this town would give me one of the five, if I
would persuade her to accept of t'other four. But she has forbid me
mentioning it to any soul living, and I have disobeyed her only to
you; and so—I'll go and call a coach. 360

GRIPE Hold—dost think, my poor Brass, one might not order it so, as
to compound° those debts for—for—twelve pence in the pound?

BRASS Sir, d'ye hear? I have already tried 'em with ten shillings, and
not a rogue will prick up his ear at it; though, after all, for three
hundred pounds all in glittering gold, I could set their chaps a- 365
watering. But where's that to be had with honour? There's the
thing, sir—I'll go and call a coach.

GRIPE Hold, once more. I have a note in my closet of two hundred,
ay—and fifty; I'll go and give it her myself.

BRASS You will, very genteel truly. Go, slap dash, and offer a woman 370
of her scruples money bolt in her face! Why, you might as well offer
her a scorpion, and she'd as soon touch it.

GRIPE Shall I carry it to her creditors then, and treat with them?

BRASS Ay; that's a rare thought.

GRIPE Is not it, Brass? 375

BRASS Only one little inconvenience by the way.

GRIPE As how?

BRASS That they are your wife's creditors as well as hers; and perhaps
it might not be altogether so well to see you clearing the debts of
your neighbour's wife, and leaving those of your own unpaid. 380

GRIPE Why that's true now.

BRASS I'm wise you see, sir.

GRIPE Thou art; and I'm but a young lover. But what shall we do
then?

BRASS Why, I'm thinking that if you give me the note, do you see, and 385
that I promise to give you an account of it—

GRIPE Ay, but look you, Brass—

BRASS But look you! Why, what d'ye think I'm a pickpocket? D'ye
think I intend to run away with your note? Your paltry note!

GRIPE I don't say so—I say only that in case— 390

BRASS Case, sir! There's no case but the case I have put you; and
since you heap cases upon cases, where there is but three hundred
rascally pounds in the case—I'll go and call a coach.

GRIPE Prithee don't be so testy; come, no more words, follow me to
my closet and I'll give thee the money.   395

BRASS A terrible effort you make indeed; you are so much in love,
your wits are all upon the wing, just a-going: and for three hundred
pounds you put a stop to their flight. Sir, your wits are worth that,
or your wits are worth nothing. Come away.

GRIPE Well, say no more, thou shalt be satisfied.   400
        Exeunt [Brass and Gripe]
        Enter Dick

DICK S't—Brass! S't—
        Re-enter Brass

BRASS Well, sir?

DICK 'Tis not well, sir, 'tis very ill, sir, we shall be all blown up.°

BRASS What? With pride and plenty?

DICK No sir, with an officious slut that will spoil all. In short, Flip-   405
panta has been telling her mistress and Araminta of my passion for
the young gentlewoman, and truly to oblige me (supposed no ill
match by the by) they are resolved to propose it immediately to her
father.

BRASS That's the devil; we shall come to papers and parchments,   410
jointures and settlements, relations meet on both sides. That's the
devil.

DICK I intended this very day to propose to Flippanta the carrying her
off: and I'm sure the young huswife would have tucked up her
coats° and have marched.   415

BRASS Ay, with the body and the soul of her.

DICK Why then what damned luck is this?

BRASS 'Tis your damned luck, not mine: I have always seen it in your
ugly phiz, in spite of your powdered periwig, pox take ye. He'll be
hanged at last. Why don't you try to get her off yet?   420

DICK I have no money, you dog; you know you have stripped me of
every penny.

BRASS Come, damn it, I'll venture one cargo more upon your rotten
bottom. But if ever I see one glance of your hempen fortune
again, I'm off of your partnership for ever—I shall never thrive   425
with him.

DICK (*aside*) An impudent rogue, but he's in possession of my estate
so I must bear with him.

BRASS Well, come, I'll raise a hundred pounds for your use, upon my
wife's jewels here (*pulling out the necklace*); her necklace shall pawn   430
for't.

DICK Remember though that if things fail, I'm to have the necklace again; you know you agreed to that.

BRASS Yes, and if I make it good, you'll be the better for't; if not, I shall. So you see where the cause° will pinch. 435

DICK Why, you barbarous dog, you won't offer to—

BRASS No words now; about your business, march. Go stay for me at the next tavern. I'll go to Flippanta and try what I can do for you.

DICK Well I'll go, but don't think to—o pox, sir—
Exit Dick

BRASS (*alone*) Will you be gone? A pretty title you'd have to sue me 440 upon truly. If I should have a mind to stand upon the defensive, as perhaps I may, I have done the rascal service enough to lull my conscience upon't I'm sure. But 'tis time enough for that. Let me see—first I'll go to Flippanta, and put a stop to this family way of matchmaking; then sell our necklace for what ready money 'twill 445 produce; and by this time tomorrow I hope we shall be in posession of—t'other jewel here; a precious jewel, as she's set in gold. I believe for the stone itself we may part with't again to a friend—for a tester.
Exit [Brass]

5.1

Gripe's house

Enter Brass and Flippanta

BRASS Well, you agree I'm in the right, don't you?

FLIPPANTA I don't know; if your master has the estate he talks of, why not do't all above board? Well, though I am not much of his mind, I'm much in his interest, and will therefore endeavour to serve him in his own way.

BRASS That's kindly said, my child, and I believe I shall reward thee one of these days with as pretty a fellow to thy husband for't, as—

FLIPPANTA Hold your prating, Jackadandy, and leave me to my business.

BRASS I obey—adieu. (*Kisses her*)

Exit Brass

FLIPPANTA Rascal!

Enter Corinna

CORINNA Ah, Flippanta, I'm ready to sink down; my legs tremble under me, my dear Flippy.

FLIPPANTA And what's the affair?

CORINNA My father's there within, with my mother and Araminta; I never saw him in so good humour in my life.

FLIPPANTA And is that it that frightens you so?

CORINNA Ah, Flippanta, they are just going to speak to him about my marrying the Colonel.

FLIPPANTA Are they so? So much the worse; they're too hasty.

CORINNA O no, not a bit. I slipped out on purpose, you must know, to give 'em an opportunity; would 'twere done already.

FLIPPANTA I tell you no; get you in again immediately and prevent it.

CORINNA My dear, dear, I am not able; I never was in such a way before.

FLIPPANTA Never in a way to be married before, ha? Is not that it?

CORINNA Ah, Lord, if I'm thus before I come to't, Flippanta, what shall I be upon the very spot?

Putting her hand to her heart

Do but feel with what a thumpaty thump it goes.

FLIPPANTA Nay, it does make a filthy bustle, that's the truth on't, child. But I believe I shall make it leap another way, when I tell you, I'm cruelly afraid your father won't consent after all.

CORINNA Why, he won't be the death o'me, will he?

FLIPPANTA I don't know, old folks are cruel; but we'll have a trick for him. Brass and I have been consulting upon the matter, and agreed upon a surer way of doing it in spite of his teeth.   35

CORINNA Ay, marry sir, that were something.

FLIPPANTA But then he must not know a word of anything towards it.

CORINNA No, no.

FLIPPANTA So, get you in immediately.   40

CORINNA (running off) One, two, three and away.

FLIPPANTA And prevent your mother's speaking on't.

CORINNA But is t'other way sure, Flippanta?

FLIPPANTA Fear nothing, 'twill only depend upon you.

CORINNA Nay then—o ho, ho, ho, how pure that is.   45

    Exit Corinna

FLIPPANTA (*alone*) Poor child! We may do what we will with her, as far as marrying her goes; when that's over 'tis possible she mayn't prove altogether so tractable. But who's here? My sharper, I think: yes.

    Enter Moneytrap

MONEYTRAP Well, my best friend, how go matters? Has the restitu-   50
tion been received, ha? Was she pleased with it?

FLIPPANTA Yes, truly, that is, she was pleased to see there was so honest a man in this immoral age.

MONEYTRAP Well, but a—does she know that 'twas I that—

FLIPPANTA Why, you must know I begun to give her a little sort of a   55
hint, and—and so—why, and so she begun to put on a sort of a severe, haughty, reserved, angry, forgiving air; but soft, here she comes. You'll see how you stand with her presently; but don't be afraid—courage!

MONEYTRAP He hem.   60

    Enter Clarissa

'Tis no small piece of good fortune, madam, to find you at home; I have often endeavoured it in vain.

CLARISSA 'Twas then unknown to me, for if I could often receive the visits of so good a friend at home, I should be more reasonably blamed for being so much abroad.   65

MONEYTRAP Madam, you make me—

CLARISSA You are the man of the world whose company I think is most to be desired. I don't compliment you when I tell you so, I assure you.

MONEYTRAP Alas, madam, your poor humble servant—   70

CLARISSA My poor humble servant however (with all the esteem I
have for him) stands suspected with me for a vile trick I doubt he
has played me, which if I could prove upon him, I'm afraid I should
punish him very severely.

MONEYTRAP I hope, madam, you'll believe I am not capable of—   75

CLARISSA Look you, look you, you are capable of whatever you please.
You have a great deal of wit, and know how to give a nice and
gallant turn to everything; but if you will have me continue your
friend, you must leave me in some uncertainty in this matter.

MONEYTRAP Madam, I do then protest to you—   80

CLARISSA Come, protest nothing about it, I am but too penetrating, as
you may perceive; but we sometimes shut our eyes, rather than
break with our friends, for a thorough knowledge of the truth of
this business would make me very seriously angry.

MONEYTRAP 'Tis very certain, madam, that—   85

CLARISSA Come, say no more on't I beseech you; for I'm in a good
deal of heat while I but think on't. If you'll walk in, I'll follow you
presently.

MONEYTRAP Your goodness, madam, is—

FLIPPANTA (*aside to Moneytrap*) Ware, horse.° No fine speeches,   90
you'll spoil all.

MONEYTRAP Thou art a most incomparable person.

FLIPPANTA Nay, it goes rarely; but get you in, and I'll say a little
something to my lady for you while she's warm.

MONEYTRAP But s't, Flippanta, how long dost think she may hold   95
out?

FLIPPANTA Phu, not a twelvemonth.

MONEYTRAP Boo.

FLIPPANTA Away, I say.
Pushing [Moneytrap] out

CLARISSA Is he gone? What a wretch it is! He never was quite such a   100
beast before.

FLIPPANTA Poor mortal, his money's finely laid out truly.

CLARISSA I suppose there may have been much such another scene
within between Araminta and my dear; but I left him so insupport-
ably brisk, 'tis impossible he can have parted with any money. I'm   105
afraid Brass has not succeeded as thou hast done, Flippanta?

FLIPPANTA By my faith but he has, and better too; he presents his
humble duty to Araminta, and has sent her—this.
Showing [Clarissa] the note

CLARISSA A bill from my love for two hundred and fifty pounds. The

monster! He would not part with ten to save his lawful wife from   110
everlasting torment.

FLIPPANTA Never complain of his avarice, madam, as long as you
have his money.

CLARISSA But is not he a beast, Flippanta? Methinks the restitution
looked better by half.   115

FLIPPANTA Madam, the man's beast enough, that's certain. But
which way will you go to receive his beastly money; for I must not
appear with his note.

CLARISSA That's true. Why, send for Mrs Amlet; that's a mighty
useful woman, that Mrs Amlet.   120

FLIPPANTA Marry is she. We should have been basely puzzled how to
dispose of the necklace without her; 'twould have been dangerous
offering it to sale.

CLARISSA It would so, for I know your master has been laying out°
for't amongst the goldsmiths. But I stay here too long. I must in and 125
coquette it a little more to my lover; Araminta will get ground on
me else.

    Exit Clarissa

FLIPPANTA And I'll go send for Mrs Amlet.

    Exit Flippanta

5.2

[Another room in Gripe's house]

*Araminta, Corinna, Gripe, and Moneytrap at a tea-table, very
gay and laughing. Clarissa comes in to them*

OMNES Ha! ha! ha! ha!

MONEYTRAP Mighty well; o mighty well indeed.

CLARISSA Save you, save you good folks; you are all in rare humour
methinks.

GRIPE Why, what should we be otherwise for, madam?   5

CLARISSA Nay, I don't know, not I, my dear, but I han't had
the happiness of seeing you so since our honeymoon was over, I
think.

GRIPE Why, to tell you the truth my dear, 'tis the joy of seeing you at
home. (*Kisses her*) You see what charms you have when you are   10
pleased to make use of 'em.

ARAMINTA Very gallant truly.

CLARISSA Nay, and what's more, you must know he's never to be otherwise henceforwards; we have come to an agreement about it.

MONEYTRAP Why here's my love and I have been upon just such another treaty too.   15

ARAMINTA Well, sure there's some very peaceful star rules at present. Pray heaven continue its reign.

MONEYTRAP Pray do you continue its reign, you ladies (*leering at Clarissa*) for 'tis all in your power.   20

GRIPE My neighbour Moneytrap says true; at least I'll confess frankly (*ogling Araminta*), 'tis in one lady's power to make me the best-humoured man on earth.

MONEYTRAP And I'll answer for another (*ogling Clarissa*) that has the same over me.   25

CLARISSA 'Tis mighty fine, gentlemen, mighty civil husbands indeed.

GRIPE Nay; what I say's true, and so true, that all quarrels being now at an end, I am willing, if you please, to dispense with all that fine company we talked of today, be content with the friendly conversation of our two good neighbours here, and spend all my toying   30
hours alone with my sweet wife.

MONEYTRAP Why, truly, I think now, if these good women pleased, we might make up the prettiest little neighbourly company between our two families, and set a defiance to all the impertinent people in the world.   35

CLARISSA (*aside*) The rascals.

ARAMINTA Indeed, I doubt you'd soon grow weary if we grew fond.

GRIPE Never, never, for our wives have wit, neighbour, and that never palls.   40

CLARISSA And our husbands have generosity, Araminta, and that seldom palls.

GRIPE So, that's a wipe for me now, because I did not give her a new-year's gift last time; but be good and I'll think of some tea-cups for you next year.   45

MONEYTRAP And perhaps I mayn't forget a fan, or as good a thing—hum, hussy?

CLARISSA Well, upon these encouragements, Araminta, we'll try how good we can be.

GRIPE Well, this goes most rarely. (*Aside*) Poor Moneytrap, he little   50
thinks what makes his wife so easy in his company.

MONEYTRAP (*aside*) I can but pity poor neighbour Gripe. Lard, Lard, what a fool does his wife and I make of him?

CLARISSA (*aside to Araminta*) Are not these two wretched rogues, Araminta?   55
ARAMINTA (*aside to Clarissa*) They are indeed.
    Enter Jessamin
JESSAMIN Sir, here's Mr Clip the goldsmith desires to speak with you.
GRIPE Cods so, perhaps some news of your necklace, my dear.
CLARISSA That would be news indeed.   60
GRIPE Let him come in.
    [*Exit Jessamin*]
    Enter Mr Clip
GRIPE Mr Clip, your servant; I'm glad to see you. How do you do?
CLIP At your service, sir, very well. Your servant, Madam Gripe.
CLARISSA (*aside*) Horrid fellow!
GRIPE Well, Mr Clip, no news yet of my wife's necklace?   65
CLIP If you please to let me speak with you in the next room, I have something to say to you.
GRIPE Ay, with all my heart. Shut the door after us.
    They come forward, and the scene shuts behind them
    Well, any news?
CLIP Look you, sir, here's a necklace brought me to sell, at least; very   70
like that you described to me.
GRIPE Let's see't. *Victoria!*° The very same. Ah my dear Mr Clip. (*Kisses him*) But who brought it you? You should have seized him.
CLIP 'Twas a young fellow that I know; I can't tell whether he may be guilty, though it's like enough. But he has only left it me now to   75
show a brother of our trade, and will call upon me again presently.
GRIPE Wheedle him hither, dear Mr Clip. Here's my neighbour Moneytrap in the house; he's a justice, and will commit him presently.
CLIP 'Tis enough.   80
    Enter Brass
GRIPE O, my friend Brass!
BRASS Hold, sir, I think that's a gentleman I'm looking for. Mr Clip, your servant. What, are you acquainted here? I have just been at your shop.
CLIP I only stepped here to show Mr Gripe the necklace you left.   85
BRASS (*to Gripe*) Why, sir, do you understand jewels? I thought you had dealt only in gold. But I smoke the matter. Hark you—a word in your ear—you are going to play the gallant again, and make a purchase on't for Araminta; ha, ha?
GRIPE Where had you the necklace?   90

BRASS Look you, don't trouble yourself about that. It's in commission
    with me,° and I can help you to a pennyworth° on't.

GRIPE A pennyworth on't, villain? (*Strikes at him*)

BRASS Villain! A hey, a hey. Is't you or me, Mr Clip, he's pleased to
    compliment?   95

CLIP What do you think on't, sir?

BRASS Think on't? Now the devil fetch me if I know what to think
    on't.

GRIPE You'll sell a pennyworth, rogue, of a thing you have stolen from
    me!   100

BRASS Stolen! Pray, sir, what wine have you drank today? It has a very
    merry effect upon you.

GRIPE You villain! Either give me an account how you stole it, or—

BRASS O ho, sir, if you please don't carry your jest too far; I don't
    understand hard words, I give you warning on't. If you han't a   105
    mind to buy the necklace, you may let it alone. I know how to
    dispose on't. What a pox!

GRIPE O, you shan't have that trouble, sir. Dear Mr Clip, you may
    leave the necklace here. I'll call at your shop and thank you for your
    care.   110

CLIP Sir, your humble servant. (*Going*)

BRASS O ho, Mr Clip, if you please, sir, this won't do. (*Stopping him*) I
    don't understand raillery in such matters.

CLIP I leave it with Mr Gripe; do you and he dispute it.
        Exit Clip

BRASS Ay, but 'tis from you, by your leave, sir, that I expect it. (*Going*   115
    after him)

GRIPE You expect, you rogue, to make your escape, do you? But I have
    other accounts besides this to make up with you. To be sure the dog
    has cheated me of the two hundred and fifty pound. Come, villain,
    give me an account of—

BRASS Account of! Sir, give me an account of my necklace, or I'll   120
    make such a noise in your house I'll raise the devil in't.

GRIPE Well said, courage.

BRASS Blood and thunder, give it me, or—

GRIPE Come, hush, be wise, and I'll make no noise of this affair.

BRASS You'll make no noise! But I'll make a noise, and a damned noise   125
    too. O, don't think to—

GRIPE I tell thee I will not hang thee.

BRASS But I tell you I will hang you if you don't give me my necklace.
    I will, rot me.

GRIPE Speak softly, be wise, how came it thine? Who gave it thee?   130
BRASS A gentleman, a friend of mine.
GRIPE What's his name?
BRASS His name? I'm in such a passion I have forgot it.
GRIPE Ah, brazen rogue—thou hast stole it from my wife; 'tis the
same she lost six weeks ago.   135
BRASS This has not been in England a month.
GRIPE You are a son of a whore.
BRASS Give me my necklace.
GRIPE Give me my two hundred and fifty pound note.
BRASS Yet I offer peace. One word without passion; the case stands   140
thus. Either I am out of my wits, or you are out of yours; now 'tis
plain I am not out of my wits, *ergo*° —
GRIPE My bill, hang dog, or I'll strangle thee.
        They struggle
BRASS Murder, murder.
        Enter Clarissa, Araminta, Corinna, Flippanta, and Moneytrap
FLIPPANTA What's the matter? What's the matter here?   145
GRIPE I'll matter him.
CLARISSA Who makes thee cry out thus, poor Brass?
BRASS Why, your husband, madam, he's in his altitudes° here.
GRIPE Robber.
BRASS Here, he has cheated me of a diamond necklace.   150
CORINNA Who, papa? Ah dear me.
CLARISSA Prithee what's the meaning of this great commotion,° my
dear?
GRIPE The meaning is that—I'm quite out of breath—this son of a
whore has got your necklace, that's all.   155
CLARISSA My necklace!
GRIPE That birdlime there—stole it.
CLARISSA Impossible!
BRASS Madam, you see master's a little—touched, that's all. Twenty
ounces of blood let loose would set all right again.   160
GRIPE Here, call a constable presently. Neighbour Moneytrap, you'll
commit him.
BRASS D'ye hear? D'ye hear? See how wild he looks? How his eyes roll
in his head? Tie him down, or he'll do some mischief or other.
GRIPE Let me come at him.   165
CLARISSA Hold! Prithee, my dear, reduce things to a little temper-
ance, and let us coolly into the secret of this disagreeable rupture.
GRIPE Well then, without passion—why, you must know—but I'll

have him hanged—you must know that he came to Mr Clip, to Mr
Clip the dog did—with a necklace to sell; so Mr Clip having notice   170
before that—can you deny this, sirrah—that you had lost yours,
brings it to me. Look at it here, do you know it again? (*To Brass*) Ah
you traitor!

BRASS He makes me mad; here's an appearance of something now to
the company, and yet nothing in't in the bottom.   175

    Enter Constable

CLARISSA [*aside to Flippanta, showing the necklace*] Flippanta!

FLIPPANTA [*aside to Clarissa*] 'Tis i'faith; here's some mystery in
this—we must look about us.

CLARISSA [*aside to Flippanta*] The safest way is point blank to disown
the necklace.   180

FLIPPANTA [*aside to Clarissa*] Right, stick to that.

GRIPE Well, madam, do you know your old acquaintance, ha?

CLARISSA Why, truly, my dear, though (as you may all imagine) I
should be very glad to recover so valuable a thing as my necklace,
yet I must be just to all the world; this necklace is not mine.   185

BRASS Huzza—here Constable, do your duty; Mr Justice, I demand
my necklace, and satisfaction of him.

GRIPE I'll die before I part with it. I'll keep it, and have him hanged.

CLARISSA But be a little calm, my dear, do my bird, and then thou'lt
be able to judge rightly of things.   190

GRIPE O good lack; o good lack.

CLARISSA No, but don't give way to fury and interest both; either of
'em are passions strong enough to lead a wise man out of the way.
The necklace not being really mine, give it the man again, and come
drink a dish of tea.   195

BRASS Ay, madam says right.

GRIPE Oons, if you, with your addle head, don't know your own
jewels, I with my solid one do. And if I part with it, may famine be
my portion.

CLARISSA But don't swear and curse thyself at this fearful rate, don't 200
my dove. Be temperate in your words, and just in all your actions;
'twill bring a blessing upon you and your family.

GRIPE Bring thunder and lightning upon me and my family, if I part
with my necklace.

CLARISSA Why, you'll have the lightning burn your house about your   205
ears, my dear, if you go on in these practices.

MONEYTRAP (*aside*) A most excellent woman this.

    Enter Mrs Amlet

GRIPE I'll keep my necklace.

BRASS Will you so? Then here comes one has a title to it if I han't; let Dick bring himself off with her as he can. Mrs Amlet you are come in a very good time; you lost a necklace t'other day, and who do you think has got it? 210

MRS AMLET Marry, that know I not; I wish I did.

BRASS Why then here's Mr Gripe has it, and swears 'tis his wife's.

GRIPE And so I do, sirrah—look here, mistress, do you pretend this is yours? 215

MRS AMLET Not for the round world I would not say it; I only kept it to do madam a small courtesy, that's all.

CLARISSA (aside to Flippanta) Ah, Flippanta, all will out now.

GRIPE Courtesy! What courtesy? 220

MRS AMLET A little money only that madam had present need of; please to pay me that and I demand no more.

BRASS (aside) So here's fresh game. I have started a new hare I find.

GRIPE (to Clarissa) How, forsooth, is this true?

CLARISSA You are in a humour at present, love, to believe anything, so I won't take the pains to contradict it. 225

BRASS (aside) This damned necklace will spoil all our affairs; this is Dick's luck again.

GRIPE Are you not ashamed of these ways? Do you see how you are exposed before your best friends here? Don't you blush at it? 230

CLARISSA I do blush, my dear, but 'tis for you, that here it should appear to the world, you keep me so bare of money I am forced to pawn my jewels.

GRIPE Impudent huswife! (Raising his hand to strike her)

CLARISSA Softly chicken; you might have prevented all this, by giving me the two hundred and fifty pound you sent to Araminta e'en now. 235

BRASS You see, sir, I delivered your note. How I have been abused today!

GRIPE (aside) I'm betrayed—jades on both sides, I see that.

MONEYTRAP But, madam, madam, is this true I hear? Have you taken a present of two hundred and fifty pound? Pray what were you to return for these pounds, madam, ha? 240

ARAMINTA Nothing, my dear; I only took 'em to reimburse you of about the same sum you sent to Clarissa.

MONEYTRAP Hum, hum, hum. 245

GRIPE How, gentlewoman? Did you receive money from him?

CLARISSA O, my dear, 'twas only in jest. I knew you'd give it again to his wife.

MRS AMLET But amongst all this tintamar, I don't hear a word of my
hundred pounds. Is it madam will pay me, or master?   250

GRIPE I pay? The devil shall pay.

CLARISSA Look you, my dear, malice apart, pay Mrs Amlet her
money, and I'll forgive you the wrong you intended my bed with
Araminta. Am not I a good wife now?

GRIPE I burst with rage, and will get rid of this noose though I tuck   255
myself up in another.

MONEYTRAP Nay, pray, e'en tuck me up with you.
    Exeunt Moneytrap and Gripe [and Constable]

CLARISSA and ARAMINTA Bye dearies.
    Enter Dick

CORINNA Look, look Flippanta, here's the Colonel come at last.

DICK Ladies I ask your pardon I have stayed so long, but—   260

MRS AMLET Ah rogue's face, have I got thee? Old good-for-nought!
Sirrah, sirrah, do you think to amuse° me with your marriages and
your great fortunes? Thou hast played me a rare prank, by my
conscience. Why, you ungracious rascal, what do you think will be
the end of all this? Now heaven forgive me, but I have a great mind   265
to hang thee for't.

CORINNA She talks to him very familiarly, Flippanta.

FLIPPANTA So methinks, by my faith.

BRASS (*aside*) Now the rogue's star is making an end of him.

DICK (*aside*) What shall I do with her?   270

MRS AMLET Do but look at him, my dames; he has the countenance
of a cherubim, but he's a rogue in his heart.

CLARISSA What is the meaning of all this, Mrs Amlet?

MRS AMLET The meaning, good lack. Why this all-to-be-powdered
rascal here is my son an't please you; ha, graceless? Now I'll make   275
you own your mother, vermin.

CLARISSA What, the Colonel your son?

MRS AMLET 'Tis Dick, madam, that rogue Dick I have so often told
you of, with tears trickling down my old cheeks.

ARAMINTA The woman's mad; it can never be.   280

MRS AMLET Speak rogue, am I not thy mother? Ha? Did I not bring
thee forth? Say then.

DICK What will you have me say? You had a mind to ruin me, and you
have done't; would you do any more?

CLARISSA Then, sir, you are son to good Mrs Amlet?   285

MRS AMLET And have had the assurance to put upon us all this while?

FLIPPANTA And the confidence to think of marrying Corinna?

BRASS And the impudence to hire me for your servant, who am as well born as yourself.

CLARISSA Indeed I think he should be corrected 290

ARAMINTA Indeed I think he deserves to be cudgelled.

FLIPPANTA Indeed I think he might be pumped.

BRASS Indeed I think he will be hanged.

MRS AMLET Good lack-a-day, good lack-a-day, there's no need to be so smart upon him neither. If he is not a gentleman, he's a gentle- 295 man's fellow. Come hither, Dick, they shan't run thee down neither. Cock up thy hat, Dick, and tell 'em, though Mrs Amlet is thy mother, she can make thee amends, with ten thousand good pounds to buy thee some lands, and build thee a house in the midst on't.

OMNES How! 300

CLARISSA Ten thousand pounds, Mrs Amlet?

MRS AMLET Yes forsooth; though I should lose the hundred you pawned your necklace for. Tell 'em of that, Dick.

CORINNA Look you, Flippanta, I can hold no longer, and I hate to see the young man abused. And so, sir, if you please, I'm your friend 305 and servant, and what's mine is yours, and when our estates are put together, I don't doubt but we shall do as well as the best of 'em.

DICK Say'st thou so, my little queen? Why then if dear mother will give us her blessing, the parson shall give us a tack.° We'll get her a score of grandchildren, and a merry house we'll make her. 310

They kneel to Mrs Amlet

MRS AMLET Ah—ha, ha, ha, ha, the pretty pair, the pretty pair; rise my chickens, rise, rise and face the proudest of 'em. And if madam does not deign to give her consent, a fig for her, Dick. Why, how now?

CLARISSA Pray, Mrs Amlet, don't be in a passion; the girl is my 315 husband's girl, and if you can have his consent, upon my word you shall have mine, for anything belongs to him.

FLIPPANTA Then all's peace again, but we have been more lucky than wise.

ARAMINTA And I suppose, for us, Clarissa, we are to go on with our 320 dears, as we used to do.

CLARISSA Just in the same tract, for this late treaty of agreement with 'em was so unnatural, you see it could not hold. But 'tis just as well with us, as if it had. Well, 'tis a strange fate, good folks. But while you live, everything gets well out of a broil, but a husband. 325

Epilogue

Spoke by Mrs Barry

I've heard wise men in politics lay down
What feats by little England might be done,
Were all agreed, and all would act as one.
Ye wives a useful hint from this might take,
The heavy, old, despotic kingdom shake, 5
And make your matrimonial *monsieurs* quake.
Our heads are feeble, and we're cramped by laws;
Our hands are weak, and not too strong our cause:
Yet would those heads and hands, such as they are,
In firm confed'racy resolve on war,° 10
You'd find your tyrants—what I've found my dear.
What only two united can produce
You've seen tonight, a sample for your use.
Single, we found we nothing could obtain;
We join our force—and we subdued our men. 15
Believe me, my dear sex, they are not brave;
Try each your man, you'll quickly find your slave.
I know they'll make campaigns, risk blood and life,
But this is a more terrifying strife;
They'll stand a shot, who'll tremble at a wife. 20
Beat then your drums, and your shrill trumpets sound,
Let all your visits of your feasts resound,
And deeds of war in cups of tea go round.
The stars are with you, fate is in your hand,
In twelve months' time you've vanquished half the land; 25
Be wise, and keep 'em under good command.
This year will to your glory long be known,
And deathless ballads hand your triumphs down;
Your late achievements ever will remain,
For though you cannot boast of many slain, 30
Your pris'ners show, you've made a brave campaign.

A JOURNEY TO LONDON

THE CHARACTERS OF THE PLAY

Sir Francis Headpiece,° a country gentleman
Lord Loverule
Sir Charles
Uncle Richard, uncle to Sir Francis
Squire Humphry, son to Sir Francis
Colonel Courtly
John Moody, servant to Sir Francis
James, servant to Uncle Richard
[George and Tom, servants to Sir Francis]
[Moneybag, steward to Lord Loverule]
[Shortyard, a mercer]°
[Captain Toupee]°
[Servants to Mrs Motherly]

Lady Headpiece
Miss Betty, her daughter
Lady Arabella, wife to Lord Loverule
Clarinda, a young unmarried lady
Mrs Motherly,° one that lets lodgings
Martilla, her niece
[Deborah, maid to Mrs Motherly]
[Doll Tripe,° cook to the Headpieces]
[Mrs Handy, maid to Lady Headpiece]
[Trusty, maid to Lady Arabella]

1.1

Uncle Richard's house

Enter Uncle Richard alone

UNCLE RICHARD What prudent cares does this deep foreseeing nation take for the support of its worshipful° families! In order to which, and that they may not fail to be always significant and useful in their country, it is a settled foundation-point, that every child that is born shall be a beggar—except one; and that he—shall be a fool. My grandfather was bred a fool, as the country report; my father was a fool—as my mother used to say; my brother was a fool, to my own knowledge, though a great justice of the peace; and he has left a son, that will make his son a fool, or I am mistaken. The lad is now fourteen years old, and but just out of his psalter.° As to his honoured father, my much esteemed nephew, here I have him (*showing a letter*) in this profound epistle (which I have just now received); there is the top and bottom of him. Forty years and two is the age of him; in which it is computed by his butler, his own person has drank two and thirty ton of ale. The rest of his time has been employed in persecuting all the poor four-legged creatures round, that would but run away fast enough from him to give him the high-mettled pleasure of running after them. In this noble employ, he has broke his right arm, his left leg, and both his collar-bones—once he broke his neck, but that did him no harm; a nimble hedge-leaper, a brother of the stirrup that was by, whipped off of his horse and mended it. His estate being left him with two join-tures and three weighty mortgages upon it, he, to make all easy, and pay his brother's and sister's portions, married a profuse young housewife for love, with never a penny of money. Having done all this, like his brave ancestors for the support of the family, he now finds children and interest-money make such a bawling about his ears that he has taken the friendly advice of his neighbour the good Lord Courtlove, to run his estate two thousand pounds more in debt, that he may retrieve his affairs by being a Parliament-man and bringing his wife to London, to play off a hundred pounds at dice with ladies of quality before breakfast. But let me read this wise-acre's letter, once over again. [*Reads*] 'Most honoured uncle: I do not doubt but you have much rejoiced at my success in my election. It has cost me some money, I own: but what of all that! I am a

5

10

15

20

25

30

35

Parliament-man, and that will set all to rights. I have lived in the
country all my days, 'tis true; but what then! I have made speeches
at the sessions,° and in the vestry° too, and can elsewhere perhaps,
as well as some others that do; and I have a noble friend hard by,
who has let me into some small knowledge of what's what at West-   40
minster and so, that I may be always at hand to serve my country, I
have consulted with my wife about taking a house at London, and
bringing her and my family up to town; which, her opinion is, will
be the rightest thing in the world.' My wife's opinion about
bringing her to London? I'll read no more of thee—beast.   45
    Strikes the letter down with his stick
    Enter James hastily

JAMES Sir, sir, do you hear the news? They are all a-coming.

UNCLE RICHARD Ay sirrah, I hear it, with a pox to it.

JAMES Sir, here's John Moody arrived already; he's stumping about
the streets in his dirty boots, and asking every man he meets if they
can tell where he may have a good lodging for a Parliament-man,   50
till he can hire such a house as becomes him. He tells them his lady
and all the family are coming too, and that they are so nobly
attended, they care not a fig for anybody. Sir, they have added two
cart-horses to the four old geldings, because my lady will have it
said she came to town in her coach and six, and—ha, ha—heavy   55
George the ploughman rides postilion.

UNCLE RICHARD Very well; the journey begins as it should do. James.

JAMES Sir.

UNCLE RICHARD Dost know whether they bring all the children with
them?   60

JAMES Only Squire Humphry and Miss Betty, sir; the other six are
put to board at half-a-crown a week a head, with Joan Growse at
Smoke-dunghill Farm.

UNCLE RICHARD The Lord have mercy upon all good folks;
what work will these people make? Dost know when they'll be   65
here?

JAMES John says, sir, they'd have been here last night, but that the old
wheezy-belly horse tired, and the two fore-wheels came crash down
at once in Waggonrut Lane. Sir, they were cruelly loaden, as I
understand; my lady herself, he says, laid on four mail-trunks,   70
besides the great deal-box, which fat Tom sat upon behind.

UNCLE RICHARD Soh!

JAMES Then within the coach there was Sir Francis, my lady, the
great fat lap-dog, Squire Humphry, Miss Betty, my lady's maid

Mrs Handy, and Doll Tripe the cook; but she puked with sitting   75
backward, so they mounted her into the coach-box.

UNCLE RICHARD Very well.

JAMES Then sir, for fear of a famine before they should get to the baiting-place,° there was such baskets of plumcake, Dutch ginger-
bread, Cheshire cheese, Naples biscuits, macaroons, neats' tongues,   80
and cold boiled beef—and in case of sickness, such bottles of
usquebaugh,° black-cherry brandy, cinnamon-water, sack, tent,
and strong-beer, as made the old coach crack again.

UNCLE RICHARD Well said!

JAMES And for defence of this good cheer, and my lady's little pearl   85
necklace, there was the family basket-hilt sword,° the great Turkish
scimitar, the old blunderbuss, a good bag of bullets, and a great
horn of gunpowder.

UNCLE RICHARD Admirable!

JAMES Then for band-boxes, they were so bepiled up to Sir Francis's   90
nose, that he could only peep out at a chance hole with one eye, as if
he were viewing the country through a perspective-glass. But sir, if
you please, I'll go look after John Moody a little, for fear of accidents; for he never was in London before, you know, but one week,
and then he was kidnapped into a house of ill repute, where he   95
exchanged all his money and clothes for a—um. So I'll go look after
him, sir.

          Exit [James]

UNCLE RICHARD Nay, I don't doubt but this wise expedition will be
attended with more adventures than one. This noble head and sup-
porter of his family will, as an honest country gentleman, get credit   100
enough amongst the tradesmen to run so far in debt in one session
as will make him just fit for a jail when he's dropped at the next
election. He will make speeches in the house, to show the government of what importance he can be to them, by which they will see
he can be of no importance at all; and he will find in time, that he   105
stands valued at (if he votes right) being sometimes—invited to
dinner. Then his wife (who has ten times more of a jade about her
than she yet knows of) will so improve in this rich soil, she will, in
one month, learn every vice the finest lady in the town can teach
her. She will be extremely courteous to the fops who make love to   110
her in jest, and she will be extremely grateful to those who do it in
earnest. She will visit all ladies that will let her into their houses,
and she will run in debt to all the shopkeepers that will let her into
their books. In short, before her husband has got five pound by a

speech at Westminster, she will have lost five hundred at cards and   115
dice in the parish of St James's.° Wife and family to London with a
pox!

Going off

1.2

[A room in Mrs Motherly's house]

Enter James and John Moody

JAMES Dear John Moody, I am so glad to see you in London once
more.

JOHN MOODY And I you, dear Mr James. Give me a kiss. [*They kiss*]
Why, that's friendly.

JAMES I wish they had been so, John, that you met with when you   5
were here before.

JOHN MOODY Ah—murrain upon all rogues and whores, I say; but I
am grown so cunning now, the deel himself can't handle me. I have
made a notable bargain for these lodgings here; we are to pay but
five pounds a week, and have all the house to ourselves.   10

JAMES Where are the people that belong to it to be then?

JOHN MOODY O, there's only the gentlewoman, her two maids, and a
cousin—a very pretty civil young woman truly; and the maids are
the merriest grigs—

JAMES Have a care, John.   15

JOHN MOODY O, fear nothing, we did so play together last night.

JAMES Hush, here comes my master.

Enter Uncle Richard

UNCLE RICHARD What! John has taken these lodgings, has he?

JAMES Yes sir, he has taken 'em.

UNCLE RICHARD Oh John! How dost do, honest John? I am glad to   20
see thee with all my heart.

JOHN MOODY I humbly thank your worship. I'm staut still, and a
faithful awd servant to th' family. Heaven prosper aw that belong
to't.

UNCLE RICHARD What, they are all upon the road?   25

JOHN MOODY As mony as the awd coach would hauld, sir; the Lord
send 'em well to tawn.

UNCLE RICHARD And well out on't again, John, ha!

JOHN MOODY Ah sir! You are a wise man, so am I; home's home, I

say. I wish we get any good here. I's sure we ha' got little upo' the   30
road. Some mischief or other, aw the day long. Slap goes one thing,
crack goes another; my lady cries out for driving fast; the awd
cattle° are for going slow; Roger whips, they stand still and kick;
nothing but a sort of a contradiction aw the journey long. My lady
would gladly have been here last night sir, though there were no   35
lodgings got; but her ladyship said, she did naw care for that—
she'd lie in the inn where the horses stood, as long as it was in
London.

UNCLE RICHARD These ladies, these ladies, John—

JOHN MOODY Ah sir, I have seen a little of 'em, though not so much   40
as my betters. Your worship is naw married yet?

UNCLE RICHARD No, John, no; I'm an old bachelor still.

JOHN MOODY Heavens bless you and preserve you, sir.

UNCLE RICHARD I think you have lost your good-woman, John?

JOHN MOODY No sir, that have I not; Bridget sticks to me still. Sir,   45
she was for coming to London too, but no, says I, there may be
mischief enough done without you.

UNCLE RICHARD Why that was bravely spoken, John, and like a man.

JOHN MOODY Sir, were my measter but hafe the mon that I am,
gadswookers—though he'll speak stautly too sometimes, but then   50
he conno hawd it; no, he conno hawd it.

    Enter Maid

MAID Mr Moody, Mr Moody, here's the coach come.

JOHN MOODY Already? No, sure.

MAID Yes, yes, it's at the door, they are getting out; my mistress is run
to receive 'em.   55

JOHN MOODY And so will I, as in duty bound.

    Exeunt John and Maid

UNCLE RICHARD And I will stay here, not being in duty bound, to do
the honours of this house.

    *Enter Sir Francis, Lady [Headpiece], Squire Humphry, Miss
    Betty, Mrs Handy, Doll Tripe,° John Moody, and Mrs
    Motherly [with Deborah]*

LADY HEADPIECE Do you hear, Moody, let all the things be first laid
down here, and then carried where they'll be used.   60

JOHN MOODY They shall, an't please your ladyship.

LADY HEADPIECE What, my Uncle Richard here to receive us! This is
kind indeed: sir, I am extremely glad to see you.

UNCLE RICHARD Niece, your servant. (*Salutes her*) I am extremely
sorry to see you in the worst place I know in the world for a good   65

woman to grow better in. Nephew, I am your servant too; but I
don't know how to bid you welcome.

SIR FRANCIS I am sorry for that, sir.

UNCLE RICHARD Nay, 'tis for your own sake; I'm not concerned.

SIR FRANCIS I hope, uncle, I shall give you such weighty reasons for   70
what I have done, as shall convince you I am a prudent man.

UNCLE RICHARD (*aside*) That wilt thou never convince me of, whilst
thou shalt live.

SIR FRANCIS Here Humphry, come up to your uncle. Sir, this is your
godson.   75

SQUIRE HUMPHRY Honoured uncle and godfather, I crave leave to
ask your blessing. (*Kneels*)

UNCLE RICHARD (*aside*) Thou art a numbskull, I see already. [*Aloud*]
There, thou hast it.

> *Puts his hand on his head*

And if it will do thee any good, may it be, to make thee at least as   80
wise a man as thy father.

LADY HEADPIECE Miss Betty, don't you see your uncle?

UNCLE RICHARD And for thee my dear, mayst thou be at least as good
a woman as thy mother.

MISS BETTY I wish I may ever be so handsome, sir.   85

UNCLE RICHARD (*aside*) Ha! Miss Pert! Now that's a thought that
seems to have been hatched in the girl on this side Highgate.°

SIR FRANCIS Her tongue is a little nimble, sir.

LADY HEADPIECE That's only from her country education, Sir
Francis. She has been kept there too long. I therefore brought her   90
to London, sir, to learn more reserve and modesty.

UNCLE RICHARD O, the best place in the world for it. Every woman
she meets will teach her something of it. There's the good
gentlewoman of the house, looks like a knowing person; even she
perhaps will be so good to read her a lesson, now and then, upon   95
that subject. (*Aside*) An errant° bawd, or I have no skill in
physiognomy.

MRS MOTHERLY Alas, sir, Miss won't stand long in need of my poor
instructions; if she does, they'll be always at her service.

LADY HEADPIECE Very obliging indeed, Mrs Motherly.   100

SIR FRANCIS Very kind and civil truly; I believe we are got into a
mighty good house here.

UNCLE RICHARD (*aside*) For good business° very probable. [*Aloud*]
Well niece, your servant for tonight; you have a great deal of affairs
upon your hands here, so I won't hinder you.   105

LADY HEADPIECE I believe, sir, I shan't have much less every day, while I stay in this town, of one sort or other.

UNCLE RICHARD Why, 'tis a town of much action indeed.

MISS BETTY And my mother did not come to it to be idle, sir.

UNCLE RICHARD Nor you neither, I dare say, young mistress.   110

MISS BETTY I hope not, sir.

UNCLE RICHARD Um! Miss Mettle.
          Going, Sir Francis following him
Where are you going, nephew?

SIR FRANCIS Only to attend you to the door, sir.

UNCLE RICHARD Phu! No ceremony with me; you'll find I shall use   115
none with you, or your family.

SIR FRANCIS I must do as you command me, sir.
          Exit [Uncle Richard]

MISS BETTY This Uncle Richard, papa, seems but a crusty sort of an old fellow.

SIR FRANCIS He is a little odd, child, but you must be very civil to   120
him, for he has a great deal of money, and nobody knows who he may give it to.

LADY HEADPIECE Phu, a fig for his money; you have so many projects of late about money, since you are a Parliament-man. We must make ourselves slaves to his testy humours seven years perhaps, in   125
hopes to be his heirs; and then he'll be just old enough to marry his maid. But pray let us take care of our things here; are they all brought in yet?

MRS HANDY Almost, my lady; there are only some of the band-boxes behind, and a few odd things.   130

LADY HEADPIECE Let 'em be fetched in presently.
          [Enter servants, with bandboxes and other household articles]

MRS HANDY They are here; come, bring the things in. Is there all yet?

SERVANT All but the great basket of apples, and the goose pie.
          Enter [Doll Tripe the] Cookmaid°

COOK Ah my lady! We're aw undone, the goose pie's gwon.

ALL Gone?   135

SIR FRANCIS The goose pie gone? How?

COOK Why sir, I had got it fast under my arm to bring it in, but being almost dark, up comes two of these thin starved London rogues. One gives me a great kick o' the—here,
          Laying her hand upon her backside
while t'other hungry varlet twitcht° the dear pie out of my hands,   140
and away they run dawn street like two greyhounds. I cried out fire!

267

But heavy George and fat Tom are after 'em with a vengeance; they'll sawce their jackets for 'em,° I'll warrant 'em.

Enter George with a bloody face, and Tom

So, have you catcht 'em?

GEORGE Catcht 'em! The gallows catch 'em for me. I had naw run 145
hafe the length of our bearn, before somewhat fetcht me such a wherry across the shins, that dawn came I flop o' my feace all along in the channel, and thought I should ne'er ha' gotten up again; but Tom has skaward after them, and cried murder as he'd been stuck.° 150

COOK Yes, and straight upo' that, swap comes somewhat across my forehead, with such a force that dawn came I, like an ox.

SQUIRE HUMPHRY So, the poor pie's quite gone then.

TOM Gone, young measter? Yeaten I believe by this time. These I suppose are what they call sharpers in this country. 155

SQUIRE HUMPHRY It was a rare good pie.

COOK As e'er these hands put pepper to.

LADY HEADPIECE Pray Mrs Motherly, do they make a practice of these things often here?

MRS MOTHERLY Madam, they'll twitch a rump of beef out of a boil- 160
ing copper;° and for a silver tankard, they make no more conscience of that than if it were a Tunbridge sugar-box.°

SIR FRANCIS I wish the coach and horses, George, were safe got to the inn. Do you and Tom take special care that nobody runs away with them as you go thither. 165

GEORGE I believe sir, aur cattle woant yeasily be run away with tonight; but we'st take best care we con of them, poor sauls!

[*Exit Cookmaid*]
Exit [*George*]

SIR FRANCIS Do so, pray now.

SQUIRE HUMPHRY Feather, I had rather they had run away with heavy George than the goose pie; a slice of it before supper tonight 170
would have been pure.

LADY HEADPIECE This boy is always thinking of his belly.

SIR FRANCIS But my dear, you may allow him to be a little hungry after a journey.

LADY HEADPIECE Pray, good Sir Francis, he has been constantly eat- 175
ing in the coach, and out of the coach, above seven hours this day. I wish my poor girl could eat a quarter as much.

MISS BETTY Mama, I could eat a good deal more than I do, but then I should grow fat mayhap, like him, and spoil my shape.

LADY HEADPIECE Mrs Motherly, will you be so kind to tell them   180
where they shall carry the things.

MRS MOTHERLY Madam, I'll do the best I can. I doubt our closets
will scarce hold 'em all, but we have garrets and cellars, which, with
the help of hiring a storeroom, I hope may do. (*To Tom*) Sir, will
you be so good to help my maids a little in carrying away the   185
things?

TOM With all my heart, forsooth, if I con but see my way; but these
whoresons have awmost knockt my eyen awt.

> [*Tom and servants carry*] *off the things*

MRS MOTHERLY Will your ladyship please to refresh yourself with a
dish of tea, after your fatigue? I think I have pretty good.   190

LADY HEADPIECE If you please, Mrs Motherly.

SQUIRE HUMPHRY Would not a good tankard of strong beer, nutmeg,
and sugar do better, feather, with a toast and some cheese?

SIR FRANCIS I think it would, son; here, John Moody, get us a tankard
of good hearty stuff presently.   195

JOHN MOODY Sir, here's Norfolk-nog to be had at next door.

SQUIRE HUMPHRY That's best of all, feather; but make haste with it,
John.

> *Exit* [*John*] *Moody*

LADY HEADPIECE Well, I wonder, Sir Francis, you will encourage
that lad to swill his guts thus with such beastly, lubberly liquor; if it   200
were Burgundy, or Champagne, something might be said for't.
They'd perhaps give him some wit and spirit; but such heavy,
muddy stuff as this will make him quite stupid.

SIR FRANCIS Why you know, my dear, I have drank good ale and
strong beer these thirty years, and by your permission I don't know   205
that I want wit.

MISS BETTY But you might have had more, papa, if you'd have been
governed by my mother.

> *Enter John Moody with a tankard* [*and other necessaries for*
> *supper*]
> [*Exit John Moody*]

SIR FRANCIS Daughter, he that is governed by his wife has no wit at
all.   210

MISS BETTY Then I hope I shall marry a fool, father, for I shall love to
govern dearly.

SIR FRANCIS Here Humphry, here's to thee. (*Drinks*) You are too pert,
child; it don't do well in a young woman.

LADY HEADPIECE Pray Sir Francis, don't snub her. She has a fine   215 growing spirit, and if you check her so, you'll make her as dull as her brother there.

SQUIRE HUMPHRY (*after drinking a long draught*) Indeed mother, I think my sister is too forward.

MISS BETTY You? You think I'm too forward? What have you to do to   220
think, brother Heavy? You are too fat to think of anything but your belly.

LADY HEADPIECE Well said, Miss; he's none of your master, though he's your elder brother.

Enter George

GEORGE Sir, I have no good opinion of this tawn; it's made up of   225
mischief, I think.

SIR FRANCIS Why, what's the matter now?

GEORGE I'se tell your worship; before we were gotten to the street end, a great luggerheaded cart, with wheels as thick as a good brick wall, layd hawld of the coach, and has pood it aw to bits. An this be   230
London, wa'd we were all weel i'th' country again.

MISS BETTY What have you to do, sir, to wish us all in the country again, lubber? I hope we shan't go in the country again these seven years, mama, let twenty coaches be pulled to pieces.

SIR FRANCIS Hold your tongue, Betty. Was Roger in no fault in this?   235

GEORGE No sir, nor I neither. 'Are not you ashamed,' says Roger to the carter, 'to do such an unkind thing to strangers?' 'No,' says he, 'you bumpkin.' Sir, he did the thing on very purpose, and so the folks said that stood by; but they said your worship need na be concerned, for you might have a lawsuit° with him when you   240
pleased, that would not cost you above a hundred pounds, and mayhap you might get the better of him.

SIR FRANCIS I'll try what I can do with him. Egad, I'll make such—

SQUIRE HUMPHRY Feather, have him before the Parliament.

SIR FRANCIS And so I will. I'll make him know who I am. Where does   245
he live?

GEORGE I believe in London, sir.

SIR FRANCIS What's the villain's name?

GEORGE I think I heard somebody call him Dick.

SIR FRANCIS Where did he go?   250

GEORGE Sir, he went home.

SIR FRANCIS Where's that?

GEORGE By my troth I do naw knaw. I heard him say he had nothing more to do with us tonight, and so he'd go home and smoke a pipe.

LADY HEADPIECE Come, Sir Francis, don't put yourself in a heat;   255

accidents will happen to people in travelling abroad to see the
world. Eat your supper heartily, go to bed, sleep quietly, and tomorrow see if you can buy a handsome second-hand coach for present
use, bespeak a new one, and then all's easy.

> *Exeunt [Sir Francis, Lady Headpiece, Squire Humphry, Miss*
> *Betty, Mrs Motherly, and George]*
> *[Deborah, alone]*
> *Enter Colonel Courtly*

COLONEL COURTLY Who's that? Deborah?   260

DEBORAH At your service, sir.

COLONEL COURTLY What, do you keep open house here? I found the
street door as wide as it could gape.

DEBORAH Sir, we are all in a bustle; we have lodgers come in tonight,
the house full.   265

COLONEL COURTLY Where's your mistress?

DEBORAH Prodigious busy with her company, but I'll tell Mrs Martilla you are here. I believe she'll come to you.

COLONEL COURTLY That will do as well.

> *Exit [Deborah]*

Poor Martilla! She's a very good girl, and I have loved her a great   270
while, I think; six months it is, since like a merciless highwayman I
made her deliver all she had about her. She begged hard, poor
thing, I'd leave her one small bauble. Had I let her keep it, I believe
she had still kept me. Could women but refuse their ravenous
lovers that one dear destructive moment, how long might they   275
reign over them! But for a bane to both their joys and ours, when
they have indulged us with such favours as make us adore them,
they are not able to refuse us that one which puts an end to our
devotion.

> *Enter Martilla*

COLONEL COURTLY Martilla, how dost thou do, my child?   280

MARTILLA As well as a losing gamester can.

COLONEL COURTLY Why, what have you lost?

MARTILLA I have lost you.

COLONEL COURTLY How came you to lose me?

MARTILLA By losing myself.   285

COLONEL COURTLY We can be friends still.

MARTILLA Dull ones.

COLONEL COURTLY Useful ones perhaps. Shall I help thee to a good
husband?

MARTILLA Not if I were rich enough to live without one.   290

COLONEL COURTLY I'm sorry I am not rich enough to make thee so; but we won't talk of melancholy things. Who are these folks your aunt has got in her house?

MARTILLA One Sir Francis Headpiece and his lady, with a son and daughter.   295

COLONEL COURTLY Headpiece! Cotso, I know 'em a little. I met with 'em at a race in the country two years since; a sort of blockhead, is not he?

MARTILLA So they say.

COLONEL COURTLY His wife seemed a mettled gentlewoman, if she   300
had had but a fair field to range in.

MARTILLA That she won't want now, for they stay in town the whole winter.

COLONEL COURTLY Oh that will do, to show all her parts in.
      Enter Mrs Motherly
How do you do, my old acquaintance?   305

MRS MOTHERLY At your service you know always, Colonel.

COLONEL COURTLY I hear you have got good company in the house.

MRS MOTHERLY I hope it will prove so; he's a Parliament-man only, Colonel—you know there's some danger in that.°

COLONEL COURTLY O, never fear; he'll pay his landlady, though he   310
don't pay his butcher.

MRS MOTHERLY His wife's a clever woman.

COLONEL COURTLY So she is.

MRS MOTHERLY How do you know?

COLONEL COURTLY I have seen her in the country, and I begin to   315
think I'll visit her in town.

MRS MOTHERLY You begin to look like a rogue.

COLONEL COURTLY What, your wicked fancies are stirring already?

MRS MOTHERLY Yours are, or I'm mistaken. But I'll have none of your pranks played upon her.   320

COLONEL COURTLY Why she's no girl, she can defend herself.

MRS MOTHERLY But what if she won't?

COLONEL COURTLY Why then she can blame neither you nor me.

MRS MOTHERLY You'll never be quiet till you get my windows broke;° but I must go and attend my lodgers, so good night.   325

COLONEL COURTLY Do so, and give my service to my lady, and tell her, if she'll give me leave, I'll do myself the honour tomorrow to come and tender my services to her, as long as she stays in town. (*Aside*) If it ben't too long.

MRS MOTHERLY I'll tell her what a devil you are, and advise her to   330
    have a care of you.
       Exit [Mrs Motherly]
COLONEL COURTLY Do, that will make her every time she sees me
    think of what I'd be at. Dear Martilla, good night. I know you
    won't be my hindrance; I'll do you as good a turn some time or
    other. Well, I am so glad you don't love me too much.   335
MARTILLA When that's our fate, as too too oft we prove,
       How bitterly we pay the past delights of love.
      [Exeunt]

2.1

Enter Lord Loverule, and Lady Arabella, he following her

LADY ARABELLA Well, look you my lord, I can bear it no longer;
nothing still but about my faults, my faults! An agreeable subject
truly!

LORD LOVERULE But madam, if you won't hear of your faults, how is
it likely you should ever mend 'em? 5

LADY ARABELLA Why, I don't intend to mend 'em. I can't mend 'em,
I have told you so a hundred times; you know I have tried to do it,
over and over, and it hurts me so I can't bear it. Why, don't you
know, my lord, that whenever, just to please you only, I have gone
about to wean myself from a fault—one of my faults I mean that I 10
love dearly—han't it put me so out of humour, you could scarce
endure the house with me?

LORD LOVERULE Look you, my dear, it is very true that in weaning
oneself from—

LADY ARABELLA Weaning? Why ay, don't you see that even in wean- 15
ing poor children from the nurse, it's almost the death of 'em? And
don't you see your true religious people, when they go about to
wean themselves, and have solemn days of fasting and praying on
purpose to help them, does it not so disorder them, there's no
coming near 'em; are they not as cross as the devil? And then they 20
don't do the business neither; for next day their faults are just
where they were the day before.

LORD LOVERULE But madam, can you think it a reasonable thing to
be abroad till two a' clock in the morning, when you know I go to
bed at eleven? 25

LADY ARABELLA And can you think it a wise thing, to talk your own
way now, and go to° bed at eleven, when you know I am likely to
disturb you by coming there at three?

LORD LOVERULE Well, the manner of women's living of late is insupportable, and some way or other— 30

LADY ARABELLA It's to be mended, I suppose. Pray, my lord, one
word of fair argument. You complain of my late hours, I of your
early ones; so far we are even, you'll allow. But which gives us the
best figure in the eye of the polite world? My two a' clock speaks
life, activity, spirit, and vigour; your eleven has a dull, drowsy, 35

stupid, good-for-nothing sound with it. It savours much of a mechanic, who must get to bed betimes, that he may rise early to open his shop. Faugh!

LORD LOVERULE I thought to go to bed early and rise so, was ever esteemed a right practice for all people. 40

LADY ARABELLA Beasts do it.

LORD LOVERULE Fie, fie, madam, fie; but 'tis not your ill hours alone disturb me, but the ill company who occasion those ill hours.

LADY ARABELLA And pray what ill company may those be?

LORD LOVERULE Why, women that lose their money, and men that 45 win it: especially when 'tis to be paid out of their husbands' estate; or if that fail, and the creditor be a little pressing, the lady will perhaps be obliged to try if the gentleman instead of gold will accept of a trinket.°

LADY ARABELLA My lord, you grow scurrilous, and you'll make me 50 hate you. I'll have you to know I keep company with the politest people in the town, and the assemblies I frequent are full of such.

LORD LOVERULE So are the churches now and then.

LADY ARABELLA My friends frequent them often, as well as the assemblies. 55

LORD LOVERULE They would do it oftener if a groom of the chamber° there were allowed to furnish cards and dice to the company.

LADY ARABELLA You'd make a woman mad.

LORD LOVERULE You'd make a man a fool. 60

LADY ARABELLA If heaven has made you otherwise, that won't be in my power.

LORD LOVERULE I'll try if I can prevent your making me a beggar at least.

LADY ARABELLA A beggar! Croesus!° I'm out of patience—I won't 65 come home till four tomorrow morning.

LORD LOVERULE I'll order the doors to be locked at twelve.

LADY ARABELLA Then I won't come home till tomorrow night.

LORD LOVERULE Then you shall never come home again, madam.

Exit [Lord Loverule]

LADY ARABELLA There he has knocked me down. My father upon 70 our marriage said wives were come to that pass he did not think it fit they should be trusted with pin-money; and so would not let this man settle one penny upon his poor wife, to serve her at a dead lift° for separate maintenance.°

Enter Clarinda

CLARINDA Good-morrow, madam; how do you do today? You seem to   75
be in a little fluster.

LADY ARABELLA My lord has been in one, and as I am the most
complaisant poor creature in the world, I put myself into one too,
purely to be suitable company to him.

CLARINDA You are prodigious good; but surely it must be mighty   80
agreeable when a man and his wife can give themselves the same
turn of conversation.

LADY ARABELLA O, the prettiest thing in the world.

CLARINDA But yet, though I believe there's no life so happy as a
married one in the main, yet I fancy, where two people are so very   85
much together, they must often be in want of something to talk
upon.

LADY ARABELLA Clarinda, you are the most mistaken in the world;
married people have things to talk of, child, that never enter into
the imagination of others. Why now, here's my lord and I, we han't   90
been married above two short years you know, and we have already
eight or ten things constantly in bank, that whenever we want
company, we can talk of any one of them for two hours together,
and the subject never the flatter. It will be as fresh next day, if we
have occasion for it, as it was the first day it entertained us.   95

CLARINDA Why that must be wonderful pretty.

LADY ARABELLA O, there's no life like it. This very day now, for
example, my lord and I, after a pretty cheerful *tête à tête* dinner, sat
down by the fire-side, in an idle, indolent, pick-tooth way for a
while, as if we had not thought of one another's being in the room.   100
At last, stretching himself, and yawning twice, 'My dear,' says he,
'you came home very late last night.' ''Twas but two in the morning,' says I. 'I was in bed' (yawning) 'by eleven,' says he. 'So you are
every night,' says I. 'Well,' says he, 'I am amazed, how you can sit
up so late.' 'How can you be amazed,' says I, 'at a thing that hap-   105
pens so often?' Upon which, we entered into conversation. And
though this is a point has entertained us above fifty times already,
we always find so many pretty new things to say upon't, that I
believe in my soul it will last as long as we live.

CLARINDA But in such sort of family dialogues—though extremely   110
well for passing of time—don't there now and then enter some
little witty sort of bitterness?

LADY ARABELLA O yes, which don't do amiss at all. A little something that's sharp moderates the extreme sweetness of matrimonial
society, which would else perhaps be cloying. Though to tell you   115

the truth, Clarinda, I think we squeezed a little too much lemon
into it this bout; for it grew so sour at last, that I think I almost told
him he was a fool; and he talked something oddly of turning me out
of doors.

CLARINDA O, but have a care of that. 120

LADY ARABELLA Why, to be serious, Clarinda, what would you have a
woman do in my case? There is no one thing he can do in this world
to please me—except giving me money, and that he is growing
weary of; and I at the same time (partly by nature, and partly
perhaps by keeping the best company) do with my soul love almost 125
everything that he hates. I dote upon assemblies, adore masquerades,° my heart bounds at a ball; I love play to distraction, cards
enchant me, and dice—put me out of my little wits. Dear, dear
hazard,° what music there is in the rattle of the dice, compared to a
sleepy opera! Do you ever play at hazard, Clarinda? 130

CLARINDA Never. I don't think it sits well upon women; it's very
masculine, and has too much of a rake. You see how it makes the
men swear and curse. Sure it must incline the women to do the
same too, if they durst give way to it.

LADY ARABELLA So it does. But hitherto, for a little decency, we keep 135
it in; and when in spite of our teeth an oath gets into our mouths,
we swallow it.

CLARINDA That's enough to burst you; but in time perhaps you'll let
'em fly as they do.

LADY ARABELLA Why 'tis probable we may, for the pleasure of all 140
polite women's lives now, you know, is founded upon entire liberty
to do what they will. But shall I tell you what happened t'other
night? Having lost all my money but ten melancholy guineas, and
throwing out for them, what do you think slipped from me?

CLARINDA An oath? 145

LADY ARABELLA Gudsoons!

CLARINDA O Lord! O Lord! Did not it frighten you out of your wits?

LADY ARABELLA Clarinda, I thought a gun had gone off. But I forget,
you are a prude,° and design to live soberly.

CLARINDA Why 'tis true; both my nature and my education do in a 150
good degree incline me that way.

LADY ARABELLA Well, surely to be sober is to be terribly dull. You
will marry, won't you?

CLARINDA I can't tell but I may.

LADY ARABELLA And you'll live in town? 155

CLARINDA Half the year I should like it very well.

LADY ARABELLA And you would live in London half a year, to be sober in it?

CLARINDA Yes.

LADY ARABELLA Why can't you as well go and be sober in the country?   160

CLARINDA So I would the t'other half year.

LADY ARABELLA And pray, what pretty scheme of life would you form now, for your summer and winter sober entertainments?

CLARINDA A scheme that, I think, might very well content us.   165

LADY ARABELLA Let's hear it.

CLARINDA I could in summer, pass my time very agreeably, in riding soberly, in walking soberly, in sitting under a tree soberly, in gardening soberly, in reading soberly, in hearing a little music soberly, in conversing with some agreeable friends soberly, in working   170 soberly, in managing my family and children (if I had any) soberly, and possibly by these means I might induce my husband to be as sober as myself.

LADY ARABELLA Well Clarinda, thou art a most contemptible creature. But let's have the sober town scheme too, for I am charmed   175 with the country one.

CLARINDA You shall, and I'll try to stick to my sobriety there too.

LADY ARABELLA If you do, you'll make me sick of you. But let's hear it however.

CLARINDA I would entertain myself in observing the new fashions   180 soberly, I would please myself in new clothes soberly, I would divert myself with agreeable friends at home and abroad soberly, I would play at quadrille° soberly, I would go to court soberly, I would go to some plays soberly, I would go to operas soberly, and I think I could go once, or, if I liked my company, twice, to a masquerade soberly.   185

LADY ARABELLA If it had not been for that last piece of sobriety, I was going to call for some surfeit-water.°

CLARINDA Why, don't you think, that with the further aid of breakfasting, dining, supping, and sleeping (not to say a word of devotion) the four-and-twenty hours might roll over in a tolerable   190 manner?

LADY ARABELLA How I detest that word, tolerable! And so will a country relation of ours that's newly come to town, or I'm mistaken.

CLARINDA Who is that?   195

LADY ARABELLA Even my dear Lady Headpiece.

CLARINDA Is she come?

LADY ARABELLA Yes, her sort of a tolerable husband has gotten to be
    chosen Parliament-man at some simple town or other, upon which
    she has persuaded him to bring her and her folks up to London.   200
CLARINDA That's good; I think she was never here before.
LADY ARABELLA Not since she was nine years old; but she has had an
    outrageous mind to it ever since she was married.
CLARINDA Then she'll make the most of it I suppose, now she is
    come.   205
LADY ARABELLA Depend upon that.
CLARINDA We must go and visit her.
LADY ARABELLA By all means; and maybe you'll have a mind to offer
    her your tolerable scheme for her London diversion this winter. If
    you do, mistress, I'll show her mine too, and you shall see: she'll so   210
    despise you and adore me, that if I do but chirrup to her, she'll hop
    after me like a tame sparrow, the town round. But there's your
    admirer I see coming in; I'll oblige him, and leave you to receive
    part of his visit, while I step up to write a letter. Besides, to tell you
    the truth, I don't like him half so well as I used to do; he falls off of   215
    late from being the company he was, in our way. In short, I think
    he's growing to be a little like my lord.
        Exit [Lady Arabella]
        Enter Sir Charles
SIR CHARLES Madam, your servant; they told me Lady Arabella was
    here.
CLARINDA She's only stepped up to write a letter; she'll come down   220
    presently.
SIR CHARLES Why, does she write letters? I thought she had never
    time for't. Pray how may she have disposed of the rest of the day?
CLARINDA A good deal as usual. She has visits to make till six; she's
    then engaged to the play; from that till court-time she's to be at   225
    cards at Mrs Idle's; after the drawing-room, she takes a short sup-
    per with Lady Hazard, and from thence they go together to the
    assembly.
SIR CHARLES And are you to do all this with her?
CLARINDA The visits and the play, no more.   230
SIR CHARLES And how can you forbear all the rest?
CLARINDA 'Tis easy to forbear what we are not very fond of.
SIR CHARLES I han't found it so. I have passed much of my life in this
    hurry of the ladies, yet was never so pleased as when I was at quiet
    without 'em.   235
CLARINDA What then induced you to be with 'em?

SIR CHARLES Idleness, and the fashion.

CLARINDA No mistresses in the case?

SIR CHARLES To speak honestly, yes. When one is in a toyshop, there
was no forbearing the baubles; so I was perpetually engaging with   240
some coquette or other, whom I could love perhaps just enough to
put it into her power to plague me.

CLARINDA Which power I suppose she sometimes made use of.

SIR CHARLES The amours of a coquette, madam, generally mean
nothing farther. I look upon them and prudes to be nuisances much   245
alike, though they seem very different; the first are always disturbing the men, and the latter always abusing the women.

CLARINDA And all I think is to establish the character of being
virtuous.

SIR CHARLES That is, being chaste they mean, for they know no other   250
virtue; therefore indulge themselves in everything else that's
vicious. They against nature keep their chastity, only because they
find more pleasure in doing mischief with it than they should have
in parting with it. But madam, if both these characters are so
odious, how highly to be valued is that woman who can attain all   255
they aim at, without the aid of the folly or vice of either?
      Enter Lady Arabella

LADY ARABELLA Your servant, sir. I won't ask your pardon for leaving you alone a little with a lady that I know shares so much of your
good opinion.

SIR CHARLES I wish, madam, she could think my good opinion of   260
value enough to afford me a small part in hers.

LADY ARABELLA I believe, sir, every woman who knows she has place
in a fine gentleman's good opinion will be glad to give him one in
hers, if she can. But however you two may stand in one another's,
you must take another time if you desire to talk farther about it, or   265
we shan't have enough to make our visits in; and so your servant,
sir. Come Clarinda.

SIR CHARLES I'll stay and make my lord a visit, if you will give me
leave.

LADY ARABELLA You have my leave, sir, though you were a lady.   270
      Exit [Lady Arabella] with Clarinda
      Enter Lord Loverule

LORD LOVERULE Sir Charles, your servant; what, have the ladies left
you?

SIR CHARLES Yes, and the ladies in general I hope will leave me too.

LORD LOVERULE Why so?

SIR CHARLES That I mayn't be put to the ill manners of leaving them 275
first.

LORD LOVERULE Do you then already find your gallantry inclining to
an ebb?

SIR CHARLES 'Tis not that I am yet old enough to justify myself in an
idle retreat, but I have got, I think, a sort of surfeit on me, that 280
lessens much the force of female charms.

LORD LOVERULE Have you then been so glutted with their favours?

SIR CHARLES Not with their favours, but with their service; it is
unmerciful. I once thought myself a tolerable time-killer; I drank, I
played, I intrigued, and yet I had hours enough for reasonable uses. 285
But he that will list himself a lady's man of mettle now, she'll work
him so at cards and dice, she won't afford him time enough to play
with her at anything else, though she herself should have a tolerable
good mind to it.

LORD LOVERULE And so the disorderly lives they lead make you 290
incline to a reform of your own.

SIR CHARLES 'Tis true; for bad examples, if they are but bad enough,
give us as useful reflections as good ones do.

LORD LOVERULE 'Tis pity anything that's bad should come from
women. 295

SIR CHARLES 'Tis so indeed, and there was a happy time when both
you and I thought there never could.

LORD LOVERULE Our early first conceptions of them, I well remember, were that they never could be vicious, nor never could be old.

SIR CHARLES We thought so then: the beauteous form we saw them 300
cast in seemed designed a habitation for no vice, nor no decay. All I
had conceived of angels, I conceived of them; true, tender, gentle,
modest, generous, constant, I thought was writ in every feature;
and in my devotions, heaven, how did I adore thee, that blessings
like them should be the portion of such poor inferior creatures as I 305
took myself, and all men else (compared with them) to be. But
where's that adoration now?

LORD LOVERULE 'Tis with such fond young fools as you and I were
then.

SIR CHARLES And with such it ever will be. 310

LORD LOVERULE Ever. The pleasure is so great, in believing women
to be what we wish them, that nothing but a long and sharp experience can ever make us think them otherwise. That experience,
friend, both you and I have had; but yours has been at other men's
expense, mine—at my own. 315

SIR CHARLES Perhaps you'd wonder, should you find me disposed to run the risk of that experience too.

LORD LOVERULE I should indeed.

SIR CHARLES And yet 'tis possible I may. Know, at least, I still have so much of my early folly left to think there's yet one woman fit to   320
make a wife of: how far such a one can answer the charms of a mistress, married men are silent in, so pass—for that, I'd take my chance. But could she make a home easy to her partner, by letting him find there a cheerful companion, an agreeable intimate, a useful assistant, a faithful friend, and (in its time perhaps) a tender   325
mother, such change of life, from what I lead, seems not unwise to think of.

LORD LOVERULE Not unwise to purchase, if to be had for millions; but—

SIR CHARLES But what?   330

LORD LOVERULE If the reverse of this should chance to be the bitter disappointment, what would the life be then?

SIR CHARLES A damned one.

LORD LOVERULE And what relief?

SIR CHARLES A short one; leave it, and return to that you left, if you   335
can't find a better.

LORD LOVERULE (aside) He says right—that's the remedy, and a just one. For if I sell my liberty for gold, and I am foully° paid in brass, shall I be held to keep the bargain?

SIR CHARLES What are you thinking of?   340

LORD LOVERULE Of what you have said.

SIR CHARLES And was it well said?

LORD LOVERULE I begin to think it might.

SIR CHARLES Think on; 'twill give you ease. The man who has courage enough to part with a wife need not much dread the   345
having one; and he that has not ought to tremble at being a husband. But perhaps I have said too much; you'll pardon however the freedom of an old friend, because you know I am so. So, your servant.

Exit [Sir Charles]

LORD LOVERULE Charles, farewell; I can take nothing as ill-meant   350
that comes from you. Nor ought my wife to think I mean amiss to her if I convince her I'll endure no longer that she should thus expose herself and me. No doubt 'twill grieve her sorely. Physic's a loathsome thing, till we find it gives us health, and then we are thankful to those who made us take it. Perhaps she may do so by   355

me. If she does 'tis well; if not, and she resolves to make the house ring with reprisals, I believe (though the misfortune's great) he'll make a better figure in the world who keeps an ill wife out of doors, than he that keeps her within.

    [*Exit Lord Loverule*]

3.1

[A room in Mrs Motherly's house]

Enter Lady Headpiece and Mrs Motherly

LADY HEADPIECE So, you are acquainted with Lady Arabella, I find.

MRS MOTHERLY Oh madam, I have had the honour to know her ladyship almost from a child, and a charming woman she has made.

LADY HEADPIECE I like her prodigiously. I had some acquaintance with her in the country two years ago; but she's quite another woman here. 5

MRS MOTHERLY Ah madam, two years' keeping company with the polite people of the town will do wonders in the improvement of a lady, so° she has it but about her.

LADY HEADPIECE Now 'tis my misfortune, Mrs Motherly, to come late to school. 10

MRS MOTHERLY Oh, don't be discouraged at that madam; the quickness of your ladyship's parts will easily recover your loss of a little time.

LADY HEADPIECE O! You flatter me! But I'll endeavour by industry 15
and application to make it up; such parts as I have shall not lie idle. My Lady Arabella has been so good to offer me already her introduction to those assemblies where a woman may soonest learn to make herself valuable to everybody.

MRS MOTHERLY (*aside*) But her husband. [*Aloud*] Her ladyship, 20
madam, can indeed better than anybody introduce you where everything that accomplishes a fine lady is practised to the last perfection; madam, she herself is at the very tip top of it. 'Tis pity, poor lady, she should meet with any discouragements.

LADY HEADPIECE Discouragements! From whence pray? 25

MRS MOTHERLY From home sometimes—my lord a—

LADY HEADPIECE What does he do?

MRS MOTHERLY But one should not talk of people of quality's family concerns.

LADY HEADPIECE O, no matter, Mrs Motherly, as long as it goes no 30
farther. My lord, you were saying—

MRS MOTHERLY Why, my lord, madam, is a little humoursome, they say.

LADY HEADPIECE Humoursome?

MRS MOTHERLY Yes, they say he's humoursome. 35

LADY HEADPIECE As how, pray?

MRS MOTHERLY Why, if my poor lady perhaps does but stay out at night, maybe four or five hours after he's in bed, he'll be cross.

LADY HEADPIECE What, for such a thing as that?

MRS MOTHERLY Yes, he'll be cross; and then, if she happens, it may   40
be, to be unfortunate at play, and lose a great deal of money, more than she has to pay, then madam—he'll snub.

LADY HEADPIECE Out upon him, snub such a woman as she is? I can tell you, Mrs Motherly, I that am but a country lady, should Sir Francis take upon him to snub me, in London, he'd raise a spirit   45
would make his hair stand an end.

MRS MOTHERLY Really madam, that's the only way to deal with 'em.
          Enter Miss Betty
And here comes pretty Miss Betty, that I believe will never be made a fool of, when she's married.

MISS BETTY No, by my troth won't I. What, are you talking of my   50
being married, mother?

LADY HEADPIECE No, Miss; Mrs Motherly was only saying what a good wife you would make when you were so.

MISS BETTY The sooner it's tried, mother, the sooner it will be known. Lord, here's the Colonel, madam.   55
          Enter Colonel [Courtly]

LADY HEADPIECE Colonel, your servant.

MISS BETTY Your servant, Colonel.

COLONEL COURTLY Ladies, your most obedient—I hope, madam, the town air continues to agree with you?

LADY HEADPIECE Mighty well, sir.   60

MISS BETTY Oh prodigious well, sir. We have bought a new coach, and an ocean of new clothes, and we are to go to the play tonight, and tomorrow we go to the opera, and next night we go to the assembly, and then the next night after, we—

LADY HEADPIECE Softly, Miss. Do you go to the play tonight,   65
Colonel?

COLONEL COURTLY I did not design it, madam; but now I find there is to be such good company, I'll do myself the honour, if you'll give me leave, ladies, to come and lead you to your coach.

LADY HEADPIECE It's extremely obliging.   70

MISS BETTY It is indeed mighty well-bred. Lord, Colonel, what a difference there is between your way and our country companions; one of them would have said, 'What, you are aw gooing to the playhouse then?' 'Yes,' says we, 'won't you come and lead us out?'

'No, by good feggings,'° says he, 'ye ma' e'en ta' care o'your sells,   75
y'are awd enough'; and so he'd ha' gone to get drunk at the tavern
against we came home to supper.

MRS MOTHERLY Ha, ha, ha! Well, sure madam, your ladyship is the
happiest mother in the world to have such a charming companion
to your daughter.   80

COLONEL COURTLY The prettiest creature upon earth!

MISS BETTY D'ye hear that, mother? Well, he's a fine gentleman
really, and I think a man of admirable sense.

LADY HEADPIECE Softly Miss, he'll hear you.

MISS BETTY If he does, madam, he'll think I say true, and he'll like   85
me never the worse for that, I hope. Where's your niece Martilla,
Mrs Motherly? Mama, won't you carry Martilla to the play with
us?

LADY HEADPIECE With all my heart, child.

COLONEL COURTLY She's a very pretty civil sort of woman, madam,   90
and Miss will be very happy in having such a companion in the
house with her.

MISS BETTY So I shall indeed, sir, and I love her dearly already; we
are growing very great together.

LADY HEADPIECE But what's become of your brother, child? I han't   95
seen him these two hours; where is he?

MISS BETTY Indeed, mother, I don't know where he is; I saw him
asleep about half an hour ago by the kitchen fire.

COLONEL COURTLY Must not he go to the play too?

LADY HEADPIECE Yes, I think he should go, though he'll be weary   100
on't before it's half done.

MISS BETTY Weary? Yes, and then he'll sit, and yawn, and stretch like
a greyhound by the fireside, 'till he does some nasty thing or other,
that they'll turn him out of the house, so it's better to leave him at
home.   105

MRS MOTHERLY O, that were pity, Miss. Plays will enliven him—see,
here he comes, and my niece with him.

Enter Squire Humphry and Martilla

COLONEL COURTLY Your servant, sir; you come in good time. The
ladies are all going to the play, and wanted you to help gallant them.

SQUIRE HUMPHRY And so 'twill be nine a' clock, before one shall get   110
ony supper.

MISS BETTY Supper! Why your dinner is not out of your mouth yet,
at least 'tis all about the brims of it. See how greasy his chops is,
mother.

286

LADY HEADPIECE Nay, if he han't a mind to go, he need not. You may   115
   stay here till your father comes home from the Parliament house,
   and then you may eat a broiled bone together.

MISS BETTY Yes, and drink a tankard of strong beer together, and
   then he may tell you all he has been doing in the Parliament house,
   and you may tell him all you have been thinking of when you were   120
   asleep in the kitchen; and then if you'll put it all down in writing,
   when we come from the play I'll read it to the company.

SQUIRE HUMPHRY Sister, I don't like your joking, and you are not a
   well-behaved young woman; and although my mother encourages
   you, my thoughts are, you are not too big to be whipped.   125

MISS BETTY How, sirrah?

SQUIRE HUMPHRY There's a civil young gentlewoman stands there,
   is worth a hundred of you. And I believe she'll be married before
   you.

MISS BETTY Cots my life, I have a good mind to pull your eyes out.   130

LADY HEADPIECE Hold, Miss, hold, don't be in such a passion
   neither.

MISS BETTY Mama, it is not that I am angry at anything he says to
   commend Martilla, for I wish she were to be married tomorrow,
   that I might have a dance at her wedding; but what need he abuse   135
   me for? (*Aside*) I wish the lout had mettle enough to be in love with
   her, she'd make pure sport with him. [*To Squire Humphry*] Does
   your Heaviness find any inclinations moving towards the lady you
   admire? Speak! Are you in love with her?

SQUIRE HUMPHRY I am in love with nobody; and if anybody be in   140
   love with me, mayhap they had as good be quiet.

MISS BETTY Hold your tongue; I'm quite sick of you. Come, Martilla,
   you are to go to the play with us.

MARTILLA Am I, Miss? I am ready to wait upon you.

LADY HEADPIECE I believe it's time we should be going, Colonel, is   145
   not it?

COLONEL COURTLY Yes, madam, I believe it is.

LADY HEADPIECE Come then; who is there?

   Enter Tom

   Is the coach at the door?

TOM It has been there this hafe haur, so please your ladyship.   150

MISS BETTY And are all the people in the street gazing at it, Tom?

TOM That are they, madam; and Roger has drank so much of his own
   beveridge that he's e'en as it were gotten a little drunk.

LADY HEADPIECE Not so drunk, I hope, but that he can drive us?

TOM Yes, yes, madam, he drives best when he's a little uppish. When   155
Roger's head turns, raund go the wheels, i'faith.

MISS BETTY Never fear, mama; as long as it's to the playhouse, there's
no danger.

LADY HEADPIECE Well, daughter, since you are so courageous, it
shan't be said I make any difficulty; and if the Colonel is so gallant   160
to have a mind to share our danger, we have room for him, if he
pleases.

COLONEL COURTLY Madam, you do me a great deal of honour, and
I'm sure you give me a great deal of pleasure.

MISS BETTY Come, dear mama, away we go.   165
        Exeunt [*Lady Headpiece, Colonel Courtly, Miss Betty, and Tom*]

SQUIRE HUMPHRY (*to Martilla*) I did not think you would have
gone.

MARTILLA O, I love a play dearly.
        Exit [*Martilla*]

MRS MOTHERLY I wonder, Squire, that you would not go to the play
with 'em.   170

SQUIRE HUMPHRY What needed Martilla have gone? They were
enow without her.

MRS MOTHERLY O, she was glad to go to divert herself; and besides,
my lady desired her to go with them.

SQUIRE HUMPHRY And so I am left alone.   175

MRS MOTHERLY Why, should you have cared for her company?

SQUIRE HUMPHRY Rather than none.

MRS MOTHERLY (*aside*) On my conscience, he's ready to cry. This is
matter to think of; but here comes Sir Francis.
        Enter Sir Francis
How do you do, sir? I'm afraid these late Parliament hours won't   180
agree with you.

SIR FRANCIS Indeed, I like them not, Mrs Motherly; if they would
dine at twelve a' clock, as we do in the country, a man might be able
to drink a reasonable bottle between that and supper-time.

MRS MOTHERLY That would be much better indeed, Sir Francis.   185

SIR FRANCIS But then when we consider that what we undergo is in
being busy for the good of our country°—o, the good of our country is above all things! What a noble and glorious thing it is, Mrs
Motherly, that England can boast of five hundred zealous gentlemen, all in one room, all of one mind, upon a fair occasion, to go all   190
together by the ears° for the good of their country! Humphry,
perhaps you'll be a senator in time, as your father is now; when you

are, remember your country. Spare nothing for the good of
your country; and when you come home, at the end of the sessions,
you will find yourself so adored, that your country will come   195
and dine with you every day in the week. O, here's my Uncle
Richard.

 Enter Uncle Richard

MRS MOTHERLY I think, sir, I had best get you a mouthful of something to stay your stomach till supper.

SIR FRANCIS With all my heart, for I'm almost famished.   200

 Exit [Mrs Motherly]

SQUIRE HUMPHRY And so shall I before my mother comes from the
playhouse, so I'll go get a buttered toast.

 Exit [Squire Humphry]

SIR FRANCIS Uncle, I hope you are well.

UNCLE RICHARD Nephew, if I had been sick, I would not have come
abroad; I suppose you are well, for I sent this morning, and was   205
informed you went out early. Was it to make your court to some of
the great men?

SIR FRANCIS Yes uncle, I was advised to lose no time, so I went to one
great man, whom I had never seen before.

UNCLE RICHARD And who had you got to introduce you?   210

SIR FRANCIS Nobody; I remembered I had heard a wise man say, 'My
son, be bold'; so I introduced myself.

UNCLE RICHARD As how, I pray?

SIR FRANCIS Why thus, uncle: 'Please your lordship,' says I, 'I am Sir
Francis Headpiece, of Headpiece Hall, and member of Parliament   215
for the ancient borough of Gobble Guinea° sir.' 'Your humble servant,' says my lord, 'though I have not the honour to know your
person, I have heard you are a very honest gentleman, and I am
very glad your borough has made choice of so worthy a representa-
tive; have you any service to command me?' Those last words,   220
uncle, gave me great encouragement; and though I know you have
not any very great opinion of my parts, I believe you won't say I
missed it now.

UNCLE RICHARD I hope I shall have no cause.

SIR FRANCIS 'My lord,' says I, 'I did not design to say anything to   225
your lordship today about business; but since your lordship is so
kind and free, as to bid me speak if I have any service to command
you, I will.'

UNCLE RICHARD So.

SIR FRANCIS 'I have,' says I, 'my lord, a good estate, but it's a little aut   230

289

at elbows, and as I desire to serve my king, as well as my country, I
shall be very willing to accept of a place at court.'

UNCLE RICHARD This was bold indeed.

SIR FRANCIS I'cod, I shot him flying, uncle; another man would have
been a month before he durst have opened his mauth about a place.   235
But you shall hear. 'Sir Francis,' says my lord, 'what sort of a place
may you have turned your thoughts upon?' 'My lord,' says I, 'beggars must not be choosers; but some place about a thousand a year,
I believe, might do pretty weel to begin with.' 'Sir Francis,' says he,
'I shall be glad to serve you in anything I can'; and in saying these   240
words he gave me a squeeze by the hand, as much as to say, I'll do
your business. And so he turned to a lord that was there, who
looked as if he came for a place too.

UNCLE RICHARD And so your fortune's made.

SIR FRANCIS Don't you think so, uncle?   245

UNCLE RICHARD Yes, for just so mine was made—twenty years ago.

SIR FRANCIS Why, I never knew you had a place, uncle.

UNCLE RICHARD Nor I neither upon my faith, nephew: but you have
been down at the House since you made your court, have not you?

SIR FRANCIS O yes; I would not neglect the House, for ever so much.   250

UNCLE RICHARD And what may they have done there today, I pray?

SIR FRANCIS Why truly, uncle, I cannot well tell what they did, but
I'll tell you what I did. I happened to make a little sort of a mistake.

UNCLE RICHARD How was that?

SIR FRANCIS Why you must know, uncle, they were all got into a sort   255
of a hodge-podge argument for the good of the nation, which I did
not well understand. However, I was convinced, and so resolved to
vote aright, according to my conscience. But they made such a
puzzling business on't, when they put the question,° as they call it,
that I believe I cried ay when I should have cried no; for a sort of a   260
Jacobite that sate next me took me by the hand and said, 'Sir, you
are a man of honour, and a true Englishman, and I should be glad to
be better acquainted with you', and so he pulled me along with the
crowd into the lobby with him, when, I believe, I should have
stayed where I was.   265

UNCLE RICHARD And so, if you had not quite made your fortune
before, you have clenched it now. (*Aside*) Ah thou head of the
Headpieces! [*Aloud*] How now, what's the matter here?

> *Enter Lady Headpiece,* [*Miss Betty, Colonel Courtly, Roger, and*
> *Tom*] *all in disorder, some dirty, some lame, some bloody*

SIR FRANCIS Mercy on us! They are all killed.

MISS BETTY Not for a thousand pounds; but we have been all down in   270
the dirt together.

LADY HEADPIECE We have had a sad piece of work on't, Sir Francis;
overturned in the channel, as we were going to the playhouse.

MISS BETTY Over and over, papa; had it been coming from the
playhouse I should not have cared a farthing.   275

SIR FRANCIS But child you are hurt; your face is all bloody.

MISS BETTY O sir, my new gown is all dirty.

LADY HEADPIECE The new coach is all spoiled.

MISS BETTY The glasses are all to bits.

LADY HEADPIECE Roger has put out his arm.   280

MISS BETTY Would he had put out his neck, for making us lose the
play.

SQUIRE HUMPHRY Poor Martilla has scratched her little finger.

LADY HEADPIECE And here's the poor Colonel; nobody asks what he
has done. I hope, sir, you have got no harm?   285

COLONEL COURTLY Only a little wounded with some pins I met with
about your ladyship.

LADY HEADPIECE I am sorry anything about me should do you harm.

COLONEL COURTLY If it does, madam, you have that about you, if
you please, will be my cure. I hope your ladyship feels nothing   290
amiss?

LADY HEADPIECE Nothing at all, though we did roll about together
strangely.

COLONEL COURTLY We did indeed. [Aside] I'm sure we rolled so,
that my poor hands were got once—I don't know where they were   295
got. But her ladyship I see will pass by slips.

SIR FRANCIS It would have been pity the Colonel should have
received any damage in his services to the ladies. He is the most
complaisant man to 'em, uncle; always ready when they have
occasion for him.   300

UNCLE RICHARD Then I believe, nephew, they'll never let him want
business.

SIR FRANCIS O, but they should not ride the free horse to death°
neither. Come Colonel, you'll stay and drink a bottle, and eat a little
supper with us, after your misfortune?   305

COLONEL COURTLY Sir, since I have been prevented from attending
the ladies to the play, I shall be very proud to obey their commands
here at home.

SIR FRANCIS A prodigious civil gentleman, uncle; and yet as bold as
Alexander upon occasion.   310

UNCLE RICHARD Upon a lady's occasion.

SIR FRANCIS Ha, ha, you are a wag, uncle; but I believe he'd storm anything.

UNCLE RICHARD (*aside*) Then I believe your citadel may be in danger.

SIR FRANCIS Uncle, won't you break your rule for once, and sup from home? 315

UNCLE RICHARD The company will excuse me, nephew, they'll be freer without me; so good night to them and you.

LADY HEADPIECE Good night to you, sir, since you won't stay. Come Colonel. 320

UNCLE RICHARD (*aside*) Methinks this facetious Colonel is got upon a pretty, familiar, easy foot already with the family of the Headpieces—hum.

> *Exit* [*Uncle Richard*]

SIR FRANCIS Come, my lady, let's all in, and pass the evening cheerfully. And d'ye hear, wife—a word in your ear—I have got a 325 promise of a place at court, of a thousand a year, he, hem.

> [*Exeunt*]

4.1

[Lord Loverule's house]

Enter Lady Arabella, as just up, walking pensively to her toilet, followed by Trusty

LADY ARABELLA Well, sure never woman had such luck—these devilish dice! Sit up all night; lose all one's money, and then—how like a hag I look.

Sits at her toilet, turning her purse inside out

Not a guinea—worth less by a hundred pounds than I was at one a' clock this morning—and then—I was worth nothing. What is to be done, Trusty?

TRUSTY I wish I were wise enough to tell you, madam; but if there comes in any good company to breakfast with your ladyship, perhaps you may have a run of better fortune.

LADY ARABELLA But I han't a guinea to try my fortune. Let me see— who was that impertinent man, that was so saucy last week about money, that I was forced to promise, once more, he should have what I owed him this morning?

TRUSTY O, I remember, madam; it was your old mercer° Shortyard, that you turned off a year ago, because he would trust you no longer.

LADY ARABELLA That's true; and I think I bid the steward keep thirty guineas out of some money he was paying me, to stop his odious mouth.

TRUSTY Your ladyship did so.

LADY ARABELLA Prithee, Trusty, run and see whether the wretch has got the money yet; if not, tell the steward I have occasion for it myself. Run quickly!

Trusty runs to the door

TRUSTY Ah, madam, he's just a paying it away now, in the hall.

LADY ARABELLA Stop him! Quick, quick, dear Trusty.

TRUSTY Hem, hem, Mr Moneybag, a word with you quickly.

MONEYBAG (*within*) I'll come presently.

TRUSTY Presently won't do; you must come this moment.

MONEYBAG [*within*] I'm but just paying a little money.

TRUSTY Cods my life, paying money? Is the man distracted? Come here, I tell you, to my lady this moment, quick.

Moneybag comes to the door with a purse in his hand

My lady says you must not pay the money today; there's a mistake
in the account, which she must examine—and she's afraid too there
was a false guinea or two left in the purse, which might disgrace
her.   35
    Twitches the purse from him
But she's too busy to look for 'em just now, so you must bid Mr
What-d'ye-call-'em come another time.
    [*Exit Moneybag*]
There they are, madam. (*Gives her the money*) The poor things were
so near gone, they made me tremble; I fancy your ladyship will give
me one of those false guineas for good luck. (*Takes a guinea*) Thank   40
you, madam.

LADY ARABELLA Why, I did not bid you take it.

TRUSTY No, but your ladyship looked as if you were just going to bid
me, so I took it to save your ladyship the trouble of speaking.

LADY ARABELLA Well, for once—but hark—I think I hear the man   45
making a noise yonder.

TRUSTY Nay, I don't expect he'll go out of the house quietly. I'll
listen.

LADY ARABELLA Do.
    [*Trusty*] *goes to the door*

TRUSTY He's in a bitter passion with poor Moneybag; I believe he'll   50
beat him—Lord, how he swears!

LADY ARABELLA And a sober citizen too! That's a shame.

TRUSTY He says he will speak with you, madam, though the devil
held your door—Lord! He's coming hither full drive, but I'll lock
him out.   55

LADY ARABELLA No matter, let him come. I'll reason with him.

TRUSTY But he's a saucy fellow for all that.
    Enter Shortyard
What would you have, sir?

SHORTYARD I would have my due, mistress.

TRUSTY That would be—to be well cudgelled, master, for coming so   60
familiarly where you should not come.

LADY ARABELLA Do you think you do well, sir, to intrude into my
dressing-room?

SHORTYARD Madam, I sold my goods to you in your dressing-room; I
don't know why I mayn't ask for my money there.   65

LADY ARABELLA You are very short,° sir.

SHORTYARD Your ladyship won't complain of my patience being
so?

LADY ARABELLA I complain of nothing that ought not to be complained of; but I hate ill manners. 70

SHORTYARD So do I, madam—but this is the seventeenth time I have been ordered to come, with good manners, for my money, to no purpose.

LADY ARABELLA Your money, man! Is that the matter? Why it has lain in the steward's hands this week for you. 75

SHORTYARD Madam, you yourself appointed me to come this very morning for it.

LADY ARABELLA But why did you come so late then?

SHORTYARD So late! I came soon enough, I thought.

LADY ARABELLA That thinking wrong makes us liable to a world of 80 disappointments; if you had thought of coming one minute sooner, you had had your money.

SHORTYARD Gad bless me, madam; I had the money as I thought. I'm sure it was telling out,° and I was writing a receipt for't.

TRUSTY Why there you thought wrong again, master. 85

LADY ARABELLA Yes, for you should never think of writing a receipt till the money is in your pocket.

SHORTYARD Why, I did think 'twas in my pocket.

TRUSTY Look you, thinking again! Indeed Mr Shortyard, you make so many blunders, 'tis impossible but you must suffer by it, in your 90 way of trade. I'm sorry for you, and you'll be undone.

SHORTYARD And well I may, when I sell my goods to people that won't pay me for 'em till the interest of my money eats out all my profit. I sold them so cheap, because I thought I should be paid the next day. 95

TRUSTY Why there again! There's another of your thoughts; paid the next day, and you han't been paid this twelvemonth, you see.

SHORTYARD Oons, I han't been paid at all, mistress.

LADY ARABELLA Well, tradesmen are strange unreasonable creatures; refuse to sell people any more things, and then quarrel with 'em 100 because they don't pay for those they have had already. Now what can you say to that, Mr Shortyard?

SHORTYARD Say! Why—'sdeath madam, I don't know what you talk of. I don't understand your argument.

LADY ARABELLA Why, what do you understand, man? 105

SHORTYARD Why, I understand that I have had above a hundred pounds due to me a year ago; that I came by appointment just now to receive it; that it proved at last to be but thirty instead of a hundred and ten; and that while the steward was telling ev'n that

out, and I was writing the receipt, comes Mrs Pop here, and the   110
money was gone. But I'll be bantered no longer if there's law in
England. Say no more, Shortyard.

    Exit [Shortyard]

TRUSTY What a passion the poor devil's in!

LADY ARABELLA Why truly one can't deny but he has some present
cause for a little ill humour; but when one has things of so much   115
greater consequence on foot, one can't trouble oneself about making such creatures easy. So call for breakfast, Trusty, and set the
hazard-table ready. If there comes no company I'll play a little by
myself.

    Enter Lord Loverule

LORD LOVERULE Pray what offence, madam, have you given to a man   120
I met with just now as I came in?

LADY ARABELLA People who are apt to take offence do it for small
matters, you know.

LORD LOVERULE I shall be glad to find this so, but he says you have
owed him above a hundred pounds this twelvemonth; that he has   125
been here forty times by appointment for it, to no purpose; and that
coming here this morning upon positive assurance from yourself,
he was tricked out of the money while he was writing a receipt for
it, and sent away without a farthing.

LADY ARABELLA Lord, how these shopkeepers will lie!   130

LORD LOVERULE What then is the business? For some ground the
man must have to be in such a passion.

LADY ARABELLA I believe you'll rather wonder to see me so calm,
when I tell you he had the insolence to intrude into my very dressing-room here, with a story without head or tail; you know, Trusty,   135
we could not understand one word he said, but when he swore—
good Lord! How the wretch did swear!

TRUSTY I never heard the like, for my part.

LORD LOVERULE And all this for nothing?

LADY ARABELLA So it proved, my lord, for he got nothing by it.   140

LORD LOVERULE His swearing I suppose was for his money, madam.
Who can blame him?

LADY ARABELLA If he swore for money,° he should be put in the
pillory.

LORD LOVERULE Madam, I won't be bantered, nor sued by this man   145
for your extravagancies. Do you owe him the money or not?

LADY ARABELLA He says I do, but such fellows will say anything.

LORD LOVERULE (*aside*) Provoking! [*To Lady Arabella*] Did not I desire an account from you of all your debts but six months since, and give you money to clear them? 150

LADY ARABELLA My lord, you can't imagine how accounts make my head ache.

LORD LOVERULE That won't do; the steward gave you two hundred pounds besides, but last week. Where's that?

LADY ARABELLA Gone. 155

LORD LOVERULE Gone! Where?

LADY ARABELLA Half the town over I believe by this time.

LORD LOVERULE Madam, madam, this can be endured no longer, and before a month passes expect to find me—

LADY ARABELLA Hist my lord, here's company. 160

Enter Captain Toupee

Captain Toupee, your servant. What, nobody with you? Do you come quite alone?

CAPTAIN TOUPEE 'Slife, I thought to find company enough here. My lord, your servant. What a deuce, you look as if you had been up all night. I'm sure I was in bed but three hours; I would you'd give me 165 some coffee.

LADY ARABELLA Some coffee there; tea too, and chocolate.

[*Exit Trusty*]

CAPTAIN TOUPEE (*singing a minuet and dancing*) Well, what a strange fellow am I to be thus brisk, after losing all my money last night— but upon my soul you look sadly. 170

LADY ARABELLA No matter for that, if you'll let me win a little of your money this morning.

CAPTAIN TOUPEE What, with that face? Go, go wash it, go wash it, and put on some handsome things. You looked a good likely woman last night—I would not much have cared if you had run five hun- 175 dred pounds in my debt; but if I play with you this morning, egad I'd advise you to win, for I won't take your personal security at present for a guinea.

LORD LOVERULE [*aside*] To what a nauseous freedom do women of quality of late admit these trifling fops? And there's a morning 180 exercise will give 'em claim to greater freedoms still. (*Points to hazard table*) Some course must be taken.

Exit [Lord Loverule]

CAPTAIN TOUPEE What, is my lord gone? He looked methought as if he did not delight much in my company. Well, peace and plenty attend him for your ladyship's sake, and those who have now and 185 then the honour to win a hundred pounds of you.

Goes to the table singing, and throws°

LADY ARABELLA (*twitching the box from him*) What, do you intend to win all the money upon the table . . . seven's the main . . . set me a million, Toupee.

CAPTAIN TOUPEE I set you two, my queen . . . six to seven.   190

LADY ARABELLA Six . . . the world's my own.

BOTH Ha, ha, ha.

LADY ARABELLA O that my lord had but spirit enough about him to let me play for a thousand pounds a night. But here comes country company.   195

> *Enter Lady Headpiece, Miss Betty, Mrs Motherly, and Colonel Courtly*

Your servant, madam, Good morrow to you.

LADY HEADPIECE And to you, madam. We are come to breakfast with you. Lord, are you got to those pretty things already? (*Points to the dice*)

LADY ARABELLA You see we are not such idle folks in town as you country ladies take us to be; we are no sooner out of our beds, but   200
we are at our work.

MISS BETTY Will dear Lady Arabella give us leave, mother, to do a stitch or two with her? (*Takes the box and throws*)

CAPTAIN TOUPEE The pretty lively thing!

LADY ARABELLA With all her heart; what says your mama?   205

LADY HEADPIECE She says, she don't love to sit with her hands before her when other people's are employed.

CAPTAIN TOUPEE And this is the prettiest little sociable work; men and women can all do together at it.

LADY HEADPIECE Colonel, you are one with us, are you not?   210

LADY ARABELLA O, I'll answer for him; he'll be out at nothing.

CAPTAIN TOUPEE In a facetious way; he is the politest person. He will lose his money to the ladies so civilly, and will win theirs with so much good breeding; and he will be so modest to 'em before company, and so impudent to 'em in a dark corner. Ha!   215
Colonel!

LADY HEADPIECE So I found him, I'm sure, last night. Mercy on me, an ounce of virtue less than I had, and Sir Francis had been undone.

CAPTAIN TOUPEE Colonel, I smoke you.   220

COLONEL COURTLY And a fine character you give the ladies of me to help me.

CAPTAIN TOUPEE I give 'em just the character of you they like, modest and brave. Come ladies, to business. Look to your money— every woman her hand upon her purse.° 225

MISS BETTY Here's mine, captain.

CAPTAIN TOUPEE O the little soft velvet one; and it's as full . . . Come Lady Blowze,° rattle your dice, and away with 'em.

LADY ARABELLA Six . . . at all . . . five to six . . . five . . . eight . . . at all again . . . nine to eight . . . nine . . . 230
Enter Sir Francis, and stands gazing at 'em
Seven's the main . . . at all for ever. (*Throws out*)

MISS BETTY Now Mama, let's see what you can do.
Lady Headpiece takes the box

LADY HEADPIECE Well, I'll warrant you, daughter.

MISS BETTY If you do, I'll follow a good example.

LADY HEADPIECE Eight's the main . . . don't spare me gentlemen, I 235 fear you not . . . have at you all . . . seven to eight . . . seven.

CAPTAIN TOUPEE Eight, lady, eight . . . five pounds if you please.

LADY ARABELLA Three, kinswoman.

COLONEL COURTLY Two, madam.

MISS BETTY And one for Miss, Mama . . . and now let's see what I 240 can do. (*Aside*) If I should win enough this morning to buy me another new gown—o bless me! There they go—seven . . . come Captain, set me boldly, I want to be at a handful.

CAPTAIN TOUPEE There's two for you Miss.

MISS BETTY I'll at 'em, though I die for't. 245

SIR FRANCIS Ah my poor child, take care. (*Runs to stop the throw*)

MISS BETTY There.

CAPTAIN TOUPEE Out . . . twenty pounds, young lady.

SIR FRANCIS False dice, sir.

CAPTAIN TOUPEE False dice, sir? I scorn your words . . . twenty 250 pounds, madam.

MISS BETTY Undone, undone!

SIR FRANCIS She shan't pay you a farthing, sir; I won't have Miss cheated.

CAPTAIN TOUPEE Cheated, sir? 255

LADY HEADPIECE What do you mean, Sir Francis, to disturb the company and abuse the gentleman thus?

SIR FRANCIS I mean to be in a passion.

LADY HEADPIECE And why will you be in a passion, Sir Francis?

SIR FRANCIS Because I came here to breakfast with my lady there 260 before I went down to the house, expecting to find my family set round a civil table with her upon some plum cake, hot rolls, and a cup of strong beer; instead of which, I find these good women staying their stomachs with a box and dice, and that man there, with the strange periwig, making a good hearty meal upon my wife 265 and daughter—

   Cætera desunt°

THE COUNTRY HOUSE

A Farce

THE CHARACTERS OF THE PLAY

Mr Barnard.
Mr Griffard, brother to Mr Barnard
Erast, in love with Mariane
Dorant, son to Mr Barnard
The Marquis
The Baron de Messy
Janno, cousin to Mr Barnard
Collin, servant to Mr Barnard
Charly, a boy
A Soldier
Servant to Dorant
Servant to Erast
A Cook
Three gentlemen, friends to Dorant

Madam Barnard
Mariane, her daughter
Mawkin,° sister to Janno
Lisett, servant to Mariane

1.1

[Mr Barnard's country house in Normandy]

Enter Erast and his Servant, with Lisett

LISETT Once more I'll tell ye, sir, if you've any consideration in the world for her, you must be gone this minute.

ERAST My dear Lisett, let me but see her; let me but speak to her only.

LISETT You may do what you will. Here you are in our house, and I do believe she's as impatient to see you as you can be to see her; but— 5

ERAST But why won't you give us that satisfaction then?

LISETT Because I know the consequence; for when you once get together, the devil himself is not able to part ye. You'll stay so long till you're surprised, and what shall become of us then?

SERVANT Why, then we shall be thrown out at the window, I suppose. 10

LISETT No, but I shall be turned out of doors.

ERAST How unfortunate am I! These doors are open to all the world, and only shut to me.

LISETT Because you come for a wife, and at our house we don't care for people that come for wives. 15

SERVANT What would you have us come for then?

LISETT Because such people generally want portions.

SERVANT Portion! No, no, never talk of portions. My master nor I neither don't want portions; *[to Erast]* and if you'd follow my advice, a regiment of fathers should not guard her. 20

LISETT What's that?

SERVANT Why, if you'll contrive that my master may run away with your mistress, I don't much care, faith, if I run away with you.

LISETT Don't you so, rogue's face? But I hope to be better provided for. 25

ERAST Hold your tongue. But where is her brother? He is my bosom friend, and would be willing to serve me.

LISETT I told you before that he has been abroad a-hunting, and we han't seen him these three days. He seldom lies at home, to avoid his father's ill humour; so that it is not your mistress only that our 30 old covetous cuff° teases—there's nobody in the family but feels the effects of his ill humour. By his good will he would not suffer a creature to come within his doors, or eat at his table; and then if there be but a rabbit extraordinary for dinner, he thinks himself ruined for ever. 35

ERAST Then I find you pass your time comfortably in this family.

LISETT Not so bad as you imagine neither, perhaps; for, thank heaven, we have a mistress that's as bountiful as he's stingy, one that will let him say what he will, and yet does what she will. But hark, here's somebody coming; it is certainly he. 40

ERAST Can't you hide us somewhere?

LISETT Here, here, get you in here as fast as you can.

SERVANT Thrust me in too.

> [Lisett] puts [Erast and Servant] into the closet
> Enter Mariane

LISETT O, is it you?

MARIANE So, Lisett, where have you been? I've been looking for ye all 45
over the house. Who are those people in the garden with my mother-in-law? I believe my father won't be very well pleased to see 'em there.

LISETT And here's somebody else not far off that I believe your father won't be very well pleased with neither. (*Calls*) Come, sir! 50
Sir!

> Enter Erast and Servant

MARIANE (*cries out*) O heavens!

LISETT Come, lovers, I can allow you but a short bout on't this time. You must do your work with a jerk—one whisper, two sighs, and a kiss. Make haste I say, and I'll stand sentry for ye in the 55
meantime.

> Exit Lisett

MARIANE Do you know what you expose me to, Erast? What do you mean?

ERAST To die, madam, since you receive me with so little pleasure.

MARIANE Consider what would become of me if my father should see 60
you here.

ERAST What would you have me do?

MARIANE Expect with patience some happy turn of affairs. My mother-in-law is kind and indulgent to a miracle, and her favour, if well managed, may turn to our advantage. And could I prevail upon 65
myself to declare my passion to her, I don't doubt but she'd join in our interest.

ERAST Well, since we've nothing to fear from her, and your brother you know is my intimate friend, therefore you may conceal me somewhere about the house for a few days. I'll hide anywhere. 70

SERVANT [*aside*] Ay, but who must have the care of bringing us victuals?

ERAST Thrust us into the cellar—up into the garret; I don't care where it is, so that it be but under the same roof with ye.

SERVANT But I don't say so, for that jade Lisett will have the feeding of us, and I know what kind of diet she keeps. I believe we shan't be like the fox in the fable.° Our bellies won't be so full but we shall be able to creep out at the same hole we got in at.

ERAST Must I then be gone? Must I return to Paris?

Enter Lisett

LISETT Yes, that you must, and immediately too, for here's my master coming in upon ye.

ERAST What shall I do?

LISETT Begone this minute.

MARIANE Stay in the village till you hear from me; none of our family know that you are here.

ERAST Shall I see you sometimes?

MARIANE I han't time to answer you now.

LISETT Make haste, I say; are you bewitched?

ERAST Will you write to me?

MARIANE I will if I can.

LISETT Begone, I say. Is the devil in you?

[*Thrusting Erast and his Servant out*]

Come this way; your father's just stepping in upon us.

Exeunt [Lisett and Mariane]

Enter Mr Barnard beating Collin

MR BARNARD Rogue! Rascal! Did not I command you? Did not I give you my orders, sirrah?

COLLIN Why, you give me orders to let nobody in; and madam, her gives me orders to let everybody in—why, the devil himself can't please you both, I think.

MR BARNARD But, sirrah, you must obey my orders, not hers.

COLLIN Why, the gentlefolks asked for her; they did not ask for you— what do ye make such a noise about?

MR BARNARD For that reason, sirrah, you should not let 'em in.

COLLIN Hold, sir, I'd rather see you angry than her, that's true. For when you're angry you have the de'il in ye, that's true enough; but when madam's in passion she has the de'il and his dam both in her belly.

MR BARNARD You must mind what I say to you, sirrah, and obey my orders.

COLLIN Ay, ay, measter—but let's not quarrel with one another; you're always in such a plaguey humour.

305

MR BARNARD What are these people that are just come? 110

COLLIN Nay, that know not I; but, as fine folk they are as ever eye beheld, heaven bless 'em.

MR BARNARD Did you hear their names?

COLLIN Noa, noa, but in a coach they ceam all besmeared with gould; with six breave horses, the like on 'em ne'er did I set eyes 115 on. 'Twould do a man's heart good to look on those fine beasts, measter.

MR BARNARD How many persons are there?

COLLIN Four—two as fine men as ever woman bore, and two as dainty deames as a man would desire to lay his lips to. 120

MR BARNARD And all this crew sets up at my house.

COLLIN Noa, noa, measter, the coachman is gone into the village to set up his coach at some inn, for I told him our coach-house was full of faggots, but he'll bring back the six horses, for I told him we had a rear good steable. 125

MR BARNARD (*beating him*) Did you so, rascal? Did you so?

COLLIN Doant, doant, sir. It would do you good to see those cattle. I' faith they look as if they had ne'er kept Lent.

MR BARNARD Then they shall learn religion at my house. Sirrah, do you take care they sup without oats tonight. What will become of 130 me? Since I bought this damned country house, I spend more in a summer than would maintain me seven year.

COLLIN Why, if you spend money han't you good things for it all the whole country raund? Come they not all to see you? Mind how you're beloved, measter. 135

MR BARNARD Pox take such love!

Enter Lisett

How now, what do you want?

LISETT Sir, there's some company in the garden with my mistress, who desire to see you.

MR BARNARD Devil take 'em, what business have they here? But who 140 are they?

LISETT Why, sir, there's the fat abbot that always sets so long at dinner, and drinks his two bottles by way of whet.

MR BARNARD I wish his church was in his belly, that his guts might be half full before he came—and who else? 145

LISETT Then there's the young marquis that won all my lady's money at cards.

MR BARNARD Pox take him too.

LISETT Then there's the merry lady that's always in good humour.

MR BARNARD Very well.   150

LISETT Then there's she that threw down all my lady's china t'other
day, and then laughed at it for a jest.

MR BARNARD Which I paid above fifty pounds for in earnest. Very
well, and pray how did madam receive all this fine company? With a
hearty welcome and a curtsey with her bum down to the ground,   155
ha?

LISETT No indeed, sir, she was very angry with 'em.

MR BARNARD How! Angry with 'em, say you?

LISETT Yes indeed, sir, for she expected they would have stayed here a
fortnight; but it seems things happen so unluckily that they can't   160
stay here above ten days.

MR BARNARD Ten days! How! What! Four persons with a coach and
six, and a kennel of hungry hounds in liveries, to live upon me ten
days!

    Exit Lisett
    Enter a Soldier

So, what do you want?   165

SOLDIER Sir, I come from your nephew, Captain Hungary.°

MR BARNARD Well, what does he want?

SOLDIER He gives his service to you, sir, and sends you word that he'll
come and dine with you tomorrow.

MR BARNARD Dine with me! No, no, friend, tell him I don't dine at all   170
tomorrow; it is my fast day—my wife died on't.

SOLDIER And he has sent you here a pheasant and a couple of
partridges.

MR BARNARD How's that, a pheasant and partridges, say you? Let's
see—very fine birds truly—let me consider—tomorrow is not my   175
fast day, I mistook; tell my nephew he shall be welcome—and d'ye
hear? (*To Collin*) Do you take these fowl and hang them up in a
cool place—and take this soldier in and make him drink—make
him drink, do ye see—a cup—ay, a cup of small beer—do ye
hear?   180

COLLIN Yes, sir. Come along; our small beer is rare good.

SOLDIER But sir, he bad me tell ye that he'll bring two or three of his
brother officers along with him.

MR BARNARD How's that! Officers with him? Here, come back—take
the fowl again. I don't dine tomorrow, and so tell him.   185

    Gives [the Soldier] the basket

Go, go.

    Thrusts him out

SOLDIER Sir, sir, that won't hinder them from coming, for they
retired off the camp; and because your house is near 'em, sir, they
resolve to come.

MR BARNARD Go, begone rogue!   190

    Thrusts him out

There's a rogue now, that sends me three lean carrion birds, and
brings half a dozen rogues to eat them.

    Enter [Mr Barnard's] brother [Mr Griffard]

MR GRIFFARD Brother, what is the meaning of these doings? If you
don't order your affairs better, you'll have your fowl taken out of
your very yard, and carried away before your face.   195

MR BARNARD Can I help it, brother? But what's the matter now?

MR GRIFFARD There's a parcel of fellows have been hunting about
your grounds all this morning, broke down your hedges, and are
now coming into your house—don't you hear them?

MR BARNARD No, I did not hear them; but who are they?   200

MR GRIFFARD Three or four rakehelly officers, with your nephew at
the head of 'em.

MR BARNARD O the rogue! He might well send me fowl, but is it not a
vexatious thing that I must stand still and see myself plundered at
this rate, and have a carrion of a wife that thinks I ought to thank all 205
these rogues that come to devour me? But can't you advise me
what's to be done in this case?

MR GRIFFARD I wish I could, for it goes to my heart to see you thus
treated by a crew of vermin who think they do you a great deal of
honour in ruining of you.   210

MR BARNARD Can there be no way found to redress this?

MR GRIFFARD If I were you, I'd leave this house quite, and go to
town.

MR BARNARD What, leave my wife behind me? Ay, that would be
mending the matter indeed!   215

MR GRIFFARD Why don't you sell it then?

MR BARNARD Because nobody will buy it; it has got as ill a name as if
it had the plague. It has been sold over and over, and every family
that has lived in it has been ruined.

MR GRIFFARD Then send away all your beds and furniture, except   220
what is absolutely necessary for your family. You'll save something
by that, for then your guests can't stay with you all night, however.

MR BARNARD I've tried that already, and it signified nothing. For they
all got drunk and lay in the barn, and next morning laughed it off
for a frolic.   225

MR GRIFFARD Then there is but one remedy left that I can think of.

MR BARNARD What's that?

MR GRIFFARD You must e'en do what's done when a town's a-fire—
blow up your house that the mischief may run no further. But who
is this gentleman?   230

MR BARNARD I never saw him in my life before, but for all that, I hold
fifty pound he comes to dine with me.

    Enter the Marquis

MARQUIS My dear Mr Barnard, I'm your most humble servant.

MR BARNARD I don't doubt it, sir.

MARQUIS What is the meaning of this, Mr Barnard? You look as   235
coldly upon me as if I were a stranger.

MR BARNARD Why truly, sir, I'm very apt to do so by persons I never
saw in my life before.

MARQUIS You must know, Mr Barnard, I'm come on purpose to drink
a bottle of wine with you.   240

MR BARNARD That may be, sir, but it happens that at this time I am
not at all dry.

MARQUIS I left the ladies at cards waiting for supper. For my part, I
never play, so I come to see my dear Mr Barnard; and I'll assure
you, I undertook this journey only to have the honour of your   245
acquaintance.

MR BARNARD You might have spared yourself that trouble, sir.

MARQUIS Don't you know, Mr Barnard, that this house of yours is a
little paradise?

MR BARNARD Then rot me if it be, sir.   250

MARQUIS For my part, I think a pretty retreat in the country is one of
the greatest comforts in life; I suppose you never want good company, Mr Barnard?

MR BARNARD No, sir, I never want company; for you must know I
love very much to be alone.   255

MARQUIS Good wine you must keep above all things. Without good
wine and good cheer I would not give a fig for the country.

MR BARNARD Really, sir, my wine is the worst you ever drank in your
life, and you'll find my cheer but very indifferent.

MARQUIS No matter, no matter, Monsieur Barnard. I've heard much   260
of your hospitality, there's a plentiful table in your looks—and your
wife is certainly the best woman in the world.

MR BARNARD Rot me if she be, sir.

    Enter Collin

COLLIN Sir, sir, yonder's the Baron de Messy has lost his hawk in our

garden. He says it is pearched upon one of the trees. May we let 265
him have'n again, sir?

MR BARNARD Go tell him that—

COLLIN Nay, you may tell him yourself, for here he comes.

Enter the Baron de Messy

BARON Sir, I'm your most humble servant, and ask you a thousand
pardons that I should live so long in your neighbourhood, and come 270
upon such an occasion as this to pay you my first respects.

MR BARNARD It is very well, sir, but I think people may be very good
neighbours without visiting one another.

BARON Pray how do you like our country?

MR BARNARD Not at all. I'm quite tired on't. 275

MARQUIS [*aside*] Is it not the Baron? It is certainly he.

BARON How, my dear Marquis! Let me embrace you.

MARQUIS My dear Baron, let me kiss you.

They run and embrace

BARON We have not seen one another since we were schoolfellows,
before. 280

MARQUIS The happiest rencounter!

MR GRIFFARD These gentlemen seem to be very well acquainted.

MR BARNARD Yes, but I know neither one nor t'other of them.

MARQUIS Baron, let me present to you one of the best-natured
men in the world! Mr Barnard here, the flower of hospitality. I 285
congratulate you upon having so good a neighbour.

MR BARNARD Sir!

BARON It is an advantage I am proud of.

MR BARNARD Sir!

BARON Come, gentlemen, you must be very intimate; let me have the 290
honour of bringing you better acquainted.

MR BARNARD Sir!

BARON Dear Marquis, I shall take it as a favour if you'll do me that
honour.

MR BARNARD Sir! 295

MARQUIS With all my heart. Come, Baron, now you are here we can
make up the most agreeable company in the world—faith, you shall
stay and pass a few days with us.

MR BARNARD Now methinks this son of a whore does the honour of
my house° to a miracle. 300

BARON I don't know what to say; but I should be very glad you'd
excuse me.

MARQUIS Faith, I can't.

310

BARON Dear Marquis.

MARQUIS Egad, I won't.   305

BARON Well, since it must be so—but here comes the lady of the family.

Enter Madam Barnard

MARQUIS Madam, let me present to you the flower of France.

BARON Madam, I shall think myself the happiest person in the world in your ladyship's acquaintance; and the little estate I have in this   310 country I esteem more than all the rest, because it lies so near your ladyship.

MADAM BARNARD Sir, your most humble servant.

MARQUIS Madam, the Baron de Messy is the best-humoured man in the world. I've prevailed with him to give us his company a few   315 days.

MADAM BARNARD I'm sure you could not oblige Mr Barnard or me more.

MR BARNARD (*aside*) That's a damned lie, I'm sure.

BARON I'm sorry, madam, I can't accept of the honour, but it falls out   320 so unlucky, for I've some ladies at my house that I can't possibly leave.

MARQUIS No matter, no matter, Baron. You have ladies at your house, we have ladies at our house. Let's join companies. Come let's send for them immediately; the more the merrier.   325

MR BARNARD An admirable expedient, truly!

BARON Well, since it must be so, I'll go for them myself.

MARQUIS Make haste, dear Baron, for we shall be impatient for your return.

BARON Madam, your most humble servant. But I won't take my leave   330 of you—I shall be back again immediately. Monsieur Barnard, I'm your most humble servant; since you will have it so, I'll return as soon as possible.

MR BARNARD I have it so! 'Sbud, sir, you may stay as long as you please. I'm in no haste for ye.   335

Exeunt Baron and Marquis

MR BARNARD Madam, you are the cause that I am not master of my own house.

MADAM BARNARD Will you never learn to be reasonable, husband?

The Marquis returns

MARQUIS The Baron is the best-humoured man in the world—only a little too ceremonious, that's all. I love to be free and generous.   340 Since I came to Paris I've reformed half the court.

MADAM BARNARD You are of the most agreeable humour in the world.

MARQUIS Always merry—but what have you done with the ladies?

MADAM BARNARD I left them at cards.   345

MARQUIS Well, I'll wait upon 'em. But madam, let me desire you not put yourself to any extraordinary expense upon our accounts. You must consider we have more than one day to live together.

MR BARNARD You are pleased to be merry, Marquis.

MARQUIS Treat us without ceremony. Good wine and poultry you   350
have of your own; wild fowl and fish are brought to your door. You need not send abroad for anything but a piece of butcher's meat or so—let us have no extraordinaries.

    Exit [Marquis]

MR BARNARD If I had the feeding of you, a thunderbolt should be your supper.   355

MADAM BARNARD Husband, will you never change your humour? If you go on at this rate, it will be impossible to live with ye.

MR BARNARD Very true, for in a little time I shall have nothing to live upon.

MADAM BARNARD Do you know what a ridiculous figure you make?   360

MR BARNARD You'll make a great deal worse when you han't money enough to pay for the washing of your smocks.

MADAM BARNARD It seems you married me only to dishonour me. How horrible this is!

MR BARNARD I tell ye, you'll ruin me! Do you know how much   365
money you spend in a year?

MADAM BARNARD Not I truly; I don't understand arithmetic.

MR BARNARD Arithmetic? O Lud! O Lud! Is it so hard to comprehend, that he who spends a shilling and receives but sixpence must be ruined in the end?   370

MADAM BARNARD I never troubled my head with accounts, nor never will; but if you did but know what ridiculous things the world says of ye—

MR BARNARD Rot the world—'twill say worse of me when I'm in a jail.   375

MADAM BARNARD A very Christian-like saying, truly.

MR BARNARD Don't tell me of Christian—adsbud, I'll turn Jew, and nobody shall eat at my table that is not circumcised.

    Enter Lisett

LISETT Madam, there's the Duchess of Twangdillo° just set down near our door. Her coach was overturned.   380

MADAM BARNARD I hope her grace has received no hurt.

LISETT No, madam, but her coach is broke.

MR BARNARD Then there's a smith in town may mend it.

LISETT They say 'twill require two or three days to fit it up.

MADAM BARNARD I'm glad on't with all my heart, for then I shall 385
enjoy the pleasure of her grace's good company—I'll wait upon
her.

MR BARNARD Very fine doings!

Exeunt severally

2.1

[Mr Barnard's house]
Enter Mr Barnard

MR BARNARD Now heaven be my comfort, for my house is hell. *[Starts]* How now, what do you want? Who are you?

Enter Servant with a portmanteau

SERVANT Sir, here's your cousin Janno and cousin Mawkin come from Paris.

MR BARNARD What a plague do they want?   5

[Exit Servant]
Enter Janno leading in Mawkin

JANNO Come, sister, come along. O here's cousin Barnard—cousin Barnard, your servant—here's my sister Mawkin and I are come to see you.

MAWKIN Ay, cousin, here's brother Janno and I are come from Paris to see you. Pray how does cousin Mariane do?   10

JANNO My sister and I waunt well at Paris, so my father sent us here for two or three weeks to take a little country air.

MR BARNARD You could not come to a worse place, for this is the worst air in the whole country.

MAWKIN Nay, I'm sure my father says it is the best.   15

MR BARNARD Your father's a fool I tell ye, 'tis the worst

JANNO Nay, cousin, I fancy you're mistaken now; for I begin to find my stomach come to me already. In a fortnight's time you'll see how I'll lay about me.

MR BARNARD I don't at all doubt it.   20

MAWKIN Father would have sent sister Flip and little brother Humphry, but the Calash would not hold us all, and so they don't come till tomorrow with mother.

JANNO Come sister, let's put up our things in our chamber, and after you have washed my face, and put me on a clean neckcloth, we'll go   25
and see how our cousins do.

MAWKIN Ay, come along, we'll go and see cousin Mariane.

JANNO Cousin, we shan't give you much trouble. One bed will serve us, for sister Mawkin and I always lie together.

MAWKIN But, cousin, mother prays you that you'd order a little cock-   30
broth° for brother Janno and I, to be got ready as soon as may be.

JANNO Ay, *à propos*, cousin Barnard, that's true. My mother desires that we may have some cock-broth to drink two or three times a day between meals, for my sister and I are sick folks.

MAWKIN And some young chickens too the doctor said would bring   35
us to our stomachs very soon.

JANNO You fib now, sister. It waunt young chickens, so it waunt; it was plump partridges. Sure, the doctor said so.

MAWKIN Ay, so it was brother. Come, let's go see our cousins.

JANNO Ay, come along sister. Cousin Barnard, don't forget the   40
cock-broth.

    Exeunt Janno and Mawkin

MR BARNARD What the devil does all this mean? Mother, and sister Flip, and little brother Humphry, and chickens, and pigeons, and cock-broth, and fire from hell to dress 'em all.

    Enter Collin

COLLIN O measter, o measter, you'll not chide today as you are usen   45
to do; no, marry will you not. See now what it is to be wiser than one's measter.

MR BARNARD What would this fool have?

COLLIN Why thanks, and money to boot, an folk were grateful.

MR BARNARD What's the matter?   50

COLLIN Why the matter is: if you have store of company in your house, why you have store of meat to put in their bellies.

MR BARNARD How so? How so?

COLLIN A large and steatly stag, with a pair of horns of his head, heavens bless you, your worship might have seen to wear 'em,   55
comes towards our geat a puffing and blowing like cew° in hard labour. 'Now,' says I to myself, says I, 'if my measter refuse to let this fine youth come in, why then he's a fool de ye see'; so I opens him the geat, pulls off my hat with both my hands, and said 'You're welcome, kind sir, to our house.'   60

MR BARNARD Well, well!

COLLIN Well, well, ay, and so it is well as you shall straightway find. So in a trots, and makes directly towards our barn, and goes bounce, bounce, against the door, as boldly as if he had been measter on't. He turns 'en about and twacks 'n down in the stra, as   65
who would say, here will I lay me 'till tomorrow morning; but he had no fool to deal with—for to the kitchen goes I, and takes me down a musket, and with a brace of balls, I hits'n such a slap in the face, that he ne'er spoke a word more to me. Have I done well or no, measter?   70

MR BARNARD Yes, you have done very well for once.

COLLIN But this was not all, for a parcel of dogs came yelping after
their companion, as I suppose. So I goes to our back yard door,
and as many as came by, 'shoo' says I, and drive 'em into the
gearden, so there they are safe as in a pound. Ha, ha, but I can   75
but think what a power of pasties we shall have at our house—ha,
ha.

> (*Exit Collin*)

MR BARNARD I see providence takes some care of me. This could
never have happened in a better time.

> *Enter Cook*

COOK Sir, sir, in the name of wonder, what do you mean? Is it by your   80
orders that all those dogs were let into the garden.

MR BARNARD How!

COOK I believe there's forty or fifty dogs tearing up the lettuce and
cabbage by the root. I believe before they've done they'll root up
the whole garden.   85

MR BARNARD This is that rogue's doings.

COOK This was not all, sir, for three or four of 'em came into the
kitchen, and tore half the meat off the spit that was for your worship's supper.

MR BARNARD The very dogs plague me.   90

COOK And then there's a crew of hungry footmen devoured what the
dogs left, so that there's not a bit left for your worship's supper—
not a scrap, not one morsel, sir.

> *Exit Cook*

MR BARNARD Sure I shall hit on some way to get rid of this crew.

> *Enter Collin*

COLLIN Sir, sir, here's the devil to do without. Yonder, a parcel of   95
fellows swear they'll have our venison, and 'sblead I swear they shall
have none on't, so stand to your arms, measter.

MR BARNARD (*beating him*) Ay, you've done finely; rogue, rascal, have
you not?

COLLIN 'Sblead I say they shan't have our venison. I'll die before I'll   100
part with it.

> *Exit* [*Collin*]
> *Enter* [*Barnard's*] *brother* [*Mr Griffard*]

MR GRIFFARD Brother, there's some gentlemen within ask for you.

MR BARNARD What gentlemen? Who are they?

MR GRIFFARD The gentlemen that have been hunting all this
morning. They're now gone up to your wife's chamber.   105

MR BARNARD The devil go with 'em.

MR GRIFFARD There's but one way to get rid of this plague, and that
is as I told you before—to set your house on fire.

MR BARNARD That's doing myself an injury, not them.

MR GRIFFARD There's dogs, horses, masters, and servants all intend   110
to stay here till tomorrow morning, that they may be near the
woods to hunt the earlier. Besides, I overheard 'em. They're in a
kind of a plot against you.

MR BARNARD What did they say?

MR GRIFFARD You'll be angry if I should tell ye?   115

MR BARNARD Can I be more angry than I am?

MR GRIFFARD Then they said it was the greatest pleasure in the world
to ruin an old lawyer in the country, who had got an estate by
ruining honest people in town.

MR BARNARD There's rogues for ye!   120

MR GRIFFARD I'm mistaken if they don't play you some trick or other.

MR BARNARD Hold, let me consider.

MR GRIFFARD What are you doing?

MR BARNARD I'm conceiving—I shall bring forth° presently. Oh, I
have it, it comes from hence: wit was its father, and invention its   125
mother. If I had thought on't sooner, I should have been happy.

MR GRIFFARD What is it?

MR BARNARD Come, come along I say, you must help me to put it in
execution.

Enter Lisett

LISETT Sir, my mistress desires you to walk up. She is not able, all   130
alone, to pay the civilities due to so much good company.

MR BARNARD O the carrion! What, does she play her jests upon me
too! But mum, he laughs best that laughs last.

LISETT What shall I tell her, sir? Will you come?

MR BARNARD Yes, yes, tell her I'll come, with a pox to her.   135

Exeunt Mr Barnard and [Mr Griffard]

LISETT Nay, I don't wonder he should be angry—they do try his
patience, that's the truth on't.

Enter Mariane

What, madam, have you left your mother and the company?

MARIANE So much tittle tattle makes my head ache. I don't wonder
my father should not love the country, for besides the expense he's   140
at, he never enjoys a minute's quiet.

LISETT But let's talk of your own affairs. Have you writ to your lover?

MARIANE No, for I have not had time since I saw him.

LISETT Now you have time then, about it immediately, for he's a sort

of a desperate spark and a body does not know what he may do if he   145
should not hear from you; besides you promised him, and you must
behave yourself like a woman of honour, and keep your word.

MARIANE I'll about it this minute.

      Enter Charly

CHARLY Cousin, cousin, cousin, where are you going? Come back, I
have something to say to you.   150

LISETT What does this troublesome boy want?

CHARLY What's that to you what I want? Perhaps I have something to
say to her that will make her laugh. Why sure, what need you care?

MARIANE Don't snub my cousin, Charly—well, what is't?

CHARLY Who do you think I met as I was coming here, but that   155
handsome gentleman I've seen at church ogle you like any devil.

MARIANE Hush, softly cousin.

LISETT Not a word of that for your life.

CHARLY O, I know I should not speak on't before folks. You know I
made signs to you above that I wanted to speak to you in private,   160
did not I, cousin?

MARIANE Yes, yes, I saw you.

CHARLY You see I can keep a secret. I am no girl, mun! I believe I
could tell ye fifty and fifty to that, of my sister Sis°—o, she's the
devil of a girl! But she gives me money and sugar-plums; and those   165
that are kind to me fare the better for it, you see cousin.

MARIANE I always said my cousin Charly was a good-natured boy.

LISETT Well, and did he know you?

CHARLY Yes, I think he did know me; for he took me in his arms, and
did so hug me and kiss me—between you and I, cousin, I believe   170
he's one of the best friends I have in the world.

MARIANE Well, but what did he say to you?

CHARLY Why, he asked me where I was going. I told him I was coming to see you. 'You're a lying young rogue,' says he. 'I'm sure you
dare not go see your cousin'; for you must know, my sister was with   175
me, and it seems he took her for a crack, and I being a forward boy,
he fancied I was going to make love to her under a hedge, ha, ha.

MARIANE So.

CHARLY So he offered to lay me a *Louis d'Or*° that I was not coming
to you. So 'done,' says I; 'done,' says he—and so 'twas a bet, you   180
know.

MARIANE Certainly.

CHARLY So my sister's honour being concerned, and having a mind
to win his *Louis d'Or*, d'ye see, I bad him follow me, that he might

see whether I came in or no; but he said he'd wait for me at the little   185
garden door that opens into the fields, and if I would come through
the house and meet him there, he'd know by that whether I had
been in or no.

MARIANE Very well.

CHARLY So I went there, opened the door, and let him in—   190

MARIANE What then?

CHARLY Why, then he paid me the *Louis d'Or*, that's all.

MARIANE Why, that was honestly done.

CHARLY And then he talked to me of you, and said you had the
charmingest bubbies, and every time he named 'em, 'ha!' says he, as   195
if he had been supping hot milk tea.

MARIANE But was this all?

CHARLY No, for he had a mind, you must know, to win his *Louis d'Or*
back again. So he laid me another, that I dare not come back and
tell you that he was there. So cousin, I hope you won't let me lose,   200
for if you don't go to him and tell him that I've won, he won't pay
me.

MARIANE What, would you have me go and speak to a man?

CHARLY Not for any harm, but to win your poor cousin a *Louis d'Or*.
I'm sure you will, for you're a modest young woman, and may go   205
without danger. Well, cousin, I'll swear you look very handsome
today, and have the prettiest bubbies there. Do let me touch 'em;
I'll swear I must.

MARIANE What does the young rogue mean? I swear I'll have you
whipped.   210

> *Exeunt Charly, Mariane*
> *Enter Collin*

COLLIN Ha, ha! Od, the old gentleman's a wag efaith; he'll be even
with 'em for all this, ha—

LISETT What's the matter? What does the fool laugh at?

COLLIN We an't in our house now Lisett; we're in an inn; ha, ha!

LISETT How in an inn?   215

COLLIN Yes, in an inn. My measter has gotten an old rusty sword, and
hung it up at our geat, and writ underneath, with a piece of char-
coal, with his own fair hand: *At the Sword Royal; Entertainment for
Man and Horse*. Ha, ha—

LISETT What whim is this?   220

COLLIN Thou and I live at the Sword Royal, ha, ha—

LISETT I'll go tell my mistress of her father's extravagance.

> *Exit Lisett*

Enter Mr Barnard and [Mr Griffard]

MR BARNARD Ha, ha! Yes I think this will do. [*To Collin*] Sirrah, now you may let in all the world; the more the better.

COLLIN Yes, sir. Odsflesh! We shall break all the inns in the country, 225
for we have a breave handsome landlady, and a curious young lass to her daughter. O, here comes my young measter; we'll make him chamberlain. Ha, ha—

Enter Dorant

MR BARNARD What's the matter, son? How comes it that you are all alone? You used to do me the favour to bring some of your friends 230
along with ye.

DORANT Sir, there are some of 'em coming. I only rid before to beg you to give 'em a favourable reception.

MR BARNARD Ay, why not? It is both for your honour and mine; you shall be master. 235

DORANT Now, sir, we have an opportunity of making all the gentle-men in the country our friends.

MR BARNARD I'm glad on't with all my heart; pray, how so?

DORANT There's an old quarrel to be made up between two families, and all the company is to meet at our house. 240

MR BARNARD Ay, with all my heart, but pray what is the quarrel?

DORANT O, sir, a very ancient quarrel. It happened between their great grandfathers about a duck.

MR BARNARD A quarrel of consequence truly.

DORANT And 'twill be a great honour to us if this should be 245
accommodated at our house.

MR BARNARD Without doubt.

DORANT Dear sir, you astonish me with this goodness. How shall I express this obligation? I was afraid, sir, you would not like it.

MR BARNARD Why so? 250

DORANT I thought, sir, you did not care for the expense.

MR BARNARD O Lord, I'm the most altered man in the world from what I was. I'm quite another thing, mun; but how many are there of 'em?

DORANT Not above nine or ten of a side, sir. 255

MR BARNARD O, we shall dispose of them easily enough.

DORANT Some of 'em will be here presently; the rest I don't expect till tomorrow morning.

MR BARNARD I hope they're good companions—jolly fellows, that love to eat and drink well. 260

DORANT The merriest, best-natured creatures in the world, sir.

MR BARNARD I'm very glad on't, for 'tis such men I want. But come, brother, you and I will go and prepare for their reception.
> *Exeunt Mr Barnard and [Mr Griffard]*

DORANT Bless me, what an alteration is here? How my father's temper is altered within these two or three days! Do you know the meaning of this? 265

COLLIN Why, the meaning on't is—ha, ha—

DORANT Can you tell me the cause of this sudden change, I say?

COLLIN Why the cause on't is—ha, ha—

DORANT What do you laugh at, sirrah? Do you know? 270

COLLIN Ha—because the old gentleman's a drole,° that's all.

DORANT Sirrah, if I take cudgel—

COLLIN Nay, sir, don't be angry for a little harmless mirth—But here are your friends.
> *Enter three gentlemen*

DORANT Gentlemen, you are welcome to Pasty Hall; see that these gentlemen's horses are taken care of. 275

FIRST GENTLEMAN A very fine dwelling this.

DORANT Yes, the house is tolerable.

SECOND GENTLEMAN And a very fine lordship belongs to it.

DORANT The land is good. 280

THIRD GENTLEMAN This house ought to have been mine, for my grandfather sold it to his father, from whom your father purchased it.

DORANT Yes, the house has gone through a great many hands.

FIRST GENTLEMAN A sign there has been always good housekeeping in it. 285

DORANT And I hope there ever will.
> *Enter Mr Barnard and [Mr Griffard], dressed like drawers*

MR BARNARD Gentlemen, do you call? Will you please to see a room, gentlemen? Here somebody; take off the gentlemen's boots there.

DORANT Father! Uncle? What is the meaning of this? 290

MR BARNARD Here, show a room! Or will you please walk into the kitchen first, and see what you like for dinner.

FIRST GENTLEMAN Make no preparations, sir; your own dinner will suffice.

MR BARNARD Very well, I understand ye, let's see, how many are there of ye? [*Counts them*] One, two, three, four? Well, gentlemen, it is but half-a-crown apiece for yourselves, and sixpence apiece for your servants. Your dinner shall be ready in half an hour. Here, show the gentlemen into the Apollo.° 295

SECOND GENTLEMAN What, sir, does your father keep an inn?   300

MR BARNARD The Sword Royal, at your service, sir.

DORANT But, father, let me speak to ye. Will you shame me?

MR BARNARD My wine is very good, gentlemen, but to be plain with
    ye, it is dear.

DORANT O, I shall run distracted.   305

MR BARNARD You seem not to like my house, gentlemen. You may try
    all the inns in the country and not be better entertained; but I own
    my bills run high.

DORANT Gentlemen, let me beg the favour of ye.

FIRST GENTLEMAN Ay, my young squire of the Sword Royal, you   310
    shall receive some favours from us.

DORANT Dear *Monsieur la Garantiere*!

FIRST GENTLEMAN Here, my horse there.

DORANT *Monsieur la Rose!*

SECOND GENTLEMAN Damn ye, you prig.   315

DORANT *Monsieur Trofignac!*

THIRD GENTLEMAN Go to the devil.

　　　　　Exeunt gentlemen

DORANT O, I'm disgraced forever.

MR BARNARD Now, son, this will teach you how to live.

DORANT Your son! I deny the kindred; I'm the son of a whore, and I'll   320
    burn your house about your ears, you old rogue you.

　　　　　Exit [Dorant]

MR BARNARD Ha, ha—

MR GRIFFARD The young gentleman's in a passion.

MR BARNARD They're all gone for all that, and the Sword Royal's the
    best general in Christendom.   325

　　　　　Enter Dorant's Servant, talking with Lisett

LISETT What, that tall gentleman I saw in the garden with ye?

SERVANT The same. He's my master's uncle, and ranger of all the
    king's forests. He intends to leave my master all he has.

MR BARNARD Don't I know this scoundrel? What, is his master here?
    What do you do here, rascal?   330

SERVANT I was asking which must be my master's chamber.

MR BARNARD Where is your master?

SERVANT Above stairs with your wife and daughter; and I want to
    know where he's to lie, that I may put up his things.

MR BARNARD Do you so, rascal?   335

SERVANT A very handsome inn this! Here, drawer, fetch me a pint of
    wine.

MR BARNARD Take that, rascal! Do you banter us? (*Kicks him out*)
>   *Enter Mrs Barnard*

MRS BARNARD What is the meaning of this, husband? Are not you
>   ashamed to turn your house into an inn—and is this a dress for my   340
>   husband, and a man of your character?

MR BARNARD I'd rather wear this dress than be ruined.

MRS BARNARD You're nearer being so than you imagine; for there are
>   some persons within that have it in their power to punish you for
>   your ridiculous folly.   345
>   *Enter Erast leading in Mariane*

MR BARNARD How, sirs? What means this? Who sent you here?

ERAST It was the luckiest star in your firmament that sent me here.

MR BARNARD Then I doubt that at my birth, the planets were but in a
>   scurvy disposition.°

ERAST The killing one of the king's stags° that run hither for refuge is   350
>   enough to overturn a fortune much better established than yours.
>   However, sir, if you consent to give me your daughter, for her sake I
>   will secure you harmless.

MR BARNARD No, sir. No man shall have my daughter that won't take
>   my house too.   355

ERAST Sir, I will take your house, pay you the full value on't, and you
>   shall remain as much its master as ever.

MR BARNARD No, sir, that won't do neither. You must be master on't
>   yourself, and from this minute begin to do the honours on't in your
>   own person.   360

ERAST Sir, I do consent.

MR BARNARD Upon that condition, and in order to get rid of my
>   house, here—take my daughter. And now, sir, if you think you've a
>   hard bargain, I don't care if I toss you in my wife, to make you
>   amends.   365

>   —Since all things now are sped,
>   My son in anger, and my daughter wed,
>   My house disposed of, which was the cause of strife,
>   I now may hope to lead a happy life,
>   If I can part with my engaging wife.   370

>   *Exeunt*

EXPLANATORY NOTES

For full details of the editions by Coleman, Cordner, Dobrée, Lowder-baugh, Smith, and Zimansky referred to in these notes, see the Select Bibliography.

The Relapse

TITLE PAGE

The play to which *The Relapse* was a reaction, and to which the term 'relapse' in the title refers, Colley Cibber's *Love's Last Shift; or, The Fool in Fashion*, was premièred at Drury Lane Theatre. The precise date is unknown, but Cibber (*An Apology for the Life of Mr Colley Cibber*, ed. R. W. Lowe, 2 vols. (London: J. C. Nimmo, 1889), i. 212–14) says that the playwright Thomas Southerne promoted it to the theatre manager Christopher Rich and it was acted in January 1696. Publication followed soon after, advertised in the *London Gazette* 3157 (10–13 February 1695/6—see *The London Stage 1660–1800. A Calender of Plays etc.*, ed. William von Lennop (Carbondale: Southern Illinois University Press, 1965), i. 457–8). For the relationship between this play and *The Relapse*, see Introduction, pp. x–xii.

PREFACE

2 *the town*: by 'town', Vanbrugh means the fashionable elite who live in the newly developing areas of London. After the Great Fire of 1666, there was large-scale development by aristocrats of great palaces and estates close to St James's into fashionable residential housing, in the areas of Piccadilly, St James's Street, the Haymarket and Pall Mall. A passage from John Dryden's 1673 play *Marriage à la Mode* gives the sense of a hierarchy of social spaces inhabited by, respectively, the courtier, town resident, fussy city dweller (finical cit), and country dweller:

DORALICE That's very true; your little courtier's wife, who speaks to the king but once a month, need but go to a town lady, and there she may vapour and cry 'The king and I' at every word. Your town lady, who is laughed at in the circle, takes her coach into the city, and there she's called Your Honour, and has a banquet from the merchant's wife, whom she laughs at for her kindness. And as for my finical cit, she removes but to her country house, and there insults

over the country gentlewoman that never comes up, who treats her
with frumity and custard, and opens her dear bottle of mirabilis
beside, for a gill-glass of it at parting. (2.1.140–8)

11 *blasphemy and bawdy*: strenuous agitation against the licentiousness of the
English stage had been occurring for some years before the first performance of the play (see Introduction, pp. viii–ix). The issue gained a higher
profile shortly after the play, when in 1698 Jeremy Collier published his *A
Short View of the Immorality and Profaneness of the English Stage*. This
provoked V. into defending his writing in a prose treatise called *A Short
Vindication of the* Relapse *and the* Provok'd Wife, *from Immorality and
Prophaneness* (1698). Whether this was an effective riposte to Collier
remains a very live issue in discussion of V.'s work. Collier's tactic of
quoting extensively from the plays to condemn the playwrights out of
their own mouths was original, and forced them onto the back foot. V.
tried to exculpate himself on an instance-by-instance basis, not the most
successful way to refute Collier. For a discussion of V.'s method of self-
defence, see Michael Cordner, 'Playwright versus Priest: Profanity and
the Wit of Restoration Comedy', in Deborah Payne Fisk (ed.), *The Cambridge Companion to English Restoration Theatre* (Cambridge: CUP, 2000),
209–25.

14 *by racking of mysteries*: i.e. even by torturing meaning out of the text as
one might an obscure passage in Scripture. V.'s enemies would have
found this deployment of a biblical analogy further evidence of his
inveterate and habitual profanity.

17 *closet*: Samuel Johnson's *Dictionary* (1755) defines this as 'a small room of
privacy'. Closets had a dubious reputation—places where women in particular could be free from patriarchal scrutiny, where they might keep
letters and read romances. To put the words 'closet' and 'innocent' in the
same sentence, as V. does here, is provocative.

22 *bawdy jest . . . ejaculation*: precisely what V. does in the sentence, by
punning on the grammatical and indecent senses of the word
'ejaculation'.

26 *Saints*: an ironic reference to all who put on a show of outward purity and
piety. The anti-stage agitation united on a common platform people from
differing religious groups who otherwise did not agree on very much,
such as the dissenters and non-juring former members of the Church of
England; for example Jeremy Collier, who would not take the oath of
allegiance to William and Mary after 1688.

42 *honest gentlemen of the town*: this has some of the French associations of
'honnête homme', 'man of breeding'. V. has in mind those young men of
gentlemanly status or bearing who are usually presented in comedies
of the period as succeeding very well with the ladies, and in life
generally—in contrast to those deemed 'fops'.

46 *spleen*: in the ancient tradition of medicine descending from the writings of the Greek Hippocrates (*c.*460–377 BC), there were four fluids or 'humours' that the body needed to keep in balance: blood, water, black bile, and yellow bile. When black bile predominated, the mood became melancholy. Black bile was thought to be seated in the spleen. By the later seventeenth century, 'spleen' had become the name of a melancholic or depressive complaint or illness fashionable amongst the upper classes.

50 *fine gentleman of the play*: the actor who played Worthy on the first night (probably 21 November 1696) was George Powell (?1688–1714), who had a bad reputation for being an unpleasant drunkard. His advances to Mrs Rogers, playing Amanda, were more realistic than is required by dramatic art! Cibber tells a story about Powell complaining that Cibber had a much better costume for Lord Foppington in *The Relapse* than he himself had in *Caesar Borgia*. Cibber was quick to point out the relative profitability of the roles. (Philip H. Highfill, Jr., Kalman A. Burnim, and Edward A. Langhans, *A Biographical Dictionary of Actors, Actresses, Musicians, Dancers, Managers & Other Stage Personnel in London, 1660–1800* (Carbondale: Southern Illinois UP, 1987), xii. 110.)

51 *Nantes brandy*: Nantes, the largest city in Brittany, was France's busiest port during this period. Before the rise of Cognac and the Charente as the main brandy-producing area of France, the thin wines from the hinterland of Nantes were very prominent in brandy manufacture, easily shipped out of the port. In the 1690s, when England was at war with France, French wines were heavily discriminated against by import duty, though smuggling was rife.

THE CHARACTERS OF THE PLAY

Sir Novelty Fashion: is the fop invented by, and played by, Colley Cibber in *Love's Last Shift*. V.'s joke for the sequel is that he has bought himself a title and has been elevated to Lord Foppington. Fopington was a name used by Aphra Behn in *The City-Heiress* (1682), though the character does not resemble Vanbrugh's. Sir Timothy Treat-all, the republican, true-blue Protestant protagonist of Behn's play, refers to Fopington (who is the untrustworthy hanger-on of his nephew Wilding) disparagingly as amongst 'such Tarmagant Tories as these, who are the very Vermine of a young Heir, and for one Tickling give him a thousand Bites' (1.1.33–5: *The Works of Aphra Behn*, ed. Janet Todd (London: Pickering, 1996), vii. 11).

Young Fashion: Cordner suggests that the surprising casting of a woman, Mrs Kent, in this role, was perhaps intended to soften the impact of Young Fashion's encounters with Coupler, the ageing homosexual pimp. These would be even more shocking if Young Fashion had been played by a man.

Loveless: in the first quarto edition of the play (1697), the name is given as 'Loveless' in the list of characters—the name Cibber uses in *Love's Last Shift*. However, the first stage direction in the 1697 edition is 'Enter Lovelace reading'.

Sir Tunbelly Clumsy: a 'tun' is a cask used for wine or beer. Falstaff puns on the word in conversation with Prince Hal: 'There is a devil haunts thee in the likeness of a fat old man; a tun of man is thy companion' (*Henry IV, Part 1*, 2.4.498).

Lory: a contraction of Lawrence. Laurence Sterne, for example, was addressed as 'Lory' by his close friends and family.

La Verole: 'La vérole' is French for syphilis, but is used also in the sense of 'very disagreeable person'. Q1 prints the name without the acute accent.

Miss Hoyden: 'hoyden' means 'a rude, or ill-bred girl; a boisterous noisy girl, a romp' (*OED*).

FIRST PROLOGUE

Miss Cross: Letitia Cross, who had played Cupid and sung in Cibber's *Love's Last Shift*, played Hoyden. There is some controversy about her age, but she was probably 19. She seems to have been associated with 'hoydenish' roles. In 1698 she eloped to France, and the actor and writer Joe Haines, who provided the epilogue to Farquhar's *Love and a Bottle* (1699), blamed this on Jeremy Collier. Lines 36–40: 'Oh Collier! Collier! Thou'st frighted away Miss C—s. | She, to return our Foreigner's Complizance, | At Cupid's Call, has made a Trip to France. | Love's Fire-Arm's here are since not worth a sous, | We've lost the only Touch-hole of our House'. (A 'touch-hole' is the vent of a firearm through which the charge is ignited; here with an indecent pun on a woman's genitals.)

3 *six weeks' space*: V.'s play was finished by April 1696, so it presumably was written within six weeks of publication of *Love's Last Shift*. But this prologue is part of a very lively debate in seventeenth-century aesthetics about whether it was desirable to write quickly, conducted often in play prologues and prefaces. Whereas in the era of Shakespeare and Jonson it had been desirable to claim that one dashed plays and poems off, rapid composition in the late seventeenth century was more likely to be perceived as part of a trading or commercial ethos. Thomas Shadwell, for example, frequently complained, as V. does here, that he simply did not have enough time to produce a considered and thoughtful dramatic composition.

17 *lug in resty nature's spite*: in the first quarto, 'resty' is given as 'wresty', but the meaning is *OED* 2: 'disinclined for action or exertion; sluggish, indolent, lazy'. Such authors have to overcome great inertia to write, just as

some beaux do to respond to challenges. Cowardice in responding to challenges is an aspect of Sir John Brute's character in *The Provoked Wife*.

28 *Hotspurs*: a hot-headed rebel in Shakespeare's *Henry IV Part 1*.

PROLOGUE ON THE THIRD DAY

On the third day of a production the takings normally went to the author, but V. apparently gave his share to the players. Commercial earnings from the theatre presumably did not suit his self-image.

5 *interest*: advantage; vested interest.

16 *by tedious form*: in the old-fashioned, prescribed manner.

21 *crowding on the stage*: a printed Bill of 2 March 1708 is one of several attempts to prevent this undesirable practice: 'Whereas we are informed that frequent disorders have been occasioned of late in our theatres in the Haymarket and Drury Lane by persons coming behind the scenes and standing upon the stage during the performance of plays and operas, by which means they cannot be acted to the best advantage: our will and pleasure therefore is, and we do hereby strictly require and command the managers, sharers, etc. of both our theatres in the Haymarket and Drury Lane that they suffer no person whatever hereafter to come behind the scenes, or be upon the stage, either before or during the acting any play or opera, excepting the actors and servants necessary for the performance thereof, upon pain of our highest displeasure' (D. Thomas and A. Hare, *Theatre in Europe: A Documentary History. Restoration and Georgian England, 1660–1788* (Cambridge: Cambridge University Press, 1989), 180).

22 *sped*: succeeded.

26 *comb*: given that wigs were covered with meal powder, combing would have been a very noticeable activity.

37 *grimaces*: affected facial expressions intended to charm.

43 *interlude*: during the sixteenth century, this term was used often of plays having a morality bias. V.'s use of it here is self-consciously old-fashioned, and perhaps he now refers to trivial forms of between-acts entertainment.

1.1 S.D. *Enter Loveless reading*: often in plays of this period, reading is associated with libertinism—even if today we don't necessarily consider lechers to be great readers! Seventeenth-century libertinism was perceived to be a position arrived at rationally, and this in turn involved doing some reading—especially Thomas Hobbes's *Leviathan* (1651). Hobbes insisted that all judgements about what is good and evil are subjective: 'whatsoever is the object of any mans Appetite or Desire; that is it, which for his part he calleth Good: And the object of his Hate, and Aversion, Evill; And of his Contempt, Vile and Inconsiderable. For these words of Good,

Evill, and Contemptible, are ever used with relation to the person that useth them: There being nothing simply and absolutely so' (Part 1 ch. 6). So, at the beginning of Thomas Shadwell's *The Virtuoso* (1676), Bruce, like Loveless, enters reading, in this case the notorious ancient 'material-ist' Lucretius, from whom he quotes at length in Latin and whose writing he goes on to discuss with his fellow rake Longvil. In April 1695, Con-greve's *Love for Love* had its première, beginning 'Valentine in his Chamber, Reading'. He is reading the Stoic philosophers Epictetus and Seneca, and commences a discussion with his man Jeremy on what those philosophers teach us about living without means:

> JEREMY Does your Epictetus, or your Seneca here, or any of these
>   poor rich Rogues, teach you how to pay your Debts without Money?
>   Will they shut up the Mouths of your Creditors? Will Plato be bail
>   for you? (1.1).

What Loveless is reading is not absolutely clear. The view that external reality is created by the mind's ideas, rather than vice versa, is post-Cartesian (i.e. after Descartes). Loveless's expression of an idealist position is, however, very ambiguous and not, finally, very philosophical. He may simply be saying that happiness is a state of mind. It could be applied just as easily to his former dissipation as to his current state of contrition and moral reform. The point of the opening scene is its ambi-guity. For that reason, I have retained the question mark in line 2 from Q1 rather than amending it to an exclamation mark as is more common editorial practice.

5 *luxury*: the primary meaning of the term is 'lasciviousness' or 'lust' (*OED* 1); overindulgence in what is choice or costly is a later meaning. Loveless certainly has the older meaning in mind.

13 *duties of dependence*: waiting upon powerful men at court, etc.

33 *ponderous lump of clay*: i.e. the body.

34 *appetites we know not of*: it is not entirely promising, perhaps, that when Loveless imagines the emancipated soul of Christian immortality, he thinks of it as having even more exotic appetites than it had when embodied!

55 *rock of reason*: Anglican theology was insistent on the rationality of Chris-tian belief. 'Reason' could, however, be made to reinforce the promptings of desire rather than to undermine them, and in contemporary libertine philosophy often was.

71 *needs*: is necessary.

73 *heart*: I have emended the pointing from Q1, where the passage reads: 'You know then all that needs to give you Rest, | For Wife's the strongest Claim that you can urge. | When you would plead your Title to my Heart, | On this you may depend;'. The lines flow more smoothly in the version I have printed.

78 *gossip*: 'gossips' were godfathers/mothers to children, and hence were spiritually intimate with the families for whom they acted. From this derives the more modern sense of 'gossip' as tattle or indiscreet talk about other people's affairs. It is unusual to use the word as a verb with an abstract noun like 'fears'. Loveless is certainly speaking in a rhetorical, almost poetic style here.

82 *erect their heads*: mount another rebellion (continuing the conceit of Amanda's fears being 'traitors' involved in plots against their mistress).

102 *the helmet proved*: i.e. tested. Loveless's reference to a 'helmet' here might suggest that he is considering himself in the light of the epic hero. Heroes in the great epics frequently had impenetrable helmets. One such was Mambrino in Ariosto's sixteenth-century epic *Orlando furioso*. This one gained celebrity because Cervantes has fun with it in *Don Quixote*, when the Don mistakes a barber's basin for this famous piece of armour. The image arguably renders Loveless faintly ridiculous; although depending on the actor's delivery, Loveless could also be humorously invoking the idea of the epic hero to mock Amanda's anxiety about the riskiness of the metropolis.

106 *essay*: trial (pronounced 'essày').

112 *wild enthusiasts*: 'enthusiasm' was a form of religious zeal attributed to fanatics and sectaries—those who made much of states of grace or inner spiritual conviction.

114 *stubborn atheist*: although Loveless means that he will be an unbeliever in this libertine creed, Amanda may not be much cheered by his use of this word. No atheist was a *virtuous* atheist!

132 *undigested composition*: chaotic make-up.

142 *fiery trial*: the metaphor here is probably alchemical, but there are suggestions also of religious martyrdom and ordeal by fire. Such suggestions continue the sense of Loveless's self-importance, the mock-epic undercurrent, that bubbles through the scene.

144 *false allay*: unstable compound—alloy.

1.2 s.D. *Whitehall*: interesting to note that in 1701 V. built himself a house on the site of a fire in the Palace of Whitehall close to the river. He would have used exactly the same steps to the river as he imagines Young Fashion and Lory using here. The house was satirized by Jonathan Swift, who called it 'A thing resembling a goose-pie' in l. 104 of a poem entitled 'Vanbrug's House. Built from the Ruins of Whitehall That Was Burnt' (1708). See Pat Rogers (ed.), *The Complete Poems of Jonathan Swift* (Harmondsworth: Penguin, 1983), 99.

7 *Gravesend*: travellers from France usually came from Dover to Gravesend overland, then by barge up the Thames.

7–8 *thirty shillings . . . privy purse . . . two half crowns*: thirty shillings (£1.50 in current coin) was a heavy reckoning. A schoolteacher or a curate's annual income was around £50. The 'privy purse' was the allowance paid by Parliament to the monarch, so this is a heavily ironic remark from Lory. Two half-crowns was five shillings (25 pence).

11 *guinea*: the value of the guinea fluctuated between 20 and 21 shillings until it was fixed at one pound one shilling (£1.05) in 1717. Guineas were relatively new coins, introduced by Charles II in 1662 and made from Guinea gold.

20 *half a piece*: half a guinea.

30 *Tug*: the name here means 'toil, struggle; go laboriously' (*OED* v. 4).

30–1 *Drab Alley at Wapping*: Wapping, being an area frequented by sailors, was also an area frequented by prostitutes. Ned Ward describes in *The London Spy* an encounter with a group of sailors thus: 'Sometimes we met in the street with a boat's crew, just come on shore in search of those land debaucheries which the sea denies 'em, looking such wild, staring, gamesome, uncouth animals, that a litter of squab rhinoceroses, dressed up in human apparel, could not have made a more ungainly appearance. They were so mercurial in their actions, and rude in their behaviour, that a woman could not pass by 'em without a sense of shame or fear or danger' (Ned Ward, *The London Spy* (4th edn. 1709), ed. Kenneth Fenwick (London: Folio Society, 1955), Part XIV, pp. 249–50). A 'drab' is a slang term for a prostitute: so Mrs Tug perhaps would not have wanted to 'pass by' Ward's sailors.

47 *redeem your annuity*: Young Fashion has either mortgaged the capital sum or the future payments of an invested annuity to raise ready cash. He needs his brother to pay back the money provided (and presumably interest) so that he can again have access to this source of income.

50 *powder puff*: for powdering the wig.

56 *Jacobite*: Young Fashion is loyal to the exiled James II, and therefore ineligible for the armed forces. Jacobites were Tories in the 1690s. His brother is of the opposite (Whig) persuasion, as Young Fashion learns in the next scene when it transpires that he has bought a title. The Tory/Whig tension is another motive (even if a latent one) for the coldness between the two brothers.

57 *take orders*: become a clergyman.

67 *generosity*: i.e. generosity in living up to a standard beyond his means
   rents: salaries.

69 *menus plaisirs*: little pleasures. 'The French Bureau des Menus Plaisirs arranged court entertainments for the king' (Cordner).

72 *farthing*: a small coin worth a quarter of an old penny. Phased out in 1961.

73 *de haut en bas*: literally, 'from high to low' i.e. with condescension.

75 *tickle him*: catching trout by tickling the underbelly of the fish and immobilizing it.

85 *engage*: guarantee; give [my] word.

1.3 S.D. *nightgown*: dressing-gown.

12 *C'est quelque chose de beau, que le diable m'emporte*: 'Tis a fine thing, devil take me:

13 *pewk*: spelt thus in Q1. Modern editors usually amend to 'puke', but I have not done so because as becomes clear, Foppington consistently tortures his vowels and this may be the first instance.

13–15 *Sir Navelty . . . pawnd*: one of the most interesting aspects of this text is the way in which, by substituting 'a' for 'o', and 'aw' for 'ou', V. has tried to indicate how Cibber actually performed the text, or how a later actor might render Foppington's affected speech. In the 1967 RSC production of the play at the Aldwych, Donald Sinden gave a magnificent performance in the part; and in a volume of his memoirs, *Laughter in the Second Act* (London: Futura, 1985), he writes as follows: 'As we know that the expletive 'Slife is a corruption of God's life and Zounds a corruption of God's wounds, so Lord Foppington's famous phrase Stap me vitals is derived from Stop my vitals (constipate me) but I know of no other instance of the word stop being spelt stap. The script contained several other o's spelt as a's. I tried to understand the author's intention in spelling it that way and I think I found the answer. The danger is in thinking that stap should rhyme with slap. Vanbrugh obviously intended his character to use an affected mode of speech—one might almost say, aristocratic: orf instead of off; hice instead of house—and to pronounce stop as stahp. I delighted in this discovery and throughout the play I pronounced every o as ah. I even carried it a step further by making every a into awe. Surprisingly it was still intelligible' (p. 218). In the 2001 National Theatre production, however, Alex Jennings playing Foppington dismissed this way of rendering the text. Neither he nor director Trevor Nunn considered that the audience, already coping with seventeenth-century English, would find a clear semiotic significance in the distortions.

15 *ten thousand pawnd*: confirmation that he has purchased, rather than earned, his title. In actual fact, knighthoods were not on open sale in this period, as they had been in the reign of James I after *c.*1610. Sir Novelty must be referring to a bribe or a contribution to political funds.

16 *stap my vitals*: Donald Sinden (above note) believes this ejaculation to mean 'constipate me'—presumably, 'stop up my vital organs'. It could mean 'vittles' (victuals): deny me food. Its force does not depend on a precise meaning. Rather, it is one of a set of self-harming ejaculations ('split my windpipe') that characterize Foppington's unique idiom.

18 *please to be dress*: this stage 'Franglais' adds to the carnivalesque sense of a linguistic cocktail that is so much a feature of the play's texture.

24 *clawn*: country simpleton.

34 *levee*: a dressing ritual, usually royal, at which the monarch or potentate can receive petitions and discuss the day's business.

49 *packet's too high by a foot*: C. Willett-Cunningham and Phillis Cunningham, *Handbook of English Costume in the Seventeenth Century* (London: Faber, 1955), comment that in 1680-90, coats became closer fitting with slight waist emphasis, and pockets might actually be placed higher on the coat (p. 136). They cite Ned Ward's *The London Spy*: 'Yet he would have [his coat] in the ancient mode, with little buttons, round cuffs, narrow skirts, and pockets within two inches of the bottom'. This suggests that there is a further irony in Lord Foppington dictating the height of his pocket: this would-be arbiter of taste fails to realize that his ideas on fashion are out of date.

52 *Rat*: Foppington's pronunciation of 'rot'. This can be a little confusing in the playscript, though is plain on stage.

55 *fancy*: taste; with overtones here of idiosyncrasy.

71 *Stinkirk*: Q1 gives the word in this form, though modern editors usually amend to 'Steenkirk' or similar. I have not done so because the pun on 'stink' is perhaps intended either to mock the sempstress's ignorance or to enable her to vent some spleen on Foppington. A 'Steenkirk' was 'a very long cravat loosely tied with the ends twisted rope-wise and then passed through a buttonhole or pinned to one side of the coat by a brooch' (Cunningham and Cunningham, *Handbook of English Costume*, 148). It was named after the French victory over the English at Steenkirk in 1692, one of William III's 'Dutch wars' against the French that lasted until 1697.

76 *don't fit me*: Frank M. Patterson has pointed out that this sequence in which a shoemaker claims to know better than the wearer whether the shoe fits (absurd, but in this case the audience might sympathize because clearly Foppington rejects perfectly well-made clothes out of sheer affectation) is based directly on Molière's *Le Bourgeois Gentilhomme* (1670), 2.5. Here also, M. Jourdain takes his shoemaker to task for making shoes too tight, and the latter denies that they could possibly be too tight. (See Frank M. Patterson, 'Lord Foppington and *Le Bourgeois Gentilhomme*', *Notes & Queries*, 31 (1984), 377-8.)

77 *my thinks*: given thus in Q1; variant of 'methinks'.

94 *stockins*: given thus in Q1. I have not emended to 'stockings' because again it may suggest Foppington's affected dropping of a final consonant.

95 *chairman's*: i.e. muscular, as one would expect of those who carried passengers in sedan chairs.

99   *crown-piece*: five shillings (25p).

103   *Foretop*: 'a lock of hair (natural or in a wig) arranged ornamentally on the forehead' (Cordner). In production, something has been done with this. Around this time, forelocks were sometimes arranged like twin horns, and in Ian Judge's 1995 RSC production of the play, this motif was echoed in all of the male hairpieces, suggesting cuckolds' horns.

105   *periwig*: Lord Foppington's wig is a stage property with a very celebrated history. In *Love's Last Shift*, the wig made for Cibber as Sir Novelty Fashion was already very large, so much so that it was bought by Colonel Henry Brett as a souvenir. Alexander Pope's poem *The Dunciad* (final version 1744) is a sustained satire on Colley Cibber's career as an actor, dramatist, and impresario: and in a comical extended footnote to 1.167 ('E'er since Sir Fopling's Periwig was Praise'), Pope writes that: 'The first visible cause of the passion of the Town for our Hero [Cibber], was a fair flaxen full-bottom'd Periwig, which, he tells us, he wore in his first play of the Fool in fashion . . . This remarkable Periwig usually made its entrance upon the stage in a sedan, brought in by two chairmen, with infinite approbation of the audience' (*The Dunciad in Four Books*, ed. Valerie Rumbold (London: Longman, 1999), p. 122). Vanbrugh seems to be daring the theatre company to produce for Lord Foppington, even higher in status, an even more outsized wig—thus providing a visual equivalent for the joke of his elevation in status. Donald Sinden tells us that he had five wigs, each bigger than the last.

125   *by tale*: counting individually. 'As determined by counting individual objects or articles; by number; as distinguished from by weight, by measure' (*OED* 6). It would clearly be very stupid to deal with wigs in this way.

147   *Lady Teaser's case*: the contemporary audience would think of a fashionable 'criminal conversation' case. Around this time, husbands began to bring forward actions for damages against the seducers of their wives. Neither party was allowed to appear in court (usually King's Bench) but sworn witnesses were made to testify—very often, servants—and details were usually salacious. The Duke of Norfolk brought a celebrated case against Sir John Germain in 1691, whom he accused of seducing his Duchess. He asked for £10,000 and was awarded a derisory £66, because the jury knew him to be an adulterer who was preparing the way for a divorce.

154   *Lacket's*: Locket's Tavern near Charing Cross, an expensive and prestigious watering-hole.

158   *nice conversation*: particular or fastidious in matters of discourse or taste; refined, or difficult to please. It is quite an insult to Young Fashion to be told that he does not belong to such a fraternity.

163   S.D.   *equipage*: retinue of servants.

167 *loggerhead*: a head out of proportion to the body; a large or 'thick' head.

175 *pippin*: 'a small apple; perhaps the reference is to the Apple of Sodom or Dead-Sea apple that turns to dust when eaten' (Zimansky). The Jewish historian Josephus describes in his *Bellum judaicum* 4.8.4 fruits of Sodom that 'dissolve into smoke and ashes' when picked, giving supposed evidence of that city's destruction by fire. Josephus may have in mind the Jericho potato or Palestine nightshade. The suggestion that Coupler has something like this in mind is rendered a little more convincing by Young Fashion's calling him 'old Sodom' at l. 180; and the allusion does perhaps intensify the sense of rottenness and decrepitude attaching to Coupler.

179 *old Sodom*: Sodom was the most notorious of the five biblical Cities of the Valley, referred to many times in the Bible as the prime example of a city given over to vice. Vanbrugh's portrait of Coupler is perhaps the most explicit and outrageous representation of the sodomitically inclined 'male bawd' figure to be found on the Restoration stage. Earlier examples include Sir Joslin Jolley in Etherege's *She Wou'd If She Cou'd* (1668) and Sir Jolly Jumble in Thomas Otway's *The Soldier's Fortune* (1681).

183 *a year in Italy*: Italians had a reputation for sodomy. Coupler regrets that Young Fashion does not appear to have acquired the taste. (Coupler is both homosexual and sodomitical, it seems. He presses his attentions on Young Fashion though he is fully aware that the latter is not homosexual.)

196 *burnt in the hand*: punishment for petty criminals.

203 *Hephestion*: Hephestion was the close companion of Alexander the Great. When Hephestion died of a fever in 324 BC, Alexander went wild with grief. Amongst many tributes, he caused a funeral pyre 200 feet high to be raised, upon which the body was burned. Alexander and Hephestion were familiar on the Restoration stage from Nathaniel Lee's play *The Rival Queens* (1677), where they are represented as a homosexual couple.

221 *writings*: legal contract governing the marriage articles.

222 *pipkin's to be cracked*: vessel to be broached, i.e. Hoyden's virginity to be taken.

236 *in the country . . . off*: fifty miles at this time is enough distance to suggest that 'the country' is another planet! Vanbrugh's plays are in themselves interesting evidence of the altering relationship between town and country in this period. Fashionable Londoners looked upon 'the country' as a hell that began immediately outside the metropolitan built-up area; and the conception of life in Clumsy Hall presented later in this play partly reinforces that prejudice. Some readers of *The Relapse* find in Clumsy Hall, however, a place of fertility and teeming life much superior to the

etiolated town: see, for example, Helga Drougge, ' "The Deep Reserves of Man": Anxiety in Vanbrugh's *The Relapse*', *Studies in English Literature*, 34.3 (1994), 507–22. And an increasing trend towards suburban living was complicating the town/country polarity and hierarchy. Vanbrugh's later play *A Journey to London* (1726) is to an extent sympathetic to a family of country gentry systematically insulted and belittled on a visit to the city.

237 *parents*: there is, it seems, a Lady Clumsy though she does not appear; and Hoyden might seem to be the result of a somewhat unbalanced upbringing!

257 *muzzle*: 'to fondle with the mouth closed. A low word' (Samuel Johnson).

262 *souse*: a sou—more generally, very small coin.

272 *cup and the lip*: a variation on the saying 'there's many a slip 'twixt cup and lip', i.e. things can go wrong at the last moment. This is an ancient saying: the Greeks had a version of it.

287 *symptoms of death*: since the mention of 'conscience' in l. 283, then 'scruples', Lory suggests ironically, Young Fashion has been exhibiting the behaviour of a Christian readying his soul for death.

2.1.19 *the plays*: Loveless and Amanda debate an issue that is very prominent in contemporary discussion, and by 1698 will be given very wide circulation in Jeremy Collier's *A Short View of the Immorality and Profaneness of the English Stage*.

 26 *tares*: this word is used in early translations of the New Testament to render the Greek and Latin terms for injurious weeds that grow amongst corn. Here, as very often in the play, a term has a biblical resonance: Matthew 13:24–30 tells the Parable of the Tares.

 40 *with the addition of a relapse*: curiously, Loveless appears to have seen the very play in which he is currently a character!

115 *wish you joy*: as upon a marriage.

117 *widow*: in *Love's Last Shift*, Amanda wears her widow's weeds during Loveless's desertion of her, a sign of particular devotion and constancy.

137 *patent*: royal letter conferring his title.

164 *call you to an account*: challenge you to a duel (hence 'engage a second' earlier): prophetic, in that the scene will come very close to involving Foppington and Loveless in a duel.

226 *go to the play*: starting times for dramatic performances were getting progressively later; about 5 p.m. by this juncture.

228 *leading 'em aut*: escorting them to their coaches.

232 *raund O*: perfect circle. Foppington might possibly have in mind Shakespeare's stage as described in the prologue to *Henry V*: 'Or may we cram | Within this wooden O the very casques | That did affright the air at

Agincourt?' (ll.12–14). Perhaps more likely is the opportunity it gives him to put on a facial expression that he thinks becoming.

244–5 *shoot 'em flying*: i.e. such women are moving targets, to be taken quickly.

252–3 *compound for my appearance*: mutually agree over; reach a compromise over; settle by mutual concession.

254 *friends*: political allies.

266 *psalm*: singing of the psalm during morning service.

269 *St James's*: Michael Cordner has drawn attention to the fashionability and significance of the church of St James's, Piccadilly, in 'Time, the Churches, and Vanbrugh's Lord Foppington', *Durham University Journal*, 77 (1984–5), 11–17.

318 s.d. *Syringe*: given as Seringe in Q1.

353 *bubble*: contemporary slang for 'cheat'.

380 *Save you*: Worthy makes his entrance imitating a preacher.

386 *Bagatelle*: a trifle of no value or importance.

393 *trouble*: difficulty at law.

441 *string*: a row, but with a suggestion of child's reins or 'leading-strings'.

445–6 *find . . . in it*: profit by it.

461–2 *rivers of a modern philosopher*: Thomas Burnet published his Latin *Telluris theoria sacra* in two parts in 1681 and 1689, with the English translations (*The Sacred Theory of the Earth*) following in 1684 and 1690. This remarkable work conceived the earth upon its first creation as an entirely smooth egg, transformed at the Flood into its present state of mountains, fissures, rivers, and seas. The theory, and Burnet's arrogant certainty in delivering it, became a laughing stock for later wits. Even here, Berinthia's tone might be more than a little sceptical.

468 *commons*: fields held in common, unenclosed: women who are not in some way protected.

476 *what you call intrigues*: Amanda does not wish to admit the word for sexual liaisons—'intrigues'—into her vocabulary.

478 *practic*: practical.

493 *sound*: healthy—not afflicted by venereal disease. In Congreve's *Love for Love* (1695), when Scandal is trying to bed Mrs Foresight, she accuses him of having very many lovers. He replies laconically: 'Faith, I'm sound' (3.1.765).

502 *back-stair minister at court*: a courtier sufficiently intimate with the monarch to access his closet by the back stairs. His comings and goings would escape observation.

503–4 *ruling the roast*: 'ruling the roost'; exercising influence, with some suggestion that this is done through the ladies at court.

538 *call—a husband*: i.e. a cuckold.

579 *carding and playing*: playing cards and gambling.

582 *the spleen*: see note Preface, l. 46.

590 *widow's band*: Cordner considers this to be a headband, but it may have been worn round the neck. I have not found any examples of black bands that specifically identify women as widowed.

622 *quarter's warning*: 'contract terminable on a month's notice' (Cordner).

3.1.6 *side-box*: the theatre in which *The Relapse* was first presented was the Theatre Royal, Drury Lane, designed by Sir Christopher Wren and opened on 26 March 1674. Although no illustrations of its interior are extant, there is a longitudinal section of a playhouse drawn by Wren in the Library of All Souls College, Oxford. This shows that the side-boxes were above the two on-stage entrance doors on each side of the theatre, and that they were supported by slender columns. Those columns must have interfered with the sightlines of the high-ranking audience members who sat in the side-boxes, restricting their view of the stage action and scenery. If indeed they did, it is perhaps less surprising that Lord Foppington is more interested in himself than in the productions.

7 *masks*: i.e. women who came to the theatre carrying masks. As Cordner comments, this does not necessarily identify them as whores. Masks were used to give women some freedom of behaviour by protecting their identities to some extent. Assemblies of people wearing masks and disguises and entertaining themselves in dancing rose in popularity at the latter end of the seventeenth century.

21 *cut a caper*: execute a leap, or high step, as in a dance.

37 *pad nag*: 'a small, easy-going horse' (Cordner).

46 *à la glace*: icy cold.

75 *take a purse*: become a common highway robber.

79 *t'other*: Foppington here makes a gesture suggesting hanging or throat-cutting, probably.

91 *sweet pawder*: powder used as a cosmetic.

97 *husband*: in this sense, the manager of a household, a housekeeper.

103 *running horse*: racehorse.

111 *essence-bottle . . . musk-cat*: Young Fashion refers to his brother as the source of all perfumed smells—a scent bottle, and the very animal from which musk is derived.

121 *plats*: i.e. his strangled pronunciation of 'plots'.

143 S.D. *several*: different.

3.2.15 *drudgery*: this word had a connotation of unwelcome sexual labour in this period. One of Lord Rochester's obscene songs, for example, has the following stanza:

> Let the *Porter*, and the *Groome*,
> Things design'd for dirty *Slaves*,
> Drudge in fair Aurelia's *Womb*,
> To get supplies for Age, and Graves. (ll.5–8)

(*Poems of John Wilmot, Earl of Rochester*, ed. Keith Walker (Oxford: Blackwell, 1984), 23.)

43 *tedious growth*: slow and gradual.

45 *take*: take root; catch on.

65 *College*: Royal College of Physicians. The Royal College was rebuilt after the Great Fire in Warwick Lane.

114–15 *die together*: 'die' still had its older meaning of 'reach orgasm'. Hence John Donne's series of puns in the poem 'The Legacy': 'When I died last, and, dear, I die | As often as from thee I go'. Here, the word is the culmination of a series of images taken from medicine in which there is a sexual double entendre, running through from l. 87. 'Let me blood', for example, in l. 106, refers to blood-letting by cupping or with leeches that was a standard treatment for fever. Here, however, Loveless has in mind a different kind of relief altogether. Berinthia takes up this thread again in ll.133 ff.

129–30 S.D. *exit Loveless running*: Q1 has the stage direction a little earlier, after 'pray to heaven'. However, this passage in Q1 is set out typographically in verse. Cordner sets the whole of Berinthia's speech in prose. I agree that prose does work more successfully here, but Loveless's exit is better timed just before Berinthia's ironic descent into 'I was better pleased . . .'.

177–8 *bring me down . . . to your lure*: an image from falconry. Falconers used baited lures (bunches of feathers) to recall their birds.

179 *business*: another sexualized term.

203 *bound to help his neighbour*: there is an allusion here to the injunction in the book of Leviticus 19: 18: 'love thy neighbour as thyself', and to the various places in the New Testament where the requirement to act as a neighbour—to act charitably—is stressed, e.g. in the Parable of the Good Samaritan (Luke 10: 25–37). Worthy's parody of this would be experienced by the audience as deeply blasphemous.

218 *fond*: (1) affectionate; (2) foolish. Lear famously refers to himself as 'a very foolish, fond old man' (Shakespeare, *King Lear* 4.7.60).

229 *half-seas over*: half way there.

232 *bar*: continuing the nautical metaphor, a bank of sand, silt etc. that obstructs navigation into a river or harbour (*OED* 15a).

283 *the pip*: to be fed up, downhearted or miserable—perhaps associated with 'the pip' as a disease incident to poultry.

291 *a-pickeering*: to 'pickeer' is to make a military raid or foray.

3.3.3 *Noah's ark*: God has decided to destroy a corrupt world by Genesis 6, and in that chapter, he instructs Noah to build an ark that will accommodate his family and 'of every living thing of all flesh, two of every kind' (Genesis 6: 19). The story of the Flood continues until the end of Genesis 9.

5 *orders of building*: there were three classical Greek orders, originally represented on columns: Doric, Ionic, and Corinthian, progressing from the less adorned to the more adorned. Vanbrugh would soon become very familiar with these when he commenced his career as an architect.

11 *enchanted castle*: of many possible allusions, Lory might have in mind the Pilgrim's fate in Bunyan's *The Pilgrim's Progress* (1684), when he is incarcerated in Doubting Castle by the Giant Despair.

18 *blunderbuss*: a short gun with a large bore, capable of firing many balls or slugs but not of exact aim.

23 *Weall . . . business?*: here is yet another linguistic texture. The Clumsy family and servants have a country burr, a kind of stage 'Mummerset', that is rendered phonetically in Q1. Slightly confusingly, some of the verbal distortions are similar to Lord Foppington's. It probably functions more as a cue to actors to invent an accent than as any very precise guide to pronunciation.

36–7 *fetch . . . gunroom*: go on a wild goose chase.

58–9 *Turkey-work chairs*: chairs covered in the style of oriental carpets. English carpet-weavers developed this hand-knotting process in wool during the sixteenth century.

60 *sockets full of laurel*: as at festival times such as Christmas.

63 *shifting-day*: the day of the week upon which Hoyden would have a clean 'shift' or underskirt.

tucker: a piece of lace worn round the top of the bodice.

3.5.3 *sack wine*: a general name for a class of white wines formerly imported from Spain and the Canaries. Often it is further specified by a particular place of production, so that it can designate, for example, sherry.

10 *canonical hour*: properly speaking, the *canonicae horae* are the times of daily prayer laid down in the Roman Catholic breviary. Here, however, the phrase refers to the fact that to be legal, marriages had to be performed within the 'canonical hours' of 8 a.m. to 12 noon.

12–13 *shooting . . . bid her stand*: taking unfair advantage, as a soldier or sentry might who shoots without warning.

24 *damned star*: unlucky star.

29 *the king of Assyria*: Sir Tunbelly refers to Nebuchadnezzar, king of the Babylonians (not the Assyrians, though they were the neighbouring civilization in Mesopotamia—modern Iraq) who had a dream interpreted by the prophet Daniel to mean that he will eat grass with the oxen; and shortly afterwards a voice from heaven commands him to do so. The story is told in the Old Testament, Daniel 4: 18–37.

33–4 *stays your stomach*: satisfies his (sexual) appetite, even if he is 'sharp-set', i.e. very hungry.

4.1.14 *do as you would be done by*: this was proverbial (*A Dictionary of the Proverbs in England in the Sixteenth and Seventeenth Centuries*, ed. M. P. Tilley (Ann Arbor: University of Michigan Press, 1950), D395), but the proverb derives from Matthew 7: 12: 'Therefore all things whatsoever ye would that men should do to you, do ye even so to them.' This is related to the injunction to 'Love thy neighbour' that has already been put to perverse use by Worthy.

58 *good will*: (1) best intentions; (2) sexual desire.

76–7 *separate maintenance*: separate maintenance contracts became increasingly common in the later seventeenth and eighteenth centuries. These were normally drawn up between a husband and a wife, who usually had trustees acting for her. They were often used to enable husbands to live apart from wives whom they had no adequate grounds to divorce. Susan Staves has argued that although the proliferation of such private agreements may imply a move away from a religious-hierarchical ideology of marriage and towards a legal-contractual one, this did not necessarily mean a better deal for women. Such agreements often replaced the older common law right of 'dower' whereby a wife acquired a life interest in one-third of all her husband's land (Susan Staves, *Married Women's Separate Property in England, 1660–1833* (Cambridge, Mass.: Harvard UP, 1990), ch. 6). In this particular case, unusually, Young Fashion is hoping to obtain a separate maintenance from Hoyden rather than to confer one upon her.

89 *drop off like a leech*: it is inevitable that a character called 'Nurse' whose role is to look after a young, available female will be suggestive of Shakespeare's nurse in *Romeo and Juliet*. Thomas Otway's version of the Romeo and Juliet story, *Caius Marius* (1680), may be the missing link here. This play offers, as Irma Z. Sherwood has suggested, 'a precedent for coarsening the Romeo and Juliet material and yoking it with alien elements' ('Vanbrugh's "Romeo and Juliet": A Note on The Relapse', *Restoration and Eighteenth-Century Theatre Research*, 12.2 (1973), 41–5). A passage in Act 3 of *Caius Marius* offers a reasonably close parallel to this 'weaning' speech:

> NURSE: Well, when it [Lavinia] was a Little thing, and us'd to ly with me, it wou'd so kick, so sprawl, and so play . . . and then I would tickle it, and then it would laugh, and then it would play agen. When it had tickling and playing enough, it would go to sleep as gently as a lamb.

(Thomas Otway, *The History and Fall of Caius Marius* (1680), 29). Sherwood elaborates a series of plot and character resemblances adding up to a reading of the play as a parody of *Romeo and Juliet*. The idea of *The Relapse* as an inverted *Romeo and Juliet* is developed further, especially with respect to an integration of the main plot, in Jack D. Durant, '*The Relapse*, Shakespeare's Romeo and Otway's Marius', *Restoration and Eighteenth-Century Theatre Research*, 12.2 (1973), 46–9.

92 *proper*: fine, handsome, elegant. Cassio, in Shakespeare's *Othello*, is said by his rival Iago to be a 'proper' man.

93 *draggle-tailed*: skirt trailing on the ground—unkempt, messy.

139 *upon the hip*: proverbial (Tilley H474), meaning to gain advantage over. Again, this is one of Iago's phrases used in *Othello* 2.1.314: 'I'll have our Michael Cassio on the hip'.

141 *fat livings*: at this time, aristocrats controlled very many Church of England benefices, and had the authority to present their own appointees to those 'livings' when they fell vacant.

149–50 *bring his gown to a cassock*: a cassock is an ankle-length tunic with narrow sleeves and a belt or cincture round the waist. It was normally worn under the gown, which was a shorter garment, so Nurse's threat is not quite coherent. She seems to imply an act of shortening, cutting-off, or reducing (and the overtones of emasculation, castration are apparent); but maybe she simply means that she will tear the gown off his back.

4.2 *A song*: see separate note on the music in Vanbrugh's plays.

50 *like a text*: a passage of Scripture used as the keynote for, and illustrated by, the sermon.

52 *ecstasy*: Berinthia uses this in an almost technical sense derived from the vocabulary of religious mysticism, where it denotes a state of exaltation in which one stands outside, or transcends, the self. John Donne's poem 'The Exstasie' is amongst the best-known literary treatments of a state in which the soul temporarily leaves the body behind.

55 *application*: point in the sermon at which the preacher applies what has been said to the everyday circumstances of the congregation.

57–8 *heaven give . . . practice*: this formula was often used by preachers to round off the sermon. Berinthia's glib use of it continues her ironic claim to be her friend's spiritual adviser.

78 *pretend*: aspire (as in a 'pretender' to a throne, an aspiring candidate).

92 *far fetched, and dear bought*: proverbial. Tilley D12 gives 'Dear bought and far fetched are dainties for ladies'.

110 *expect*: wait up for.

115 *ombre*: a Spanish card game for three players, using a forty-card pack. Each player has nine cards and there is a complicated system of trumping. The first player to the right of the dealer can designate himself 'Ombre' and can choose trumps. The top three cards of trump are called matadores or 'mats', which are further designated as spadille, manille,

and basto. There are some further rules, and more terminology governing the gambling.

4.3.6 *something or other*: a ribald, and in the circumstances not very tasteful, reference to Berinthia's chamber-pot.

9 *devil . . . to assist me*: the devil's capacities to change shape, to appear as an angel of light, and to cite Scripture for his own purposes, are proverbial. Such attributes and beliefs perhaps contribute to Loveless's flippant suggestion here that the devil will be present when Berinthia prays.

13 *piquet*: a French game for two players, using a thirty-two-card pack. Each player is dealt twelve cards, and after discarding and replenishing, various scoring combinations are called e.g. carte blanche (no face cards) = 10 points.

16 *badiner*: banter, trifle.

21 *splénétique*: depressing.

22–3 *The Plotting Sisters*: Thomas Durfey's comedy *A Fond Husband; or The Plotting Sisters* was premièred in May 1677 but not published until 1685. It concerns an adulterous wife (Emilia) who deceives her husband, Peregrine Bubble, with a gentleman called Rashley, but is exposed through the jealousy of her sister Maria and Ranger, rival to Rashley.

36 *trick*: (1) device; (2) round in a card game.

4.4.21 *capitulating*: negotiating. This could be intended as a malapropism, or Lory might be assuming that Lord Foppington will overcome all obstacles.

25 *given the word for*: sent for.

50 *turning . . . lordship*: proper grammar would require 'imposture', i.e. making Lord Foppington out to be the impostor.

58 *raise the posse*: posse comitatus, the 'force of the county', i.e. the body of available men over fifteen whom the sheriff may summon or 'raise' to repress a riot, or for other purposes.

69 *scours*: flees. The word had an obscene connotation in contemporary slang. In 1690, Thomas Shadwell's play *The Scowrers* took the stage, representing the life of a 'scowrer', Sir William Rant—a drunken, fornicating vandal. The Prologue anticipates that the very word 'scowrer' will frighten the ladies: 'Scowrers! Methinks I hear some Ladies say, | How shall we bear the lewdness of this Play!' The author goes on to reassure them that: 'Tho he exposes Vice, the Play's so clean, | The nicest shall not tax it for obscene' (*Complete Works of Thomas Shadwell*, ed. Montague Summers, 5 vols. (London, 1927), 5.86).

4.5.12 *plots and roguery*: Parliament was informed of a conspiracy to assassinate King William III led by Sir George Barclay and Sir John Fenwick, in

February 1696. This was the second such attempt, and Jacobites were far from quiescent at this point.

14 *stop*: given thus in Q1. One might, for consistency's sake, emend to 'stap'. I have not done so because it may be that Vanbrugh intended this pronunciation to be inconsistent. There are several other places where in Q1, Foppington's characteristic vowel-shift is not indicated in the text, and I have not emended.

18 *sugar-candy*: a tonic.

21 *Jernie . . . ça?*: my God, what is the meaning of this?

24 *Ah . . . mort*: ah, I am dead.

4.6.6 *strollers*: the term means, generally, vagrants—those without permanent employment. In a theatrical context, it would recall the 1572 Act for the Punishment of Vagabonds. This piece of legislation created the modern theatre by requiring that travelling or 'strolling' players find the protection of a powerful aristocratic household or of local magistrates. Those who could not 'shall be taken, ajudged and deemed rogues, vagabonds and sturdy beggars'. This led to James Burbage's appeal for protection to the Earl of Leicester, and in 1576, to the opening of The Theatre, one of the first permanent London playhouses. It is therefore a very resonant insult to Foppington to call him a 'stroller'.

9 *scot and lot*: paying this earnings-related municipal tax was one of the conditions of having a vote.

10 *Williamite . . . Jacobite*: another reminder that in the background of this comedy is a fiercely divided society, not yet fully reconciled to the events of 1688–90, when powerful numbers of the English governing class determined that their rightful, divinely appointed monarch, James II, had abdicated and that a foreign prince had the right to rule in his place as William III. Those who continued to support James and his line were 'Jacobites'; those who supported William were 'Williamites'.

56 *la gouvernante*: the governess.

69 *gimmeni*: Q1 gives this form of Hoyden's favourite exclamation 'gemini!' I have not emended because it might give a clue to pronunciation.

77 *frontery*: Nurse's idiolect for 'effrontery'.

110 *country*: county, district.

154 S.D. *at one door*: the Wren cross-section referred to above, and other illustrations of contemporary stage-sets, inform us that there were two doors on each side of the stage used by actors for all entrances and exits.

192 *qualm*: sickness or faintness, but also a moral scruple.

199 *dégagé*: nonchalant.

208 *taille*: figure, appearance.

215 *châtré*: castrated.

225 *milled crowns*: 'milled' coins are machine produced rather than hammered: but the term is applied to coins having a straight-across graining on the edge. This, with the use of lettering, helped to prevent counterfeiting and clipping, i.e. filing, coins to obtain precious metal. (The legend 'decus et tutamen'—'an ornament and a safeguard'—was adopted at this time, and is still found on the edge of the English-minted pound coin.)

226 *stitched . . . tail*: entailed upon her in her father's will, but with a sexual innuendo on 'tail'.

230–1 *Christmas*: still in the 1690s, a somewhat controversial term. During the English Civil War and amongst extreme Protestants thereafter, the keeping of a feast-day to mark Christ's birth was associated with paganism and Catholicism. Christmas signified 'Christ's Mass', calling attention to the three Masses celebrated in the Catholic Church on 25 December.

239 *des affaires*: some business—with a condescending overtone.

261 *physic*: medicine. Bull's method of argument here, justifying polyandry, is clearly specious. He takes his place in the roll-call of venal stage clergymen the most memorable of whom is Ben Jonson's Zeal-of-the-Land Busy in *Bartholomew Fair*, a Puritan who is able to justify going to the Fair and tasting of its carnal delights—including the eating of roast pig, which he sanctions as a way of showing contempt for the Jews!

5.1.21–2 *Tom of Bedlam*: generic name for a madman or poor, half-crazy beggar. This is one of Edgar's guises in *King Lear*, and Bedlam beggars feature in many folk-songs. 'Bedlam' was the Royal Bethlehem Hospital, which had functioned as a lunatic asylum since the mid-sixteenth century, though it was reopened in 1675/6 in a building in Moorfields. Visitors were taken to see, and be amused by, the inmates. Since *The Relapse* is a response to Cibber's *Love's Last Shift*, it is perhaps worth noting that Cibber's father, Caius Gabriel, designed the statues of Madness and Melancholy that ornamented Bedlam's entrance.

31 S.D. *pulling off his hat*: Zimansky is right to note that this stage direction is somewhat mysterious. In Q1, it is set to the left of the first two lines of the letter's text, so that one cannot tell whether Coupler pulls off his hat, or Young Fashion does, or indeed either pulls off the other's hat. It is even more mysterious why Vanbrugh should have wanted to record this relatively trivial gesture at all.

39 *seraglio*: i.e. made him into a eunuch fit to guard a sultan's harem, following on from *châtré* earlier. The possibility of castrating his brother runs strongly in Foppington's mind.

46 *achevé*: achieved.

59 *drunken sot Lory*: if so, the audience did not see him drunk.

85 *sister*: whore.

90 *devil . . . hag*: presumably proverbial. Whereas men are ridden by their

NOTES TO PAGES 78–85

hags of wives (hag-ridden), the devil controls them. Here of course, a sexual innuendo is intended.

5.2.10 *comes from the devil*: follows on from Coupler's demonology at the end of the previous scene. Worthy is heavily associated with the devil in this play, an association that his knowledge of this kind of lore, and the ageist, misogynist nastiness of this speech does nothing to dispel. The diabolical association continues at ll.60 ff.

34 *engineer*: a designer of earthworks and military structures. Berinthia picks up and extends Worthy's military campaign imagery. Such imagery in reference to the battle of the sexes is very common in the drama of this period.

58 *devil to drive*: 'He needs must go that the devil drives'—proverbial (Tilley D278).

65–6 *virtue is its own reward*: also proverbial (Tilley V81). This commonly expressed sentiment is ironically applied here. The use and abuse of proverbial expressions in the play repays study.

108 *kissing . . . favour*: people show regard, or perform services, for those they particularly like—proverbial (Tilley K108).

159 *Babylon of wickedness, Whitehall*: Babylon gets a bad press in the Bible as a city of wickedness—perhaps not surprisingly given the harsh treatment of the Jews in captivity there. The passage most damaging to Babylon is Revelation 17: 5: 'Mystery, Babylon the great, the mother of harlots and abominations of the earth', which is actually a reference to Rome. White-hall was the principal royal palace, accommodating the king and a large entourage of relatives, courtiers, guards, servants, officials, and hangers-on. It was near the Palace of Westminster that housed the Royal Chapel of St Stephen, the effective House of Commons until it burned down in 1834. William and Mary did not use it, preferring Kensington Palace; and Whitehall burned down in 1698—see note to 1.2 (p. 330).

5.3.13 *phthisic*: a term applied to diseases of the lung.

23 *major . . . minor*: in syllogistic reasoning, a conclusion is deduced from a major premiss and a minor premiss.

49 *rogue of sanctity*: religious hypocrite.

59 *equivocations*: Roman Catholics were presumed to be able, through 'equivocation', to swear the truth of something while actually believing it to be false. This is certainly not part of official Catholic teaching. More generally, Coupler might mean using words that have double meanings. Jesuits had a reputation for this; hence 'no Roman turns'.

61 *Tyburn cart*: vehicle used to drive condemned prisoners to the gallows. Robert Hughes writes very powerfully about the spectacle of public execution:

'On the eve of Tyburn Fair (one of the colloquial names for execution-day at Tyburn gallows), it began with a prayer intoned by the sexton of the parish church of Newgate prison, St. Sepulchre's, addressed to the occupants of its condemned hold, the Stone Room . . . With the morning came the minatory prayers, the hoarse clanging bells and the procession westward along the busiest streets of London, from Newgate to Tyburn, the present site of Marble Arch. Each condemned man sat in the cart facing the rising sun, with a noose bound to his chest. At the gallows' foot, phrase by halting phrase, he had to recite Psalm 51, the "Hanging Psalm" . . . Sometimes he would append a conventional speech of repentance, known as the "dismal ditty". Then came the donning of the white shroud, an undignified and spectral garment like a coarse nightgown; the climb up the ladder; the choking drop.' (Robert Hughes, *The Fatal Shore: A History of the Transportation of Convicts to Australia, 1787–1868* (London: Collins Harvill, 1987), 31–2).

Sometimes the cart was simply driven away to complete the hanging.

69 *gown-man*: clergyman.

97 *tithe-pig*: the established church was funded by a system of 'tithes'. In biblical times, a tithe was one-tenth of all income. In Vanbrugh's time it was a less exact levy upon parishioners. A tithe-pig is an animal given to pay the tax in kind.

112 *white-leather*: soft, pliant leather. Coupler refers to the Nurse's conscience, and to her skin.

121 *Baal*: a Philistine god of vegetation and fertility, often regarded as a chief enemy of the Christian God.

134 *simony*: the practice of buying ecclesiastical preferments, benefices, or emoluments. Bull scruples at this sin, whereas he has not scrupled to marry Hoyden twice.

147 *institution and induction*: Coupler is deploying those terms in the technical usage of the Christian Church, where 'institution' is the establishment or ordination of a sacrament of the Christian Church, especially of the Eucharist, by Christ; and 'induction' is the action of formally introducing a clergyman into possession of the church to which he has been presented and instituted, together with all rights, profits, etc. pertaining to it.

5.4.16 *womans rib . . . formed of*: referring to the account in Genesis 2: 21–3 of the formation of woman from Adam's rib.

22 *slipped*: as a horse 'slips its reins' when it gets out of a rider's control.

59–60 *terror in the operation*: in Q1, the passage from 'forgive me' at ll. 50–1 to here is set as verse. Some of the lines are iambic pentameter, but most are not. On balance, I think the lines succeed better as prose.

62 *home reflections*: think positively, to some purpose.

140 *Phaeton*: Phaethon was the son of Helios, the sun god, and Clymene. He

asked his father if he could guide the solar chariot for a day, but he could not manage the horses, and they would have set the world on fire had not Zeus killed Phaethon with a thunderbolt. He fell into the Eridanus and his sisters, mourning him, became amber-dropping trees.

162 *For when . . . other cast*: i.e. when women cast off virtue, men cast off love.

5.5.10 *shapes*: figure.

11 *slam*: an ill-shaped person. The *OED* cites this passage, and considers that the term is still in use in Yorkshire.

14 *Washy*: 'of poor quality or condition; especially, liable to sweat after slight exertion' (Cordner).

41 *knotting*: making decorative bows out of ribbon or lace.

42 *Practice of Piety*: Lewis Bayly's spiritual handbook *The Practice of Piety: Directing a Christian how to walk, that he may please God* was written for the young Prince Charles early in the seventeenth century (the British Library's earliest printing is the 3rd edition of 1613) and became the most popular guide to a Christian life in the century. It is a collection of prayers and meditations, which became a byword for simple, pious living and therefore a great joke to men and women of the world, which playwrights tended to be. As an example of its tone, it has this to say on 'Houshold Piety': 'If every Housholder were thus careful, according to this duty to bring up his Children and Family in the service and fear of God in his own house, then the house of God should be better filled, and the Lords Table more frequented every Sabbath day: and the Pastor's publick preaching and labour would take more effect than it doth. The streets of Towns and Cities would not abound with so many Drunkards, Swearers, Whoremongers, and prophane Scorners of true Piety and Religion; Westminster-Hall would not be so full of Contentious, wrangling-Suits, and unchristian Debates; and the Prisons would not be every Sessions so full of Thieves, Robbers, Traitors, and Murtherers' (19th edn. (1627), 207–8).

46 *to buy pins*: the joke is on Hoyden for taking the expression 'pin money' literally, but in society at large there was quite a problem with this term. 'Pin money' was an amount often specified in a marriage contract, set aside for the wife's personal use. But disputes very frequently arose over what, exactly, it was for and some husbands required wives to purchase household necessities out of this allowance.

50 *gibberidge*: gibberish.

52 *varsal*: universal, entire.

78 S.D. *hautboys*: ancestor of the modern oboe; a high-pitched double-reeded instrument.

83 *touch and take*: catch fire at once, i.e. get pregnant easily.

93 *Ganges*: river in India, sacred to the Hindus.

99   S.D. *masque*: masques were originally courtly entertainments character-
ized by dance, music, lavish costuming, spectacle, and allegorical themes.
Their incorporation into plays written for the public stage greatly
reduced them in scale. This one takes the form of a debate between
Cupid, the wicked god of love, and Hymen, the serious-minded god of
marriage, on the relative virtues of the unmarried and the married state.
It ends in Hymen's unsettling concession that marriage need not involve
chastity at all, and that married women make better lovers! This tract for
the times is a response to Cibber's masque in *Love's Last Shift*, where
Love, Reason, Honour, and Marriage contend for supremacy. Marriage
makes an unhappy entrance, symbolically wearing a yoke, and repines at
his 'wretched life | Doom'd to this galling yoke'. Love tells him that his
happiness will be found in a virtuous wife, if he will 'mourn, | For all thy
guilty passion past'.

161 *Newgate*: the prison was rebuilt after the Great Fire and reopened in 1672
with sumptuous architectural ornaments, but the conditions were still
appalling and the inmates were subjected to systematic extortion by
prison staff.

163 *mad doctor*: i.e. one who cures the mad, rather than being mad himself!

229 *adamant*: in its history, this term has been used to refer to a substance of
mythical hardness; later more specifically identified as the diamond and
the loadstone or magnet; but the Nurse means 'the hardest possible
substance'.

249 *de bon coeur*: with a good heart, with pleasure.

254 *grimace*: show, pretence: putting a brave face on things.

260 *war*: the English and the Dutch, allied to the Holy Roman Emperor and
several other states, fought continuously against Louis XIV's imperialist
and anti-Protestant ambitions between 1689 and 1697 when the Peace of
Ryswick ended an inconclusive campaign.

263 *come to*: be reconciled.

Epilogue

5 *ab origine*: from the beginning.

22 *through*: thorough.

27 *dance the Tyburn jig*: be hanged.

30 *bawdy snuff-box*: snuff boxes adorned with dirty pictures did exist,
though no example of a seventeenth-century snuff box is known to
survive.

The Provoked Wife

THE CHARACTERS OF THE PLAY

Madamoiselle: spelt thus throughout Q1.

PROLOGUE

1–3 *the intent . . . glass*: the metaphor of the stage holding up a mirror ('glass') to 'the follies of the age' derives ultimately from Plato's theory of dialogue as imitation (mimesis) of speech; and of narrative poetry as a representation of human behaviour in Book X of *The Republic*. With respect to comic/satiric theatre, issues arose as to the motives of those who undertook this kind of imitation, and its degree of accuracy or objectivity. Several of Ben Jonson's prologues treat this topic. Writing virtually at the same time as Vanbrugh, Jonathan Swift comments that spectators no longer recognize their own faces in such 'glasses': 'Satyr is a sort of Glass, wherein Beholders do generally discover every body's Face but their Own' (Author's Preface to *The Battel . . . between the Antient and Modern Books in St James's Library*, 1710 in *A Tale of a Tub with Other Early Works, 1696–1707*, ed. Herbert Davis (Oxford: Blackwell, 1965), 140).

7 *sure to bite*: there is a further debate here in contemporary aesthetics as to how far satire should 'bite' and how far it should amuse and cajole. Juvenal was usually credited with writing 'biting' satire, whereas Horace was the model for a more benign form of the art.

8 *venomed priest*: clergymen were already attacking the stage, but it is possible that this gibe helped to bring into print Jeremy Collier's *A Short View of the Immorality and Profaneness of the English Stage* (1698) that picks Vanbrugh out as a special target.

9 *indite*: compose the words, with a pun on 'indict' meaning to bring a legal prosecution.

12 *Three plays at once*: during the 1696/7 season, three of Vanbrugh's plays took the stage: *The Relapse* (Nov. 1696); *Aesop* 1 (Jan. 1697); and *The Provok'd Wife* (Apr. 1697). There had also been a follow-up to *Aesop*, a short three-scene squib produced in March 1697. The former two were played at Drury Lane while the latter was premièred at Lincoln's Inn Fields. Vanbrugh's presence was ubiquitous at this time.

16 *to his cost . . . known you*: *Aesop* 1 was not a success.

27 *touch . . . stand*: it is not difficult to imagine the sexual thrill produced by Mrs Bracegirdle's delivery of those lines, doubtless accompanied by suitable gestures. The contrasting imagery of 'lashing' and 'tickling', pain and pleasure, in the Prologue, exploits a sado-masochistic form of eroticism.

28 *buoy*: mark out, identify.

1.1 s.d. *Enter Sir John*: in Q1, given as *Enter Sir John, solus*.

   cloying meat . . . matrimony's: very many plays of the period feature characters who express such views of marriage and use food imagery to do so.
   The sexual appetite is literalized as an appetite for food, and sexual desire
   becomes 'hunger', with its location in the stomach. This generates references to 'empty' and 'full' stomachs, to appetites sharpened and sated (or
   'taken off' and 'put on' in contemporary terms), and similar expressions.
   Deployment of this strand of imagery is usually masculinist in bias.

13 s.d. *Enter Lady Brute*: in Q1, *Enter Lady Brute, sola*. In fact she has
   entered earlier, and simply remains on stage alone.

51 *separate maintenance*: see note to *The Relapse* 4.1.76–7.

52 *monster*: cuckold. A 'monster' because the cuckold is traditionally represented as a horned beast—monstrous in the sense of being freakish or
   unnatural.

58 *judgement*: Lady Brute toys with the idea that her husband's mistreatment
   of her might be a particular act of divine Providence—a sign to her that
   her conduct is wrong. Usually, of course, such a 'sign' would not endorse
   an immoral course of action. Lady Brute is being mischievously profane.

65–7 *The argument's . . . wife?*: this refers to the 'abdication' debates following
   King James's flight from his kingdom in 1688. How was the action of
   sending for William of Orange to be justified? One way was to argue that
   a monarch was owed obedience by subjects only as long as he or she did
   not abuse their trust—for example, by turning Catholic. This was, however, an extreme Whig view that rested on theories such as John Locke's
   in *Two Treatises of Government* (1690) to the effect that the power of
   monarchs was limited by an implied contract made with the people. It
   was rejected by those who believed that subjects owed 'passive obedience'
   to their divinely appointed monarch; and it was not accepted by those
   who preferred the pragmatic path of claiming that the king had vacated
   the throne and therefore abdicated. Lady Brute's concession that 'that
   condition was not expressed' shows her awareness of the dubious and
   radical nature of her analogy between marriage and government. She
   argues herself into a pragmatic, rather than a sacramental view of marriage in the course of this speech.

71–2 *Virtue's its own reward*: proverbial (Tilley V81).

89 *Court of Chancery*: this court developed to dispense 'equity'; that is to say,
   to give judgements that were not possible under the prescribed or customary forms of common law. It was intended to be a court of 'conscience' in which the rigours of common law could be mitigated by
   fairness. Lady Brute is saying that although it is against the letter of
   religious law to commit adultery, she would be justified in doing so by any
   omnipotent judges who could see the entire picture.

91 *House of Lords*: in mentioning the House of Lords, Bellinda brings Lady Brute back to the real world. In the real world, divorces could only be granted by the passing of a private parliamentary bill. She implies that divorce is even more difficult to obtain than Lady Brute thinks.

95 *mistake in the translation*: Lady Brute continues her mischievously worldly attitude to the Scriptures by here suggesting that Bellinda's reminder of Christ's central teaching in the Sermon on the Mount (Matthew 5; Luke 6)—that we are to turn the other cheek to those who have struck us—may be a 'mistake in the translation'. During the English Civil War and the Interregnum there were many radical views expressed about the possibility of mistranslation or distortion of the biblical text. And mistranslations did occur. The 1560 'Geneva' Bible, for example, was popularly called the 'Breeches Bible' because its translation of Genesis 3: 7 has 'breeches' for the garments Adam and Eve used to cover their nakedness where earlier versions give 'aprons'. A printing of the Authorized Version published in 1631 was dubbed the 'Wicked Bible' because Exodus 20: 14 is written as 'Thou shalt commit adultery'. Perhaps this is what Lady Brute has in mind! At all events, her witticism here, taken in conjunction with the contractual view of marriage and governance expressed earlier, might suggest that she is something of a radical.

97 *prerogative*: special right or privilege. At this time, the word had political connotations: royal prerogative is the sovereign's right to dispense with common law, and its extent has been hotly contested in British constitutional history.

1.2.8 *ladyship*: thus in Q1. Since elsewhere in the text, this is given phonetically to suggest Madamoiselle's French accent, as 'latiship', some editors emend here (e.g. Coleman). I have not done so because inconsistency may be exploited by actors.

15 *gives her the démenti*: gives her the lie; is proof enough that she lies.

18 *croyez-moi*: believe me.

30 *moon have no éclat*: moon loses its brightness; no longer shines.

35 *again*: in return.

49–50 *Ah . . . aimerais*: ah my dear lady, how I would love you!

54 *penny-post*: London was the first city to develop an urban postal service when William Dockwra set up his Penny Post in 1680. This service was taken over by the government, under the Duke of York's control, in 1682. Deliveries were surprisingly frequent—every two hours, according to Smith.

80 *Ma foi*: upon my soul!

81–2 *Ah . . . moi!*: ah, how I am in love with love! [As for me, love is my favourite game!]

86 *accablées*: overwhelmed, overburdened [with amorous intention].

87 *Au contraire*: on the contrary; quite the opposite.

90 *le goût bon*: good taste; a fine instinct [for love].

96 *Green Walk in St James's*: St James's Park, occupying some 90 acres between The Mall and Birdcage Walk, was one of Charles II's favourite playgrounds and was still a fashionable place to see and be seen into the 1690s, though it was not by then the King's haunt. The 'Green Walk' was, according to Smith, 'a long avenue of lime trees ending in a knot of elms'.

104 *justement comme ça*: the very same thing

107 *Eh, pourquoi non?*: why not?

109 *Tant mieux ... nouveau*: so much the better; then it will be a new experience.

112 *Bagatelle*: trifle; thing of no value.

113 *oui, je le voudrais*: yes, I would indeed.

115 *ah ... réputation*: ah, my dear reputation.

116–17 *quand ... embarassée*: when you have [one has] once lost it, you don't [one doesn't] have to worry about it again.

119 *Qui ... chère*: and a most expensive one [literally: which costs a good deal].

122 *Je suis philosophe*: I would resign myself to it [literally: I am philosophical].

125–6 *Chaque un ... vite*: each in his own way. When something is a nuisance to me, I get rid of it quickly.

130–4 *Tenez ... scrupules*: the French in this speech of Madamoiselle's translates as follows: Do take these. Here's your scarf, your hood, your mask— that's everything ... Be off quickly! Come, madam, hurry. Gracious, what scruples!

132 *Mercure, Coquin!*: Mercure is a servant named after the Roman god of roads and rogues. The word 'coquin' means 'rascal, rogue'. Some editors (e.g. Smith, Cordner) read 'Coquin' as a name that Lady Fancyfull calls Mercure. Q1 separates the two words by a comma. I think it more likely that there are two separate servants involved.

137 *délicatesse*: delicacy.

139–41 *Belle ... donc?*: a wonderful thing indeed, that modesty of yours, when one is bent on enjoying oneself. There. You are all set, let's go! Well, what's wrong?

142 *J'ai peur*: I'm frightened.

143 *Je ... moi*: I'm not at all.

145–7 *Demeurez ... vous*: 'stay then.' 'I'm a coward.' 'The more fool you.'

149 *C'est ... sainte*: it's a delightful saint [to honour].

151–3 *Elle . . . pour*: 'it amused their children very well.' 'Honour is against it.' 'Pleasure is for it.'

157 *Vous . . . enrager*: you will drive me mad.

159 *Elle . . . aînée*: then she is very impertinent. Nature is her elder sister.

162–3 *Oui . . . Pourquoi?*: 'yes, for sure.' 'Why?'

166–7 *Ah . . . Anglaise!*: 'ah, this wicked Frenchwoman.' 'Ah, this blessed Englishwoman.'

2.1.5 *Il nous approche, madame*: he is coming this way, madam.

43 *a quaker's bargain*: Coleman cites the Quaker George Fox speaking of Quaker tradesmen in his Journal: 'the People . . . found that their Yea was Yea, and their Nay was Nay.' Bargains were quickly struck, in few words, and were binding.

51 *Allons, allons, allons*: let's go, by all means.

69 *raree-show*: a portable show such as a Punch and Judy show; more generally, a grotesque spectacle.

70–1 *Est-ce . . . ça?*: is that how they make love in England? Q1 gives 'fais', though 'fait' would be correct.

91 *Le voilà mort*: that shuts him up.

92 *clapper*: tongue, as in a bell.

94 *wash the blackamoor white*: a proverbial phrase (Tilley E186) meaning 'to attempt the impossible', not acceptable in present-day English.

107 *Magna Carta*: this was the charter signed by King John at Runnymede, Berkshire, in 1215, by which he agreed to set bounds to his prerogative and guarantee to his nobles and people certain rights. It is often considered to be the basis of English common law. An absolute monarch clearly would not respect such an instrument—as King John in fact did not. So Heartfree means that he uses Lady Fancyfull disrespectfully.

116 *Jack Pudding*: they were fairground comedians who entertained crowds by slapstick, comic acrobatics, and suchlike amusements.

168 *tiffany*: transparent silk.

175–6 *under . . . petticoat*: 'a short padded underskirt of coarse cloth' (Smith).

230 *conjunction*: means (1) union in marriage, (2) sexual union, (3) the proximity of two planets in astrology—frequently taken to be a bad omen. Congreve had had fun with the word and its sexual/astrological meanings in his play *Love for Love*, premièred in April 1695. As the old astrologer Foresight exits, leaving Scandal alone with his wife, the latter sees him off in the following terms: 'Good Night, good Mr Foresight; and I hope Mars and Venus will be in Conjunction—while your Wife and I are together' (3.1.709–11).

286 *Betty Sands*: Elizabeth Sands was a prostitute, said to be the mistress of

Czar Peter the Great of Russia during his English trip in 1698. She died in poverty in 1699, finishing her career as a Drury Lane orange-seller.

296 *whining lover*: lovers given to romanticizing their involvements, or becoming obsessive, would be called 'whining'.

303 *Locket's*: a fashionable eatery in Charing Cross, whose proprietor was Adam Locket. It was one of Lord Foppington's favourite haunts in *The Relapse*. See 1.3.154.

2.2.42 *impromptu*: it has been suggested that this may be used here as a noun (Smith), but its first recorded use as the name of a casually inspired musical composition was in 1822.

77–8 *je ne sais quoi*: literally, 'I don't know what': an indefinable 'magic ingredi-ent', an inexplicable charm, often predicated of food and art.

82 *'Chivy-Chase'*: at this time, ballads like 'Chevy Chase' were still regarded as examples of rustic or barbaric taste. In Shadwell's play *The Sullen Lovers* the line occurs: 'why you look more Comically than an old-fashion'd Fellow singing of Robin Hood or Chevy Chace.' Lady Fancy-full's liking for it betrays, therefore, her lack of sophisticated taste. The stock of the ballad form was, however, to rise dramatically during the course of the eighteenth century.

103 *penchant*: inclination.

124 *La voilà d[é]terminée*: her mind is made up.

3.1 s.d. *Scene opens*: scenery operated on movable shutters could be drawn into the wings, here discovering Sir John's dining-room.

1 s.d. *to [Rasor]*: although Q1 gives the s.d. as 'to a servant', as Cordner notes, this could provide a first entry for Rasor, who will later (5.2) carry off his drunken master as though the latter were the leavings from a table.

14 s.d. *Enter Lovewell*: in Q1, Bellinda's speech finishes after 'mind to'; there is then a long space of about 5 cm on the printed page, followed by 'Lovewell'. Lovewell is presumably called at this point. Maybe the wide space suggests that a speech prefix for Lady Brute has been omitted. I assume, however, as does Cordner, that Bellinda calls her.

20 *spleen*: (see note to *The Relapse*, Preface, l. 56).

22 *paper-mill*: previous editors have cited passages suggesting that the image of a working paper-mill as a comparison for the clacking of a woman's tongue is common. Coleman prints a particularly 'fruity' passage from Ned Ward's *The London Spy* (1709): a woman 'made such a Noise with her Bell and her Tongue together, that had half a dozen Paper-Mills been at Work within three Yards of her, they'd have signify'd no more to her clamorous Voice, than so many Lutes to a Drum, or Ladies Farts to a Peal of Ordnance'.

61–2 *Sure . . . married*: Sir John's misogyny here leads him to suggest that the devil would have found greater punishment in being shackled to a woman than in being dispatched to hell.

108 *distinguished*: publicly recognizable.

111 *Blue Posts*: there was a tavern called the Blue Posts, so called because of the distinctive colour of its doorposts, in Spring Garden, where Act 3 sc. 2 of this play is set. Sir Jolly Jumble dines there in Thomas Otway's play *The Soldier's Fortune*—a character influential upon Vanbrugh's representation of Coupler in *The Relapse*.

123 *business*: Sir John uses the word with some irony, at the expense of tradesmen and professionals who led more serious lives than he does. The sexual innuendo behind the term is picked out in the exchange with the gallants that follows.

171 *fare . . . meat*: brag of good fortune.

257 *earnest*: a first instalment; or a foretaste of more to come—as well as the usual meaning 'in earnest'—serious in intention.

260 S.D. *seem to . . . familiarly*: i.e. Heartfree and Bellinda perform so that the audience deduces that they are continuing to talk to one another, as Lady Fancyfull makes her commentary on their familiar conversation.

293 *miracles . . . ceased*: the views of Benedictus de Spinoza (1632–77) on the impossibility of miracles gave rise to controversy in the seventeenth century. An increasingly scientific, rational attitude to experience strengthened the view that phenomena were governed by an unbreakable natural law. Miracles—direct manifestations of God's presence revealed in the breaches of that law—were losing credibility. Burnet's *Sacred Theory of the Earth* (see note to *The Relapse*, 2.1.461–2) popularized the controversy in Britain.

317 S.D. *Exit . . . running*: such an exit is undignified and entirely contrary to all etiquette. Lady Fancyfull should have permitted her hostess to show her out.

362 *neighb'ring nation*: the Dutch. Dutch women were permitted a freedom in their behaviour, in terms of public displays of affection, unaccompanied walks, and candour of speech, that frequently shocked and surprised foreign observers.

365 *bring up*: promote, bring into vogue.

367 *powdered coat*: fussily decorated coat.

399 *all its product*: the sum total of what it produces.

456–7 *make . . . peace*: bonfires were lit when the negotiations of the Treaty of Ryswick brought an end to the Nine Years War between Louis XIV's France and a continental coalition including England. This actually occurred in July 1697, after much difficulty. Constant here says that he will act as if it had already happened.

456 *Bank of England*: the Bank was founded in 1694 as a private company, incorporating the subscribers to a loan of £1.2 million to the king, enabling them to deal in gold bullion and bills of exchange. As Constant's remark suggests, it was not entirely trusted at its inception, and it did seem to be going through a crisis of confidence at the time of the play's performance.

3.2 s.d. *Scene opens*: this suggests the drawing-back of stage shutters to reveal the set-up for the Blue Posts Tavern on the deeper stage. However, as Smith points out, the furniture from the previous scene in Sir John's dining-room would still be frontstage. He proposes an interval here.

3 *liberty of conscience*: in 1689, the Toleration Act 'for exempting [dissenters] from the penalties of certain laws' granted limited freedom of worship to those (except Catholics and Unitarians) who could not accept Anglican liturgy. Their civil rights were still curbed, however.

9 *What a pother of late*: the general point being made in this song is that whatever exacting debates are taking place in the religious community about freedom to worship, Lord Rake and his band of atheistical cronies find *their* freedom in drunkenness and whoremongering. For a more detailed account of the background to the song, see Michael Cordner, 'Vanbrugh's Lord Rake', *Notes and Queries*, 226 (1981), 214–16.

13 *Dispensation*: this is the king's power to suspend the law in individual cases—a very controversial issue in the reign of James II who used it to permit Catholics to hold office.

17 *penal laws*: legislation that penalized practitioners of the Roman Catholic religion. In Elizabethan England, the laws were applied savagely. In the Restoration period, the Test and Corporation Acts (1673, 1661) had the effect of excluding non-members of the Church of England from public office unless they took Anglican communion at least once a year. Catholics could not carry arms, inherit or buy property, teach in schools, or send children abroad for education. Zimansky observes that although the code was not rigidly enforced in England, it was being enforced in Ireland and the matter was topical.

35–6 *beat up their quarters*: military in origin, but became slang for visiting a brothel. Cordner considers that Rake is using the phrase in the very general sense of causing a riot.

38 *spirit of clary*: wine, clarified honey, and spices—a kind of mulled toddy.

39 *forlorn hope*: 'a picked body of men, detached to the front to begin the attack' (*OED* 1) i.e. an advance party—here, Sir John himself.

58 *privileges*: 'the constitutional rights of a freeborn Englishman' (Smith). The point of this nonsensical exchange is that an Englishman is *so* free that nobody should even have the right to raise the subject.

63–6 *within a hair's breadth . . . owe it*: again a near-nonsensical piece of inebriated paradox-mongering, but what it amounts to is that whereas the king of France, an 'absolute' monarch, has almost unlimited powers guaranteed him by royal prerogative (e.g. wide powers of taxation), Sir John's privilege of being an Englishman extends to non-payment of bills—coming to the same thing.

66 *Liberty and property*: a Whig slogan, catchphrase of the 1688 Revolution. Cordner's introduction to his 1989 edition discusses the inconsistency of Sir John's use of this phrase (pp. 19–20); how can he stand up for freedom and property rights when his conduct is anarchic and would result in the overthrow of all order?

3.3.41 *the dust*: Pepys remarks on the dust in Hyde Park in his diary entry for 22 April 1664.

70 *practise in the glass*: very frequently satirized as the height of narcissism. In *The Relapse*, Lord Foppington's favourite interior decoration is the full-length mirror. Such non-spontaneous behaviour still attracts moral condemnation.

76 *nasty thing*: indecent line or situation.

87 *some reformer or other*: the audience is probably aware that reformers are indeed busy with Vanbrugh's plays.

115 *a month's mind*: strong attraction, or inclination to do something. The phrase derives from a Catholic practice of commemorating a dead person annually—a 'twelve month's mind' (see Coleman).

123–4 *son of Bacchus*: Roman god of wine and intoxication, whose court included the female Bacchantes, nymphs, fauns, and satyrs.

137 *Spring Garden*: 'a pleasure garden in Lambeth laid out with close walls, secluded arbours, and an artificial wilderness' (Smith). The area was later called Vauxhall.

141 *billet*: note. Often occurs in plays of the period as 'billet-doux'—love letter.

4.1.16–17 *mental reservation*: a qualification to a statement that a person makes inwardly or silently. Catholics were accused of retaining such reservations when swearing loyal oaths.

17 *opinion . . . calling*: religion and trade.

28 *doctor of the parish's*: clergyman's.

61 *simony*: buying or selling ecclesiastical positions.

68 *round-house*: lock-up; place of detention.

4.2.63–4 *je ne sais quoi*: see note to 2.2.77–8.

87 *lead out*: escort the ladies in ceremonious fashion from the theatre to their coaches—regarded as affected and foppish.

109 *New Exchange*: a shopping mall on the south side of the Strand.

4.3.15–16 *unfold mysteries*: Sir John mocks the clergyman's facility for explicating obscure passages of Scripture.

42 *the Fens*: perhaps implying Cambridge University.

46 *cure*: the magistrate means 'parish' or 'benefice', but in the next line, Sir John punningly understands this to mean 'medical remedy'.

4.4.2 S.D. *and dogging them*: Q1 prints this before Constant's speech.

19 *game*: 'whores'—girls of the game.

24 *doily*: light, summery cloth named after Thomas Doyly, a London draper specializing in cheap but genteel materials.

92 *sauce to your mutton*: mutton was a slang term for a prostitute. Sir John is hoping that the gallants will catch venereal disease from the whores.

171–2 *laws dispense . . . dispense with laws*: see note to 1.1.89. Constant reprises Lady Brute's earlier argument about equity giving fairer judgements than strict law.

194 *Would you*: if you would.

224 *an*: on

232 *il n'ya rien de si naturel*: there's nothing easier (more natural).

5.1.2 *que oui*: yes indeed.

4 *Au logis*: at home.

6 *Tous ensemble*: all together.

9 *C'est . . . pas*: husband is away, that's why.

16 *En vérité . . . dommage*: truly, madam, it would be a pity.

5.2.3 S.D. *Exit Lovewell*: Q1 does not provide an exit for Lovewell, but since she enters later with news of Brute's approach, she must go out.

27 *Sound as a roach*: the roach is a proverbially healthy fish (Tilley R143).

55 S.D. *tumbles*: handles roughly, probably dishevelling her clothing.

61 *pig together*: behave like pigs. Smith gives 'lie together in one bed'.

cold tea: most editors take this to be a slang or colloquial expression for brandy. Coleman thinks the expression is literal.

82 *civil*: the word has a connotation 'polite to the point of being sexually obliging'.

95–6 *cross-purposes*: a game in which inappropriate, irrelevant answers are given to questions.

133 *place*: social precedence e.g. at table, entering and leaving rooms, etc.

171 *scavenger*: street-cleaner ('binman' in modern parlance).

5.3.14 *Il le fera*: he will oblige.

22 *Laissez-moi faire*: leave it to me.

30 *uptails-all*: 'the name of a card game and an old song; "play at uptails-all" in slang meant "have sexual intercourse" ' (Cordner).

31 *Tu . . . moi*: you're taking the mickey out of me.

32–3 *the time when . . . how*: legal jargon used in indictments.

39 *pretty poll*: parrot (i.e. garrulous woman).

waterwagtail: 'wagtail' was slang for prostitute.

43 *Doucement . . . content?*: easy . . . are you happy now?

47 *Tu parles . . . libraire*: you talk like a bookseller.

50 *valet de chambre*: gentleman's servant.

52 *Bon*: good.

54 *matter of fact*: continues the legal language—definite proof of adultery having taken place.

55 *N'importe*: no matter.

58 *Oui da*: indeed we can.

60 *Sans doute*: indeed we have.

61 *tickling*: (1) amusing; (2) sexually stimulating.

63 *Fort bien*: an excellent thing.

66 *Le diable!*: the devil!

71 *Un . . . drôlesses*: a marriage! Ah, the hussies! (Q1 has drôless.)

75–6 *liquorish whipster*: lecherous swindler.

81–2 *Écoute . . . Rasor*: listen, my poor Rasor.

93 *A ça*: to this.

94 *mal à propos*: at the wrong time.

99 *tétons*: tits.

104 *Il tombe . . . tout*: he falls on top of her and, with the devil's help, he wins it all.

120–1 *Voilà . . . diable!*: there's a true Englishman! He's in love, and he still wants to argue. Go to the devil!

124–5 *Bon . . . toi*: good. Listen then . . . You can do with me as you please.

126 *Amor vincit omnia*: (Latin) love conquers all.

128 *On le va faire*: it's being arranged.

136 *La . . . intentionnée*: here she goes. Full of good intentions!

5.4.58 *main body*: i.e. of troops.

stand buff: stand firm.

5.5.7–8 *I have . . . man*: Q1 prints 'I have much ado to be Valiant, feel very strange to go to Bed to a Man?'; *Plays* (1719) inserts 'Sure it must' before 'feel' to complete the sense.

28 *Hobbes's voyage . . . dark*: Antony Coleman argues that this refers to the
philosopher Thomas Hobbes's dictum that 'Death, is a leap into the
Dark' (*Notes and Queries*, 214 (1969), 298); and also his edition of *The
Provoked Wife*). Cordner adds that Vanbrugh referred to his own marriage as a 'great Leap in the Dark' in a letter of 1 July 1719.

39 *notes*: i.e. 'script', referring to the plot they have concocted by letter in
5.4.

40 S.D. *Enter . . . Rasor*: Rasor enters here in Q1 and that is followed in all
early editions. Smith suggests that his entrance would be more effective
ushering in the disguised Lady Fancyfull at l. 93.

68 *one way more*: i.e. a challenge.

88 *living dog . . . dead lion*: proverbial (Tilley D495).

116 *take away his life*: i.e. commit bigamy, for which the penalty was death.

165 S.D. *Enter Rasor in sackcloth*: the ritualistic set of apologies Rasor offers
are based on the penance ritual still sometimes seen in English churches,
under which penitential sinners had to beg pardon from the congregation. As Cordner points out, however, the seventeenth-century sinner
'was dressed in a white sheet and carried a white rod. Rasor's choice of
sackcloth is a throwback to the austerer days of the primitive Christians'
when penitents would wear mourning, would be disciplined by sackcloth
and ashes, and would be prostrated on the ground.

202–3 *lie upon her face . . . life*: Genesis 3.14.

214 *Que le diable . . . Rasor*: may the devil choke this scoundrel Rasor.

216 *Hungary water*: a remedy for fainting distilled from rosemary flowers.

220 *Hélas . . . fille*: alas, my poor girl.

240 *Song*: it is unclear whether the singer is Constant or someone employed
by him. Both are possible in production.

259 *dispense with*: what Heartfree perhaps means is that he would not have to
pay a bill for staying a night elsewhere, since he could now bed down with
Bellinda. Other editors have glossed this as 'tolerate' or 'agree to', but
this does not fully convince.

EPILOGUE

16 *the third day*: although V. ceded his profits to the players, it was customary
for the third-, sixth-, and ninth-day performances to be 'benefits' for the
good of the playwright.

25 *behind our scenes*: aristocratic patrons considered that they were entitled to
mingle with performers backstage. Frequently, they tried to solicit sexual
favours from actresses. There was a continual battle to expel them, led by
the Lord Chamberlain.

29–30 *But . . . adjusted*: further references to the negotiations concluding William's French wars and the Peace of Ryswick.

REVISED SCENES

See the Note on the Text for discussion of these scenes.

4.1.36–7 *Don Quixote . . . Sancho*: characters from Miguel de Cervantes Saavedra's comic-epic novel *Don Quixote de la Mancha*, published in two parts in 1605 and 1615. This parodic prose romance had enormous influence on English and other European literatures. Don Quixote is the deluded, idealistic knight-errant, while Sancho Panza is his earthy, greedy, boorish, cowardly servant.

47 *Queen of the Amazons*: in Greek mythology, the Amazons were a race of breastless female warriors (*maza*, breast), who supposedly burned off one breast in order to draw bows the better. Penthesilea is the most famous; she was killed by Achilles, according to Arctinus' *Aethiopis*. Heracles (Hercules) fetches the girdle of the Amazonian queen Hippolyte for his ninth labour.

60 *Bonduca, Queen of the Welshmen*: a female warrior-queen variously called Boadicea, Boudicca, and Bonduca led the Iceni in a rebellion against the Romans in AD 60–1. She is associated here with the Welsh presumably because native English tribes such as the Iceni were driven westwards by the Romans, and took their language with them. Cordner points out that John Fletcher's ?1613 play on the Bonduca story had been revived with alterations by George Powell and music by Henry Purcell in October 1695; the Druids sing a song called 'Britons, strike home'.

61 *leek . . . pedigree*: this mocks the Welsh penchant for genealogy, but there is also a phallic suggestion.

63 *queen*: with a pun on 'quean', an unruly woman or whore.

4.3.25 *mophrodite*: comically garbled version of 'hermaphrodite', alluding to Sir John's somewhat masculine appearance.

30 *gripen*: clenched.

37 *Bridewell*: 'a house of correction near Fleet Street, where night-walkers and other petty offenders were set to hard labour pounding hemp' (Smith).

108 *head's half-dressed*: there was considerable labour involved in setting up the elaborate headdresses of contemporary women of quality.

121 *Seven's the main*: a term from the game of hazard. For more detail, see note to *A Journey to London*, 4.1.186 S.D.

The Confederacy

Gripe, a rich money scrivener: a money scrivener raises loans and puts money out at interest for his clients, i.e. performs various financial services. Today we might say 'investment broker' or 'financial adviser'. 'Gripe' is a slang word for a usurer or miser.

Brass: name combines a reference to effrontery ('brass neck') and to money, which is one of the character's main interests in life.

Clip: can mean jewelled clasp, but with overtones also of 'clipping' coins—filing metal from coins, which was a serious offence.

luxurious: used to luxury.

Flippanta: 'flippant' means fluently spoken, impertinent and voluble; or sportive and playful.

PROLOGUE

Spoken . . . shabby poet: when the play was premièred (1705), the social status of the professional writer was very fluid. Writing for a living was not entirely respectable, and the iconography in which it was typically represented was that of poverty and prostitution. The writer was often accused of neglecting a more appropriate trade or calling, prompted to write by misplaced motives of pride or desire for fame. Although writers would soon start to earn considerable sums through their efforts in marketing their wits and their pens, Vanbrugh's prologue exploits the conception of the starving bard while juxtaposing this with the bard's 'brother' (the author himself) who is clearly very much more successful.

4 S.D. *crown of laurel*: in ancient Greek culture, the laurel was sacred to Apollo. Apollo was the god of poets, so laurel wreaths were conferred upon those whose poetry was particularly distinguished. Hence the modern 'laureate', a term that gained an official meaning in the seventeenth century when poets were first given stipends from the Royal Household in exchange for writing poetry to mark special occasions at court. Our poet is here pointing out that his literary distinction does not add up to the price of a square meal.

16 *brother*: subsequent lines show that this is Vanbrugh himself.

21 *nicked it*: hit the target.

writ for praise: the poet's brother, Vanbrugh, does not write for profit but for praise. Thus, V. distances himself from the pathetic figure that the shabby poet presents. V. let it be known that he had ceded his profits from *The Relapse* to the actors; Laurence Whistler, in *Vanbrugh: Architect and Dramatist, 1664–1726* (London: Cobden-Sanderson, 1938), 35, states that this was to repay a debt to Sir Thomas Skipwith and help the Theatre Royal.

22 *folks in black*: clergymen.

23 *souse*: suddenly, without warning—like an unexpected heavy blow.

24 *building houses*: the main reference here is probably to the commission given by Queen Anne to Vanbrugh and Congreve for the building of the Queen's Theatre in the Haymarket, which opened in 1705 and where *The Confederacy* was first performed. Members of the Society for the Reformation of Manners had written in protest to Thomas Tenison, Archbishop of Canterbury, questioning whether those were fit persons to run a theatre in view of the fact that the Bishop of Gloucester had recommended Vanbrugh to be reprimanded at the House of Lords after *The Provoked Wife*. By 1705, Vanbrugh had already worked on Castle Howard in Yorkshire for the 3rd Earl of Carlisle, and would soon commence work on Blenheim Palace for the Marlboroughs. His own house on the grounds of Whitehall had attracted some degree of ridicule—see note to *The Relapse* 1.2 S.D.

29 *set your fancy out*: furnish what you desire.

32 *this great recompense*: the laurel crown.

34 *equipped*: accoutred.

1.1.23 *pattens*: clogs, i.e. wooden-soled overshoes to protect the shoes from muddy streets.

27 *a-dunning*: collecting payments for bills.

57 *club*: share of the bill.

1.2.5 *kettle-drum*: a soldier (kettle-drum is a metonymy for military music).

23 *raise his company*: recruit a platoon of troops.

41 *turn ballad-singer*: Dick's ironic comment presumably means that if he reformed, he could go about the streets selling the kind of religious ballad that speaks of conversion.

46 *place*: a position in the Royal household or at court that was obtainable through a bribe or straightforward purchase.

91 *basset-table*: 'The card-game called basset was introduced into England in about 1677, but never caught on outside Court circles because of the enormous size of the stakes for which it was played' (Cordner). Basset is a casino game in which players put chips on a painted layout of thirteen cards, betting on whether cards drawn from a pack will win or lose by matching, or not matching, cards drawn by a banker. Just after V.'s play took the stage, Susanna Centlivre's *The Basset-Table* was premièred (November 1705). This play features a society lady, Lady Reveller, whose love of basset turns night into day, and is so great that she compromises herself with men who have lent her money. Following Centlivre's earlier

The Gamester (February 1705), the plays suggest considerable social anxiety about gaming at this time.

136 *mother-in-law*: stepmother.

1.3.25 *Fey*: faith.

mechanic mould: disposition or character of a tradesperson.

28 *splenetic*: see note to *The Relapse*, Preface, l. 46.

54 *plus elevée*: more exalted.

58 *quintessence*: originally, the 'quintessence' was the 'fifth essence' of ancient and medieval philosophy—the substance of which the heavenly bodies were composed, latent in all created things, and which alchemists could distil. What is meant here is simply the most essential element of being a lady of quality.

65 *the people*: i.e. the lower orders such as tradespeople.

75 *rising of the lights*: choking, or constriction in the throat; also possibly croup or asthma. 'Lights' are lungs (now applied to animals).

103 *patches*: pieces of silk, velvet, or taffeta attached to the face to simulate moles or beauty spots. They were usually in dark colours to set off the whiteness of the complexion. They were placed near the eyes, and on the cheek, throat, and breasts, and were carried in jewelled boxes.

iron-bodice: extreme tight-lacing.

139 *commode*: a silk-covered wire frame used from about 1675 onwards to arrange hair dressed high off the forehead and clustered in curls over the frame. Addison comments in *The Spectator* that 'There is not so variable a thing in Nature as a Lady's Head-dress: Within my own Memory I have known it rise and fall above thirty Degrees. About ten Years ago it shot up to a very great Height, insomuch that the Female Part of our Species were much taller than the Men!' (*The Spectator*, ed. D. F. Bond, 5 vols. (Oxford: Clarendon Press, 1965), i. 413).

188 *bravely*: opulently, or handsomely.

234 *gin of all trades*: like 'Jack of all trades', but with overtones of cunning or deceit deriving from the word 'gin' meaning 'trap'.

245 *let Dick alone*: leave it to Dick.

278 *The deuce!*: Q1 has 'The deux', literally the two at cards or dice. Cordner notes that the religious references in the context might suggest 'dieux' or gods.

2.1.2 *cracked chemist*: crazy or deranged alchemist.

22 *guitar master*: the five-course (ten-stringed) guitar came to the fore around 1600 and was the standard instrument until around 1800. *The New Oxford Companion to Music* (ed. Denis Arnold (OUP, 1983), i. 793) cites a certain William Turner as remarking in 1697 that 'the Fine easie

Ghittar, whose Performance is soon gained, at least after the brushing way, has . . . over-topt the nobler Lute'.

26 *coquette-patch*: see note on patches at 1.3.103 above. A 'coquette' is a teasing flirt.

50 *rubbers*: in games of skill or chance, a set. Here, the 'game' is quarrelling. In the game of bowls, for example, a 'rubber' would be an odd-numbered set of games that allowed one team victory over another.

195 *these three years*: John Ozell, translator of *M. Misson's Memoirs and Observations in his Travels over England* (London, 1719), records the following view: 'In *England*, a Boy may marry at fourteen Years old, and a Girl at twelve, in spight of Parents and Guardians, without any Possibility of dissolving their Marriage, tho' one be the Son of a Hog-driver, and the other a Duke's Daughter' (p. 82).

207 *conclave*: specifically, the assembly of cardinals met for the election of the Pope; more loosely, the entire body of cardinals.

393 *trucking*: exchanging or bartering wives as if they were commodities.

448 *extravagant*: stronger here than in the modern sense of spendthrift or unmindful of economy. Here it means exceeding all bounds of rational or proper behaviour.

3.1.4 *chequer-note*: promissory note issued by the Exchequer

bank-bill: promissory note issued by the Bank of England, to be paid on a specific date to a specific payee

5 *crooked stick*: crooked sticks with notches cut into them were issued as receipts for cash payments in pounds, shillings, and pence to the Exchequer.

7 *Zest!*: exclamation accompanying a rapid action.

24 *broke a piece of money*: broken golden coins were tokens of engagement.

36 *vartuous*: virtuous; but there is evidence for suggesting that the word was pronounced in this way at the period. In Henry Fielding's burlesque of Richardson's *Pamela* called *Shamela*, the anti-heroine repeatedly refers to her 'vartue'.

3.2.6 *not a word of the pudding*: don't mention the plot.

49 *bird-lime*: sticky (in the sense of sticky-fingered, thieving).

109 *a Roland for her Oliver*: a match; tit-for-tat.

117 *pique and repique*: in piquet, if a player can score 30 or more points prior to play and before the other player makes any score whatsoever, he can claim *repique*, and add 60 points to his score.

131 *pretty*: pleasing; we might say 'tasty' in modern slang.

134 *Huzza!*: Q1 has 'Huzzy!', which might be 'hussy', but an exclamation is more likely.

170 *break ground in form*: slowly take territory by digging trenches and laying siege.

193 *à propos*: at the right moment.

204 *play upon the square*: play honestly.

239 *business*: pickle, predicament.

386 *be*: this is how Q1 has it. A word or two seems to have been omitted—perhaps 'froward' or 'cross'.

434 *be a good prince*: directly translated from the French source—*être bon prince*, be a good fellow.

463 *Algier*: 'Algiers was then a famous pirate stronghold, which harassed Mediterranean shipping, enslaving the sailors and treating them cruelly' (Dobrée, 3.281).

464 *Turkish demand*: i.e. infidel (therefore unfair).

477 *cormorant*: legendarily greedy seabirds.

488 *ring of remembrance*: given to devoted servants on the deaths of their masters; Brass is perhaps continuing to anticipate Dick's hanging.

493 *Brillant*: one with many reflective facets; shining.

498–9 *Prince Eugene's march into Italy*: this occurred during the War of the Spanish Succession (1702–13) when William III went to war to prevent the French from incorporating the Spanish kingdom and its territories in the Netherlands and Italy into a French superstate. Britain, the United Provinces, and Austria fought as part of a 'Grand Alliance'. Prince Eugene was on campaign in Italy in 1701 and again in 1705, when the campaign culminated in the Battle of Cassona on 16 August.

521 *with a witness*: with a vengeance.

4.1.52 *Gar there*: on guard.

63 *killing pleasure*: almost too much pleasure to bear.

92 *abregée*: in a few words; in brief.

98 *tendresse*: endearments.

152 *trade you drive*: way of living in which you indulge yourself.

154 *in the fund*: at bottom.

185 *satyr*: 'satyrs are imaginary male inhabitants of the wild, comparable to the "wild men" of the European folk tradition, with some animal features, unrestrained in their desire for sex and wine, and generally represented naked' (*The Oxford Companion to Classical Civilization*, ed. Simon Hornblower and Antony Spawforth (Oxford: OUP, 1998), 638).

197 *consorts*: an old spelling of 'concert', meaning a concerted performance by a body of musicians.

212 *modes*: fashions.

220 *porter*: doorkeeper. Liveried servants to keep the front door were fashion accessories of the very rich.

229 *Swiss*: Swiss mercenary soldiers provided bodyguards for French kings, and also for the Pope in the Vatican (the *Guardia Svizzera* or Swiss Guard). But as this is borrowed from the French source play, Lowder-baugh's note on the French meaning is apposite: a 'Suisse' is a door-keeper, so named because they were recruited from amongst the Swiss.

344 *turtle*: turtle-dove.

348 *top-knot*: tuft of hair; or a knot or bow of ribbon worn on top of the head.

362 *compound*: arbitrate. Bankrupts would try to settle debts by 'compound-ing', i.e. by offering the largest proportion of the debt that they could afford to pay.

403 *blown up*: ruined, exposed.

415 *coats*: petticoats.

435 *cause*: business, affair.

5.1.90 *Ware, horse*: Q1 has 'war'—beware, watch out.

124 *laying out*: making a search.

5.2.72 *Victoria!*: victory.

91–2 *commission . . . me*: I am acting as an agent for someone.

92 *pennyworth*: bargain.

142 *ergo*: therefore.

148 *in his altitudes*: drunk.

152 *commotion*: Q1 gives 'immotion', which Cordner emends to 'emotion'. Cordner explains that the word 'immotion' appears in another play by Vanbrugh, *The Mistake*, so that the *OED* records the word as a nonce-word meaning 'impulse'. I have suggested a different, more obvious emendation.

262 *amuse*: distract, delude.

309 *give us a tack*: bind us in marriage.

EPILOGUE

10 *confed'racy*: the conceit of the entire epilogue is that there is a parallel to be drawn between the domestic 'politics' of the family and the grand politics of state. At the time of writing, the War of the Spanish Succes-sion was raging; and although the allies under Marlborough had won famous victories against the French in the Spanish Netherlands com-mencing in 1704 at Blenheim, the war effort was increasingly expensive. At home, partisan divisions between the warmongering Whigs and the Tories who thought that the campaign was being prolonged for individual profit, were splitting society. Hence the epilogue's comic

concentration on what could be achieved by acting 'as one'. The very title of the play, alluded to in this line, is politically charged, because the Grand Alliance was popularly called 'the confederacy' in contemporary newspaper reports; and in the 1690s, the alliance of Whig ministers who supported William III had been called 'the confederacy'.

A Journey to London

THE CHARACTERS OF THE PLAY

Sir Francis Headpiece: 'headpiece' means 'brain' and also 'person of intellect', clearly used ironically in respect of Sir Francis.

Shortyard, a mercer: a yard was a measuring stick, so the suggestion here is that the character gives short measure.

Captain Toupee: a toupee was a relatively new creation in hair fashion in the 1720s. It was a wig with the front hair combed up into a curl or topknot.

Mrs Motherly: 'mother' was a term frequently used as slang for a brothel madam and sometimes for a midwife. An example of the former is the notorious Mother or Madam Cresswell, who decoyed country girls and turned them into whores. She became sufficiently famous to be engraved by Marcellus Laroon, the pictorial chronicler of London tradespeople.

Doll Tripe: tripe is (1) a food made out of animal entrails, (2) has the meaning 'fat-paunched'.

1.1.2 *worshipful*: here, illustrious. The term was used in respect of city livery companies, powerful craft and trade guilds that had developed in London from the twelfth century onwards, each with its own distinctive uniform or 'livery'. Twelve 'Great Companies' dominated the hierarchy; and representatives of those companies appear as characters in V.'s plays, such as Clip the goldsmith in *The Confederacy*.

10 *psalter*: psalm book. As suggested here, those were important tools in learning literacy.

38 *sessions*: local courts

vestry: meeting of parishioners to deal with parochial affairs.

78–9 *baiting-place*: the coaching inn or other venue intended for a refreshment stop.

82 *usquebaugh*: Gaelic word for whisky.

86 *basket-hilt sword*: a sword that has an elaborate protection for the swordsman's hand, consisting of curved pieces of steel formed into a 'basket' shape.

116 *St James's*: the most fashionable district in London.

1.2.33 *cattle*: horses.

58 S.D. *Enter . . . Doll Tripe*: since there is an entrance several lines later for a 'cookmaid'—presumably Tripe—it is perhaps more sensible to delay Doll Tripe's entrance until then.

87 *Highgate*: at this time a village around 4 miles to the north of London.

96 *errant*: arrant.

103 *business*: used with a sexual connotation; commerce in prostitution.

133 S.D. *Enter . . . Cookmaid*: see note to 1.2.58 above.

140 *twitcht*: I have retained from Q1 this older form of the past participle, because it may be intended, here and in George's speeches, as a clue to dialect pronunciation.

143 *sawce . . . 'em*: thrash them.

150 *stuck*: stabbed.

160–1 *twitch . . . copper*: steal . . . copper boiling pot.

162 *Tunbridge sugar-box*: 'Tunbridge was famous for its inlaid marquetry boxes' (Dobrée). Here though the allusion represents something of modest value.

240 *lawsuit*: 'All London carts had to display officially registered numbers in order to facilitate complaints. Sir Francis and his servants do not, of course, know this' (Cordner).

309 *some danger in that*: MPs were immune to prosecution for debt.

324–5 *get my windows broke*: treatment dished out by mobs to houses that they suspected of being disorderly (brothels).

2.1.27 *and go to*: Cordner emends to 'to go to', but the Q1 reading can stand, in my view.

49 *trinket*: i.e. sexual favours.

56–7 *groom of the chamber*: principal footman in a wealthy family.

65 *Croesus*: the proverbially rich king of Lydia (western territory of Asia Minor), who flourished around 550 BC.

73 *dead lift*: in a crisis.

74 *separate maintenance*: see note to *The Relapse* 4.1.76–7.

126–7 *masquerades*: gatherings attended by participants masked and otherwise disguised.

129 *hazard*: 'A dice game in which the chances are complicated by a number of arbitrary rules' (Cordner).

149 *prude*: the term was used in a quasi-technical sense for a woman who is the opposite of a 'coquette', i.e. a woman who has a strict morality underpinned by religious values. Sir Charles calls attention to this binary opposition of female types at ll. 238 ff. The associations of 'killjoy' or one who is morbidly interested in the lovelives of others were not as strong as they now are.

183 *quadrille*: a card-game for four persons that became very fashionable in the mid-1720s.

187 *surfeit-water*: 'distilled from poppies and other herbs as a cure for indigestion' (Dobrée).

338 *foully*: deceitfully.

3.1.9 *so*: provided that.

75 *feggings*: a variant of 'feckins', itself a version of 'i'faith'.

187 *good . . . country*: Sir Francis's hopping up and down on this slogan marks him out for a member of the 'Country' party—or would do if he actually understood the phrase. In the (probable) year of this play's composition, 1726, Lord Bolingbroke had commenced the orchestration of his one-nation 'Country' opposition to Sir Robert Walpole. His estate at Dawley in Middlesex was the base-camp from which he and Nicholas Amhurst compiled the opposition organ *The Craftsman*. The vapid, quasi-Roman republicanism of Sir Francis's remarks to Humphry suggest that he has imbibed some of this rhetoric, though without realizing that it is anti-government.

191–1 *go . . . ears*: quarrel.

216 *Gobble Guinea*: calls attention to the extent to which bribery was prevalent in all eighteenth-century elections.

259 *put the question*: put the matter to the vote. Votes were taken orally, members shouting 'aye' or 'nay'; this was followed by a lobby vote if the result was unclear. The 'ayes' would leave the chamber, to be counted as they filed back in. As Sir Francis recounts, his vote has been corralled by an extreme anti-government lobby. By 1726, Jacobites were perceived to be extreme Tories who opposed the Hanoverian Succession and wished to restore the House of Stuart to the throne.

303 *ride . . . death*: take advantage of his good nature, but with an unwitting sexual suggestion.

4.1.14 *mercer*: dealer in materials. Mercers exported wool and woollen cloth, and imported silk, velvet, and linen. The mercers were the oldest of the city livery companies (see above, 1.1.2), their earliest ordinances dating to 1347 and receiving a royal charter in 1394.

66 *short*: curt, or irascible—with a play on his name.

84 *telling out*: being counted.

143 *swore for money*: Lady Arabella continues her annoying punning. To swear for money would be to give false testimony for a bribe.

186 s.d. *Goes . . . throws*: Cordner gives a clear explanation of the game of hazard that now commences. The person throwing the dice calls a

number between five and nine, then tries to throw the number (the 'main'), using two dice. If instead he throws another number between four and ten, this becomes the 'chance', and he can win the stake by repeating that number on his second throw. Throwing the 'main' on the second throw is a loser. To throw two aces, an ace and a two, or a number adding up to twelve on two dice, is also to lose. After some initial good fortune to Lady Arabella, presumably contrived by Toupee, the three women all lose; and Sir Francis is correct to suspect that the dice are loaded. They constantly throw 'at all', that is sixes.

225 *every . . . purse*: with a sexual innuendo, followed up in 'the little soft velvet one' in the next line.

228 *Lady Blowze*: 'blowsy'; unkempt or sluttish. This follows on from Toupee's earlier familiar and unpleasant remarks about Lady Arabella's appearance.

266 *Cætera desunt*: the rest is missing.

The Country House

THE CHARACTERS OF THE PLAY

Mawkin: obsolete form of 'malkin' meaning an untidy female, especially a servant or country wench; a slut, slattern, or drab, with occasionally an overtone of lewdness.

1.1.31 *cuff*: a contemptuous term for an old man, especially one of a miserly disposition.

76 *the fox in the fable*: a reference to Aesop's Fable 'The Swollen Fox', which goes as follows. 'A very hungry fox, seeing some bread and meat left by shepherds in the hollow of an oak, crept into the hole and made a hearty meal. When he finished, he was so full that he was not able to get out, and began to groan and lament his fate. Another fox passing by heard his cries, and coming up, inquired the cause of his complaining. On learning what had happened, he said to him, "Ah, you will have to remain there, my friend, until you become such as you were when you crept in, and then you will easily get out." ' Vanbrugh was very taken with Aesop. He produced two plays in 1697 in which Aesop appears as the principal character.

166 *Captain Hungary*: thus in Q1, though it is possible that what is meant is 'Hungry', given the succeeding dialogue.

299–300 *does . . . house*: acts as host, or benevolent patron.

379 *Twangdillo*: a nonsensical word seemingly cobbled together from song-refrains.

2.1.30–1 *cock-broth*: chicken soup.

56 *cew*: dialect pronunciation of 'cow'.

124 *conceiving . . . bring forth*: Mr Barnard refers to his thought process in terms of human birth processes.

164 *Sis*: Dobrée emends to 'Cicely', but I prefer to retain the reading from Q1.

179 *Louis d'Or*: French gold coin, introduced by Louis XIII (1610–43). Its value was fixed at 17 shillings in 1717.

271 *drole*: droll—a jester, or entertainer.

299 *Apollo*: like the name of a particular parlour in an inn.

349 *scurvy disposition*: not a fortunate conjunction. (In astrology, the 'conjunction' of planets at a person's birth was a determinant of their fortune.)

350 *killing . . . king's stags*: in England, hunting the king's deer was a capital offence; presumably also in France.

GLOSSARY

accountable explicable; able to be accounted for

addle muddled, confused, unsound

an if

annuity yearly allowance

apothecary one who prepares and sells medicinal preparations

assemblies social gatherings to exchange news and conversation

assurance excessive self-confidence, shading into audacity, impudence

at large free, without restraint

aut [out] at elbows cash-strapped

aversion object of dislike or repugnance

awkward oblique; perverse

babies dolls

bagatelle trifle, a thing of no value or importance

band-boxes slight boxes of cardboard covered with paper, for collars, caps, hats, and millinery

banter *v.* make fun of, ridicule

bar bank of sand, silt, etc., across the mouth of a river or harbour, which obstructs navigation

basset-table table to accommodate the card-game basset

bass-viol stringed instrument for playing the bass part in concerted music; a violoncello

bawd 'go-between', a pander

beau man of fashion and (affected) refinement

beldam loathsome old woman; hag, witch

billets-doux love notes

birdlime thief (from the glutinous substance spread upon twigs, by which birds may be caught and held fast)

blade gallant, a free-and-easy fellow, a good fellow (with an edge of good-natured contempt)

blunderbuss short gun with a large bore, firing many balls or slugs, and capable of doing execution within a limited range without exact aim

blunderhead dolt, idiot

blurt *adv.* uttered abruptly, and as if by a sudden impulse; ejaculated impulsively

boggle raise scruples, hesitate, demur

bolstering padding

bolt expresses a sudden, rapid motion (e.g. 'bolt upright')

boon companion good fellow

bottom *n.* ship, boat, vessel; sometimes refers specifically to the hull

breathing sweat profuse perspiration

brimmer brimming cup or goblet

brisk sharp-witted, pert, curt

broiled grilled

brought to bed delivered of a baby

bubbies breasts

bubble *n.* dupe; illusion

bubble *v.* fool, cheat, or humbug

buckle *v.* submit

buff firm, steadfast (from 'buff' = military uniform)

bugbears an imaginary terror or, in a weaker sense, obstacle, thorn in the flesh

bum[p]kinly clownish, rustic

buss kiss

by the ears at variance; in open opposition, sometimes violent

calash type of coach (calèche)

calling position, estate, or station in life; rank; ordinary occupation; means of getting a living

capilotade cooked-up story; hash, medley

capitulating drawing up articles of agreement

case skin or exterior

case *v.* to skin, take the skin off

cast cast off, discarded

cavalier careless in manner, offhand, free and easy

cew dialect for cow

chair hire cost of hiring a conveyance

channel passage for sewage

chastity marital fidelity

chuck v. chuckle, laugh inwardly; leap up

citizen tradesman or shopkeeper, as distinct from a gentleman

clap v. apply, place, put, set, or 'stick', with promptness and effect

clary wine spiced and honeyed

clear beautiful, beauteous, fair; not confused in mind

clenched clinched

closet inner chamber, private room

cock-broth soup made from a boiled cockerel

cod's my life not certain, but 'cods' is period slang for testicles

comfortable pleasing; affording mental or spiritual enjoyment; good to look at, cheering

commode a tall head-dress made of wire decorated with silk or lace; can also be a piece of furniture or an enclosed chamber-pot

commons common land or estate; the undivided land belonging to the members of a local community as a whole. Hence, often, the patch of unenclosed or 'waste' land which remains to represent that

commonwealths states in which the supreme power is vested in the people; republics or democratic states

complaisant obliging, politely agreeable, courteous, accommodating

composition combination of personal qualities; personality

compound n. make-up, personality

compound v. settle; compromise on a business

conduct management of a strategy

conscionable scrupulous; governed by conscience

consorts musical entertainments (early form of 'concert')

contemn treat with contempt; despise

continence self-restraint in sexual appetite

conversation manner of conducting oneself in the world or in society; behaviour, mode or course of life

coquetry female behaviour calculated to inflame the opposite sex, with no intention of responding

coronet crown denoting a dignity inferior to that of the sovereign, worn or displayed on vehicles by the nobility

cotquean coarse, vulgar scold; (of a man) effeminate, 'old woman'

coxcomb fool, simpleton; affected person

crack n. prostitute; willing wench

cramp adj. difficult to make out, understand, or decipher; crabbed

Crump crooked or hunchbacked person

cuff contemptuous term for an old man, especially one with a miserly disposition

cure n. parish or sphere of spiritual ministration

curst cantankerous; disagreeable; cross, bad-tempered; shrewish

daggles trails through the mud

daggling trailing in the mud

dam wife

dare there, in 'French'-accented English

deal-box trunk made of pine or fir

deel devil (dialect)

demonstration indubitable proof

desarts positive qualities (variant of 'deserts')

diadem crown

dilapidations ruins; of buildings, fallen masonry

disguised drunk

disparage discredit

dispatch prompt settlement of an affair

dispensation exercise of royal power to relax a particular law

dissenting separated from the communion of the Established Church of England

distemper disorder of body or mind

distract madden, drive insane

doily woollen stuff introduced for

summer wear in the latter part of the seventeenth century; cheap, but genteel material

doubt fear, expect

drawers barmen: those who draw liquor in taverns

dry nurse woman who cares for a child but does not suckle

dun make repeated and persistent demands upon, to importune; *esp.* for money due

earnest *n.* first instalment

earthed tracked to the lair (usually of a fox)

egad soft oath deriving from 'a [ah] God!'

emulation ambitious rivalry; desire to equal or surpass another's achievements

engineer one who designs and constructs military works for attack or defence

entailed settled by inheritance; transmitted by entail (i.e. the law governing inheritance of land so that it cannot be bequeathed except to specific inheritors)

equipage carriage, horses, and attendant servants

errant thoroughgoing, unmitigated (arrant)

essay attempt, endeavour

evidences witnesses

exorbitancy excessiveness, superabundance

expedition promptness, speed

facetious witty, sprightly; urbane

faggots kindling wood; twigs bound together for fuel

fain willingly, gladly

false counterfeit

fantasque fancy, whim

feggings dialect distortion of 'faith'

fiddle faddle nonsense! rot!

fiddlecome nonsensical, silly, trumpery

finical affectedly fastidious, excessively punctilious or precise, in speech, dress, manners

flat insipid, stale, tasteless

flirt *n.* sudden jerk or movement, a quick throw or cast, a darting motion

fly split into pieces

fop fool; foolishly affected person

forlorn hope body of troops detached to the front, a front line, vanguard

frisk *n.* brisk sportive movement; a frolic; a whim

frontery effrontery

froward perverse, hard to please; ill-humoured, naughty

fumbling groping (sexual)

Gad affected form of 'God'

gadding wandering in desire

gadzooks mild expletive, deriving perhaps from 'God's hooks'

gallant *n.* man of fashion and pleasure

gallant *v.* escort

gim smart, spruce

gin of all trades female equivalent of Jack of all trades

glass looking-glass; mirror

glasses coach windows

good lack! exclamation comprising 'good' as in 'good God' and 'lack' as in 'alack'

gouvernante governess, female teacher

gownman member of the clerical profession; a clergyman

great intimate

grig person full of fun

groat coin worth fourpence

Gudsoons! mild expletive, deriving from 'God's wounds'

habit fashion or mode of apparel, dress

halter rope with a noose for hanging malefactor

hazard game at dice in which the chances are complicated by a number of arbitrary rules

hedge-leaper hunter (with horse and hounds)

help off buy goods

hempen made of hemp (often with a reference to a hangman's noose)

hodge podge confused

housewifery management of household affairs; domestic economy; housekeeping

hoyden boisterous, noisy girl

humour (of a country) habitual frame of

mind or temperament; national characteristics; (of a person), mental qualities or disposition

huswife housewife; light, pert girl as in modern 'hussy'

i'cod form of 'ecod' or 'egad', an interjection having a religious root

impertinence irrelevance; impudence

impertinent irrelevant; impudent; meddlesome; trivial, absurd

importune *adj.* troublesome, vexatious

imprimis in the first place; first. Used to introduce the first of a number of items, as in an inventory or will

impudence shameless effrontery; insolent disrespect, insolence; unabashed presumption

incognito unknown; in disguise

ingenuous frank

in pickle sorry plight or predicament

in spite of his teeth despite all opposition

intelligence (exchange of) information, news; collaboration

in the fund at bottom

intrigues secret sexual relations

Jackadandy little pert or conceited fellow; a contemptuous name for a beau, fop, dandy

jade hussy; minx (otherwise, a worthless and worn-out horse)

jerk *v.* whip or scourge

jogging moving on or off

jointure property that comes to a widow

journeyman one who, having served his apprenticeship to a handicraft or trade, is qualified to work at it for days' wages

languishing assuming a tender look or expression, as an indication of loving emotion

Lard affected form of 'Lord'

law you now exclamation expressing chiefly astonishment or admiration, or (often) surprise at being asked a question

lay out for set an ambush or trap

let alone rely on

levée morning reception of visitors especially by a king or nobleman

lewd loose in morals; sexually easy

lief gladly, willingly

lighting dismounting

light on *v.* to obtain or hit on

liquorish lecherous, lustful

list *v.* enlist

lug drag, pull along with violent effort

luggerheaded thick-headed, stupid

makings exclamation: 'by the mackins'

mechanic person doing manual labour or belonging to the lower orders

mercer dealer in costly fabrics

mien physical bearing or carriage

misericord ejaculation meaning 'compassion!', 'pity!' or 'mercy!'

monster cuckold (having horns, therefore 'monstrous')

mother-in-law stepmother

mum silent

mumbled fondled with the lips; mauled or pawed

murrain plague, pestilence

muzzle *v.* to fondle with the mouth close

neats oxen

neuter neutral, unaligned

nice fastidious, dainty, difficult to please

nicked hit the target; caught exactly

niggardly miserly, stingy

nimble quick-witted; light in morals

nog a type of strong beer

obliging civil, polite, pleasing

oder other, in 'French'-accented English

officious eager to please; attentive, obliging, kind

ogle *n.* amorous, languishing, or coquettish glance

oons worn-down form of 'God's wounds'

original *n.* singular, odd or eccentric person; one who does things such as have not been done before or are not commonly done

overreached overpowered

overtaken drunk

paint facial cosmetics

parcel a set or pack

part *v.* reach a bargain

parts abilities, capacities, talents

pattens overshoes or sandals worn to raise the ordinary shoes out of mud or wet

peckadilla trifling sin or offence

period termination, conclusion

periwig artificial imitation of a head of hair (or part of one)

perquisite casual emolument, fee, or profit, attached to an office or position in addition to salary or wages; 'perks'.

perspective telescope

pert fashionably satirical or witty

phiz physiognomy—face or countenance viewed as indicator of mind or character

phthisic person having lung or throat infection, severe cough, or asthma

physiognomy art of judging character and disposition from the features of the face

pickle sorry plight or predicament

pin-money money allotted by a husband to his wife for her personal expenses

piqued moved, or excited

piquet card-game played by two persons with a pack of thirty-two cards

plenipos plenipotentiary: deputy or envoy of a sovereign

plod shoes strong, clumsy, clog-like shoes in which one walks heavily

pood dialect for 'pulled'

portion dowry brought by a woman to a marriage

portmantle portmanteau: a travelling bag or case

post *adv.* as fast as possible

postilion one who rides the near horse of the leaders when four or more are used in a carriage or post-chaise

pother disturbance, commotion, turmoil, bustle; a tumult, uproar; a noise, din

practic applied to that department of a subject, art, or science, which relates to practice

prating *n.* foolish, idle chatter

preferment advancement in position, status, or career

preparatives acts that prepare the way for other acts; draughts of liquor taken before meals

presently immediately

pretend claim authority or power or right; aspire, lay claim

privileges special rights or immunities (as a citizen)

privy-counsellor private or confidential adviser; specifically, an adviser to the sovereign

privy-purse allowance from the public revenue for the private expenses of the monarch

proper good-looking, handsome, well made

provoking stirring up

psalter a volume containing the Psalms, esp. as arranged for liturgical or devotional use

punk prostitute, strumpet, harlot.

pure general term of appreciation: fine, excellent, capital, jolly, nice, splendid

quadrille card-game played by four persons with forty cards, the eights, nines, and tens of the ordinary pack being discarded

quality people of elevated social position; social distinction

quarter-staff stout pole, from six to eight feet long and tipped with iron

raillery ridicule, banter

rakehell immoral or dissolute person ('rakc' is a contraction of 'rakchell'); thus adj. 'rakehelly'

rally to banter or make fun of

raree-show show or spectacle of any kind (originally a portable show carried in a box)

rates prices

reckoning bill at an inn or tavern

relish *v.* to be agreeable or pleasant

restitution action of restoring or giving back something to its proper owner, or of making reparation to one for loss or injury previously inflicted

resty sluggish, disinclined for action

retirement withdrawing into seclusion or privacy

right *adv.* exactly

roach freshwater fish of the carp family

romp *n.* lively, merry woman

rubbers in various games of skill or chance, a set of (usually) three games,

the last of which is played to decide
between the parties when each has
gained one; hence, two games out of
three won by the same side.
Sometimes, a set of five games, or
the winning of three of these by one
side

sack kind of white wine

sack-posset drink made from hot milk
curdled with wine and spiced

'sbud contraction of 'God's blood'

scan perceive, discern

scandalizing causing offence or
bringing into disgrace

scrivener money-lender and investor

sennight a week; thus 'this day
sennight', a week today.

seraglio inmates of a harem

sessions periodical sittings of justices of
the peace

shaking his heels running off

sharpers fradulent card-players; cheats

sharp-set acute, keen

shift *n.* woman's smock or chemise

shift *v.* change linen

shoot flying shoot birds on the wing; to
take an opportunity as it presents itself

short curt, or irascible

side-box enclosed seat at the side of a
theatre

sirrah pejorative and patronizing form
of 'sir'

skaward raced, chased (dialect for
'scoured')

skip-jack trifling, petty, flighty

slipped got out of control

small-beer weak, or poor quality
beer

smart severe, hard upon, cutting

smock-faced effeminate; pale-faced

smoke *v.* to smell out a plot; to be 'onto'
someone, suspect

snub check, reprove, or rebuke in a
sharp or cutting manner

souse suddenly, without warning; also, a
'sou' or small coin

spark young man affecting smartness or
display in dress or manners

speed fare, prosper

splenetic suffering from the spleen

sponger one who lives meanly at
another's expense; a parasite, a sponge

stagger cause (a person) to falter or
waver (in his faith or purpose)

stark arrant, thorough, unmitigated

staut stout (dialect)

stick himself commit suicide by means
of the sword

stomach appetite

stra dialect for straw

strangely extremely

stroller vagabond, vagrant; an itinerant
beggar or pedlar

surety guarantor

swap suddenly and forcibly

swingeing huge, immense, tremendous;
powerful, potent

tell count, or number (as in telling time)

telling out being counted

tent deep red Spanish wine ('tinto')

tester from *teston*; slang word for a
sixpence

text short passage from the Scriptures as
the subject of an exposition or sermon

theatre scene of action

thorough-paced thoroughly trained

tickle beat, chastise; stir up, incite

tickling risky

ticklish precarious, risky, hazardous

tight of a neat compact build, well made,
shapely

tintamar confused noise, uproar,
clamour, racket, hubbub, clatter

tire-woman dressmaker, coutumier

title claim

towards imminent

town the fashionable part of London and
its society

toying amorous dalliance

toyshop shop selling trinkets or knick-
knacks or jewellery

tract manner of proceeding; way, path

trapes slovenly or slatternly girl

trucking bargaining

truepenny trusty person; honest fellow

trull trollop, prostitute

trumpery trash, 'rubbish', nonsense

trust give credit

tumble *v.* disorder, rumple clothes

turn out of doors dismiss from service

turned off dismissed

twitch pull abruptly, pluck, jerk

udsookers mild oath, originating in a blasphemy

udswoons variant of 'God's wounds'

usquebaugh whisky

valet de chambre personal servant

vapours morbid condition supposedly caused by exhalations of air developed within the body; normally a female nervous disorder with symptoms of lassitude, depression, and low energy

vartue variant, uneducated form of 'virtue'

venery practice or pursuit of sexual pleasure

wainscot oak panelling lining the walls of a room

want *n.* lack

wheedle entice or persuade by soft flattering words

wherry sharp blow; esp. a box on the ear or slap on the face (contracted form of dialect word 'wherret')

whimsical fanciful; freakish, odd

whipster wanton, lascivious, or licentious person, a debauchee

whisk move with a light sweeping motion

widow's band flat strip of material used to bind the headdress and hair

wipe *n.* insult; slap in the face

wiseacre person who affects wisdom

with a jerk hastily

worshipful distinguished, reputable

zest! expression of keen relish or enjoyment

zoons (zounds) euphemistic abbreviation of 'by God's wounds'

American Literature

British and Irish Literature

Children's Literature

Classics and Ancient Literature

Colonial Literature

Eastern Literature

European Literature

History

Medieval Literature

Oxford English Drama

Poetry

Philosophy

Politics

Religion

The Oxford Shakespeare

A complete list of Oxford Paperbacks, including Oxford World's Classics, Oxford Shakespeare, Oxford Drama, and Oxford Paperback Reference, is available in the UK from the Academic Division Publicity Department, Oxford University Press, Great Clarendon Street, Oxford OX2 6DP.

In the USA, complete lists are available from the Paperbacks Marketing Manager, Oxford University Press, 198 Madison Avenue, New York, NY 10016.

Oxford Paperbacks are available from all good bookshops. In case of difficulty, customers in the UK can order direct from Oxford University Press Bookshop, Freepost, 116 High Street, Oxford OX1 4BR, enclosing full payment. Please add 10 per cent of published price for postage and packing.

3 1901 04488 2050